Financial Accounting
for Decision Makers

Visit the *Financial Accounting for Decision Makers*, *fifth edition* Companion Website with Grade Tracker at **www.pearsoned.co.uk/atrillmclaney** to find valuable **student** learning material including:

- Self assessment questions with Grade Tracker function to test your learning and monitor your progress
- A study guide to aid self-learning
- Revision questions and exercises to help you check your understanding
- Extensive links to valuable resources on the web
- Comments on case studies to aid interpretative and analytical skills

Financial Accounting for Decision Makers, fifth edition - Microsoft Internet Explorer

File   Edit   View   Favorites   Tools   Help

PEARSON Education   **Financial Accounting** for Decision Makers
Fifth Edition • Peter Atrill • Eddie McLaney

Home | Select Chapter: | Welcome | Go   Site Search: | Go

Welcome to the Companion Website for Financial Accounting for Decision Makers, fifth edition.

Students - select from the links in the drop-down menu above or the resource links below to access the student study materials.

- **Student resources** for each chapter, including:
    - **Self assessment questions** with Grade Tracker function to test your learning and monitor your progress.
    - **Study Guide** to aid self-learning.
    - **Exercises** to help you check your understanding.
    - **Weblinks** to valuable resources on the web.
- **Revision questions** to test your understanding of key topics.
- **General comments on case study assignments** to aid the development of interpretative and analytical skills.

Instructors - visit the Instructor Resource Centre to access password-protected resources accompanying this title.

Learn more about the book, including how to order this title or obtain an inspection copy.

Copyright © 1995-2008 Pearson Education. All Rights Reserved. Legal and Privacy Notice

Done   Internet

5th Edition

Financial Accounting
for Decision Makers

Peter Atrill

and

Eddie McLaney

FT Prentice Hall

FINANCIAL TIMES

An imprint of **Pearson Education**

Harlow, England • London • New York • Boston • San Francisco • Toronto
Sydney • Tokyo • Singapore • Hong Kong • Seoul • Taipei • New Delhi
Cape Town • Madrid • Mexico City • Amsterdam • Munich • Paris • Milan

Pearson Education Limited

Edinburgh Gate
Harlow
Essex CM20 2JE
England

and Associated Companies throughout the world

Visit us on the World Wide Web at:
www.pearsoned.co.uk

Second edition published 1999 by Prentice Hall Europe
Third edition published 2002 by Pearson Education Limited
Fourth edition 2005
Fifth edition 2008

ISBN: 978-0-273-71275-6

British Library Cataloguing-in-Publication Data
A catalogue record for this book is available from the British Library

10 9 8 7 6 5 4 3 2 1
11 10 09 08 07

Typeset in 9.5/12.5pt Stone Serif by 35
Printed and bound by Mateu Cromo Artes Graficas, Spain

The publisher's policy is to use paper manufactured from sustainable forests.

Brief contents

Supporting resources

Visit **www.pearsoned.co.uk/atrillmclaney** to find valuable online resources

Companion Website for students

- Self assessment questions with Grade Tracker function to test your learning and monitor your progress
- A study guide to aid self-learning
- Revision questions and exercises to help you check your understanding
- Extensive links to valuable resources on the web
- Comments on case studies to aid interpretative and analytical skills

For instructors

- Complete, downloadable Instructor's Manual
- PowerPoint slides that can be downloaded and used for presentations
- Progress tests, consisting of various questions and exercise material with solutions
- Additional international case studies
- Tutorial/seminar questions and solutions
- Solutions to individual chapter exercises

Also: The Companion Website with Grade Tracker provides the following features:

- Search tool to help locate specific items of content
- Online help and support to assist with website usage and troubleshooting

For more information please contact your local Pearson Education sales representative or visit **www.pearsoned.co.uk/atrillmclaney**

Contents

8 Analysing and interpreting financial statements (2)   242

9 Reporting the financial results of groups of companies   274

Guided tour of the book

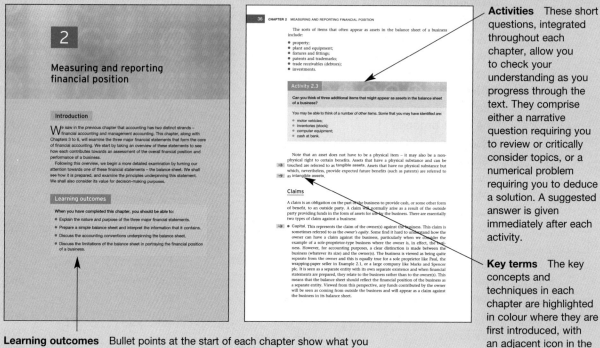

Learning outcomes   Bullet points at the start of each chapter show what you can expect to learn from that chapter, and highlight the core coverage.

Activities   These short questions, integrated throughout each chapter, allow you to check your understanding as you progress through the text. They comprise either a narrative question requiring you to review or critically consider topics, or a numerical problem requiring you to deduce a solution. A suggested answer is given immediately after each activity.

Key terms   The key concepts and techniques in each chapter are highlighted in colour where they are first introduced, with an adjacent icon in the margin to help you refer back to them.

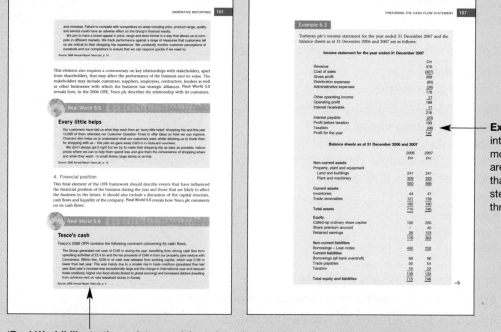

'Real World' illustrations   Integrated throughout the text, these illustrative examples highlight the practical application of accounting concepts and techniques by real businesses, including extracts from company reports and financial statements, survey data and other insights from business.

Examples   At frequent intervals throughout most chapters, there are numerical examples that give you step-by-step workings to follow through to the solution.

Self-assessment questions Towards the end of most chapters you will encounter one of these questions, allowing you to attempt a comprehensive question before tackling the end-of-chapter assessment material. To check your understanding and progress, solutions are provided at the end of the book.

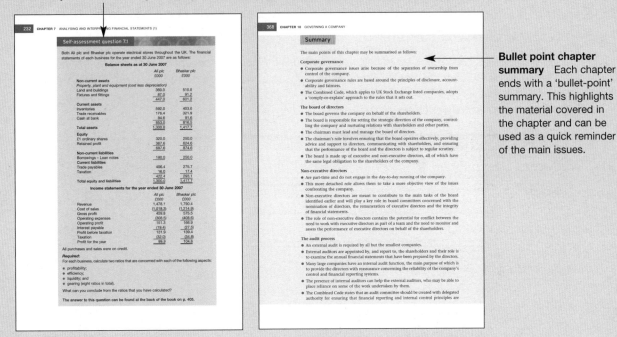

Bullet point chapter summary Each chapter ends with a 'bullet-point' summary. This highlights the material covered in the chapter and can be used as a quick reminder of the main issues.

Key terms summary At the end of each chapter, there is a listing (with page references) of all the key terms introduced in that chapter, allowing you to refer back easily to the most important points.

Review questions These short questions encourage you to review and/or critically discuss your understanding of the main topics covered in each chapter, either individually or in a group. Solutions to these questions can be found at the back of the book.

Further reading This section comprises a listing of relevant chapters in other textbooks that you might refer to in order to pursue a topic in more depth or gain an alternative perspective.

References Provides full details of sources of information referred to in the chapter.

Exercises These comprehensive questions at the end of most chapters. The more advanced questions are separately identified. Solutions to five of the questions (those with coloured numbers) are provided at the end of the book, enabling you to assess your progress. Solutions to the remaining questions are available online for lecturers only. Additional exercises can be found on the Companion Website at **www.pearsoned.co.uk/atrillmclaney**.

Guided tour of the Companion Website

Extra material has been prepared to help you study using *Financial Accounting for Decision Makers*. This material can be found on the book's Companion Website at **www.pearsoned.co.uk/atrillmclaney**.

Self assessment questions

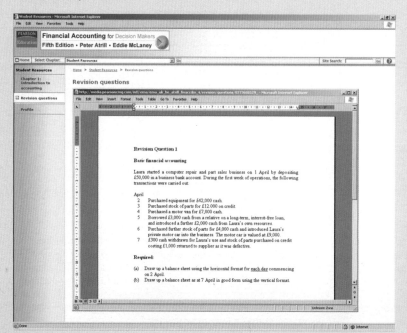

For each chapter there is a set of interactive self assessment questions, including multiple choice and fill-in-the-blanks questions. Test your learning and get automatic grading on your answers.

Revision questions

Sets of questions covering the whole book are designed to help you check your overall learning whilst you are revising.

Weblinks

A full set of relevant weblinks allows further study of each particular topic.

Preface

This text provides a comprehensive introduction to financial accounting. It is aimed both at students who are not majoring in accounting as well as those who are. Those studying introductory-level financial accounting as part of their course in business, economics, hospitality management, tourism, engineering, or some other area, should find that the book provides complete coverage of the material at the level required. Students who are majoring in accounting should find the book a useful introduction to the main principles, which can serve as a foundation for further study. The text does not focus on the technical aspects, but rather examines the basic principles and underlying concepts. The ways in which financial statements and information can be used to improve the quality of decision-making are the main focus of the book. To reinforce this practical emphasis, there are, throughout the text, numerous illustrative extracts with commentary from company reports, survey data and other sources.

In this fifth edition, we have taken the opportunity to make improvements that have been suggested by both students and lecturers who used the previous edition. We have brought up to date and expanded the number of examples from real life. We have also changed the layout of the financial statements throughout the text to reflect what we judge to be emerging practice. Changes, brought about as a result of the move towards international financial reporting standards, mean that the layouts used in previous editions no longer have to be followed by large companies. In this new edition, we have adopted the layouts that now appear to be most widely used.

Given its decision-making focus, the analysis and interpretation of financial statements lies at the heart of this text. We, therefore, have decided to expand this topic, which is now spread over two chapters. This change has allowed us to explore further topics and to provide more real-world examples and exercises. Finally, we have completely changed the last chapter of the text. Corporate governance has become a 'hot' issue in recent years and we have devoted the whole of the final chapter to an examination of this topic. The approach that we have taken is to avoid dwelling too much on the particular rules in place to govern companies but instead to examine the issues and problems arising when ownership of a company is divorced from day-to-day control.

The text is written in an 'open-learning' style. This means that there are numerous integrated activities, worked examples and questions throughout the text to help you to understand the subject fully. You are encouraged to interact with the material and to check your progress continually. Irrespective of whether you are using the book as part of a taught course or for personal study, we have found that this approach is more 'user-friendly' and makes it easier for you to learn.

We recognise that most of you will not have studied financial accounting before, and, therefore, we have tried to write in a concise and accessible style, minimising the use of technical jargon. We have also tried to introduce topics gradually, explaining everything as we go. Where technical terminology is unavoidable we try to provide clear explanations. In addition, you will find all the key terms highlighted in the text, and then listed at the end of each chapter with a page reference. All of these key terms are also listed alphabetically, with a concise definition, in the glossary given in Appendix B towards the end of the book. This should provide a convenient point of reference from which to revise.

A further important consideration in helping you to understand and absorb the topics covered is the design of the text itself. The page layout and colour scheme have been carefully considered to allow for the easy navigation and digestion of material. The layout features a large page format, an open design, and clear signposting of the various features and assessment material. More detail about the nature and use of these features is given in the 'How to use this book' section below; and the main points are also summarised, using example pages from the text, in the Guided tour on pp. xii–xiii.

We hope that you will find the book both readable and helpful.

Peter Atrill
Eddie McLaney

How to use this book

We have organised the chapters to reflect what we consider to be a logical sequence and, for this reason, we suggest that you work through the text in the order in which it is presented. We have tried to ensure that earlier chapters do not refer to concepts or terms that are not explained until a later chapter. If you work through the chapters in the 'wrong' order, you will probably encounter concepts and terms that were explained previously.

Irrespective of whether you are using the book as part of a lecture/tutorial-based course or as the basis for a more independent mode of study, we advocate following broadly the same approach.

Integrated assessment material

Interspersed throughout each chapter are numerous **Activities**. You are strongly advised to attempt all of these questions. They are designed to simulate the sort of quick-fire questions that your lecturer might throw at you during a lecture or tutorial. Activities serve two purposes:

- to give you the opportunity to check that you understand what has been covered so far;
- to encourage you to think about the topic just covered, either to see a link between that topic and others with which you are already familiar, or to link the topic just covered to the next.

The answer to each Activity is provided immediately after the question. This answer should be covered up until you have deduced your solution, which can then be compared with the one given.

Towards the middle/end of each chapter there is a **Self-assessment question**. This is more comprehensive and demanding than most of the Activities, and is designed to give you an opportunity to check and apply your understanding of the core coverage of the chapter. The solution to each of these questions is provided in Appendix C at the end of the book. As with the activities, it is important that you attempt each question thoroughly before referring to the solution. If you have difficulty with a self-assessment question, you should go over the relevant chapter again.

End-of-chapter assessment material

At the end of each chapter there are four **Review questions**. These are short questions requiring a narrative answer or discussion within a tutorial group. They are intended to help you assess how well you can recall and critically evaluate the core terms and concepts covered in each chapter. Answers to these questions are provided in Appendix E at the end of the book.

At the end of each chapter, except for Chapters 1 and 10, there are eight **Exercises**. These are mostly computational and are designed to reinforce your knowledge and understanding. Exercises are graded as either 'basic' or 'more advanced' according to their level of difficulty. The basic-level questions are fairly straightforward; the more advanced ones can be quite demanding but are capable of being successfully completed if you have worked conscientiously through the chapter and have attempted the basic exercises. Solutions to five of the exercises in each chapter are provided in Appendix D at the end of the book. A coloured exercise number identifies these five questions. Here, too, a thorough attempt should be made to answer each exercise before referring to the solution.

Solutions to the other three exercises and to the review questions in each chapter are provided in a separate *Instructors' Manual*.

To familiarise yourself with the main features and how they will benefit your study from this text, an illustrated Guided tour is provided on pp. xii–xiii.

Content and structure

The text comprises 10 main chapters. The market research for this text revealed a divergence of opinions, given the target market, on whether or not to include material on double-entry bookkeeping techniques. So as to not interrupt the flow and approach of the main chapters, Appendix A on recording financial transactions (including activities and three exercise questions) has been placed after Chapter 10.

Acknowledgements

We wish to acknowledge the generosity of ACCA in allowing material to be reproduced in Chapter 10, which was written by Peter Atrill and which first appeared in various articles in *Finance Matters*.

Publisher's acknowledgements

We are grateful to the following for permission to reproduce copyright material:

Real World 2.1 from *Brandz*, Millward Brown, (2006); Real World 3.5 and Real World 4.4 from *Annual Report*, Thorntons plc, (2005); Real World 5.1 from *Insights into IFRS 4th Edition 2007/8*, Copyright © 2007 KPMG IFRG Limited, a UK company, limited by guarantee. Printed in the UK. Reprinted with permission of KPMG IFRG Limited. All Rights Reserved. All information provided is of a general nature and is not intended to address the circumstances of any particular individual or entity. Although we endeavor to provide accurate and timely information, there can be no guarantee that such information is accurate as of the date it is received or that it will continue to be accurate in the future. No one should act upon such information without appropriate professional advice after a thorough examination of the facts of a particular situation. KPMG International is a Swiss cooperative. Member firms of the KPMG network of independent firms are affiliated with KPMG International. KPMG International provides no client services. No member firm has any authority to obligate or bind KPMG International or any other member firm vis-à-vis third parties, nor does KPMG International have any such authority to obligate or bind any member firm. For additional news and information, please access KPMG IFRG Limited's website on the Internet at http://www.kpmgifrg.com; Exercise 5.8 from *Annual Report*, Carpetright plc, (2006); Real World 6.2 from www.tescocorporate.com, Tesco plc; Real World 6.4 from *Annual Report*, LiDCO Group, (2006), special thanks to Dr. Terry O'Brien CEO; Real World 8.4 from *Annual Report*, Marks and Spencer Group PLC, (2006); NF 8.4 from Financial ratios as predictors of failure in *Empirical Research in Accounting*, Blackwell Publishing, (Beaver, W.H. 1966); Real World 9.2 from *Annual Report*, Go-Ahead Group plc, (2006); Real World 9.4 from *Annual Report*, Cadbury Schweppes plc, (2005); Real World 10.2 from www.cadburyschweppes.com, Cadbury Schweppes plc; Real World 9.4 from *Annual Report*, Wetherspoon plc, (2006); Real World 10.16 from *Annual Report*, Tesco plc, (2006).

NI Syndication Limited for extracts from Margin of Success for Clothing Retailers published in *The Times*, 20 November 2002 (Real World 1.3) and Dirty Laundry: How companies fudge the numbers published in *The Times*, 22 September 2002 (Real World 5.8); Financial Times Limited for Profit Without Honour by John Kay published in *Financial Times*, 30 June 2002 (Real World 1.6); Investors Chronicle for Amstrad AMT published in *Investors Chronicle,* 7 October 2005 (Real World 2.5); Thorntons plc for extracts from its Annual Report 2006 (Real World 2.6); VNU Business Media Europe for an extract from JJB massages results to boost profits published in *Accountancy Age,* 20 October 2005 (Real World 3.6) and Ineffective internal controls hurting GM published at www.AccountancyAge.com, 15 May 2007 (Real World 10.7); C William (Bill) Thomas for an extract from The Rise and Fall of Enron published in *The Journal of Accountancy,* vol. 194 no. 3 April 2002 (Real World 5.11 and J D Wetherspoon plc for extracts from its Annual Report 2006 (Real World 10.8).

We are grateful to the Financial Times Limited for permission to reprint the following material:

Real World 8.1 Table showing share prices of some well-known companies, © *Financial Times,* 11 November 2006.

Real World 1.1 Morrison in uphill battle to integrate Safeway, © *Financial Times,* 26 May 2005; Real World 1.5 Fair shares?, © *Financial Times,* 11 June 2005; Real World 1.7 Tsunami: finding the right figures for disaster, © *Financial Times,* 7 March 2005; Real World 2.4 Goodwill charges at record levels, © *Financial Times,* 30 May 2006; Real World 3.8 Household debt adds to rise in bank write-offs, © *Financial Times,* 28 March 2005; Real World 4.1 Monotub industries in a spin as founder gets Titan for £1, © *Financial Times,* 23 January 2003; Real World 4.8 MyTravel set to resume its dividend, © *Financial Times,* 14 March 2006; Real World 5.13 It pays to read between the lines, © *Financial Times,* 17 September 2005; Real World 6.1 Eurotunnel takes £1.3bn impairment charge, © *Financial Times,* 9 February 2004; Real World 6.3 Waterford Wedgewood face some intense questions over its cash flow, © *Financial Times,* 17 June 2004; Real World 7.3 Nissans empty products pipeline, © *Financial Times,* 6 November 2006; Real World 10.3 Morrison chairman is set to beef up corporate governance, © *Financial Times,* 23 March 2005; Real World 10.6 Fees for non-execs and chairmen rocket, © *Financial Times,* 16 October 2006; Real World 10.9 Buffett backs Cokes board pay scheme, © *Financial Times,* 6 April 2006; Real World 10.12 VW to alter management focus, © *Financial Times,* 31 August 2003; Real World 10.14 RBS will set tougher targets for executive directors pay packets, © *Financial Times,* 20 April 2006; Real World 10.15 Stock options backdating haunts Apple, © *Financial Times,* 28 December 2006; Real World 10.18 Move to oust SkyePharma chairman, © *Financial Times,* 20 January 2006; Real World 10.19 UBM investors in bonus revolt, © *Financial Times,* 4 May 2005; Real World 10.21 Few top companies follow code on corporate governance, © *Financial Times,* 28 December 2006.

1

Introduction to accounting

Introduction

In this opening chapter, we begin by considering the role and nature of accounting. We shall see that it can be a valuable tool for decision-making purposes. We shall identify the main users of accounting information and discuss the ways in which this information can improve the quality of decisions that those people make. We will then go on to consider the particular role of financial accounting and the differences that exist between financial and management accounting. As this book is concerned with accounting and financial decision-making for private-sector businesses, we shall also examine the main forms of business enterprise and consider what the key objectives of a business are likely to be.

Learning outcomes

When you have completed this chapter, you should be able to:

- Explain the nature and role of accounting.

- Identify the main users of financial information and discuss their needs.

- Distinguish between financial and management accounting.

- Identify and discuss the main forms of business enterprise.

What is accounting?

→ **Accounting** is concerned with collecting, analysing and communicating financial information. The purpose is to help people that use this information to make more informed decisions. If the financial information that is communicated is not capable of improving the quality of decisions made, there would be no point in producing it. Sometimes the impression is given that the purpose of accounting is simply to prepare financial reports on a regular basis. While it is true that accountants undertake this kind of work, it does not represent an end in itself. The ultimate purpose of the accountant's work is to give people better financial information on which to base their decisions. This decision-making perspective of accounting fits in with the theme of this book and shapes the way in which we deal with each topic.

Who are the users of accounting information?

For accounting information to be useful, the accountant must be clear *for whom* the information is being prepared and *for what purpose* the information will be used. There are likely to be various groups of people (known as 'user groups') with an interest in a particular organisation, in the sense of needing to make decisions about it. For the typical private-sector business, the most important of these groups are shown in Figure 1.1. Take a look at this figure and then try Activity 1.1 below.

Figure 1.1	Main users of financial information relating to a business

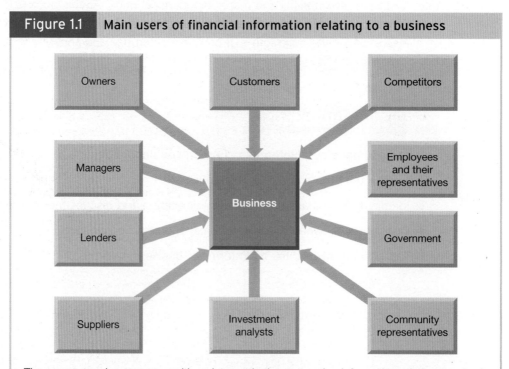

There are several user groups with an interest in the accounting information relating to a business. The majority of these are outside the business but, nevertheless, they have a stake in it. This is not meant to be an exhaustive list of potential users, however, the groups identified are normally the most important.

Activity 1.1

Ptarmigan Insurance plc (PI) is a large motor insurance business. Taking the user groups identified below, suggest, for each group, the sort of decisions likely to be made about PI and the factors to be taken into account when making these decisions.

Your answer may be as follows:

User group	Decision
Customers	Whether to take further motor policies with PI. This might involve an assessment of PI's ability to continue in business and to meet their needs, particularly in respect of any insurance claims made.
Competitors	How best to compete against PI or, perhaps, whether to leave the market on the grounds that it is not possible to compete profitably with PI. This might involve using PI's performance in various aspects as a 'benchmark' when evaluating their own performance. They might also try to assess PI's financial strength and to identify significant changes that may signal PI's future actions (for example, raising funds as a prelude to market expansion).
Employees	Whether to continue in employment with PI and, if so, whether to demand higher rewards for their labour. The future plans, profits and financial strength of the business are likely to be of particular interest when making these decisions.
Government	Whether PI should pay tax and, if so, how much, whether it complies with agreed pricing policies, whether financial support is needed and so on. In making these decisions an assessment of its profits, sales revenues and financial strength would be made.
Community representatives	Whether to allow PI to expand its premises and/or whether to provide economic support for the business. PI's ability to continue to provide employment for the community, to use community resources and to help fund environmental improvements are likely to be considered when arriving at such decisions.
Investment analysts	Whether to advise clients to invest in PI. This would involve an assessment of the likely risks and future returns associated with PI.
Suppliers	Whether to continue to supply PI and, if so, whether to supply on credit. This would involve an assessment of PI's ability to pay for any goods and services supplied.
Lenders	Whether to lend money to PI and/or whether to require repayment of any existing loans. PI's ability to pay the interest and to repay the principal sum would be important factors in such decisions.
Managers	Whether the performance of the business needs to be improved. Performance to date would be compared with earlier plans or some other 'benchmark' to decide whether action needs to be taken. Managers may also wish to decide whether there should be a change in PI's future direction. This would involve looking at PI's ability to perform and at the opportunities available to it.
Owners	Whether to invest more in PI or to sell all, or part, of the investment currently held. This would involve an assessment of the likely risks and returns associated with PI. Owners may also be involved with decisions on rewarding senior managers. The financial performance of the business would normally be considered when making such a decision.

Though this answer covers many of the key points, you may have identified other decisions and/or other factors to be taken into account by each group.

The conflicting interests of users

We have seen above that each user group looks at a business from a different perspective and has its own particular interests. This means that there is always the risk that the interests of one group will collide with those of another group. Conflict between user groups is most likely to occur over the way in which the wealth of the business is generated and/or distributed. A good example is the conflict that may arise between the managers and the owners of the business. Although managers are appointed to act in the best interests of the owners, there is always a danger that they will not do so. Instead, managers may use the wealth of the business to award themselves large pay rises, to furnish large offices or to buy expensive cars for their own use. Accounting information has an important role to play in reporting the extent to which various groups have benefited from the business. Thus, owners may rely on accounting information to check whether the pay and benefits of managers are in line with agreed policy.

A further example is the potential conflict of interest between lenders and owners. There is a risk that the funds loaned to a business will not be used for purposes that have been agreed. Lenders, therefore, may rely on accounting information to check that the funds have been applied in an appropriate manner and that the terms of the loan agreement are not being broken.

Activity 1.2

Can you think of other examples where accounting information may be used to monitor potential conflicts of interest between the various user groups identified?

Two possible examples that spring to mind are:

● employees (or their representatives) wishing to check that they are receiving a 'fair share' of the wealth created by the business and that agreed profit-sharing schemes are being adhered to;

● government wishing to check that the profits made from a contract that it has given to a business are not excessive.

You may have thought of other examples.

How useful is accounting information?

No one would seriously claim that accounting information fully meets all of the needs of each of the various user groups. Accounting is still a developing subject and we still have much to learn about user needs and the ways in which these needs should be met. Nevertheless, the information contained in accounting reports should help users make decisions relating to the business. The information should reduce uncertainty over the financial position and performance of the business. It should help to answer questions concerning the availability of funds to pay owners a return, to repay loans, to reward employees and so on.

Typically, there is no close substitute for the information provided by the financial statements. Thus, if users cannot glean the required information from the financial statements, it is often unavailable to them. Other sources of information concerning the financial health of a business are normally much less useful.

Activity 1.3

What other sources of information might users employ in an attempt to gain an impression of the financial position and performance of a business? What kind of information might be gleaned from these sources?

Other sources of information available include:

- meetings with managers of the business;
- public announcements made by the business;
- newspaper and magazine articles;
- websites, including the website of the business;
- radio and TV reports;
- information-gathering agencies (for example, agencies that assess businesses' credit worthiness or credit ratings);
- industry reports;
- economy-wide reports.

These sources can provide information on various aspects of the business, such as new products or services being offered, management changes, new contracts offered or awarded, the competitive environment within which the business operates, the impact of new technology, changes in legislation, changes in interest rates and future levels of inflation. However, the various sources of information identified are not really substitutes for accounting reports. Rather, they are best used in conjunction with the reports in order to obtain a clearer picture of the financial health of a business.

Evidence on the usefulness of accounting

There are arguments and convincing evidence that accounting information is at least *perceived* as being useful to users. Numerous research surveys have asked users to rank the importance of accounting information, in relation to other sources of information, for decision-making purposes. Generally speaking, these studies have found that users rank accounting information very highly. There is also considerable evidence that businesses choose to produce accounting information that exceeds the minimum requirements imposed by accounting regulations. (For example, businesses often produce a considerable amount of accounting information for managers, which is not required by any regulations.) Presumably, the cost of producing this additional accounting information is justified on the grounds that users find it useful. Such arguments and evidence, however, leave unanswered the question as to whether the information produced is actually used for decision-making purposes, that is: does it affect people's behaviour?

It is normally very difficult to assess the impact of accounting on decision-making. One situation arises, however, where the impact of accounting information can be observed and measured. This is where the **shares** (portions of ownership of a business) are traded on a **Stock Exchange**. The evidence reveals that, when a business makes an announcement concerning its accounting profits, the prices at which shares are traded and the volume of shares traded often change significantly. This suggests that investors are changing their views about the future prospects of the business as a result of this new information becoming available to them and that this, in turn, leads them to make a decision either to buy or sell shares in the business.

Although there is evidence that accounting reports are perceived as being useful and are used for decision-making purposes, it is impossible to measure just how useful accounting reports are to users. As a result, we cannot say with certainty whether the cost of producing those reports represents value for money. Accounting information will usually represent only one input to a particular decision and so the precise weight attached to the accounting information by the decision maker and the benefits which flow as a result, cannot be accurately assessed. We shall now go on to see, however, that it is at least possible to identify the kinds of qualities which accounting information must possess in order to be useful. Where these qualities are lacking, the usefulness of the information will be diminished.

Providing a service

One way of viewing accounting is as a form of service. Accountants provide economic information to their 'clients', who the various users identified in Figure 1.1. The quality of the service provided is determined by the extent to which the needs of the various user groups have been met. In other words, how fit for purpose is the information?

To meet these users' needs, it can be argued that accounting information should possess certain key qualities, or characteristics. These are:

- **Relevance**. Accounting information must have the ability to influence decisions. Unless this characteristic is present, there is really no point in producing the information. The information may be relevant to the prediction of future events (for example, in predicting how much profit is likely to be earned next year) or relevant in helping confirm past events (for example, in establishing how much profit was earned last year). The role of accounting in confirming past events is important because users often wish to check on the accuracy of earlier predictions that they have made. The accuracy (or inaccuracy) of earlier predictions may help users to judge the accuracy of current predictions. To influence a decision, the information must, of course, be available when the decision is being made. Thus, relevant information must be timely.

- **Reliability**. Accounting should be free from significant errors or bias. It should be capable of being relied upon by managers to represent what it is supposed to represent. Though both relevance and reliability are very important, the problem that we often face in accounting is that information that is highly relevant may not be very reliable, and that which is reliable may not be very relevant.

Activity 1.4

To illustrate this last point, let us assume that a manager has to sell a custom-built machine owned by the business and has recently received a bid for it. This machine is very unusual and there is no ready market for it.

What information would be relevant to the manager when deciding whether to accept the bid? How reliable would that information be?

The manager would probably like to know the current market value of the machine before deciding whether or not to accept the bid. The current market value would be highly relevant to the final decision, but it might not be very reliable because the machine is unique and there is likely to be little information concerning market values.

Where a choice has to be made between providing information that has either more relevance or more reliability, the maximisation of relevance is usually the guiding rule. No matter how reliable it is, it is useless if it is not relevant. On the other hand, information that is not totally reliable can be useful if it is relevant.

 ● **Comparability**. This quality will enable users to identify changes in the business over time (for example, the trend in sales revenue over the past five years). It will also help them to evaluate the performance of the business in relation to other similar businesses. Comparability is achieved by treating items that are basically the same in the same manner for accounting purposes. Comparability tends also to be enhanced by making clear the policies that have been adopted in measuring and presenting the information.

● **Understandability**. Accounting reports should be expressed as clearly as possible and should be understood by those at whom the information is aimed.

Activity 1.5

Do you think that accounting reports should be understandable to those who have not studied accounting?

It would be useful if everyone could understand accounting reports, but realistically, this is not likely to be the case. Complex financial events and transactions cannot always be reported easily. It is probably best that we regard accounting reports in the same way as we regard a report written in a foreign language. To understand either of these, we need to have had some preparation. Generally speaking, accounting reports assume that the user not only has a reasonable knowledge of business and accounting, but is also prepared to invest some time in studying the reports.

Despite the answer to Activity 1.5, the onus is clearly on accountants to provide information in a way that makes it as understandable as possible to non-accountants.

But . . . is it material?

The qualities, or characteristics, that have just been described will help us to decide whether accounting information is potentially useful. If a particular piece of information has these qualities then it may be useful. However, this does not automatically mean that it should be reported to users. We also have to consider whether the information is material, or significant. This means that we should ask whether its omission or misrepresentation in the accounting reports would really alter the decisions that users make. Thus, in addition to possessing the characteristics mentioned above, accounting information must also cross the threshold of **materiality**. If the information is not regarded as material, it should not be included within the reports as it will merely clutter them up and, perhaps, interfere with the users' ability to interpret the financial results. The type of information and amounts involved will normally determine whether it is material.

Weighing up the costs and benefits

Having read the previous sections you may feel that, when considering a piece of accounting information, provided the four main qualities identified are present and it is material it should be gathered and made available to users. Unfortunately, there is one more hurdle to jump. Something may still exclude a piece of accounting information from the reports even when it is considered to be useful. Consider Activity 1.6.

Activity 1.6

Suppose an item of information is capable of being provided. It is relevant to a particular decision, it is also reliable, comparable, can be understood by the decision maker concerned and is material.

Can you think of a reason why, in practice, you might choose not to produce the information?

The reason that you may decide not to produce, or discover, the information is that you judge the cost of doing so to be greater than the potential benefit of having the information. This cost–benefit issue will limit the extent to which accounting information is provided.

In theory, a particular item of accounting information should only be produced if the costs of providing it are less than the benefits, or value, to be derived from its use. Figure 1.2 shows the relationship between the costs and value of providing additional accounting information. The figure shows how the value of information received by the decision maker eventually begins to decline. This is, perhaps, because additional information becomes less relevant, or because of the problems that a decision maker may have in processing the sheer quantity of information provided. The costs of providing the information, however, will increase with each additional piece of information. The broken line indicates the point at which the gap between the value of information and the cost of providing that information is at its greatest. This represents the optimal amount of information that can be provided. This theoretical model, however, poses a number of problems in practice. We shall now go on to discuss these.

To illustrate the practical problems of establishing the value of information, suppose that we wish to have a car serviced at a local garage. We know that the nearest garage would charge £250 but believe that other local garages may offer the same service for a lower price. The only ways of finding out the prices at other garages are either to telephone them or to visit them. Telephone calls cost money and involve some of our time. Visiting the garages may not involve the outlay of money, but more of our time will be involved. Is it worth the cost of finding out the price of a car service at the various local garages? The answer, as we have seen, is that if the cost of discovering the price is less than the potential benefit, it is worth having that information.

Figure 1.2	Relationship between costs and the value of providing additional accounting information

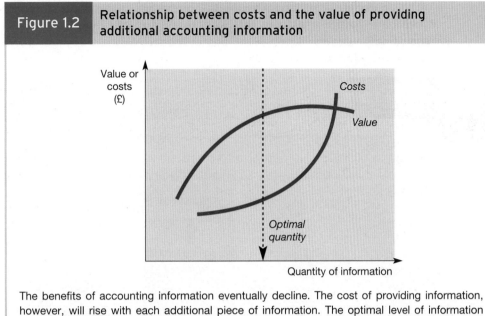

The benefits of accounting information eventually decline. The cost of providing information, however, will rise with each additional piece of information. The optimal level of information provision is where the gap between the value of the information and the cost of providing it is at its greatest.

To identify the various prices for a car service, there are various points to be considered, including:

● How many garages shall we telephone or visit?
● What is the cost of each telephone call?
● How long will it take to make all the telephone calls or visits?
● How much do we value our time?

The economic benefit of having information on the price of the service is probably even harder to assess – remember that we have not contacted any garages yet. The following points need to be considered:

● What is the cheapest price that we might be quoted for the car service?
● How likely is it that we shall be quoted a price cheaper than £250?

As we can imagine, the answers to these questions may be far from clear. When assessing the value of accounting information we are confronted with similar problems.

The provision of accounting information can be very costly, however, the costs are often difficult to quantify. The direct, out-of-pocket, costs, such as salaries of accounting staff, are not really a problem to identify, but these are only part of the total costs involved. There are also less direct costs such as the cost of the user's time spent on analysing and interpreting the information contained in reports.

The economic benefit of having accounting information is even harder to assess. It is possible to apply some 'science' to the problem of weighing the costs and benefits, but a lot of subjective judgement is likely to be involved. Whilst no one would seriously advocate that the typical business should produce no accounting information, at the same time, no one would advocate that every item of information that could be seen as possessing one or more of the key characteristics should be produced, irrespective of the cost of producing it.

The characteristics that influence the usefulness of accounting information and which have been discussed in this section and the preceding section are set out in Figure 1.3.

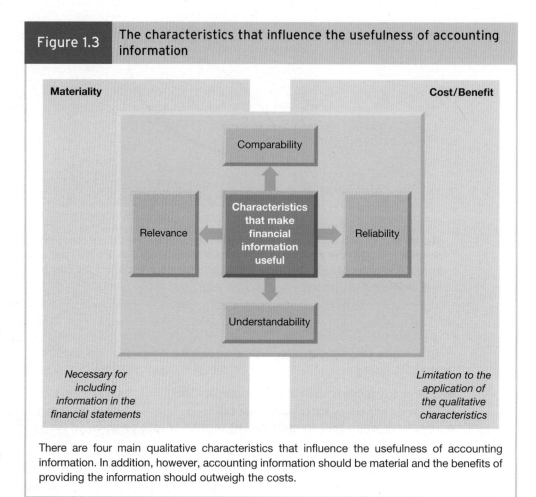

Figure 1.3   The characteristics that influence the usefulness of accounting information

There are four main qualitative characteristics that influence the usefulness of accounting information. In addition, however, accounting information should be material and the benefits of providing the information should outweigh the costs.

Accounting as an information system

We have already seen that accounting can be seen as the provision of a service to 'clients'. Another way of viewing accounting is as a part of the business's total information system. Users, both inside and outside the business, have to make decisions concerning the allocation of scarce economic resources. To try to ensure that these resources are allocated in an efficient manner, users require economic information on which to base decisions. It is the role of the accounting system to provide that information and this will involve information gathering and communication.

The **accounting information system** should have certain features that are common to all valid information systems within a business. These are:

● identifying and capturing relevant information (in this case economic information);
● recording the information collected in a systematic manner;

● analysing and interpreting the information collected;
● reporting the information in a manner that suits the needs of users.

The relationship between these features is set out in Figure 1.4.

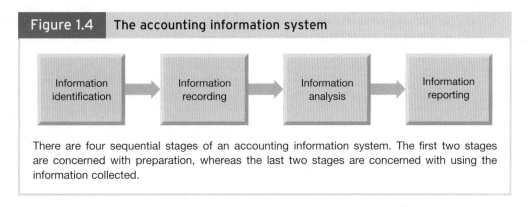

Figure 1.4 **The accounting information system**

Information identification → Information recording → Information analysis → Information reporting

There are four sequential stages of an accounting information system. The first two stages are concerned with preparation, whereas the last two stages are concerned with using the information collected.

Given the decision-making emphasis of this book, we shall be concerned primarily with the final two elements of the process – the analysis and reporting of accounting information. We shall consider the way in which information is used by, and is useful to, users rather than the way in which it is identified and recorded.

Efficient accounting systems are an essential ingredient of an efficient business. When the accounting systems fail, the results can be disastrous. **Real World 1.1** provides an example of a systems failure when two businesses combined and then attempted to integrate their respective systems.

Real World 1.1

Blaming the system

FT

When Sir Ken Morrison bought Safeway for £3.35 bn in March 2004, he almost doubled the size of his supermarket chain overnight and went from being a regional operator to a national force. His plan was simple enough. He had to sell off some Safeway stores – Morrison has to date sold off 184 stores for an estimated £1.3 bn – and convert the remaining 230 Safeway stores into Morrison's. Sir Ken has about another 50 to sell. But, nearly 15 months on, and the integration process is proving harder in practice than it looked on paper. Morrison, once known for its robust performance, has issued four profit warnings in the past 10 months. Each time the retailer has blamed Safeway. Last July, it was because of a faster than expected sales decline in Safeway stores. In March – there were two warnings that month – it was the fault of Safeway's accounting systems, which left Morrison with lower supplier incomes. This month's warning was put down to higher than expected costs from running parallel store systems. At the time of the first warning last July, Simon Procter, of the stockbrokers Charles Stanley, noted that the news 'has blown all profit forecasts out of the water and visibility is very poor from here on out'. But if it was difficult then to predict where Morrison's profits were heading, it is impossible now. Morrison itself cannot give guidance. 'No one envisaged this,' says Mr Procter. 'When I made that comment about visibility last July, I was thinking on a 12-month time frame, not a two-year one.' Morrison says the complexity of the Safeway deal has put a 'significant strain' on its ability to cope with managing internal accounts. 'This is impacting the ability of the board to forecast likely trends in profitability and the directors are therefore not currently in a position to provide reliable guidance on the level of profitability as a whole', admits the retailer.

Source: Rigby, Elizabeth 'Morrison in Uphill Battle to Integrate Safeway', FT.com, 26 May 2005.

Management and financial accounting

Accounting is usually seen as having two distinct strands. These are:

→ ● **Management accounting**, which seeks to meet the needs of managers; and
→ ● **Financial accounting**, which seeks to meet the accounting needs of all of the other users identified earlier in the chapter (see Figure 1.1).

The difference in their targeted users has led to each strand of accounting developing along different lines. The main areas of difference are as follows.

● *Nature of the reports produced.* Financial accounting reports tend to be general-purpose. That is, they contain financial information that will be useful for a broad range of users and decisions rather than being specifically designed for the needs of a particular group or set of decisions. Management accounting reports, on the other hand, are often specific-purpose reports. They are designed either with a particular decision in mind or for a particular manager.

● *Level of detail.* Financial accounting reports provide users with a broad overview of the performance and position of the business for a period. As a result, information is aggregated and detail is often lost. Management accounting reports, however, often provide managers with considerable detail to help them with a particular operational decision.

● *Regulations.* Financial accounting reports, for many businesses, are subject to accounting regulations that try to ensure they are produced with standard content and in a standard format. The law and accounting rule makers impose these regulations. As management accounting reports are for internal use only, there are no regulations from external sources concerning the form and content of the reports. They can be designed to meet the needs of particular managers.

● *Reporting interval.* For most businesses, financial accounting reports are produced on an annual basis, though large businesses may produce half-yearly reports, and a few produce quarterly ones. Management accounting reports may be produced as frequently as required by managers. In many businesses, managers are provided with certain reports on a daily, weekly or monthly basis, which allows them to check progress frequently. In addition, special-purpose reports will be prepared when required (for example, to evaluate a proposal to purchase a piece of machinery).

● *Time orientation.* Financial accounting reports reflect the performance and position of the business for the past period. In essence, they are backward looking. Management accounting reports, on the other hand, often provide information concerning future performance as well as past performance. It is an oversimplification, however, to suggest that financial accounting reports never incorporate expectations concerning the future. Occasionally, businesses will release projected information to other users in an attempt to raise capital or to fight off unwanted takeover bids. Even preparation of the routine financial accounting reports typically requires making some judgements about the future, as we shall see in Chapter 3.

● *Range and quality of information.* Financial accounting reports concentrate on information that can be quantified in monetary terms. Management accounting also produces such reports, but is also more likely to produce reports that contain information of a non-financial nature, such as physical volume of inventories, number of sales orders received, number of new products launched, physical output per employee and so on. Financial accounting places greater emphasis on the use of objective, verifiable evidence when preparing reports. Management accounting reports may use information that is less objective and verifiable, but nevertheless provide managers with the information they need.

We can see from this that management accounting is less constrained than financial accounting. It may draw from a variety of sources and use information that has varying degrees of reliability. The only real test to be applied when assessing the value of the information produced for managers is whether or not it improves the quality of the decisions made.

The distinctions between management and financial accounting suggest that there are differences between the information needs of managers and those of other users. Whilst differences undoubtedly exist, there is also a good deal of overlap between these needs.

Activity 1.7

Can you think of any broad areas of overlap between the information needs of managers and those of other users? We thought of two.

1   Managers will, at times, be interested in receiving an historical overview of business operations of the sort provided to other users.
2   Other users would be interested in receiving information relating to the future, such as the planned level of profits and non-financial information such as the state of the sales order book and the extent of product innovations.

The distinction between the two areas of accounting reflects, to some extent, the differences in access to financial information. Managers have much more control over the form and content of information they receive. Other users have to rely on what managers are prepared to provide or what the financial reporting regulations require must be provided. Though the scope of financial accounting reports has increased over time, fears concerning loss of competitive advantage and user ignorance concerning the reliability of forecast data have led businesses to resist providing other users with the same detailed and wide-ranging information available to managers.

In the past it has been argued that accounting systems are biased in favour of providing information for external users. Financial accounting requirements have been the main priority and management accounting has suffered as a result. Recent survey evidence suggests, however, that this argument has lost its force. Nowadays, management accounting systems will usually provide managers with information that is relevant to their needs rather than what is determined by external reporting requirements. Financial reporting cycles, however, retain some influence over management accounting and managers are aware of expectations of external users (see reference 1 at the end of the chapter).

Scope of this book

This book is concerned with financial accounting rather than management accounting. In Chapter 2 we begin by introducing the three principal financial statements:

- balance sheet;
- income statement (also called the profit and loss account);
- cash flow statement.

These statements are briefly reviewed before we go on to consider the balance sheet in more detail. We shall see that the balance sheet provides information concerning the wealth held by a business at a particular point in time and the claims against this wealth. Included in our consideration of the balance sheet will be an introduction to the **conventions of accounting**. Conventions are the generally accepted rules that accountants tend to follow when preparing financial statements.

Chapter 3 introduces the second of the major financial statements, the income statement. This provides information concerning the wealth created by a business during a period. In this chapter we shall be looking at such issues as how profit is measured, the point in time at which we recognise that a profit has been made and the accounting conventions that apply to this particular statement.

In the UK and throughout much of the industrialised world, the limited company is the major form of business unit. In Chapter 4 we consider the accounting aspects of limited companies. Although there is nothing of essence that makes the accounting aspects of companies different from other types of private-sector business, there are some points of detail that we need to consider. In Chapter 5 we continue our examination of limited companies and, in particular, consider the framework of rules that must be adhered to when presenting accounting reports to owners and external users.

Chapter 6 deals with the last of the three principal financial statements, the cash flow statement. This financial statement is important in identifying the financing and investing activities of the business over a period. It sets out how cash was generated and how cash was used during a period.

Reading the three statements will provide information about the performance and position of a business. It is possible, however, to gain even more helpful insights about the business by analysing the statements using financial ratios and other techniques. Combining two figures in the financial statements in a ratio and comparing this with a similar ratio for, say, another business, can often tell us much more than just reading the figures themselves. Chapters 7 and 8 are concerned with techniques for analysing financial statements.

The typical large business in the UK is a group of companies rather than just a single company. A group of companies will exist where one company controls one or more other companies. In Chapter 9 we shall see why groups exist and consider the accounting issues raised by the combination of companies into groups.

Finally, in Chapter 10, we shall consider the way in which larger businesses are governed and how directors and other senior managers are accountable to the owners and to other groups with an interest in the business.

Has accounting become too interesting?

In recent years, accounting has become front-page news and is a major talking point among those connected with the world of business. Unfortunately, the attention that accounting has attracted has been for all the wrong reasons. We have seen that investors rely on financial reports to help to keep an eye on both their investment and the managers. However, what if the managers provide misleading financial reports to investors? Recent revelations suggest that the managers of some large companies have been doing just this.

Two of the most notorious cases have been those of:

● Enron – an energy-trading business based in Texas, which was accused of entering into complicated financial arrangements in an attempt to obscure losses and to inflate profits; and

- WorldCom – a major long-distance telephone operator in the US, which was accused of reclassifying $3.9 billion of expenses so as to falsely inflate the profit figures that the business reported to its owners (shareholders) and to others.

In the wake of these scandals, there was much closer scrutiny by investment analysts and investors of the financial reports that businesses produce. This led to further businesses, in both the US and Europe, being accused of using dubious accounting practices to bolster profits.

Accounting scandals can have a profound effect on all those connected with the business. The Enron scandal, for example, ultimately led to the collapse of the company, which, in turn, resulted in lost jobs and large financial losses for lenders, suppliers and owners. Confidence in the world of business can be badly shaken by such events and this can pose problems for society as a whole. Not surprisingly, therefore, the relevant authorities tend to be severe on those who perpetrate such scandals. In the US, Bernie Ebbers, the former chief executive of WorldCom received 25 years in prison for his part in the fraud.

Various reasons have been put forward to explain this spate of scandals. Some may have been caused by the pressures on managers to meet unrealistic expectations of investors for continually rising profits, others by the greed of unscrupulous executives whose pay is linked to financial performance. However, they may all reflect a particular economic environment.

Real World 1.2 gives some comments suggesting that when all appears to be going well with a business, people can be quite gullible and over-trusting.

Real World 1.2

The thoughts of Warren Buffett

Warren Buffett is one of the world's shrewdest and most successful investors. He believes that the accounting scandals mentioned above were perpetrated during the 'new economy boom' of the late 1990s when confidence was high and exaggerated predictions were being made concerning the future. He states that during that period:

> You had an erosion of accounting standards. You had an erosion, to some extent, of executive behaviour. But during a period when everybody 'believes', people who are inclined to take advantage of other people can get away with a lot.

> He believes that the worst is now over and that the 'dirty laundry' created during this heady period is being washed away and that the washing machine is now in the 'rinse cycle'.

Source: (2002) *The Times*, Business Section, 26 September, p. 25.

Whatever the causes, the result of these accounting scandals has been to undermine the credibility of financial statements and to introduce much stricter regulations concerning the quality of financial information. We shall return to this issue in later chapters when we consider the financial statements.

The changing face of accounting

Over the past 25 years, the environment within which businesses operate has become increasingly turbulent and competitive. Various reasons have been identified to explain these changes, including:

- the increasing sophistication of customers;
- the development of a global economy where national frontiers become less important;
- rapid changes in technology;
- the deregulation of domestic markets (for example, electricity, water and gas);
- increasing pressure from owners (shareholders) for competitive economic returns;
- the increasing volatility of financial markets.

This new, more complex, environment has brought new challenges for managers and other users of accounting information. Their needs have changed and both financial accounting and management accounting have had to respond. To meet the changing needs of users there has been a radical review of the kind of information to be reported.

The changing business environment has given added impetus to the search for a clear framework and principles upon which to base financial accounting reports. Various attempts have been made to clarify the purpose of financial accounting reports and to provide a more solid foundation for the development of accounting rules. The frameworks and principles that have been developed try to address fundamental questions such as:

- 'Who are the users of financial accounting information?'
- What kinds of financial accounting reports should be prepared and what should they contain?';
- 'How should items be measured?'

In response to criticisms that the financial reports of some businesses are too opaque, accounting rule makers have tried to improve reporting rules to ensure that the accounting policies of businesses are more comparable, more transparent and portray economic reality more faithfully. Whilst this has had a generally beneficial effect, the recent accounting scandals have highlighted the limitations of accounting rules in protecting investors and others.

The internationalisation of businesses has created a need for accounting rules to have an international reach. It can no longer be assumed that users of accounting information relating to a particular business are based in the country in which the business operates or are familiar with the accounting rules of that country. Thus, there has been increasing harmonisation of accounting rules across national frontiers. A more detailed review of the developments mentioned above is included in Chapter 5.

Management accounting has also changed by becoming more outward looking in its focus. In the past, information provided to managers has been largely restricted to that collected within the business. However, the attitude and behaviour of customers and rival businesses have now become the object of much information gathering. Increasingly, successful businesses are those that are able to secure and maintain competitive advantage over their rivals.

To obtain this advantage, businesses have become more 'customer driven' (that is, concerned with satisfying customer needs). This has led to management accounting information that provides details of customers and the market, such as customer evaluation of services provided and market share. In addition, information about the costs and profits of rival businesses, which can be used as 'benchmarks' by which to gauge competitiveness, is gathered and reported.

To compete successfully, businesses must also find ways of managing costs. The cost base of modern businesses is under continual review and this, in turn, has led to the development of more sophisticated methods of measuring and controlling costs.

What kinds of business ownership exist?

The particular form of business ownership has important implications for accounting purposes and so it is useful to be clear about the main forms of ownership that can arise.

There are basically three arrangements:

● sole proprietorship
● partnership
● limited company.

We shall now consider each of these.

Sole proprietorship

→ **Sole proprietorship**, as the name suggests, is where an individual is the sole owner of a business. This type of business is often quite small in terms of size (as measured, for example, by sales revenue generated or number of staff employed), however, the number of such businesses is very large indeed. Examples of sole-proprietor businesses can be found in most industrial sectors but particularly within the service sector. Hence, services such as electrical repairs, picture framing, photography, driving instruction, retail shops and hotels have a large proportion of sole-proprietor businesses. The sole-proprietor business is easy to set up. No formal procedures are required and operations can often commence immediately (unless special permission is required because of the nature of the trade or service, such as running licensed premises). The owner can decide the way in which the business is to be conducted and has the flexibility to restructure or dissolve the business whenever it suits. The law does not recognise the sole-proprietor business as being separate from the owner, so the business will cease on the death of the owner.

Although the owner must produce accounting information to satisfy the taxation authorities, there is no legal requirement to produce accounting information relating to the business for other user groups. However, some user groups may demand accounting information about the business and may be in a position to have their demands met (for example, a bank requiring accounting information on a regular basis as a condition of a loan). The sole proprietor will have unlimited liability which means that no distinction will be made between the proprietor's personal wealth and that of the business if there are business debts that must be paid.

Partnership

→ A **partnership** exists where at least two individuals carry on a business together with the intention of making a profit. Partnerships have much in common with sole-proprietor businesses. They are often quite small in size (although some, such as partnerships of accountants and solicitors, can be large). Partnerships are also easy to set up as no formal procedures are required (and it is not even necessary to have a written agreement between the partners). The partners can agree whatever arrangements suit them concerning the financial and management aspects of the business, and the partnership can be restructured or dissolved by agreement between the partners.

Partnerships are not recognised in law as separate entities and so contracts with third parties must be entered into in the name of individual partners. The partners of a business usually have unlimited liability.

Activity 1.8

What are the main advantages and disadvantages that should be considered when deciding between a sole proprietorship and a partnership?

The main advantages of a partnership over a sole-proprietor business are:

- sharing the burden of ownership;
- the opportunity to specialise rather than cover the whole range of services (for example, a solicitors' practice, where each partner tends to specialise in a different aspect of the law);
- the ability to raise capital where this is beyond the capacity of a single individual.

The main disadvantages of a partnership compared with a sole proprietorship are:

- the risks of sharing ownership of a business with unsuitable individuals;
- the limits placed on individual decision making that a partnership will impose.

Limited company

→ **Limited companies** can range in size from quite small to very large. The number of individuals who subscribe capital and become the owners may be unlimited, which provides the opportunity to create a very large-scale business. The liability of owners, however, is limited (hence 'limited' company), which means that those individuals subscribing capital to the company are liable only for debts incurred by the company up to the amount that they have agreed to invest. This cap on the liability of the owners is designed to limit risk and to produce greater confidence to invest. Without such limits on owner liability, it is difficult to see how a modern capitalist economy could operate. In many cases, the owners of a limited company are not involved in the day-to-day running of the business and will only invest in a business if there is a clear limit set on the level of investment risk.

The benefit of limited liability, however, imposes certain obligations on such a company. To start up a limited company, documents of incorporation must be prepared that set out, amongst other things, the objectives of the business. Furthermore, a framework of regulations exists that places obligations on the way in which such a company conducts its affairs. Part of this regulatory framework requires annual financial reports to be made available to owners and lenders and usually an annual general meeting of the owners has to be held to approve the reports. In addition, a copy of the annual financial reports must be lodged with the Registrar of Companies for public inspection. In this way, the financial affairs of a limited company enter the public domain. With the exception of small companies, there is also a requirement for the annual financial reports to be subject to an audit. This involves an independent firm of accountants examining the annual reports and underlying records to see whether the reports provide a true and fair view of the financial health of the company and whether they comply with the relevant accounting rules established by law and by accounting rule makers.

All of the large household-name UK businesses (Marks and Spencer, Tesco, Shell, BskyB, BA, BT, easyJet and so on) are limited companies.

Limited companies are considered in more detail in Chapters 4 and 5.

Activity 1.9

What are the main advantages and disadvantages that should be considered when deciding between a partnership business and a limited liability company?

The main advantages of a partnership over a limited company are:

- the ease of setting up the business;
- the degree of flexibility concerning the way in which the business is conducted;
- the degree of flexibility concerning restructuring and dissolution of the business;
- freedom from administrative burdens imposed by law (for example, the annual general meeting and the need for an independent audit).

The main disadvantage of a partnership compared with a limited company is the fact that it is not possible to limit the liability of all of the partners.

This book concentrates on the accounting aspects of limited liability companies, because this type of business is by far the most important in economic terms. The early chapters will introduce accounting concepts through examples that do not draw a distinction between the different types of business. Once we have dealt with the basic accounting principles, which are the same for all three types of business, we can then go on to see how they are applied to limited companies. It must be emphasised that there are no differences in the way that all three of these forms of business keep their day-to-day accounting records. In preparing their periodic financial statements, there are certain differences that need to be considered. These differences are not ones of principle, however, but of detail.

How are businesses organised?

As we have just seen, nearly all businesses that involve more than a few owners and/or employees are set up as limited companies. This means that the finance will come from the owners (shareholders) both in the form of a direct cash investment to buy shares (in the ownership of the business) and through the owners allowing past profits, which belong to them, to be re-invested in the business. Finance will also come from lenders (banks, for example), who earn interest on their loans, and from suppliers of goods and services being prepared to supply on credit, with payment occurring a month or so after the date of supply, usually on an interest-free basis.

In larger limited companies, the owners (shareholders) are not involved in the daily running of the business; instead they appoint a board of directors to manage the business on their behalf. The board is charged with three major tasks:

● setting the overall direction and strategy for the business;
● monitoring and controlling the activities of the business; and
● communicating with owners and others connected with the business.

Each board has a chairman, elected by the directors, who is responsible for running the board in an efficient manner. In addition, each board has a chief executive officer (CEO), or managing director, who is responsible for running the business on a day-to-day basis. Occasionally, the roles of chairman and CEO are combined, although it is usually considered to be a good idea to separate them in order to prevent a single individual having excessive power.

The board of directors represents the most senior level of management. Below this level, managers are employed, with each manager given responsibility for a particular part of the business's operations.

What is the financial objective of a business?

A business is created to enhance the wealth of its owners, and throughout this book we shall assume that this is its main objective. This may come as a surprise, as there are other objectives that a business may pursue that are related to the needs of others associated with the business. For example, a business may seek to provide good working conditions for its employees, or it may seek to conserve the environment for the local community. While a business may pursue these objectives, it is normally set up with a view to increasing the wealth of its owners, and in practice the behaviour of businesses over time appears to be consistent with this objective.

Real World 1.3 provides an example of how clothes retailers pursue the search for profit.

Real World 1.3

From rags to riches

Progress in the search for profit is reported by the accounting information system. If managers find that the reported profits are inadequate, it can be an important driver for change. This change, in turn, can have a profound effect on the working lives of those both inside and outside the business.

Many clothes retailers have been concerned with profit levels in recent years. This has led them to make radical changes to the ways in which they operate. Low inflation and increased competition in the high street have forced the retailers to keep costs under strict control in order to meet their profit objectives. This has been done in various ways, including:

● moving production to cheaper countries and closing inflexible manufacturing offshoots;
● using fewer manufacturers and working more closely with manufacturers in the design of clothes. This has enabled the retailers to add details, such as embroidery or unusual design features, and to command a higher price for relatively little cost;

● improving communication to suppliers of materials and to manufacturers so that design and sourcing decisions can be made faster and more accurately. This has meant that the time to make garments has been reduced from as much as nine months to just a few weeks;

● predicting more accurately what customers want in order to avoid being left with inventories of unwanted items.

The effect of implementing these changes has been to reduce costs, and thereby improve profits, and to have more flexibility in the cost structure so that the clothes retailers are more able to weather a downturn.

Source: adapted from (2002) 'Margin of Success for Clothing Retailers', *The Times*, 20 November, p. 30.

Within a market economy there are strong competitive forces at work that ensure that failure to enhance owners' wealth will not be tolerated for long. Competition for the funds provided by the owners and competition for managers' jobs will normally mean that the owners' interests will prevail. If the managers do not provide the expected increase in ownership wealth, the owners have the power to replace the existing management team with a new team that is more responsive to owners' needs.

Does this mean that the needs of other groups associated with the business (employees, customers, suppliers, the community and so on) are not really important? The answer to this question is certainly no, if the business wishes to survive and prosper over the longer term. Satisfying the needs of other groups will normally be consistent with increasing the wealth of the owners over the longer term.

We have already discussed the importance of customers to a business. Dissatisfied customers will take their business to another supplier and this will, in turn, lead to a loss of wealth for the owners of the business losing the customers. **Real World 1.4** provides an illustration of the way in which one business acknowledges the link between customer satisfaction and creating wealth for its owners.

Real World 1.4

On a mission

A business will often express its ultimate purpose in the form of a **mission statement**. These statements are widely published and frequently adorn the websites and promotional material produced by businesses. Mission statements are usually concise and try to convey the essence of a business.

J. Sainsbury plc is a leading food retailer which recognises the importance of customers to increasing the wealth of the owners (shareholders) in its mission statement as follows:

What is Sainsbury's mission?

To meet our customers' needs effectively by providing the best quality and choice to meet their everyday shopping needs and thereby provide shareholders with good, sustainable financial returns.

Source: (2006) Investor FAQs, August, p. 2, j-sainsbury.co.uk.

A dissatisfied workforce may result in low productivity, strikes and so forth, which will in turn have an adverse effect on owners' wealth. Similarly, a business that upsets the local community by unacceptable behaviour, such as polluting the environment, may attract bad publicity, resulting in a loss of customers and heavy fines.

Real World 1.5 provides an example of how two businesses responded to potentially damaging allegations.

Real World 1.5

The price of clothes   FT

US clothing and sportswear manufacturers, Gap and Nike, have much of their clothes produced in Asia where labour tends to be cheap. However, some of the contractors that produce clothes on behalf of the two companies have been accused of unacceptable practices.

> Campaigners visited the factories and came up with damaging allegations. The factories were employing minors, they said, and managers were harassing female employees.
>
> Nike and Gap reacted by allowing independent inspectors into the factories. They promised to ensure their contractors obeyed minimum standards of employment. Earlier this year, Nike took the extraordinary step of publishing the names and addresses of all its contractors' factories on the internet. The company said it could not be sure all the abuse had stopped. It said that if campaigners visited its contractors' factories and found examples of continued malpractice, it would take action.
>
> Nike and Gap said the approach made business sense. They needed society's approval if they were to prosper. Nike said it was concerned about the reaction of potential US recruits to the campaigners' allegations. They would not want to work for a company that was constantly in the news because of the allegedly cruel treatment of those who made its products.

Source: Skapinker, Michael 'Fair Shares?', FT.com, 11 June 2005.

It is important to recognise that generating wealth for the owners is not the same as seeking to maximise the current year's profit. Wealth creation is a longer-term concept, which relates not only to this year's profit, but to that of future years as well. In the short term, corners can be cut and risks taken that improve current profit at the expense of future profit. **Real World 1.6** gives some examples of how emphasis on short-term profit can be damaging.

Real World 1.6

Short-term gains, long-term problems   FT

In recent years, many businesses have been criticised for failing to consider the long-term implications of their policies on the wealth of the owners. John Kay argues that some businesses have achieved short-term increases in wealth by sacrificing their longer-term prosperity. He points out that:

> . . . The business of Marks and Spencer, the retailer, was unparalleled in reputation but mature. To achieve earnings growth consistent with a glamour rating the company squeezed suppliers, gave less value for money, spent less on stores. In 1998, it achieved the highest (profit) margin in sales

in the history of the business. It had also compromised its position to the point where sales and profits plummeted.

Banks and insurance companies have taken staff out of branches and retrained those that remain as sales people. The pharmaceuticals industry has taken advantage of mergers to consolidate its research and development facilities. Energy companies have cut back on exploration.

We know that these actions increased corporate earnings. We do not know what effect they have on the long-run strength of the business – and this is the key point – do the companies themselves know? Some rationalisations will genuinely lead to more productive businesses. Other companies will suffer the fate of Marks and Spencer.

Source: Kay, John 'Profit without Honour', *Financial Times Weekend*, 29/30 June 2002.

Balancing risk and return

All decision-making involves the future and business decision-making is no exception. There is only one thing certain about the future, which is that we cannot be sure what is going to happen. Risk is therefore an important factor in all financial decision making, and one that must be considered explicitly in all cases. As in other aspects of life, risk and return tend to be related. Evidence shows that returns relate to risk in something like the way shown in Figure 1.5.

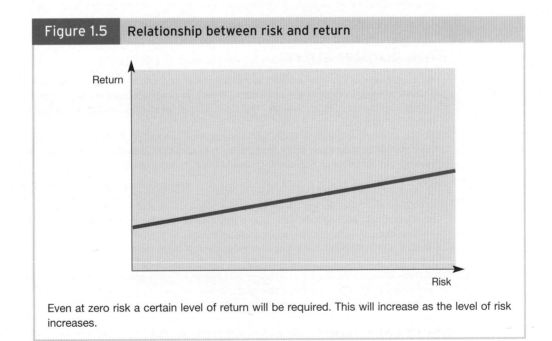

Figure 1.5 Relationship between risk and return

Even at zero risk a certain level of return will be required. This will increase as the level of risk increases.

This relationship between risk and return has important implications for setting financial objectives for a business. The owners will require a minimum return to induce them to invest at all, but will require an additional return to compensate for taking risks; the higher the risk, the higher the required return. Managers must be aware of this and must strike the appropriate balance between risk and return when setting objectives and pursuing particular courses of action.

Not-for-profit organisations

Though the focus of this book is accounting as it relates to private sector businesses, there are many organisations that do not exist mainly for the pursuit of profit. Examples include:

● charities;
● clubs and associations;
● universities;
● local government authorities;
● churches; and
● trades unions.

Such organisations also need to produce accounting information for decision-making purposes. Various user groups need accounting information about these types of organisation to help them to make decisions. These groups are often the same as, or similar to, those identified for private sector businesses. They may have a stake in the future viability of the organisation and may use accounting information to check that the wealth of the organisation is being properly controlled and used in a way that is consistent with its objectives.

Real World 1.7 provides an example of the importance of accounting to relief agencies.

Real World 1.7

When disaster strikes

FT

In the aftermath of the Asian tsunami at the turn of the year, one of the most important issues was ensuring the huge amounts of money raised were providing necessary aid and reconstruction as efficiently and effectively as possible. That does not just mean medical staff and engineers. It also means accountants.

The charity that does this is Mango: Management Accounting for Non-Governmental Organisations (NGOs). It provides accountants in the field and it provides the back-up, such as financial training, and all the other services that should result in really robust financial management in the disaster area.

'In January we had 40 requests for placements', says Denise Joseph, director of placements at Mango, 'and it was not just for the tsunami. It is an indication of the value that aid agencies place on management accountants. They play a very important role in relief efforts.'

That role will increase. The sheer scale of the money now involved ensures that. Funds for tsunami relief now stand at £365 m. In comparison, the funds raised for the Kosovo appeal in 1999 amounted to £53 m. 'It is vastly more than previous sums raised', says Ms Joseph, 'and coupled with this is the pressure to spend money very quickly. So the strain on existing financial controls and management creates extra pressures.'

Mango's work is twofold. It recruits accountants and keeps them on a register to enable a rapid response to the needs of NGOs. And it provides training courses and guidance for them.

For example, Mango has devised a Financial Management Health Check that can be downloaded by NGOs, through which they can gauge the strength of their financial systems. So far, 47,000 copies of the Health Check have been downloaded. 'Aid agencies', says Ms Joseph, 'achieve different levels of cost effectiveness. We find that if you have someone knowledgeable about financial reporting and that person is separate from the programme manager, it leads to cost savings and efficiencies.'

It is a simple principle. But it is one that can be easily forgotten in the chaos and speed of getting relief to disaster victims. Management accountants can make a huge difference both in making sure the money is spent effectively in the field and that accountability back to the donors is of a high standard.

Source: Bruce, Robert 'Tsunami: Finding the Right Figures for Disaster', FT.com, 7 March 2005.

Summary

The main points of this chapter may be summarised as follows:

What is accounting?

- Accounting provides financial information for a range of users to help them make better judgements and decisions concerning a business.

Accounting and user needs

- For accounting to be useful, there must be a clear understanding of *for whom* and *for what purpose* the information will be used.
- There may be conflicts of interest between users over the ways in which the wealth of a business is generated or distributed.
- There is evidence to suggest that accounting is both used and useful for decision-making purposes.

Providing a service

- Accounting can be viewed as a form of service as it involves providing financial information required by the various users.
- To provide a useful service, accounting must possess certain qualities, or characteristics. These are relevance, reliability, comparability and understandability. In addition, accounting information must be material.
- Providing a service to users can be costly and financial information should be produced only if the cost of providing the information is less than the benefits gained.

Accounting information

- Accounting is part of the total information system within a business. It shares the features that are common to all information systems within a business, which are the identification, recording, analysis and reporting of information.

Management and financial accounting

- Accounting has two main strands – management accounting and financial accounting.
- Management accounting seeks to meet the needs of the business's managers and financial accounting seeks to meet the needs of the other user groups.
- These two strands differ in terms of the types of reports produced, the level of reporting detail, the time horizon, the degree of standardisation and the range and quality of information provided.

Is accounting too interesting?

- In recent years, there has been a wave of accounting scandals in the US and Europe.
- This appears to reflect a particular economic environment, although other factors may also play a part.

The changing face of accounting

- Changes in the economic environment have led to changes in the nature and scope of accounting.
- Financial accounting has improved its framework of rules and there has been greater international harmonisation of accounting rules.

● Management accounting has become more outward looking and new methods for managing costs have emerged.

What kinds of business ownership exist?

There are three main forms of business unit:

● Sole proprietorship – easy to set up and flexible to operate but the owner has unlimited liability.

● Partnership – easy to set up and spreads the burdens of ownership, but partners usually have unlimited liability and there are ownership risks if the partners are unsuitable.

● Limited company – limited liability for owners but obligations imposed on the way a company conducts its affairs.

How are businesses organised and managed?

● Most businesses of any size are set up as limited companies.

● A board of directors is appointed by owners (shareholders) to oversee the running of the business.

What is the financial objective of a business?

● A business may pursue a variety of objectives but the main objective for virtually all businesses is to enhance the wealth of its owners. This does not mean, however, that the needs of other groups connected with the business, such as employees, should be ignored.

● When setting financial objectives the right balance must be struck between risk and return.

→ **Key terms**

Accounting p. 2	**Accounting information system** p. 10
Shares p. 5	**Management accounting** p. 12
Stock Exchange p. 5	**Financial accounting** p. 12
Relevance p. 6	**Conventions of accounting** p. 14
Reliability p. 6	**Sole proprietorship** p. 16
Comparability p. 7	**Partnership** p. 16
Understandability p. 7	**Limited company** p. 18
Materiality p. 7	**Mission statement** p. 21

Reference

1 Dugdale, David (2005) *Contemporary Management Accounting Practices in UK Manufacturing.* CIMA Research Publication, Vol. 1, No. 13.

Further reading

If you would like to explore the topics covered in this chapter in more depth, we recommend the following books:

Elliot, B. and Elliot, J. (2006) *Financial Accounting and Reporting*, 11th edn, Prentice Hall, Chapter 7.

Riahi-Belkaoui, A. (2004) *Accounting Theory*, 5th edn, Thomson Learning, Chapters 1, 2 and 6.

Sutton, T. (2003) *Corporate Financial Accounting and Reporting*, 2nd edn, FT Prentice Hall, Chapter 1.

Review questions

Answers to these questions can be found at the back of the book on pp. 409–10.

1.1 Identify the main users of accounting information for a university. Do these users, or the way in which they use accounting information, differ very much from the users of accounting information for private-sector businesses?

1.2 What, in economic principle, should determine what accounting information is produced? Should economics be the only issue here? (Consider who are the users of accounting information.)

1.3 Financial accounting statements tend to reflect past events. In view of this, how can they be of any assistance to a user in making a decision when decisions, by their very nature, can only be made about future actions?

1.4 'Accounting reports should be understandable. As some users of accounting information have a poor knowledge of accounting, we should produce simplified financial reports to help them.' To what extent do you agree with this view?

2

Measuring and reporting financial position

Introduction

We saw in the previous chapter that accounting has two distinct strands – financial accounting and management accounting. This chapter, along with Chapters 3 to 6, will examine the three major financial statements that form the core of financial accounting. We start by taking an overview of these statements to see how each contributes towards an assessment of the overall financial position and performance of a business.

Following this overview, we begin a more detailed examination by turning our attention towards one of these financial statements – the balance sheet. We shall see how it is prepared, and examine the principles underpinning this statement. We shall also consider its value for decision-making purposes.

Learning outcomes

When you have completed this chapter, you should be able to:

- Explain the nature and purpose of the three major financial statements.

- Prepare a simple balance sheet and interpret the information that it contains.

- Discuss the accounting conventions underpinning the balance sheet.

- Discuss the limitations of the balance sheet in portraying the financial position of a business.

The major financial statements - an overview

The major financial accounting statements aim to provide a picture of the financial position and performance of a business. To achieve this, a business's accounting system will normally produce three particular statements on a regular, recurring basis. These three are concerned with answering the following questions:

● What cash movements (that is, cash in and cash out) took place over a particular period?
● How much wealth (that is, profit) was generated, or lost, by the business over that period? (Profit (loss) is defined as the increase (decrease) in wealth arising from trading activities.)
● What is the accumulated wealth of the business at the end of that period and what form does the wealth take?

To address each of the above questions, there is a separate financial statement. The financial statements are:

● The **cash flow statement**;
● The **income statement** (also known as the profit and loss account);
● The **balance sheet** (also known as the statement of financial position).

When taken together, they provide an overall picture of the financial health of the business.

Perhaps the best way to introduce these financial statements is to look at an example of a very simple business. From this, we shall be able to see the sort of information that each of the statements can usefully provide. It is, however, worth pointing out that, whilst a simple business is our starting point, the principles that we consider apply equally to the largest and most complex businesses. This means that we shall frequently encounter these principles again in later chapters.

Example 2.1

Paul was unemployed and unable to find a job. He, therefore, decided to embark on a business venture. Christmas was approaching, and so he decided to buy gift wrapping paper from a local supplier and to sell it on the corner of his local high street. He felt that the price of wrapping paper in the high street shops was excessive. This provided him with a useful business opportunity.

He began the venture with £40 in cash. On Monday, Paul's first day of trading, he bought wrapping paper for £40 and sold three-quarters of it for £45 cash.

What cash movements took place during Monday?
For Monday, a cash flow statement showing the cash movements for the day can be prepared as follows:

Cash flow statement for Monday

	£
Opening balance (cash introduced)	40
Add Cash from sales of wrapping paper	45
	85
Less Cash paid to buy wrapping paper	40
Closing balance of cash	45

How much wealth (that is, profit) was generated by the business during Monday?

An *income statement (profit and loss account)* can be prepared to show the wealth (profit) generated on Monday. The wealth generated will represent the difference between the value of the sales made and the cost of the goods (that is, wrapping paper) sold:

Income statement (profit and loss account) for Monday

	£
Sales revenue	45
Less Cost of goods sold ($^3/_4$ of £40)	30
Profit	15

Note that it is only the cost of the wrapping paper *sold* that is matched against the sales revenue in order to find the profit, and not the whole of the cost of wrapping paper acquired. Any unsold inventories (in this case 1/4 of £40 = £10) will be charged against the future sales revenue that it generates.

What is the accumulated wealth at Monday evening?

To establish the accumulated wealth at the end of Monday's trading, we can draw up a *balance sheet (statement of financial position)*. This will list the resources held at the end of that day:

Balance sheet (statement of financial position) as at Monday evening

	£
Cash (closing balance)	45
Inventories of goods for resale ($^1/_4$ of £40)	10
Total business wealth	55

We can see from the financial statements in Example 2.1 that each statement provides part of a picture portraying the financial performance and position of the business. We begin by showing the cash movements. Cash is a vital resource that is necessary for any business to function effectively. Cash is required to meet debts that may become due and to acquire other resources (such as inventories). Cash has been described as the 'lifeblood' of a business, and movements in cash are usually given close scrutiny by users of financial statements.

However, it is clear that reporting cash movements alone would not be enough to portray the financial health of the business. The changes in cash over time do not tell us how much profit was generated. The income statement provides us with information concerning this aspect of performance. For example, we saw that during Monday the cash balance increased by £5, but the profit generated, as shown in the income statement, was £15. The cash balance did not increase by the amount of the profit made because part of the wealth generated (£10) was held in the form of inventories.

A balance sheet can be drawn up as at the end of Monday's trading, which should provide an insight to the total wealth of the business. Cash is only one form in which wealth can be held. In the case of this business, wealth is also held in the form of inventories (also known as stock). Hence, when drawing up the balance sheet, both forms of wealth held will be listed. In the case of a large business, there may be many other forms in which wealth will be held, such as land and buildings, equipment, motor vehicles and so on.

Let us now continue with our example.

Example 2.1 (continued)

On Tuesday, Paul bought more wrapping paper for £20 cash. He managed to sell all of the new inventories and all of the earlier inventories, for a total of £48.

The cash flow statement for Tuesday will be as follows:

Cash flow statement for Tuesday

	£
Opening balance (from Monday evening)	45
Add Cash from sales of wrapping paper	48
	93
Less Cash paid to buy wrapping paper	20
Closing balance	73

The income statement for Tuesday will be as follows:

Income statement for Tuesday

	£
Sales revenue	48
Less Cost of goods sold (£20 + £10)	30
Profit	18

The balance sheet as at Tuesday evening will be:

Balance sheet as at Tuesday evening

	£
Cash (closing balance)	73
Inventories	–
Total business wealth	73

We can see that the total business wealth increased to £73 by the Tuesday evening. This represents an increase of £18 (that is, £73 – £55) over Monday's figure – which, of course, is the amount of profit made during Tuesday as shown on the income statement.

Activity 2.1

On Wednesday, Paul bought more wrapping paper for £46 cash. However, it was raining hard for much of the day and sales were slow. After Paul had sold half of his total inventories for £32, he decided to stop trading until Thursday morning.

Have a go at drawing up the three financial statements for Paul's business for Wednesday.

Cash flow statement for Wednesday

	£
Opening balance (from the Tuesday evening)	73
Add Cash from sales of wrapping paper	32
	105
Less Cash paid to buy wrapping paper	46
Closing balance	59

Income statement for Wednesday

	£
Sales revenue	32
Less Cost of goods sold (¹/₂ of £46)	23
Profit	9

Balance sheet as at Wednesday evening

	£
Cash (closing balance)	59
Inventories (¹/₂ of £46)	23
Total business wealth	82

Note that the total business wealth had increased by £9 (that is, the amount of Wednesday's profit) even though the cash balance had declined. This is because the business is holding more of its wealth in the form of inventories rather than cash, compared with the position on Tuesday evening.

We can see that the income statement and cash flow statement are both concerned with measuring flows (of wealth and cash respectively) during a particular period (for example, a particular day, a particular month or a particular year). The balance sheet, however, is concerned with the financial position at a particular moment in time.

Figure 2.1 illustrates this point. The financial statements (income statement, cash flow statement and balance sheet) are often referred to as the **final accounts** of the business.

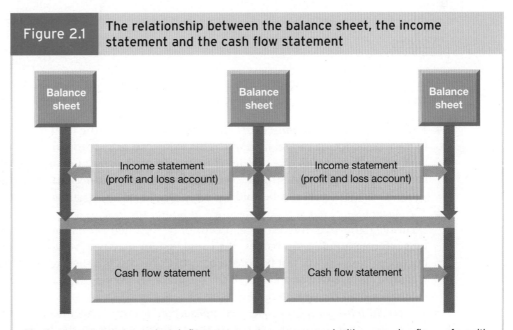

Figure 2.1   The relationship between the balance sheet, the income statement and the cash flow statement

The income statement and cash flow statement are concerned with measuring flows of wealth and cash (respectively) over time. The balance sheet, however, is concerned with measuring the stock of wealth at a particular moment in time.

For external users (that is virtually all except the managers of the business concerned), these statements are normally backward looking because they are based on information concerning past events and transactions. This can be useful in providing feedback on past performance, and in identifying trends that provide clues to future performance. However, the statements can also be prepared using projected data to help assess likely future profits, cash flows and so on. The financial statements are normally prepared on a projected basis for internal decision-making purposes only. Managers are usually reluctant to publish these projected statements for external users, as they may reveal valuable information to competitors.

Now that we have an overview of the financial statements, we shall consider each statement in more detail. We shall go straight on to look at the balance sheet. Chapter 3 looks at the income statement, Chapter 6 goes into more detail on the cash flow statement. (Chapters 4 and 5 consider the balance sheets and income statements of limited companies.)

The balance sheet

The purpose of the balance sheet is simply to set out the financial position of a business at a particular moment in time (hence, its alternative name *statement of financial position*). We saw above that the balance sheet will reveal the forms in which the wealth of the business is held and how much wealth is held in each form. We can, however, be more specific about the nature of the balance sheet by saying that it sets out the **assets** of the business on the one hand, and the **claims** against the business on the other. Before looking at the balance sheet in more detail, we need to be clear about what these terms mean.

Assets

An asset is essentially a resource held by the business. For a particular item to be treated as an asset for accounting purposes, it should have the following characteristics:

- *A probable future benefit must exist.* This simply means that the item must be expected to have some future monetary value. This value can arise through its use within the business or through its hire or sale. Thus, an obsolete piece of equipment that could be sold for scrap would still be considered an asset, whereas an obsolete piece of equipment that could not be sold for scrap would not be regarded as one.
- *The business must have an exclusive right to control the benefit.* Unless the business has exclusive rights over the resource, it cannot be regarded as an asset. Thus, for a business offering holidays on barges, the canal system may be a very valuable resource, but as the business will not be able to control the access of others to the canal system, it cannot be regarded as an asset of the business. (However, the barges owned by the business would be regarded as assets.)
- *The benefit must arise from some past transaction or event.* This means that the transaction (or other event) giving rise to the business's right to the benefit must have already occurred, and will not arise at some future date. Thus, an agreement by a business to buy a piece of equipment at some future date would not mean the item is currently an asset of the business.

● *The asset must be capable of measurement in monetary terms.* Unless the item can be measured in monetary terms, with a reasonable degree of reliability, it will not be regarded as an asset for inclusion on the balance sheet. Thus, the title of a magazine (for example, *Hello!* or *Vogue*) that was created by its publisher may be extremely valuable to that publishing business, but this value is usually difficult to quantify. It will not, therefore, be treated as an asset.

Note that all four of these conditions must apply. If one of them is missing, the item will not be treated as an asset, for accounting purposes, and will not appear on the balance sheet.

We can see that these conditions will strictly limit the kind of items that may be referred to as 'assets' in the balance sheet. Certainly not all resources exploited by a business will be assets of the business for accounting purposes. Some, like the canal system or the magazine title *Hello!*, may well be assets in a broader sense, but not for accounting purposes. Once an asset has been acquired by a business, it will continue to be considered an asset until the benefits are exhausted or the business disposes of it in some way.

Activity 2.2

Indicate which of the following items could appear as an asset on the balance sheet of a business. Explain your reasoning in each case.

1 £1,000 owing to the business by a customer who is unable to pay.
2 The purchase of a patent from an inventor that gives the business the right to produce a new product. Production of the new product is expected to increase profits over the period during which the patent is held.
3 The business hiring a new marketing director who is confidently expected to increase profits by over 30 per cent during the next three years.
4 The purchase of a machine that will save the business £10,000 each year. It is currently being used by the business but it has been acquired on credit and is not yet paid for.

Your answer should be along the following lines:

1 Under normal circumstances a business would expect a customer to pay the amount owed. Such an amount is therefore typically shown as an asset under the heading 'trade receivables' (or 'debtors'). However, in this particular case the customer is unable to pay. Hence the item is incapable of providing future benefits, and the £1,000 owing would not be regarded as an asset. Debts that are not paid are referred to as 'bad debts'.
2 The purchase of the patent would meet all of the conditions set out above and, therefore, would be regarded as an asset.
3 The hiring of a new marketing director would not be considered as the acquisition of an asset. One argument against its classification as an asset is that the business does not have exclusive rights of control over the director. (Nevertheless, it may have an exclusive right to the services that the director provides.) Perhaps a stronger argument is that the value of the director cannot be measured in monetary terms with any degree of reliability.
4 The machine would be considered an asset even though it is not yet paid for. Once the business has agreed to buy the machine, and has accepted it, the machine is legally owned by the business even though payment is still outstanding. (The amount outstanding would be shown as a claim, as we shall see below.)

The sorts of items that often appear as assets in the balance sheet of a business include:

● property;
● plant and equipment;
● fixtures and fittings;
● patents and trademarks;
● trade receivables (debtors);
● investments.

Activity 2.3

Can you think of three additional items that might appear as assets in the balance sheet of a business?

You may be able to think of a number of other items. Some that you may have identified are:

● motor vehicles;
● inventories (stock);
● computer equipment;
● cash at bank.

Note that an asset does not have to be a physical item – it may also be a non-physical right to certain benefits. Assets that have a physical substance and can be touched are referred to as **tangible assets**. Assets that have no physical substance but which, nevertheless, provide expected future benefits (such as patents) are referred to as **intangible assets**.

Claims

A claim is an obligation on the part of the business to provide cash, or some other form of benefit, to an outside party. A claim will normally arise as a result of the outside party providing funds in the form of assets for use by the business. There are essentially two types of claim against a business:

● **Capital**. This represents the claim of the owner(s) against the business. This claim is sometimes referred to as the *owner's equity*. Some find it hard to understand how the owner can have a claim against the business, particularly when we consider the example of a sole-proprietor-type business where the owner *is*, in effect, the business. However, for accounting purposes, a clear distinction is made between the business (whatever its size) and the owner(s). The business is viewed as being quite separate from the owner and this is equally true for a sole proprietor like Paul, the wrapping-paper seller in Example 2.1, or a large company like Marks and Spencer plc. It is seen as a separate entity with its own separate existence and when financial statements are prepared, they relate to the business rather than to the owner(s). This means that the balance sheet should reflect the financial position of the business as a separate entity. Viewed from this perspective, any funds contributed by the owner will be seen as coming from outside the business and will appear as a claim against the business in its balance sheet.

As we have just seen, the business and the owner are separate for accounting purposes, irrespective of the type of business concerned. It is also true that the operation of the capital section of the balance sheet is broadly the same irrespective of the type of business concerned. As we shall see in Chapter 4, with limited companies the owner's claim figure must be analysed according to how each part of it first arose. For example, companies must make a distinction between that part of the owner's claim that arose from retained profits and that part that arose from the owners putting in cash to start up the business, usually by buying shares in the company.

→ ● **Liabilities**. Liabilities represent the claims of all other individuals and organisations, apart from the owner(s). Liabilities must have arisen from past transactions or events such as supplying goods or lending money to the business. When a liability is settled it will normally be through an outflow of assets (usually cash).

Once a claim from the owners or outsiders has been incurred by a business, it will remain as an obligation until it is settled.

Now that the meaning of the terms *assets* and *claims* has been established, we can go on and discuss the relationship between the two. This relationship is quite straightforward. If a business wishes to acquire assets, it will have to raise the necessary funds from somewhere. It may raise the funds from the owner(s) or from other outside parties or from both. Example 2.2 illustrates this relationship.

Example 2.2

Jerry and Company start a business by depositing £20,000 in a bank account on 1 March. This amount was raised partly from the owner (£6,000) and partly from borrowing (£14,000). Raising funds in this way will give rise to a claim on the business by both the owner (capital) and the lender (liability). If a balance sheet of Jerry and Company is prepared following the above transactions, it will appear as follows:

Jerry and Company
Balance sheet as at 1 March

	£		£
Assets		Claims	
Cash at bank	20,000	Capital (owner's equity)	6,000
		Liability – borrowing	14,000
	20,000		20,000

We can see from the balance sheet that the total claims are the same as the total assets. Thus:

Assets = Capital + Liabilities

This equation – which is often referred to as the *balance sheet equation* – will always hold true. Whatever changes may occur to the assets of the business or the claims against it, there will be compensating changes elsewhere that will ensure that the balance sheet always 'balances'. By way of illustration, consider the following transactions for Jerry and Company:

→

Example 2.2 continued

2 March   Bought a motor van for £5,000, paying by cheque.

3 March   Bought inventories (that is, goods to be sold) on one month's credit for £3,000. (This means that the inventories will be bought on 3 March, but payment will not be made to the supplier until 3 April.)

4 March   Repaid £2,000 of the amount borrowed to the lender, by cheque.

6 March   Owner introduced another £4,000 into the business bank account.

A balance sheet may be drawn up after each day in which transactions have taken place. In this way, the effect can be seen of each transaction on the assets and claims of the business. The balance sheet as at 2 March will be as follows:

Jerry and Company
Balance sheet as at 2 March

Assets	£	Claims	£
Cash at bank (20,000 – 5,000)	15,000	Capital	6,000
Motor van	5,000	Liabilities – borrowing	14,000
	20,000		20,000

As can be seen, the effect of buying the motor van is to decrease the balance at the bank by £5,000 and to introduce a new asset – a motor van – to the balance sheet. The total assets remain unchanged. It is only the 'mix' of assets that has changed. The claims against the business remain the same because there has been no change in the way in which the business has been funded.

The balance sheet as at 3 March, following the purchase of inventories, will be as follows:

Jerry and Company
Balance sheet as at 3 March

Assets	£	Claims	£
Cash at bank	15,000	Capital	6,000
Motor van	5,000	Liabilities – borrowing	14,000
Inventories (stock)	3,000	Liabilities – trade payable	3,000
	23,000		23,000

The effect of buying inventories has been to introduce another new asset (inventories) to the balance sheet. In addition, the fact that the goods have not yet been paid for means that the claims against the business will be increased by the £3,000 owed to the supplier, who is referred to as a *trade payable* (or trade creditor) on the balance sheet.

Activity 2.4

Try drawing up a balance sheet for Jerry and Company as at 4 March.

The balance sheet as at 4 March, following the repayment of part of the loan, will be as follows:

Jerry and Company
Balance sheet as at 4 March

Assets		£	Claims		£
Cash at bank (15,000 – 2,000)		13,000	Capital		6,000
Motor van		5,000	Liabilities – borrowing (14,000 – 2,000)		12,000
Inventories (stock)		3,000	Liabilities – trade payable (creditor)		3,000
		21,000			21,000

The repayment of £2,000 of the borrowing will result in a decrease in the balance at the bank of £2,000 and a decrease in the lender's claim against the business by the same amount.

Activity 2.5

Try drawing up a balance sheet as at 6 March for Jerry and Company

The balance sheet as at 6 March, following the introduction of more funds, will be as follows:

Jerry and Company
Balance sheet as at 6 March

Assets		£	Claims		£
Cash at bank (13,000 + 4,000)		17,000	Capital (6,000 + 4,000)		10,000
Motor van		5,000	Liabilities – borrowing		12,000
Inventories (stock)		3,000	Liabilities – trade payable (creditor)		3,000
		25,000			25,000

The introduction of more funds by the owner will result in an increase in the capital of £4,000 and an increase in the cash at bank by the same amount.

Example 2.2 illustrates the point that the balance sheet equation (assets equals capital plus liabilities) will always hold true, because it reflects the fact that, if a business wishes to acquire more assets, it must raise funds equal to the cost of those assets. The funds raised must be provided by the owners (capital), or by others (liabilities) or by a combination of the two. Hence the total cost of assets acquired should always equal the total capital plus liabilities.

It is worth pointing out that, in real life, businesses do not normally draw up a balance sheet after each day, as shown in the example above. Such an approach is not likely to be useful, given the relatively small number of transactions each day. We have done this in our examples to see the effect on the balance sheet, transaction by transaction. In real life, a balance sheet for the business is usually prepared at the end of a defined reporting period.

Determining the length of the reporting interval will involve weighing up the costs of producing the information against the perceived benefits of the information for decision-making purposes. In practice, the reporting interval will vary between businesses; it could be monthly, quarterly, half-yearly or annually. For external reporting purposes, an annual reporting cycle is the norm (although certain businesses, typically larger ones, report more frequently than this). However, for internal reporting purposes to managers, many businesses produce monthly financial statements.

The effect of trading operations on the balance sheet

In the example we considered earlier, we dealt with the effect on the balance sheet of a number of different types of transactions that a business might undertake. These transactions covered the purchase of assets for cash and on credit, the repayment of a loan, and the injection of capital. However, one form of transaction, trading, has not yet been considered. To deal with the effect of trading transactions on the balance sheet, let us return to our earlier example.

Example 2.2 (continued)

The balance sheet that we drew up for Jerry and Company as at 6 March was as follows:

Jerry and Company
Balance sheet as at 6 March

Assets	£	Claims	£
Cash at bank	17,000	Capital	10,000
Motor van	5,000	Liabilities – borrowing	12,000
Inventories (stock)	3,000	Liabilities – trade payable (creditor)	3,000
	25,000		25,000

On 7 March, the business managed to sell all of the inventories for £5,000 and received a cheque immediately from the customer for this amount. The balance sheet on 7 March, after this transaction has taken place, will be as follows:

Jerry and Company
Balance sheet as at 7 March

Assets	£	Claims	£
Cash at bank (17,000 + 5,000)	22,000	Capital [10,000 + (5,000 – 3,000)]	12,000
Motor van	5,000	Liabilities – borrowing	12,000
Inventories (stock) (3,000 – 3,000)	–	Liabilities – trade payable (creditor)	3,000
	27,000		27,000

We can see that the inventories (£3,000) have now disappeared from the balance sheet, but the cash at bank has increased by the selling price of the inventories (£5,000). The net effect, therefore, has been to increase assets by £2,000 (that is £5,000 – £3,000). This increase represents the net increase in wealth (the profit) that has arisen from trading. Also note that the capital of the business has increased by £2,000, in line with the increase in assets. This increase in capital reflects the fact that increases in wealth, as a result of trading or other operations, will be to the benefit of the owners and will increase their stake in the business.

Activity 2.6

What would have been the effect on the balance sheet if the inventories had been sold on 7 March for £1,000 rather than £5,000?

The balance sheet on 7 March would be as follows:

Jerry and Company
Balance sheet as at 7 March

	£		£
Assets		**Claims**	
Cash at bank (17,000 + 1,000)	18,000	Capital [10,000 + (1,000 − 3,000)]	8,000
Motor van	5,000	Liabilities − borrowing	12,000
Inventories (stock) (3,000 − 3,000)	−	Liabilities − trade payable (creditor)	3,000
	23,000		23,000

As we can see, the inventories (£3,000) will disappear from the balance sheet, but the cash at bank will rise by only £1,000. This will mean a net reduction in assets of £2,000. This reduction represents a loss arising from trading and will be reflected in a reduction in the capital of the owner.

We can see that any decrease in wealth (loss) arising from trading or other transactions will lead to a reduction in the owner's stake in the business. If the business wished to maintain the level of assets as at 6 March, it would be necessary to obtain further funds from the owner or from borrowing, or both.

What we have just seen means that the balance sheet equation can be extended as follows:

Assets = Capital at the start of the period + Profit (or − Loss) for the period + Liabilities

As we have seen, the profit (or loss) for the period impacts on the balance sheet as an addition to (or a reduction of) capital. Any funds introduced or withdrawn by the owner for living expenses or other reasons also affect capital, but are shown separately. By doing this, we provide more comprehensive information for users of the financial statements. If Jerry and Company sold the inventories for £5,000, as in Example 2.2, and further assume that the owner withdrew £1,500 for his or her own use, the capital of the owner would appear as follows on the balance sheet:

	£
Capital (owner's equity)	
Opening balance	10,000
Add Profit	2,000
	12,000
Less Drawings	1,500
Closing balance	10,500

If the drawings were in cash, the balance of cash would decrease by £1,500 in the balance sheet.

Note that, like all balance sheet items, the amount of capital is cumulative. This means that any profit made that is not taken out as drawings by the owner(s) remains in the business. These retained (or 'ploughed-back') profits have the effect of expanding the business.

The classification of assets

If the items on the balance sheet are listed haphazardly, with assets listed on one side and claims on the other, though it may be mathematically correct, it can be confusing. To help users to understand more clearly the information that is presented, assets and claims are usually grouped into categories. Assets may be categorised as being either current or non-current.

Current assets

→ **Current assets** are basically assets that are held for the short term. To be more precise, they are assets that meet any of the following conditions:

- they are held for sale or consumption in the normal course of a business's operating cycle;
- they are expected to be sold within the next year;
- they are held primarily for trading;
- they are cash, or near cash such as easily marketable, short-term investments.

The most common current assets are inventories (stock), customers who owe money for goods or services supplied on credit (known as trade receivables or debtors), and cash.

Perhaps it is worth making the point here that most sales made by most businesses are made on credit. This is to say that the goods pass to, or the service is rendered to, the customer at one point but the customer pays later. Retail sales are the only significant exception to this general point.

For businesses that sell goods, rather than render a service, the current assets of inventories, trade receivables and cash are interrelated. They circulate within a business as shown in Figure 2.2. We can see that cash can be used to buy inventories, which are then sold on credit. When the credit customers (trade receivables) pay, the business receives an injection of cash, and so on.

| Figure 2.2 | The circulating nature of current assets |

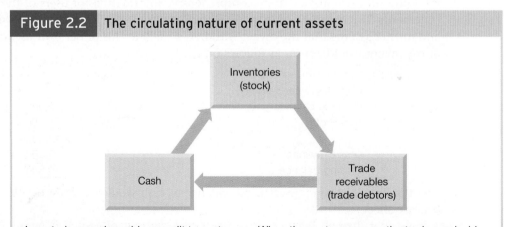

Inventories may be sold on credit to customers. When the customers pay, the trade receivables will be converted into cash, which can then be used to purchase more inventories, and so the cycle begins again.

For purely service businesses, the situation is similar, except that inventories are not involved.

Non-current assets

→ **Non-current assets** (also called fixed assets) are simply assets that do not meet the definition of current assets. Generally speaking, they are held for long-term operations.

This distinction between assets that are continuously circulating within the business and assets used for long-term operations may be helpful when trying to assess the appropriateness of the mix of assets held. Most businesses will need a certain amount of both types of asset to operate effectively.

Activity 2.7

Can you think of two examples of assets that may be classified as non-current assets for an insurance business?

Examples of assets that may be defined as being non-current are:

- property;
- plant and equipment;
- motor vehicles;
- computers;
- computer software;
- reference books.

This is not an exhaustive list. You may have thought of others.

It is important to appreciate that how a particular asset is classified (that is, between current and non-current) may vary according to the nature of the business. This is because the *purpose* for which a particular type of asset is held may differ from business to business. For example, a motor vehicle manufacturer will normally hold inventories of the finished motor vehicles produced for resale, and would therefore classify them as part of the current assets. On the other hand, a business that uses motor vehicles for delivering its goods to customers (that is, as part of its long-term operations) would classify them as non-current assets.

Activity 2.8

The assets of Kunalun and Co., a large advertising agency, are as follows:

- cash at bank;
- fixtures and fittings;
- office equipment;
- motor vehicles;
- property;
- computer equipment;
- work-in-progress (that is, partly completed work for clients).

Which of these do you think should be defined as non-current assets, and which should be defined as current assets?

→

Activity 2.8 continued

Your answer should be as follows:

Non-current assets	Current assets
Fixtures and fittings	Cash at bank
Office equipment	Work-in-progress
Motor vehicles	
Property	
Computer equipment	

The classification of claims

As we have already seen, claims are normally classified into capital (owner's claim) and liabilities (claims of outsiders). Liabilities are further classified as either current or non-current:

→ ● **Current liabilities** are basically amounts due for settlement in the short term. To be more precise, they are liabilities that meet any of the following conditions:
  – they are expected to be settled within the normal course of the business's operating cycle;
  – they are due to be settled within 12 months after the date of the balance sheet on which they appear;
  – they are held primarily for trading purposes;
  – there is no right to defer settlement for at least 12 months after the date of the balance sheet on which they appear.
→ ● **Non-current liabilities** represent amounts due that do not meet the definition of current liabilities.

Note that it is quite common for non-current liabilities to become current liabilities. For example, borrowings that are due to be repaid in 18 months after the date of a particular balance sheet will appear as a non-current liability, but as a current one in the balance sheet as at one year later. (This assumes that the borrowings have not been paid off in the meantime.)

This classification of liabilities can help gain a clearer impression of the ability of the business to meet its maturing obligations (that is, claims that must shortly be met). The value of the current liabilities (that is the amounts that must be paid within the normal operating cycle), can be compared with the value of the current assets (that is the assets that are either cash or will turn into cash within the same period).

The classification of liabilities should also help to highlight how the long-term finance of the business is raised. If a business relies on long-term borrowings to finance the business, the financial risks associated with the business will increase. This is because these borrowings will bring a commitment to make interest payments and capital repayments and the business may be forced to stop trading if this commitment is not fulfilled. Thus, when raising long-term finance, a business must strike the right balance between non-current liabilities and owner's capital. We shall consider this issue in more detail in Chapter 7.

Activity 2.9

Can you think of one example of a current liability and one of a non-current liability?

An example of a current liability would be amounts owing to suppliers for goods supplied on credit (known as trade payables or trade creditors) or a bank overdraft (a form of short-term bank borrowing that is repayable on demand). An example of a non-current liability would be a long-term loan.

Balance sheet layouts

Now that we have looked at the classification of assets and liabilities, we shall consider the layout of the balance sheet. Although there is an almost infinite number of ways in which the same balance sheet information could be presented, we shall consider two basic layouts. The first of these follows the style we adopted with Jerry and Company earlier (see p. 37). A more comprehensive example of this style is shown in Example 2.3.

Within each category of asset (non-current and current) shown in Example 2.3, the items are listed in reverse order of liquidity (nearness to cash). Thus, the assets that are furthest from cash are listed first and the assets that are closest to cash are listed last. In the case of non-current assets, property is listed first as that is usually the most difficult to turn into cash and motor vans are listed last as there is usually a ready market for them. In the case of current assets, we have already seen that inventories are converted to trade receivables and then trade receivables are converted to cash. Hence, under the heading of current assets, inventories are listed first, followed by trade receivables and finally cash itself. This ordering of assets is a normal practice, which is followed irrespective of the layout used.

Note that, in addition to a grand total for assets held, sub-totals for non-current assets and current assets are shown. Sub-totals are also used for non-current liabilities and current liabilities when more than one item appears within these categories.

Example 2.3

Brie Manufacturing
Balance sheet as at 31 December 2006

	£000		£000
Non-current assets		**Capital (owner's equity)**	
Property	45	Opening balance	50
Plant and equipment	30	*Add* Profit	14
Motor vans	19		64
	94	*Less* Drawings	4
			60
		Non-current liabilities	
		Long-term borrowings	50
Current assets		**Current liabilities**	
Inventories	23	Trade payables	37
Trade receivables	18		
Cash at bank	12		
	53		
Total assets	147	**Total equity and liabilities**	147

An obvious alternative to the balance sheet illustrated in Example 2.3 would be to show claims on the left and assets on the right. Some people prefer this approach because the claims can be seen as the source of finance for the business and the assets show how that finance has been deployed. It could be seen as more logical to show sources first and uses second.

The balance sheet illustrated in Example 2.3 has a *horizontal layout*, with assets on one side and claims on the other. In recent years, however, a *vertical layout* has become the norm. As the name suggests, this type of layout presents the information vertically rather than horizontally with assets being shown above capital and liabilities. One approach is to start with non-current assets and work downwards towards current liabilities at the end. The balance sheet of Brie Manufacturing, which was arranged using a horizontal layout in Example 2.3, can be rearranged in a vertical layout as shown in Example 2.4.

Example 2.4

Brie Manufacturing
Balance sheet as at 31 December 2006

	£000
Non-current assets	
Property	45
Plant and equipment	30
Motor vans	19
	94
Current assets	
Inventories	23
Trade receivables	18
Cash at bank	12
	53
Total assets	147
Capital (owner's equity)	
Opening balance	50
Add Profit	14
	64
Less Drawings	4
	60
Non-current liabilities	
Long-term borrowings	50
Current liabilities	
Trade payables	37
Total equity and liabilities	147

Although some vertical layouts are slightly different than the one illustrated, we shall stick with this particular format throughout the book. It is easy to understand and is increasingly used in practice.

The following information relates to Simonson Engineering as at 30 September 2006:

	£
Plant and equipment	25,000
Trade payables	18,000
Short-term borrowing	26,000
Inventories	45,000
Property	72,000
Long-term borrowing	51,000
Trade receivables	48,000
Capital at 1 October 2005	117,500
Cash in hand	1,500
Motor vehicles	15,000
Fixtures and fittings	9,000
Profit for the year to 30 September 2006	18,000
Drawings for the year to 30 September 2006	15,000

Required:
Prepare a balance sheet for the business using a vertical layout.

The answer to this question can be found at the back of the book on p. 400.

The balance sheet and time

As we have already seen, the balance sheet is a statement of the financial position of the business at *a specified point in time*. The balance sheet has been compared to a photograph. A photograph 'freezes' a particular moment in time and will represent the situation only at that moment. Hence, events may be quite different immediately before and immediately after the photograph was taken. Similarly, the balance sheet represents a 'snapshot' of the business at a particular moment. When examining a balance sheet, therefore, it is important to establish the date at which it has been drawn up. This information should be prominently displayed in the balance sheet heading, as shown above in Example 2.4. The more recent the balance sheet date, the better, when we are trying to assess the current financial position.

A business will normally prepare a balance sheet as at the close of business on the last day of its accounting year. In the UK, businesses are free to choose their accounting year. When making a decision on which year-end date to choose, commercial convenience can often be a deciding factor. For example, a business operating in the retail trade may choose to have a year-end date early in the calendar year (for example 31 January) because trade tends to be slack during that period and more staff time is available to help with the tasks involved in the preparation of the annual financial statements (such as checking the amount of inventories held). Since trade is slack, it is also a time when the amount of inventories held by the retail business is likely to be unusually low as compared with other times of the year. Thus the balance sheet, though showing a fair view of what it purports to show, may not show a picture of what is more typically the position of the business over the rest of the year.

Accounting conventions and the balance sheet

Accounting has a number of rules or conventions that have evolved over time. They have evolved as attempts to deal with practical problems experienced by preparers and users of financial statements, rather than to reflect some theoretical ideal. In preparing the balance sheets earlier, we have followed various **accounting conventions**, although they have not been explicitly mentioned. We shall now identify and discuss the major conventions that we have applied.

Business entity convention

For accounting purposes, the business and its owner(s) are treated as being quite separate and distinct. This is why owners are treated as being claimants against their own business in respect of their investment in the business. The **business entity convention** must be distinguished from the legal position that may exist between businesses and their owners. For sole proprietorships and partnerships, the law does not make any distinction between the business and its owner(s). For limited companies, on the other hand, there is a clear legal distinction between the business and its owners. (As we shall see in Chapter 4, the limited company is regarded as having a separate legal existence.) For accounting purposes these legal distinctions are irrelevant, and the business entity convention applies to all businesses.

Historic cost convention

This convention holds that the value of assets shown on the balance sheet should be based on their **historic cost** (that is, acquisition cost). This method of measuring asset value takes preference over other methods based on some form of current value. Many people, however, find the **historic cost convention** difficult to support, as outdated historic costs are unlikely to help in the assessment of current financial position. It is often argued that recording assets at their current value would provide a more realistic view of financial position and would be relevant for a wide range of decisions. However, a system of measurement based on current values can present a number of problems.

Activity 2.10

Can you think of reasons why current value accounting may pose problems for both preparers and users of financial statements?

The term 'current value' can be defined in a number of ways. For example, it can be defined broadly as either the current replacement cost or the current realisable value (selling price) of an asset. These two types of valuation may result in quite different figures being produced to represent the current value of an item. (Think, for example, of second-hand car values: there is often quite a difference between buying and selling prices.) In addition, the broad terms 'replacement cost' and 'realisable value' can be defined in different ways. We, therefore, must be clear about what kind of current value accounting we wish to use.

There are also practical problems associated with attempts to implement any system of current value accounting. For example, current values, however defined, are often difficult to establish with any real degree of objectivity. This may mean that the figures produced are heavily dependent on the opinion of managers. Unless the current value figures are capable of some form of independent verification, there is a danger that the financial statements will lose their credibility among users.

By reporting assets at their historic cost, it is argued that more reliable information is produced. Reporting in this way reduces the need for judgements, as the amount paid for a particular asset is usually a matter of demonstrable fact. Information based on past costs, however, may not always be relevant to the needs of users.

Later in the chapter, we shall consider the valuation of assets in the balance sheet in more detail. We shall see that the historic cost convention is not always rigidly adhered to, and departures from this convention are becoming more frequent.

Prudence convention

→ The **prudence convention** holds that caution should be exercised when making accounting judgements. Uncertainty about the future is dealt with by recording all losses at once and in full; this refers to both actual losses and expected losses. Profits, on the other hand, are only recognised when they actually arise. Greater emphasis is, therefore, placed on expected losses than on expected profits. To illustrate the application of this convention, let us assume that certain inventories held by a business prove unpopular with customers and so a decision is made to sell them below their original cost. The prudence convention requires that the expected loss from future sales be recognised immediately rather than when the goods are eventually sold. If, however, these inventories could have been sold above their original cost, profit would only be recognised at the time of sale.

The prudence convention evolved to counteract the excessive optimism of some managers and owners and is designed to prevent an overstatement of financial position. There is, however, a risk that it will introduce a bias towards understatement of financial position.

Activity 2.11

What problems might arise if an excessively prudent view is taken of the financial position and performance of a business?

Excessive prudence will lead to an overstatement of losses and an understatement of profits and financial position. This will obscure the underlying financial reality and may lead users to make bad decisions. The owners, for example, may sell their stake in the business at a lower price than they would have received if a fairer picture of the financial health of the business had been presented.

In recent years, the prudence convention has weakened its grip on accounting and has become a less dominant force. Nevertheless, it remains an important convention.

Going concern convention

→ The **going concern convention** holds that the financial statements should be prepared on the assumption that the business will continue operations for the foreseeable future, unless this is known not to be true. In other words, it is assumed that there is no intention, or need, to sell off the non-current assets of the business. Such a sale may arise where the business is in financial difficulties and needs to pay amounts borrowed that are due for repayment. This convention is important because the market (sale) value of many non-current assets is often low in relation to the values at which they appear in the balance sheet. This means that were a forced sale to occur, there is the likelihood that assets will be sold for less than their balance sheet value. Such anticipated losses should be fully recorded as soon as the business's going concern status is called into question. However, where there is no expectation of a need to sell off the assets, the value of non-current assets can continue to be shown at their recorded values (that is, based on historic cost). This convention therefore provides some support for the historic cost convention under normal circumstances.

Dual aspect convention

→ The **dual aspect convention** asserts that each transaction has two aspects, both of which will affect the balance sheet. Thus, the purchase of a motor car for cash results in an increase in one asset (motor car) and a decrease in another (cash). The repayment of a loan results in the decrease in a liability (borrowing) and the decrease in an asset (cash).

Activity 2.12

What are the two aspects of each of the following transactions?

- Purchase £1,000 inventories on credit.
- Owner withdraws £2,000 in cash.
- Repayment of borrowings of £3,000.

Your answer should be as follows:

- Inventories increase by £1,000, trade payables increase by £1,000.
- Capital reduces by £2,000, cash reduces by £2,000.
- Borrowings reduce by £3,000, cash reduces by £3,000.

Recording the dual aspect of each transaction ensures that the balance sheet will continue to balance.

Money measurement

We saw earlier that a resource will only be regarded as an asset and included on the balance sheet if it can be measured in monetary terms, with a reasonable degree of reliability. Some resources of a business, however, do not meet this criterion and so are excluded from the balance sheet. As a result, the scope of the balance sheet is limited.

Activity 2.13

Can you think of resources of a business that cannot usually be measured reliably in monetary terms?

In answering this activity you may have thought of the following:

- the quality of the human resources of the business;
- the reputation of the business's products;
- the location of the business;
- the relationship a business enjoys with its customers;

There have been occasional attempts to measure and report resources of a business that are normally excluded from the balance sheet so as to provide a more complete picture of financial position. These attempts, however, invariably fail the reliability test. We saw in Chapter 1 that a lack of reliability affects the quality of financial statements. Unreliable measurement can lead to inconsistency in reporting and can create uncertainty among users, which in turn undermines the credibility of the financial statements.

Some key resources of a business that normally defy reliable measurement are discussed below.

Goodwill and brands

Some intangible, non-current assets are similar to tangible, non-current assets; they have a clear and separate identity and the cost of acquiring the asset can be reliably measured. Examples normally include patents, trademarks, copyrights and licences. Other intangible non-current assets, however, are quite different. They lack a clear and separate identity and reflect a hotchpotch of attributes, which are part of the essence of the business. Goodwill and product brands are often examples of assets that lack a clear and separate identity.

The term 'goodwill' is often used to cover various attributes such as the quality of the products, the skill of employees and the relationship with customers. The term 'product brands' is also used to cover various attributes, such as the brand image, the quality of the product, the trademark and so on. Where goodwill and product brands have been generated internally by the business, it is often difficult to determine their cost, or to measure their current market value or even to be clear that they really exist. They are, therefore, excluded from the balance sheet.

When they are acquired through an arm's-length transaction, however, the problems of uncertainty about their existence and measurement are resolved. (An 'arm's-length' transaction is one that is undertaken between two unconnected parties.) If goodwill is acquired when taking over another business, or if a business acquires a particular product brand from another business, these items will be separately identified and a price agreed for them. Under these circumstances, they can be regarded as assets by the business that acquired them and included on the balance sheet.

To agree a price for acquiring goodwill or product brands means that some form of valuation must take place and this raises the question as to how it is done. Usually, the valuation will be based on estimates of future earnings from holding the asset, a process that is fraught with difficulties. Nevertheless, a number of specialist businesses now exist that are prepared to take on this challenge. **Real World 2.1** reveals how one specialist business ranked and valued the top 10 brands in the world.

Real World 2.1

Valuing brands

Millward Brown Optimor, part of WPP marketing services group, recently produced a report which ranked and valued the top 10 world brands for 2007 as follows:

Ranking	Brand	Value ($m)
1	Google	66,434
2	GE (General Electric)	61,880
3	Microsoft	54,951
4	Coca-Cola	44,134
5	China Mobile	41,214
6	Marlboro	39,166
7	Wal-Mart	36,880
8	Citi	33,706
9	IBM	33,572
10	Toyota	33,427

We can see that the valuations placed on the brands owned are quite staggering.

Source: 2007 Brandz Top 100 most powerful brands MillwardBrown Optimor 2007 P. 10.

Human resources

Attempts have been made to place a monetary measurement on the human resources of a business, but without any real success. There are, however, certain limited circumstances in which human resources are measured and reported in the balance sheet. These circumstances normally arise with professional football clubs. Whilst football clubs cannot own players, they can own the rights to the players' services. Where these rights are acquired by compensating other clubs for releasing the players from their contracts, an arm's length transaction arises and the amounts paid provide a reliable basis for measurement. This means that the rights to services can be regarded as an asset of the club for accounting purposes (assuming, of course, the player will also bring benefits to the club).

Real World 2.2 describes how one leading club reports its investment in players on the balance sheet.

Real World 2.2

Rio's on the team sheet and on the balance sheet

Manchester United Football Club (MUFC) has acquired several key players as a result of paying transfer fees to other clubs. In common with most UK football clubs, MUFC reports the cost of acquiring those rights to the players' services on its balance sheet. The club's balance sheet for 2005 shows the cost of registering its squad of players as £137.5 million. The item of players' registrations is shown as an intangible asset in the balance sheet as it is the rights to services not the players that are the assets. This figure of £137.5 million includes the cost of bought-in players such as Rio Ferdinand (for £31.1 m from Leeds United) but not 'home-grown' players, such as Wes Brown, Darren Fletcher and Paul Scholes. These players are not included because MUFC did not pay a transfer fee for them and so no clear-cut value can be placed on their services.

Source: Manchester United PLC Annual Report 2005.

Monetary stability

When using money as the unit of measurement, we normally fail to recognise the fact that it will change in value over time. In the UK and throughout much of the world, however, inflation has been a persistent problem. This has meant that the value of money has declined in relation to other assets. In past years, high rates of inflation have resulted in balance sheets, which were prepared on an historic cost basis, reflecting figures for assets that were much lower than if current values were employed. Rates of inflation have been relatively low in recent years and so the disparity between historic cost values and current values has been less pronounced. Nevertheless, it can still be significant and has added fuel to the debate concerning how to measure asset values on the balance sheet. It is to this issue that we now turn.

Valuing assets on the balance sheet

It was mentioned earlier that, when preparing the balance sheet, the historic cost convention is normally applied for the reporting of assets. However, this point requires further elaboration as, in practice, it is not simply a matter of recording each asset on the balance sheet at its original cost. We shall see that things are a little more complex than this. Before discussing the valuation rules in some detail, however, we should point out that these rules are based on international accounting standards, which are rules that are generally accepted throughout much of the world. The nature and role of accounting standards will be discussed in detail in Chapter 5.

Tangible non-current assets (property, plant and equipment)

→ Tangible non-current assets normally consist of **property, plant and equipment**, and we shall refer to them in this way from now on. This is a rather broad term that covers all items mentioned in its title plus other items such as motor vehicles and fixtures and fittings. All of these items are, in essence, the 'tools' used by the business to generate wealth; that is, they are used to produce or supply goods and services or for administration purposes. They are held for the longer term, which means for more than one accounting period.

Initially these items are recorded at their historic cost, which will include any amounts spent on getting them ready for use. However, they will normally be used up over time as a result of wear and tear, obsolescence and so on. The amount used up, which is referred to as *depreciation*, must be measured for each accounting period that the assets are held. Although we shall leave a detailed examination of depreciation until Chapter 3, we need to know that when an asset has been depreciated, this must be reflected in the balance sheet.

The total depreciation that has accumulated over the period since the asset was acquired must be deducted from its cost. This net figure (that is, the cost of the asset less the total depreciation to date) is referred to as the *carrying amount, net book value* or *written down value*. The procedure just described is not really a contravention of the historic cost convention. It is simply recognition of the fact that a proportion of the historic cost of the non-current asset has been consumed in the process of generating benefits for the business.

Although using historic cost (less any depreciation) is the 'benchmark treatment' for recording these assets, an alternative is allowed. Property, plant and equipment can be
→ recorded using **fair values** provided that these values can be measured reliably. The 'fair values', in this case, are usually the current market values (that is, the exchange values in an arm's-length transaction). By using fair value, a more up-to-date figure than the depreciated cost figure is provided to users, which may be more relevant to their needs. It may also place the business in a better light, as assets such as property may have increased significantly in value over time. Of course, increasing the balance sheet value of an asset does not make that asset more valuable. Nevertheless, perceptions of the business may be altered by such a move.

One consequence of revaluing non-current assets is that the depreciation charge will be increased. This is because the depreciation charge is based on the increased value of the asset.

Real World 2.3 shows that one well-known business revalued its land and buildings and, by doing so, greatly improved the look of its balance sheet.

Real World 2.3

Retailer marks up land and buildings

The balance sheet of Marks and Spencer plc, a major high street retailer, as at 1 April 2006 reveals land and buildings at a net book value, or carrying amount, of £2,310.0 m. These land and buildings were revalued by a firm of independent surveyors two years earlier and this has been reflected in subsequent balance sheets. The effect of the revaluation was to give an uplift of £530.9 m against the previous carrying amount.

Source: Marks and Spencer plc, Annual Report 2006, p. 74, www.marksandspencer.com.

Activity 2.14

Refer to the vertical format balance sheet of Brie Manufacturing shown earlier (p. 46). What would be the effect of revaluing the property to a figure of £110,000 on the balance sheet?

The effect on the balance sheet would be to increase the property to £110,000 and the gain on revaluation (that is, £110,000 − £45,000 = £65,000) would be added to the capital of the owner, as it is the owner who will benefit from the gain. The revised balance sheet would therefore be as follows:

Brie Manufacturing
Balance sheet as at 31 December 2006

	£000
Non-current assets (Property, plant and equipment)	
Property	110
Plant and equipment	30
Motor vans	19
	159
Current assets	
Inventories (stock)	23
Trade receivables (debtors)	18
Cash at bank	12
	53
Total assets	212
Capital (owner's equity)	
Opening balance	50
Add Revaluation gain	65
Profit	14
	129
Less Drawings	4
	125
Non-current liabilities	
Long-term borrowing	50
Current liabilities	
Trade payables (creditors)	37
Total equity and liabilities	212

Once assets are revalued, the frequency of revaluation then becomes an important issue as assets recorded at out-of-date values can mislead users. Using out-of-date revaluations on the balance sheet is the worst of both worlds. It lacks the objectivity and verifiability of historic cost; it also lacks the realism of current values. Revaluations should therefore be frequent enough to ensure that the carrying amount of the revalued asset does not differ materially from its fair value at the balance sheet date.

When an item of property, or plant, or equipment is revalued on the basis of fair values, all assets within that particular group must be revalued. Thus, it is not acceptable to revalue some property but not others. Although this provides some degree of consistency within a particular group of assets, it does not, of course, prevent the balance sheet from containing a mixture of valuations.

Intangible non-current assets

For these assets, the 'benchmark treatment' is, once again, that they are measured initially at historic cost. What follows, however, will depend on whether the asset has a finite or an infinite useful life. (Purchased goodwill can provide an example of an asset with an infinitely useful life.) Where the asset has a finite life, any depreciation (or *amortisation* as it is usually termed for intangible non-current assets) following acquisition will be deducted from its cost. Where, however, the asset has an infinite life, it will not be amortised. Instead, it will be tested annually to see whether there has been any fall in value. This point is discussed in more detail in the following section.

Again, the alternative of revaluing intangible assets using fair values is available. However, this can only be used where an active market exists that allows fair values to be properly determined. In practice, this is a rare occurrence.

The impairment of non-current assets

There is always a risk that both types of non-current asset (tangible and intangible) may suffer a significant fall in value. This may be due to factors such as changes in market conditions, technological obsolescence and so on. In some cases, this fall in value may lead to the carrying amount, or net book value, of the asset being higher than the amount that could be recovered from the asset through its continued use or through its sale. When this occurs, the asset value is said to be impaired and the general rule is to reduce the asset on the balance sheet to its recoverable amount. Unless this is done, the asset will be overstated on the balance sheet.

Activity 2.15

With which one of the accounting conventions, that we discussed earlier, is this accounting treatment consistent?

The answer is the prudence convention, which states that actual or anticipated losses should be recognised in full.

In many situations, a business may use either historic cost, less any depreciation, or a value-based measure when reporting its non-current assets. However, where the former is greater than the latter, the business has no choice; the use of depreciated historic cost is not an option. **Real World 2.4** provides an example of where the application of the 'impairment rule', as it is called, resulted in huge write-downs (that is, reductions in the balance sheet value of the assets) for a well-known mobile phone operator.

Real World 2.4

Talking telephone numbers   FT

The scale of Vodafone's binge of spending on telecom assets at the turn of the century can still be seen six years later after the mobile phone operator on Tuesday announced major write-downs of goodwill for a third successive year.

The £23.5 bn write-down in the carrying value of goodwill, flagged earlier this year, is one of the largest corporate write-downs on record.

But it is the £101 bn purchase of Germany's Mannesmann in 2000, and the Italian operations it partly inherited from the deal, that has caused the problems.

Broken down, Vodafone ascribed a write-down value of £19.4 bn for its assets in Germany, £3.6 bn for its Italian operations and £515 m for the assets in Sweden. The latter already had an impairment charge of £475 m a year ago, and Vodafone has since sold it to Norway's Telenor Mobile.

Vodafone blamed the write-down on the revision of its longer term prospects in the German and Italian markets, which are being hit by tough price competition.

Source: 'Goodwill Charges at Record Levels', FT.com, 30 May 2006.

We saw earlier that intangible, non-current assets with infinite lives must be tested annually to see whether there has been any impairment. Other non-current assets, however, must be also tested where events suggest that impairment has taken place.

Inventories (stock)

It is not only non-current assets that run the risk of a significant fall in value. The inventories of a business could also suffer this fate, which could be caused by factors such as reduced selling prices, obsolescence, deterioration, damage and so on. Where a fall in value means that the amount likely to be recovered from the sale of the inventories will be lower than their cost, this loss must be reflected in the balance sheet. Thus, if the net realisable value (that is, selling price less any selling costs) falls below the historic cost of inventories held, the former should be used as the basis of valuation. This reflects, once again, the influence of the prudence convention on the balance sheet.

Real World 2.5 reveals how one well-known business wrote down the inventories of one of its products following a sharp reduction in selling prices.

Real World 2.5

You're fired!

'You're fired!' is what some investors might like to tell Amstrad, run by Apprentice star, Sir Alan Sugar . . . Shares in the company fell nearly 10 per cent as it revealed that sales of its much-vaunted videophone have failed to take off.

Amstrad launched the E3, a phone allowing users to hold video calls with each other, in a blaze of publicity last year. But, after cutting the price from £99 to £49, Amstrad sold just 61,000 E3s in the year to June and has taken a £5.7 m stock (inventories) write down.

Source: (2005) 'Amstrad (AMT)', *Investors Chronicle*, 7 October.

The published financial statements of large businesses will normally show the basis on which inventories are valued. **Real World 2.6** shows how one well-known business reports this information.

Real World 2.6

Reporting inventories

The 2006 financial statements of Thorntons plc, the chocolate makers, include the following explanation concerning inventories:

> Inventories are recorded at the lower of cost and net realisable value. Cost includes materials, direct labour and an attributable proportion of manufacturing overheads, based on normal operating capacity, according to the stage of production reached. Net realisable value is the estimated value which would be realised after deducting all costs of completion, marketing and selling. Provision is made to reduce the cost to net realisable value having regard to the age and condition of inventory, as well as its saleability.

Source: Thorntons plc, Annual Report 2006, p. 25.

Interpreting the balance sheet

We have seen that the conventional balance sheet has a number of limitations. This has led some users of financial information to conclude that the balance sheet has little to offer in the way of useful information. However, this is not really the case. The balance sheet can provide useful insights about the financing and investing activities of a business. We shall consider this in detail in Chapters 7 and 8 when we deal with the analysis and interpretation of the financial statements.

Summary

The main points of the chapter may be summarised as follows:

The major financial statements
- There are three major financial statements – the cash flow statement, the income statement (profit and loss account) and the balance sheet (statement of financial position).
- The cash flow statement shows the cash movements over a particular period.
- The income statement shows the wealth (profit) generated over a particular period.
- The balance sheet shows the accumulated wealth at a particular point in time.

The balance sheet
- This sets out the assets of the business, on the one hand, and the claims against those assets, on the other.
- Assets are resources of the business that have certain characteristics, such as the ability to provide future benefits.
- Claims are obligations on the part of the business to provide cash, or some other benefit, to outside parties.

- Claims are of two types – capital and liabilities.
- Capital represents the owner's claim and liabilities represent the claims of others, apart from the owner.

Classification of assets and liabilities

- Assets are normally categorised as being current or non-current.
- Current assets are cash or near cash or are held for sale or consumption in the normal course of business, or for trading, or for the short term.
- Non-current assets are assets that are not current assets. They are normally held for the long-term operations of the business.
- Liabilities are normally categorised as being current or non-current liabilities.
- Current liabilities represent amounts due in the normal course of the business's operating cycle, or are held for trading, or are to be settled within 12 months, or cannot be deferred for at least 12 months after the end of the reporting period.
- Non-current liabilities represent amounts due that are not current liabilities.

Balance sheet layouts

- The horizontal layout sets out the assets on one side of the balance sheet and the capital and liabilities on the other side.
- The vertical layout begins with the assets at the top of the balance sheet and places capital and liabilities underneath.

Accounting conventions

- Accounting conventions are the rules of accounting that have evolved to deal with practical problems experienced by those preparing financial statements.
- The main conventions relating to the balance sheet include business entity, historic cost, prudence, going concern and dual aspect.

Money measurement

- Using money as the unit of measurement limits the scope of the balance sheet.
- Certain resources such as goodwill, product brands and human resources are difficult to measure. An 'arm's-length transaction' is normally required before such assets can be reliably measured and reported on the balance sheet.
- Money is not a stable unit of measurement – it changes in value over time.

Asset valuation

- The 'benchmark treatment' is to show property, plant and equipment at historic cost less any amounts written off for depreciation. However, fair values may be used rather than depreciated cost.
- The 'benchmark treatment' for intangible non-current assets is to show the items at historic cost. Only assets with a finite life will be amortised (depreciated) and fair values will rarely be used.
- Where the recoverable amount from tangible non-current assets is below their carrying amount, this lower amount is reflected in the balance sheet.
- Inventories are shown at the lower of cost or net realisable value.

→ **Key terms**

Cash flow statement p. 30	Current liabilities p. 44
Income statement p. 30	Non-current liabilities p. 44
Balance sheet p. 30	Accounting conventions p. 48
Final accounts p. 33	Business entity convention p. 48
Assets p. 34	Historic cost p. 48
Claims p. 34	Historic cost convention p. 48
Tangible assets p. 36	Prudence convention p. 49
Intangible assets p. 36	Going concern convention p. 50
Capital p. 36	Dual aspect convention p. 50
Liabilities p. 37	Property, plant and equipment
Current assets p. 42	p. 54
Non-current (fixed) assets p. 42	Fair values p. 54

Further reading

If you would like to explore the topics covered in this chapter in more depth, we recommend the following books:

Elliott, B. and Elliott, J. (2006) *Financial Accounting and Reporting*, 11th edn, Prentice Hall, Chapters 16 and 18.

Kirk, R. J. (2005) *International Financial Reporting Standards in Depth, Volume 1: Theory and Practice*, CIMA Publishing, Chapters 2 and 3.

IASB International Financial Reporting Standards (IFRSs), International Accounting Standards Board, IAS 16 (revised December 2003), IAS 36 (revised March 2004) and IAS 38 (revised March 2004).

Sutton, T. (2004) *Corporate Financial Accounting and Reporting*, 2nd edn, Financial Times Prentice Hall, Chapters 2 and 8.

Review questions

Answers to these questions can be found at the back of the book on pp. 410–11.

2.1 An accountant prepared a balance sheet for a business. In the balance sheet, the capital of the owner was shown next to the liabilities. This confused the owner, who argued: 'My capital is my major asset and so should be shown as an asset on the balance sheet.' How would you explain this misunderstanding to the owner?

2.2 'The balance sheet shows how much a business is worth' Do you agree with this statement? Discuss.

2.3 What is meant by the balance sheet equation? How does the form of this equation differ between the horizontal and vertical balance sheet layout?

2.4 In recent years there have been attempts to place a value on the 'human assets' of a business in order to derive a figure that can be included on the balance sheet. Do you think humans should be treated as assets? Would 'human assets' meet the conventional definition of an asset for inclusion on the balance sheet?

Exercises

Exercises 2.5 to 2.8 are more advanced than 2.1 to 2.4. Those exercises with a coloured number have answers at the back of the book, starting on p. 418.

If you wish to try more exercises, visit the students' side of the Companion Website.

2.1 On Thursday, the fourth day of his business venture, Paul, the street trader in wrapping paper (see earlier in the chapter, p. 30), bought more inventories (stock) for £53 cash. During the day he sold inventories that had cost £33 for a total of £47.

Required:
Draw up the three financial statements for Paul's business venture for Thursday.

2.2 The 'total business wealth' belongs to Paul because he is the sole owner of the business. Can you explain how the figure for total business wealth by Thursday evening has arisen? You will need to look back at the events of Monday, Tuesday and Wednesday (in this chapter on pp. 30 to 33) to do this.

2.3 Whilst on holiday in Bridlington, Helen had her credit cards and purse stolen from the beach while she was swimming. She was left with only £40, which she had kept in her hotel room, but she had three days of her holiday remaining. She was determined to continue her holiday and decided to make some money to enable her to do so. She decided to sell orange juice to holiday-makers using the local beach. On day 1 she bought 80 cartons of orange juice at £0.50 each for cash and sold 70 of these at £0.80 each. On the following day she bought 60 cartons at £0.50 each for cash and sold 65 at £0.80 each. On the third and final day she bought another 60 cartons at £0.50 each for cash. However, it rained and, as a result, business was poor. She managed to sell 20 at £0.80 each but sold off the rest of her inventories at £0.40 each.

Required:
Prepare an income statement and cash flow statement for each day's trading and prepare a balance sheet at the end of each day's trading.

2.4 On 1 March, Joe Conday started a new business. During March he carried out the following transactions:

1 March   Deposited £20,000 in a bank account
2 March   Bought fixtures and fittings for £6,000 cash, and inventories £8,000 on credit
3 March   Borrowed £5,000 from a relative and deposited it in the bank
4 March   Bought a motor car for £7,000 cash and withdrew £200 in cash for his own use
5 March   A further motor car costing £9,000 was bought. The motor car bought on 4 March was given in part exchange at a value of £6,500. The balance of purchase price for the new car was paid in cash
6 March   Conday won £2,000 in a lottery and paid the amount into the business bank account. He also repaid £1,000 of the loan

Required:
Draw up a balance sheet for the business at the end of each day.

2.5 The following is a list of the assets and claims of Crafty Engineering Ltd at 30 June last year:

	£000
Trade payables	86
Motor vehicles	38
Long-term loan from Industrial Finance Co.	260
Equipment and tools	207
Short-term borrowings	116
Inventories	153
Property	320
Trade receivables	185

Required:
(a) Prepare the balance sheet of the business as at 30 June last year from the above information using the vertical layout. (*Hint*: There is a missing item that needs to be deduced and inserted.)
(b) Discuss the significant features revealed by this financial statement.

2.6 The balance sheet of a business at the start of the week is as follows:

Assets	£	Claims	£
Property	145,000	Capital	203,000
Furniture and fittings	63,000	Short-term borrowing (Bank overdraft)	43,000
Inventories	28,000	Trade payables	23,000
Trade receivables	33,000		
	269,000		269,000

During the week the following transactions take place:

(a) Inventories sold for £11,000 cash; these inventories had cost £8,000.
(b) Sold inventories for £23,000 on credit; these inventories had cost £17,000.
(c) Received cash from trade receivables totalling £18,000.
(d) The owners of the business introduced £100,000 of their own money, which was placed in the business bank account.
(e) The owners brought a motor van, valued at £10,000, into the business.
(f) Bought inventories on credit for £14,000.
(g) Paid trade payables £13,000.

Required:
Show the balance sheet after all of these transactions have been reflected.

2.7 The following is a list of assets and claims of a manufacturing business at a particular point in time:

	£
Short-term borrowing	22,000
Property	245,000
Inventories of raw materials	18,000
Trade payables	23,000
Plant and equipment	127,000
Loan from Manufacturing Finance Co. (long-term borrowing)	100,000
Inventories of finished goods	28,000
Delivery vans	54,000
Trade receivables	34,000

Required:
Write out a balance sheet in the standard vertical form incorporating these figures. *Hint*: there is a missing item that needs to be deduced and inserted.

2.8 You have been talking to someone who had read a few chapters of an accounting text some years ago. During your conversation the person made the following statements:

(a) The income statement shows how much cash has come into and left the business during the accounting period and the resulting balance at the end of the period.

(b) In order to be included in the balance sheet as an asset, an item needs to be worth something in the market – that is all.

(c) The balance sheet equation is:

$$\text{Assets} + \text{Capital} = \text{Liabilities}$$

(d) Non-current assets are things that cannot be moved.

(e) Goodwill has an indefinite life and so should not be amortised.

Required:
Comment critically on each of the above statements, going into as much detail as you can.

3

Measuring and reporting financial performance

Introduction

In this chapter, we shall continue our examination of the major financial statements by looking at the income statement. This statement was briefly considered in Chapter 2 and we shall now examine it in some detail. We shall see how it is prepared and how it links with the balance sheet. We shall also consider some of the key measurement problems to be faced when preparing the income statement.

Learning outcomes

When you have completed this chapter, you should be able to:

● Discuss the nature and purpose of the income statement.

● Prepare an income statement from relevant financial information.

● Discuss the main recognition and measurement issues that must be considered when preparing the income statement.

● Explain the main accounting conventions underpinning the income statement.

The income statement

In Chapter 2, we examined the nature and purpose of the balance sheet. We saw that this statement is concerned with setting out the financial position of a business at a particular moment in time. However, it is not usually enough for users of the financial statements to have information relating only to the amount of wealth held by a business at one moment in time. Businesses exist for the primary purpose of generating wealth, or profit, and it is the profit generated *during a period* that is the main concern of many users of financial statements. Although the amount of profit generated is of particular interest to the owners of a business, other groups such as managers, employees and suppliers will also have an interest in the profit-generating ability of the business. The purpose of the income statement – or profit and loss account, as it is sometimes called – is to measure and report how much **profit** (wealth) the business has generated over a period. As with the balance sheet that we examined in Chapter 2, the principles of preparation are the same irrespective of whether the income statement is for a sole proprietorship business or for a limited company.

The measurement of profit requires that the total revenue of the business, generated during a particular period, be identified. **Revenue** is simply a measure of the inflow of economic benefits arising from the ordinary activities of a business. These benefits, which accrue to the owners, will result in either an increase in assets (such as cash or amounts owed to the business by its customers) or a decrease in liabilities. Different forms of business enterprise will generate different forms of revenue. Some examples of the different forms that revenue can take are as follows:

- sales of goods (for example, of a manufacturer);
- fees for services (for example, of a solicitor);
- subscriptions (for example, of a club);
- interest received (for example, of an investment fund).

The total expenses relating to each period must also be identified. **Expense** is really the opposite of revenue. It represents the outflow of economic benefits arising from the ordinary activities of a business. This loss of benefits will result in either a decrease in assets (such as cash) or an increase in liabilities (such as amounts owed to suppliers). Expenses are incurred in the process of generating revenue, or attempting to generate it. The nature of the business will again determine the type of expenses that will be incurred. Examples of some of the more common types of expenses are:

- the cost of buying goods that are subsequently sold – known as *cost of sales* or *cost of goods sold*;
- salaries and wages;
- rent and rates;
- motor vehicle running expenses;
- insurances;
- printing and stationery;
- heat and light;
- telephone and postage and so on.

The **income statement** simply shows the total revenue generated during a particular period and deducts from this the total expenses incurred in generating that revenue. The difference between the total revenue and total expenses will represent either profit (if revenue exceeds expenses) or loss (if expenses exceed revenue). Thus, we have:

> **Profit (loss) for the period = Total revenue for the period *less* Total expenses incurred in generating the revenue**

The period over which profit or loss is measured is usually known as the *accounting period*, but sometimes known as the 'reporting period' or 'financial period'.

Real World 3.1 below shows the various forms of revenue generated by a leading football club.

Real World 3.1

Away the lads!

Newcastle United is a well-known football club in the English Premiership. For the year to 31 July 2005, the club generated revenue totalling £87.0 m. A breakdown of this amount is provided in Figure 3.1 below.

Figure 3.1	Revenues generated by Newcastle United during the year ended 31 July 2005

Branded products (£7.6m) 9%
Catering (£6.8m) 8%
Match (£35.3m) 40%
Sponsorship (£9.4m) 11%
32% Television and broadcasting (£27.9m)

The two main sources of income are match receipts and TV and broadcasting receipts. Together, these account for nearly 73 per cent of the total revenue generated.

Source: Adapted from a diagram in Newcastle United plc, Annual Report 2005.

The income statement and the balance sheet

The income statement and the balance sheet should not be viewed in any way as substitutes for one another. Rather they should be seen as performing different functions. The balance sheet is, as stated earlier, a statement of the financial position of a business at a single moment in time – a 'snapshot' of the make up of the wealth held by the business. The income statement, on the other hand, is concerned with the *flow* of wealth over a period of time. The two statements are, however, closely related.

The income statement links the balance sheets at the beginning and the end of an accounting period. Thus, at the start of a new accounting period, the balance sheet shows the opening financial position. After an appropriate period, an income statement is prepared to show the wealth generated over that period. A balance sheet is then also prepared to reveal the new financial position at the end of the period. This balance sheet will incorporate the changes in wealth that have occurred since the previous balance sheet was drawn up.

We saw in Chapter 2 (page 40) that the effect on the balance sheet of making a profit (loss) means that the equation can be extended as follows:

$$\text{Assets} = \text{Capital} + \text{Profit (or} - \text{Loss)} + \text{Liabilities}$$

The amount of profit or loss for the period affects the balance sheet as an adjustment to capital.

The above equation can be extended to:

$$\text{Assets} = \text{Capital} + \text{(Sales revenue} - \text{Expenses)} + \text{Liabilities}$$

In theory, it would be possible to calculate the profit (or loss) for the period by making all adjustments for revenue and expenses through the capital section of the balance sheet. However, this would be rather cumbersome. A better solution is to have an 'appendix' to the capital section, in the form of an income statement. By deducting expenses from revenue for the period, the income statement derives the profit (loss) for adjustment in the capital item in the balance sheet. This figure represents the net effect of trading for the period. By providing this 'appendix', a detailed and more informative view of performance is presented to users.

The income statement layout

The layout of the income statement will vary according to the type of business to which it relates. To illustrate an income statement, let us consider the case of a retail business (that is, a business that buys goods in their completed state and resells them). This type of business usually has straightforward operations and, as a result, the income statement is relatively easy to understand.

Example 3.1 sets out a typical layout for the income statement of a retail business.

Example 3.1

Better-Price Stores
Income statement for the year ended 31 October 2007

	£
Sales revenue	232,000
Cost of sales	(154,000)
Gross profit	78,000
Salaries and wages	(24,500)
Rent and rates	(14,200)
Heat and light	(7,500)
Telephone and postage	(1,200)
Insurance	(1,000)
Motor vehicle running expenses	(3,400)
Depreciation – fixtures and fittings	(1,000)
Depreciation – motor van	(600)
Operating profit	24,600
Interest received from investments	2,000
Loan interest	(1,100)
Profit for the year	25,500

We can see that trading revenue, which arises from selling the goods, is the first item to appear. Deducted from this item is the cost of sales (also called the cost of the goods sold) during the period. Note that brackets are used to denote when an item is to be deducted. This convention is used by accountants in preference to + or − signs and will be used throughout the text.

Gross profit

→ This first part of the income statement is concerned with calculating the **gross profit** for the period. It is simply the difference between the trading revenue and cost of sales and represents the profit from buying and selling goods without taking into account any other revenues or expenses associated with the business.

Operating profit

From the gross profit, other expenses (overheads) that have been incurred in operating the business (salaries and wages, rent and rates and so on) are deducted.

→ The resulting figure is known as the **operating profit** for the accounting period. This represents the wealth generated during the period from the normal activities of the business.

Operating profit does not take account of any income that the business may have from activities that are not included in its normal operations. Better-Price Stores (Example 3.1) is a retailer, so the interest on some spare cash that the business has lent is not part of its operating profit.

Costs of financing the business are also ignored in the calculation of the operating profit.

Profit for the year

Having established the operating profit, we add any non-operating income (such as interest receivable) and deduct any interest payable on borrowings made by the

→ business, to arrive at the **profit for the year** (or **net profit**). This is the income that is attributable to the owner(s) of the business and which will be added to capital in the balance sheet. As can be seen, profit for the year is a residual – that is, the amount remaining after deducting all expenses incurred in generating the sales revenue for the period and taking account of non-operating income.

Some further issues

Having set out the main principles involved in preparing an income statement, we need to consider some further points.

Cost of sales

→ The **cost of sales** (or cost of goods sold) figure for a period can be identified in different ways. In some businesses, the cost of sales is identified at the time a sale has been made. Sales are closely matched with the cost of those sales and so identifying the cost of sales figure for inclusion in the income statement is not a problem. Many large retailers (for example, supermarkets) have point-of-sale (checkout) devices that not only record each sale but also simultaneously pick up the cost of the goods that are the subject of the particular sale. Other businesses that sell a relatively small number of high-value items (for example, an engineering business that produces custom-made equipment) also tend to match sales revenue with the cost of the goods sold at the time of the sale. However, some businesses (for example, small retailers) do not usually find it practical to match each sale to a particular cost of sales figure as the accounting period progresses. They find it easier to identify the cost of sales figure at the end of the accounting period.

Deriving the cost of sales after the end of the accounting period

To understand how this is done, it is important to recognise that the cost of sales figure represents the cost of goods that were *sold* by the business during the period rather than the cost of goods that were *bought* by that business during the period. Part of the goods bought during a particular period may remain in the business, as inventories, and not be sold until a later period. To derive the cost of sales for a period, it is necessary to know the amount of opening and closing inventories (stock) for the period and the cost of goods bought during the period. Example 3.2 below illustrates how the cost of sales is derived.

Example 3.2

Better-Price Stores, which we considered in Example 3.1 above, began the accounting year with unsold inventories of £40,000 and during that year bought inventories at a cost of £189,000. At the end of the year, unsold inventories of £75,000 were still held by the business.

The opening inventories at the beginning of the year *plus* the goods bought during the year will represent the total goods available for resale. Thus:

	£
Opening inventories	40,000
Goods bought	189,000
Goods available for resale	229,000

The closing inventories will represent that portion of the total goods available for resale that remains unsold at the end of the period. Thus, the cost of goods actually sold during the period must be the total goods available for resale *less* the inventories remaining at the end of the period. That is:

	£
Goods available for resale	229,000
Closing inventories	(75,000)
Cost of sales (or cost of goods sold)	154,000

These calculations are sometimes shown on the face of the income statement as in Example 3.3.

Example 3.3

	£	£
Sales revenue		232,000
Cost of sales		
Opening inventories	40,000	
Goods bought	189,000	
	229,000	
Closing inventories	(75,000)	(154,000)
Gross profit		78,000

The above is just an expanded version of the first section of the income statement for Better-Price Stores, as set out in Example 3.1. We have simply included the additional information concerning inventories balances and purchases for the year provided in Example 3.2.

Classification of expenses

The classifications for the revenue and expense items, as with the classifications of various assets and claims in the balance sheet, are often a matter of judgement by those who design the accounting system. Thus, the income statement set out in Example 3.1 could have included the insurance expense with the telephone and postage expense under a single heading – say, general expenses. Such decisions are normally based on how useful a particular classification will be to users. This will usually mean, however, that expense items of material size will be shown separately. For businesses that trade as limited companies, there are rules that dictate the classification of various items appearing in the financial statements for external reporting purposes. These rules will be discussed in Chapter 5.

Activity 3.1

The following information relates to the activities of H & S Retailers for the year ended 30 April 2007:

	£
Motor vehicle running expenses	1,200
Rent received from subletting	2,000
Closing inventories	3,000
Rent and rates payable	5,000
Motor vans (cost less depreciation)	6,300
Annual depreciation – motor vans	1,500
Heat and light	900
Telephone and postage	450
Sales revenue	97,400
Goods purchased	68,350
Insurance	750
Loan interest payable	620
Balance at bank	4,780
Salaries and wages	10,400
Opening inventories	4,000

Prepare an income statement for the year ended 30 April 2007. (*Hint*: not all items shown above should appear on this statement.)

Your answer to this activity should be as follows:

H & S Retailers
Income statement for the year ended 30 April 2007

	£	£
Sales revenue		97,400
Cost of sales		
Opening inventories	4,000	
Purchases	68,350	
	72,350	
Closing inventories	(3,000)	(69,350)
Gross profit		28,050
Rent receivable		2,000
Salaries and wages		(10,400)
Rent and rates		(5,000)
Heat and light		(900)
Telephone and postage		(450)
Insurance		(750)
Motor vehicle running expenses		(1,200)
Depreciation – motor van		(1,500)
Operating profit		9,850
Loan interest		(620)
Profit for the year		9,230

Note that neither the motor vans nor the bank balance are included in this statement. Rent receivable has been treated as part of the normal operations of the business.

In the case of the balance sheet, we saw that the information could be presented using either a horizontal or a vertical layout. This is also true of the income statement. Where a horizontal layout is used, expenses are listed on the left-hand side and revenues on the right, the difference being either profit or loss. The vertical layout has been used in our examples so far because it is easier to understand and, for this reason, it is now almost always used in practice.

The accounting period

We have seen already that for reporting to those outside the business, a financial reporting cycle of one year is the norm, though some large businesses will produce a half-yearly, or interim, financial statement to provide more frequent feedback on progress. For those who manage a business, however, it is important to have much more frequent feedback on performance. Thus it is quite common for income statements to be prepared on a quarterly, monthly, weekly or even daily basis in order to show how things are progressing.

Recognising revenue

A key issue in the measurement of profit concerns the point at which revenue is recognised. Revenue arising from the sale of goods or provision of a service could be recognised at various points. Where, for example, a motor car dealer receives an order for a new car from one of its business clients, the associated revenue could be recognised by the dealer:

- at the time that the order is placed by the customer;
- at the time that the car is collected by the customer; or
- at the time that the customer pays the dealer.

These three points could well be quite far apart, particularly where the order relates to a specialist car that is sold to the customer on credit.

The point chosen is not simply a matter of academic interest: it can have a profound impact on the total revenues, and therefore total profits, reported for a particular accounting period. If the car transaction straddled the end of an accounting period, the choice made between the three possible times for recognising the revenue could determine whether the revenue is included as revenue of an earlier accounting period or a later one.

When dealing with the sale of goods or the provision of services, the main criteria for recognising revenue are that:

- the amount of revenue can be measured reliably;
- it is probable that the economic benefits will be received.

An additional criterion, however, must be applied where the revenue comes from the sale of goods, which is that:

- ownership and control of the items should pass to the buyer.

Activity 3.2 below provides an opportunity to apply these criteria to a practical problem.

Activity 3.2

A manufacturing business sells goods on credit (that is, the customer pays for the goods some time after they are received). Below are four points in the production/selling cycle at which revenue might be recognised by the business:

1 when the goods are produced;
2 when an order is received from a customer;
3 when the goods are delivered to, and accepted by, the customer;
4 when the cash is received from the customer.

A significant amount of time may elapse between these different points. At what point do you think the business should recognise revenue?

All of the three criteria mentioned above will usually be fulfilled at point 3; when the goods are passed to, and accepted by, the customer. This is because

- the selling price and the settlement terms will have been agreed and therefore revenue can be reliably measured;
- delivery and acceptance of the goods leads to ownership and control passing to the buyer;
- transferring ownership gives the seller legally enforceable rights that makes it probable the buyer will pay.

We can see that the effect of applying these criteria is that a sale on credit is usually recognised *before* the cash is received. Thus, the total sales revenue figure shown in the income statement may include sales transactions for which the cash has yet to be received. The total sales revenue figure in the income statement for a period will often, therefore, be different from the total cash received from sales during that period.

Where goods are sold for cash rather than on credit, the revenue will normally be recognised at the point of sale. It is at this point that all the criteria will usually be met. For cash sales, there will be no difference in timing between reporting sales revenue and cash received.

Real World 3.2 sets out the revenue recognition criteria for one well-known manufacturing and retail business, which specialises in healthcare products.

Real World 3.2

Selling point

Revenue comprises sales and services to external customers (excluding VAT and other sales taxes). Consideration received from customers is only recorded as revenue when the group has completed full performance in respect of that consideration.

In respect of the Boots loyalty scheme, the Advantage Card, when points are issued to customers the retail value of those points expected to be redeemed is deferred. When the points are used by the customer they are recorded as revenue.

Sales of gift vouchers are only included in revenue when the vouchers are redeemed.

Source: Boots Group plc Annual report 2006.

Long-term contracts

Some contracts, both for goods and services can last for more than one accounting period. If the business providing the goods or services were to wait until the contract is completed before recognising any revenue, the income statement could give a misleading impression of profitability in the various accounting periods covered by the contract. This is a particular problem for businesses that undertake major long-term contracts, where a single contract could represent a large proportion of their total activities.

Construction contracts

Construction contracts often extend over a long period of time. Suppose a customer enters into a contract with a builder to build a new factory that will take three years to complete. In such a situation, it is possible to recognise revenue *before* the factory is completed, provided that the building work can be broken down into a number of stages and each stage can be measured reliably. Let us assume that building the factory could be broken down into the following stages:

- Stage 1 – clearing and levelling the land and putting in the foundations.
- Stage 2 – building the walls.
- Stage 3 – putting on the roof.
- Stage 4 – putting in the windows and completing all the interior work.

Each stage can be awarded a separate price with the total for all the stages being equal to the total contract price for the factory. This means that, as each stage is completed, the builder can recognise the price for that stage as revenue and bill the customer accordingly.

If the builder were to wait until the factory was completed before recognising revenue, the income statement covering the final year of the contract would recognise all the revenue and the income statements for each preceding year would recognise no revenue. This would give a misleading impression as it would not reflect the work done during each period.

Real World 3.3 sets out the revenue recognition criteria for one large construction business.

Real World 3.3

Tracking revenue

Jarvis plc is a construction business that is involved in road and rail infrastructure renewal.
 The point at which revenue on long-term contracts is recognised by the business is as follows:

> When the outcome of a long-term contract can be estimated reliably, contract revenue is recognised by reference to the degree of completion of each contract, based on the amounts certified and to be certified by the customer.

Source: Jarvis plc Annual Report and Accounts 2006, p. 43.

Services

Revenue from contracts for services may also be recognised in stages. Suppose a consultancy business has a contract to install a new computer system for the government, which will take several years to complete. Revenue can be recognised *before* the contract is completed as long as the contract can be broken down into stages and the particular stages of completion can be measured reliably. This is really the same approach as that used in the construction contract mentioned above.

Sometimes a continuous service is provided to a customer; for example, a telecommunications business may provide open access to the internet to those who subscribe to the service. In this case, revenue is usually recognised as the service is rendered. Benefits from providing the service are usually assumed to flow evenly over time and so revenue is recognised evenly over the subscription period.

Where it is not possible to break down a service into particular stages of completion, or to assume that benefits from providing the service accrue evenly over time, revenue will not usually be recognised until the service is fully completed. A solicitor handling a house purchase for a client provides such an example.

Real World 3.4 provides an example of how one major business recognises revenue from providing services.

Real World 3.4

Broadcasting revenue

British Sky Broadcasting Group plc is a major satellite broadcaster that generates various forms of revenue. Here are the ways in which some of its revenues are recognised:

● pay-per-view revenues – when the event (movie or football match) is viewed;
● direct-to-home subscription services – as the services are provided;
● cable revenues – as the services are provided;
● advertising revenues – when the advertising is broadcast;
● installations and digibox revenues – when the goods or services have been provided.

Source: British Sky Broadcasting Group plc Annual Report and Accounts 2006, p. 84.

When a service is provided, there will normally be a timing difference between the recognition of revenue and the receipt of cash. Revenue for providing services is often recognised *before* the cash is received, just like the sale of goods on credit. However, there are occasions when it is the other way around, usually because the business demands payment before providing the service.

Activity 3.3

Can you think of any examples of where cash may be demanded in advance of a service being provided? (*Hint*: try to think of services that you may use.)

Examples of where cash is received in advance of the service being provided may include:

● rent received from letting premises;
● telephone line rental charges;
● TV licence (BBC) or subscription (for example, Sky) fees; and
● subscriptions received for the use of health clubs or golf clubs.

You may have thought of others.

Recognising expenses

Having decided on the point at which revenue is recognised, we can now turn to the issue of the recognition of expenses. The **matching convention** in accounting is designed to provide guidance concerning the recognition of expenses. This convention states that expenses should be matched to the revenue that they helped to generate. In other words, the expenses that are associated with a particular revenue must be taken into account in the income statement for the same accounting period as that in which that revenue is included in the total sales revenue figure. Applying this convention may mean that a particular expense reported in the income statement for a period may not be the same figure as the cash paid for that item during the period. The expense reported might be either more or less than the cash paid during the period. Let us consider two examples that illustrate this point.

When the expense for the period is more than the cash paid during the period

Example 3.4

Domestic Ltd sells household electrical appliances. It pays its sales staff a commission of 2 per cent of sales revenue generated. Total sales revenue for last year amounted to £300,000. This will mean that the commission to be paid in respect of the sales for the year will be £6,000. However, by the end of the period, the amount of sales commission that had actually been paid to staff was £5,000. If the business reported only the amount paid, it would mean that the income statement would not reflect the full expense for the year. This would contravene the *matching convention* because not all of the expenses associated with the revenue of the year would have been matched in the income statement. This will be remedied as follows:

- Sales commission expense in the income statement will include the amount paid plus the amount outstanding (that is, £6,000 = £5,000 + £1,000).
- The amount outstanding (£1,000) represents an outstanding liability at the balance sheet date and will be included under the heading **accrued expenses**, or 'accruals', in the balance sheet. As this item will have to be paid within 12 months of the balance sheet date, it will be treated as a current liability.
- The cash will already have been reduced to reflect the commission paid (£5,000) during the period.

These points are illustrated in Figure 3.2.

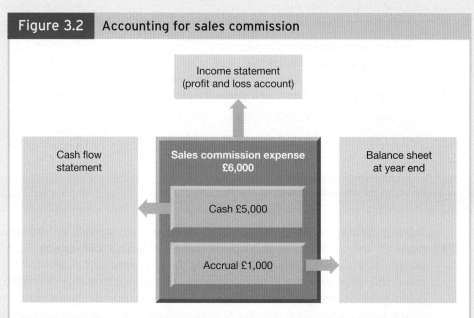

| Figure 3.2 | Accounting for sales commission |

This illustrates the main points of Example 3.4. We can see that the sales commission expense of £6,000 (which appears in the income statement) is made up of a cash element £5,000 and an accrued element £1,000. The cash element appears in the cash flow statement and the accrued element will appear as a year-end liability in the balance sheet.

In principle, all expenses should be matched to the period in which the sales revenue to which they relate is reported. However, it is sometimes difficult to match closely certain expenses to sales revenue in the same precise way that we have matched sales commission to sales revenue. It is unlikely, for example, that electricity charges incurred can be linked directly to particular sales in this way. As a result, the electricity charges incurred by, say, a retailer would be matched to the *period* to which they relate. Example 3.5 illustrates this.

Example 3.5

Domestic Ltd has reached the end of its accounting year and has only paid electricity for the first three quarters of the year (amounting to £1,900). This is simply because the electricity company has yet to send out bills for the quarter that ends on the same date as Domestic Ltd's year end. The amount of Domestic Ltd's bill for the last quarter is £500. In this situation, the amount of the electricity expense outstanding is dealt with as follows:

● Electricity expense in the income statement will include the amount paid, plus the amount of the bill for the last quarter (that is, £1,900 + £500 = £2,400) in order to cover the whole year.
● The amount of the outstanding bill (£500) represents a liability at the balance sheet date and will be included under the heading 'accruals' or 'accrued expenses' in the balance sheet. This item would normally have to be paid within 12 months of the end of the accounting year and will, therefore, be treated as a current liability.
● The cash will already have been reduced to reflect the electricity paid (£1,900) during the period.

This treatment will have the desired effect of increasing the electricity expense to the correct figure for the year in the income statement. It will also have the effect of showing that, at the end of the accounting year, Domestic Ltd owed the amount of the last quarter's electricity bill. Dealing with the outstanding amount in this way reflects the dual aspect of the item and will ensure that the balance sheet equation is maintained.

Domestic Ltd may wish to draw up its income statement before it is able to discover how much it owes for the last quarter's electricity. In this case it is quite normal to make a reasonable estimate of the amount of the bill and to use this estimated amount as described above.

Activity 3.4

How will the payment of the electricity bill for the last quarter be dealt with in the accounting records of Domestic Ltd?

When the electricity bill is eventually paid, it will be dealt with as follows:

● Reduce cash by the amount of the bill.
● Reduce the amount of the accrued expense as shown on the balance sheet by the same amount.

If an estimated figure is used and there is a slight error in the estimate, a small adjustment (either negative or positive depending on the direction of the error) can be made to the following year's expense. Dealing with the estimation error in this way is not strictly correct, but the amount is likely to be insignificant.

Activity 3.5

Can you think of other expenses for a retailer, apart from electricity charges, that cannot be linked directly to sales revenue and for which matching will therefore be done on a time basis?

You may have thought of the following examples:

● rent and rates;
● insurance;
● interest payments;
● licence fees payable.

This is not an exhaustive list. You may have thought of others.

When the amount paid during the year is more than the full expense for the period

It is not unusual for a business to be in a situation where it has paid more during the year than the full expense for that year. Example 3.6 below illustrates how we deal with this.

Example 3.6

Images Ltd, an advertising agency, normally pays rent for its premises quarterly in advance (on 1 January, 1 April, 1 July and 1 October). On the last day of the last accounting year (31 December), it paid the next quarter's rent (£4,000) to the following 31 March, which was a day earlier than required. This would mean that a total of five quarters' rent was paid during the year. If Images Ltd reports all of the cash paid as an expense in the income statement, this would be more than the full expense for the year. This would contravene the matching convention because a higher figure than the expenses associated with the revenue of the year would appear in the income statement.

The problem is overcome by dealing with the rental payment as follows:

● Show the rent for four quarters as the appropriate expense in the income statement (that is, 4 × £4,000 = £16,000).
● The cash (that is, 5 × £4,000 = £20,000) would already have been paid during the year.
● Show the quarter's rent paid in advance (£4,000) as a prepaid expense under assets in the balance sheet. (The prepaid expense will appear as a current asset in the balance sheet, under the heading **prepaid expenses** or 'prepayments'.)

In the next accounting period, this prepayment will cease to be an asset and will become an expense in the income statement of that period. This is because the rent prepaid relates to that period and will be 'used up' during that period.

These points are illustrated in Figure 3.3.

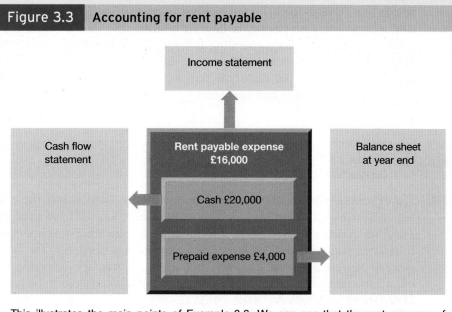

Figure 3.3   Accounting for rent payable

This illustrates the main points of Example 3.6. We can see that the rent expense of £16,000 (which appears in the income statement) is made up of four quarters' rent at £4,000 per quarter. This is the amount that relates to the period and is 'used up' during the period. The cash paid of £20,000 (which appears in the cash flow statement) is made up of the cash paid during the period, which is five quarters at £4,000 per quarter. Finally, the prepayment of £4,000 (which appears on the balance sheet) represents the payment made on 31 December and relates to the next financial year.

In practice, the treatment of accruals and prepayments will be subject to the **materiality convention** of accounting. This convention states that, where the amounts involved are immaterial, we should consider only what is reasonable. This may mean that an item will be treated as an expense in the period in which it is paid, rather than being strictly matched to the revenue to which it relates. For example, a business may find that, at the end of an accounting period, a bill of £5 has been paid for stationery that has still yet to be delivered. For a business of any size, the time and effort involved in recording this as a prepayment would not be justified by the little effect that this would have on the measurement of profit or financial position. The amount would, therefore, be treated as an expense when preparing the income statement for the current period and ignored in the following period.

Profit, cash and accruals accounting

As we have just seen, revenue does not usually represent cash received and expenses are not the same as cash paid. As a result, the profit figure (that is, total revenue minus total expenses) will not normally represent the net cash generated during a period. It is therefore important to distinguish between profit and liquidity. Profit is a measure of achievement, or productive effort, rather than a measure of cash generated. Although making a profit will increase wealth, as we have already seen in Chapter 2, cash is only one form in which that wealth may be held.

   The above points are reflected in the **accruals convention** of accounting, which asserts that profit is the excess of revenue over expenses for a period, not the excess of cash receipts over cash payments. Leading on from this, the approach to accounting that is based on the accruals convention is frequently referred to as **accruals accounting**. Thus, the balance sheet and the income statement are both prepared on the basis of accruals accounting. The cash flow statement, on the other hand, is not, as it simply deals with cash receipts and payments.

Depreciation

The expense of **depreciation**, which appeared in the income statement in Activity 3.1, requires further explanation. Most non-current assets do not have a perpetual existence. They are eventually used up in the process of generating revenue for the business. In essence, depreciation is an attempt to measure that portion of the cost (or fair value) of a non-current asset that has been used up in generating the revenue recognised during a particular period. The depreciation charge is considered to be an expense of the period to which it relates. Depreciation tends to be relevant both to *tangible non-current assets* (property, plant and equipment) and to *intangible non-current assets*. We should be clear that the principle is the same for both types of non-current asset. We shall deal with each of these two in turn.

Tangible non-current assets (property, plant and equipment)

To calculate a depreciation charge for a period, four factors have to be considered:

- the cost (or fair value) of the asset;
- the useful life of the asset;
- the residual value of the asset;
- the depreciation method.

The cost (or fair value) of the asset

The cost of an asset will include all costs incurred by the business to bring the asset to its required location and to make it ready for use. Thus, in addition to the costs of acquiring the asset, any delivery costs, installation costs (for example, setting up a new machine) and legal costs incurred in the transfer of legal title (for example, in purchasing property) will be included as part of the total cost of the asset. Similarly, any costs incurred in improving or altering an asset in order to make it suitable for its intended use within the business will also be included as part of the total cost.

Activity 3.6

Andrew Wu (Engineering) Ltd bought a new motor car for its marketing director. The invoice received from the motor car supplier revealed the following:

	£
New BMW 325i	26,350
Delivery charge	80
Alloy wheels	660
Sun roof	200
Petrol	30
Number plates	130
Road fund licence	165
	27,615
Part exchange – Reliant Robin	(1,000)
Amount outstanding	26,615

What is the total cost of the new car that will be treated as part of the business's property, plant and equipment?

The cost of the new car will be as follows:

	£
New BMW 325i	26,350
Delivery charge	80
Alloy wheels	660
Sun roof	200
Number plates	130
	27,420

This cost includes delivery charges and number plates, as they are a necessary and integral part of the asset. Improvements (alloy wheels and sun roof) are also regarded as part of the total cost of the motor car. The petrol and road fund licence, however, represent costs of operating the asset rather than a part of the total cost of acquiring it and making it ready for use: hence, these amounts will be charged as an expense in the period incurred (although part of the cost of the licence may be regarded as a prepaid expense in the period incurred).

The part-exchange figure shown is part payment of the total amount outstanding and so is not relevant to a consideration of the total cost.

The fair value of an asset was defined in Chapter 2 as the exchange value that could be obtained in an arm's-length transaction. We have already seen that assets may only be revalued to fair value if this can be measured reliably. When a revaluation is carried out, all items within the same class must be revalued and revaluations must be kept up to date.

The useful life of the asset

A tangible non-current asset has both a *physical life* and an *economic life*. The physical life will be exhausted through the effects of wear and tear and/or the passage of time. It is possible, however, for the physical life to be extended considerably through careful maintenance, improvements and so on. The economic life is decided by the effects of technological progress and by changes in demand. After a while, the benefits of using the asset may be less than the costs involved. This may be because it is unable to compete with newer assets, or because it is no longer relevant to the needs of the business. The economic life of a non-current tangible asset may be much shorter than its physical life. For example, a computer may have a physical life of eight years and an economic life of three years.

It is the economic life that will determine the expected useful life for the purpose of calculating depreciation. Forecasting the economic life, however, may be extremely difficult in practice: both the rate at which technology progresses and shifts in consumer tastes can be swift and unpredictable.

Residual value (disposal value)

When a business disposes of a tangible non-current asset that may still be of value to others, some payment may be received. This payment will represent the **residual value**, or *disposal value*, of the asset. To calculate the total amount to be depreciated, the residual value must be deducted from the cost of the asset. The likely amount to be received on disposal can, once again, be difficult to predict. The best guide is often past experience of similar assets sold.

Depreciation method

Once the amount to be depreciated (that is, the cost, or fair value, of the asset less any residual value) has been estimated, the business must select a method of allocating this depreciable amount between the accounting periods covering the asset's useful life. Although there are various ways in which the total depreciation may be allocated and, from this, a depreciation charge for each period derived, there are really only two methods that are commonly used in practice.

The first of these is known as the **straight-line method**. This method simply allocates the amount to be depreciated evenly over the useful life of the asset. In other words, an equal amount of depreciation is charged for each year the asset is held.

Example 3.7

To illustrate this method, consider the following information:

Cost of machine	£40,000
Estimated residual value at the end of its useful life	£1,024
Estimated useful life	4 years

To calculate the depreciation charge for each year, the total amount to be depreciated must be calculated. This will be the total cost less the estimated residual value: that is, £40,000 – £1,024 = £38,976. Having done this, the annual depreciation charge can be derived by dividing the amount to be depreciated by the estimated useful life of the asset of four years. The calculation is therefore:

$$\frac{£38,976}{4} = £9,744$$

Thus, the annual depreciation charge that appears in the income statement in relation to this asset will be £9,744 for each of the four years of the asset's life.

The amount of depreciation relating to the asset will be accumulated for as long as the asset continues to be owned by the business. This accumulated depreciation figure will increase each year as a result of the annual depreciation amount charged to the income statement. This accumulated amount will be deducted from the cost of the asset on the balance sheet. At the end of the second year, for example, the accumulated depreciation will be £9,744 × 2 = £19,488, and the asset details will appear on the balance sheet as follows:

	£
Machine at cost	40,000
Accumulated depreciation	(19,488)
	20,512

The balance of £20,512 shown above is referred to as the **carrying amount** (sometimes also known as the **written-down value** or **net book value**) of the asset. It represents that portion of the cost (or fair value) of the asset that has still to be charged as an expense (written off) in future years. It must be emphasised that this figure does not represent the current market value, which may be quite different.

The straight-line method derives its name from the fact that the carrying amount of the asset at the end of each year, when plotted against time, will result in a straight line, as shown in Figure 3.4.

Figure 3.4	Graph of carrying amount against time using the straight-line method

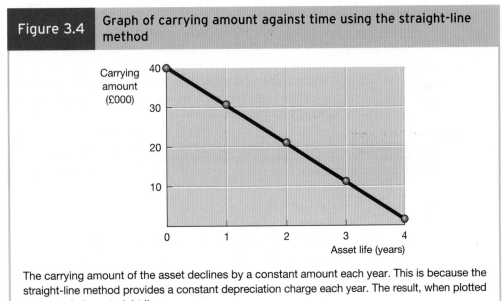

The carrying amount of the asset declines by a constant amount each year. This is because the straight-line method provides a constant depreciation charge each year. The result, when plotted on a graph, is a straight line.

The second approach to calculating depreciation for a period, found in practice, is referred to as the **reducing-balance method**. This method applies a fixed percentage rate of depreciation to the carrying amount of an asset each year. The effect of this will be high annual depreciation charges in the early years and lower charges in the later years. To illustrate this method, let us take the same information used in Example 3.7. It can be shown that using a fixed percentage of 60 per cent of the carrying amount to determine the annual depreciation charge will have the effect of reducing the carrying amount to £1,024 after four years.

The calculations will be as follows:

	£
Cost of machine	40,000
Year 1 Depreciation charge (60%* of cost)	(24,000)
Carrying amount	16,000
Year 2 Depreciation charge (60% of carrying amount)	(9,600)
Carrying amount	6,400
Year 3 Depreciation charge (60% of carrying amount)	(3,840)
Carrying amount	2,560
Year 4 Depreciation charge (60% of carrying amount)	(1,536)
Residual value	1,024

* See box below for an explanation of how to derive the fixed percentage.

Deriving the fixed percentage

Deriving the fixed percentage to be applied requires the use of the following formula:

$$P = (1 - \sqrt[n]{R/C}) \times 100\%$$

where: P = the depreciation percentage;
  n = the useful life of the asset (in years);
  R = the residual value of the asset;
  C = the cost, or fair value, of the asset.

The fixed percentage rate will, however, be given in all examples used in this text.

We can see that the pattern of depreciation is quite different for the two methods. If we plot the carrying amount of the asset, which has been derived using the reducing-balance method, against time, the result will be as shown in Figure 3.5.

Figure 3.5	Graph of carrying amount against time using the reducing-balance method

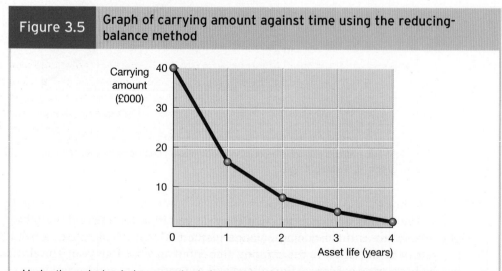

Under the reducing-balance method, the carrying amount of an asset falls by a larger amount in the earlier years than in the later years. This is because the depreciation charge is based on a fixed-rate percentage of the carrying amount.

Activity 3.7

Assume that the machine used in the example above was owned by a business that made a profit before depreciation of £20,000 for each of the four years in which the asset was held.

Calculate the profit for the business for each year under each depreciation method, and comment on your findings.

Your answer should be as follows:

Straight-line method

	(a) Profit before depreciation £	(b) Depreciation £	(a – b) Profit £
Year 1	20,000	9,744	10,256
Year 2	20,000	9,744	10,256
Year 3	20,000	9,744	10,256
Year 4	20,000	9,744	10,256

Reducing-balance method

	(a) Profit before depreciation £	(b) Depreciation £	(a – b) Profit/ (loss) £
Year 1	20,000	24,000	(4,000)
Year 2	20,000	9,600	10,400
Year 3	20,000	3,840	16,160
Year 4	20,000	1,536	18,464

The straight-line method of depreciation results in a constant profit figure over the four-year period. This is because both the profit before depreciation and the depreciation charge are constant over the period. The reducing-balance method, however, results in a changing profit figure over time, despite the fact that in this example the pre-depreciation profit is the same each year. In the first year a loss is reported, and thereafter a rising profit is reported.

Although the *pattern* of profit over the four-year period will be quite different, depending on the depreciation method used, the *total* profit for the period (£41,024) will remain the same. This is because both methods of depreciating will allocate the same amount of total depreciation (£38,976) over the four-year period. It is only the amount allocated *between years* that will differ.

In practice, the use of different depreciation methods may not have such a dramatic effect on profits as suggested in Activity 3.7 above. Where a business replaces some of its assets each year, the total depreciation charge calculated under the reducing-balance method will reflect a range of charges (from high through to low), as assets will be at different points in the replacement cycle. This could mean that each year's total depreciation charge may not be significantly different from the total depreciation charge that would be derived under the straight-line method.

Selecting a depreciation method

How does a business choose which depreciation method to use for a particular asset? The answer is the one that best matches the depreciation expense to the pattern of economic benefits that the asset provides. Where these benefits are provided evenly over time (buildings, for example), the straight-line method is usually appropriate. Where assets lose their efficiency (such as certain types of machinery), the benefits provided will decline over time and so the reducing-balance method may be more appropriate. Where the pattern of economic benefits provided by the asset is uncertain, the straight-line method is normally chosen.

There is an international financial reporting standard (or international accounting standard) to deal with the depreciation of property, plant and equipment. As we shall see in Chapter 5, the purpose of accounting standards is to narrow areas of accounting difference and to ensure that information provided to users is transparent and comparable. The relevant standard endorses the view that the depreciation method chosen should reflect the pattern of economic benefits provided but does not specify particular methods to be used. It states that the useful life, depreciation method and residual values of non-current assets should be reviewed at least annually and adjustments made where appropriate.

Real World 3.5 sets out the depreciation policies of Thorntons plc.

Real World 3.5

Depreciation policies in practice

Thorntons plc, the manufacturer and retailer of confectionery, uses the straight-line method to depreciate nearly all its non-current assets. In practice, this appears to be the most widely used method of depreciation. The financial statements for the year ended 30 June 2006 show the period over which different classes of tangible non-current assets are depreciated as follows:

In equal annual instalments

Factory freehold premises	50 years
Short leasehold land and buildings	Period of the lease
Retail fixtures and fittings	5 years
Retail equipment	4 to 5 years
Retail store improvements	Up to 10 years
Other equipment and vehicles	3 to 7 years
Manufacturing plant and machinery	12 to 15 years
Computer software and licences	3 to 5 years

We can see that there are wide variations in the expected useful lives of the various non-current assets held.

Source: Thorntons plc, Annual Report and Accounts 2006, p. 24.

The approach taken to calculating depreciation is summarised in Figure 3.6.

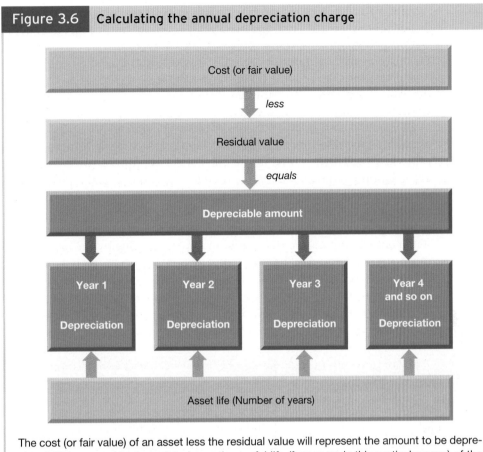

Figure 3.6   Calculating the annual depreciation charge

The cost (or fair value) of an asset less the residual value will represent the amount to be depreciated. This amount is depreciated over the useful life (four years in this particular case) of the asset using an appropriate depreciation method.

Depreciating intangible assets

Where an intangible asset has a finite life, the approach taken for the depreciation (or *amortisation* as it is usually called with intangibles) is broadly the same as that for property, plant and equipment (tangible non-current assets). The asset is amortised (depreciated) over its useful life and the amortisation method used should reflect the pattern of benefits provided. Some differences arise, however, because of the valuation problems surrounding these assets. Intangible assets are normally reported at cost rather than their fair value. They are rarely revalued because there is usually no active market from which to establish fair values. For similar reasons, the residual value of an intangible asset is normally assumed to be zero.

We saw in Chapter 2 that some intangible assets, which may include acquired goodwill, have an indefinite useful life. These assets are not amortised but instead are tested for impairment at least annually. Whilst intangible assets with finite lives and property, plant and equipment are also subject to impairment testing, this will only occur when there is some indication that impairment has taken place.

Depreciation and the replacement of non-current assets

There seems to be a misunderstanding in the minds of some people that the purpose of depreciation is to provide the funds for the replacement of an asset when it reaches the end of its useful life. However, this is not the purpose of depreciation as conventionally defined. It was mentioned earlier that depreciation represents an attempt to allocate the cost, or fair value, (less any residual value) of an asset over its expected useful life. The resulting depreciation charge in each accounting period represents an expense, which is then used in the calculation of profit for the period. Calculating the depreciation charge for a period is therefore necessary for the proper measurement of financial performance, and must be done whether or not the business intends to replace the asset in the future.

If there is an intention to replace the asset, the depreciation charge in the income statement will not ensure that liquid funds are set aside by the business specifically for this purpose. Although the effect of a depreciation charge is to reduce profit, and, therefore, to reduce the amount available for withdrawal by the owners, the amounts retained within the business as a result may be invested in ways that are unrelated to the replacement of the specific asset.

Depreciation and judgement

When reading the above sections on depreciation, it may have struck you that accounting is not as precise and objective as is sometimes suggested. There are areas where subjective judgement is required, and depreciation provides a good illustration of this.

Activity 3.8

What kinds of judgements must be made to calculate a depreciation charge for a period?

In answering this activity, you may have thought of the following:

● the expected residual or disposal value of the asset;
● the expected useful life of the asset;
● the choice of depreciation method.

Making different judgements on these matters would result in a different pattern of depreciation charges over the life of the asset, and therefore in a different pattern of reported profits. However, underestimations or overestimations that are made in relation to the above will be adjusted for in the final year of an asset's life, and so the total depreciation charge (and total profit) over the asset's life will not be affected by estimation errors.

Real World 3.6 describes the effect of extending the useful life of property, plant and equipment on the short-term profits of one large business.

Real World 3.6

Sports massage

JJB Sports plc, a leading retailer, reported interim financial results for the six months ended 30 June 2005 that caused some disquiet among investors and analysts. The business changed the estimates for the useful life of its property, plant and equipment when calculating depreciation. It explained that this was due to new requirements to adopt International Financial Reporting Standards (IFRSs) when preparing financial statements. The article below, however, suggests that not everyone believed this.

JJB Massages Results to Boost Profits

High street retailer JJB Sports massaged last week's disappointing interim results by changing its depreciation calculations, in order to boost flagging profits by £4.3 m.

Analysts admitted that they were caught on the hop, as the company reported a 35.8 per cent drop in operating profits from £27.4 m to £17.6 m for six months ended June 2005 on revenues down 6 per cent to £340.4 m. Operating profits would have plummeted even further to £14.3 m had the company not changed its accounting for depreciation. 'The company explained the change as coming out of its IFRS conversion review, but it was clearly there for other reasons,' said Teather & Greenwood retail analyst Sanjay Vidyarthi.

JJB said that an impairment review ahead of its IFRS transition had forced a rethink on the carrying value of property, plant and equipment.

It concluded that these items had useful economic lives that more closely matched the length of the short-term lease of the property, rather than the 10-year economic life, which had formed the basis of the depreciation charge in previous accounting periods.

Richard Ratner, head of equity research at Seymour Pierce, said: 'They said the way they had depreciated assets previously was not correct but I haven't seen any other companies make this kind of change.'

JJB's share price fell from 168.2 p before the results to 164.7 p at the end of last week.

Source: (2005) 'JJB Massages Results to Boost Profits', *Accountancy Age*, 20 October, p. 3.

Activity 3.9

Sally Dalton (Packaging) Ltd bought a machine for £40,000. At the end of its useful life of four years, the amount received on sale was £4,000. When the asset was bought the business received two estimates of the likely residual value of the asset, which were: (a) £8,000; and (b) zero.

Show the pattern of annual depreciation charges over the four years and the total depreciation charges for the asset under each of the two estimates. The straight-line method should be used to calculate the annual depreciation charges.

The depreciation charge, assuming estimate (a), will be £8,000 a year ((that is, £40,000 – 8,000)/4). The depreciation charge, assuming estimate (b), will be £10,000 a year (that is, £40,000/4). As the actual residual value is £4,000, estimate (a) will lead to underdepreciation of £4,000 (that is, £8,000 – £4,000) over the life of the asset, and estimate (b) will lead to overdepreciation of £4,000 (that is, £0 – £4,000). These under- and overestimations will be dealt with in year 4.

→

Activity 3.9 continued

The pattern of depreciation and total depreciation charges will therefore be:

		Estimate	
		(a)	*(b)*
Year		£	£
1	Annual depreciation	8,000	10,000
2	Annual depreciation	8,000	10,000
3	Annual depreciation	8,000	10,000
4	Annual depreciation	8,000	10,000
		32,000	40,000
4	Under/(over)depreciation	4,000	(4,000)
	Total depreciation	36,000	36,000

The final adjustment for underdepreciation of an asset is often referred to as 'loss (or deficit) on sale of non-current asset', as the amount actually received is less than the residual value. Similarly, the adjustment for overdepreciation is often referred to as 'profit (or surplus) on sale of non-current asset'.

Costing inventories

The way in which we measure the cost of inventories (or stock) is important because the cost of inventories sold during a period will affect the calculation of profit and the remaining inventories held at the end of the period will affect the portrayal of financial position in the balance sheet. In the previous chapter, we saw that historic cost is often the basis for reporting assets, and so it is tempting to think that determining the cost of inventories held is very straightforward. However, in a period of *changing prices*, the costing of inventories can be a problem.

A business must determine the cost of the inventories sold during the period and the cost of the inventories remaining at the end of the period. To do this, some assumption must be made about the way in which the inventories are physically handled. The assumption made need have nothing to do with how the inventories are *actually* handled; it is concerned only with providing useful accounting information.

Two common assumptions used are:

- **first in, first out (FIFO)** – the earliest inventories held are the first to be used;
- **last in, first out (LIFO)** – the latest inventories held are the first to be used.

Another approach to deriving the cost of inventories is to assume that inventories entering the business lose their separate identity, and any issues of inventories reflect the average cost of the inventories that are held. This is the **weighted average cost (AVCO)** method, where the weights used in deriving the average cost figures are the quantities of each batch of inventories bought. Example 3.8 provides a simple illustration of the way in which each method is applied.

Information Services & Systems
Swansea University

Issues Summary
05/10/2014 20:48

Id :: 1008078061

Item 1006465204
Financial accounting for decision makers [print and electi
13/10/2014

Total Number of Issued Items 1

Thank you for using Self Service
For renewals contact 01792 295178

Example 3.8

A business that supplies coal to factories has the following transactions during a period:

		Tonnes	Cost/tonne
1 May	Opening inventories	1,000	£10
2 May	Bought	5,000	£11
3 May	Bought	8,000	£12
		14,000	
6 May	Sold	(9,000)	
	Closing inventories	5,000	

First in, first out (FIFO)

Using the first in, first out approach, the first 9,000 tonnes of coal are treated as if these are the ones to be sold. This will consist of the opening inventories (1,000 tonnes), the purchases made on 2 May (5,000 tonnes) and some of the purchases made on 3 May (3,000 tonnes). The remainder of the 3 May purchases (5,000 tonnes) will comprise the closing inventories. Thus, we have:

	Cost of sales			Closing inventories		
	Tonnes	Cost/tonne £	Total £000	Tonnes	Cost/tonne £	Total £000
1 May	1,000	10	10.0			
2 May	5,000	11	55.0			
3 May	3,000	12	36.0	5,000	12	60.0
Cost of sales			101.0	Closing inventories		60.0

Last in, first out (LIFO)

Using the last in, first out approach, the later purchases will be treated as if these are the first to be sold. This is the 3 May purchases (8,000 tonnes) and some of the 2 May purchases (1,000 tonnes). The earlier purchases (the rest of the 2 May purchase and the opening inventories) will comprise the closing inventories. Thus, we have:

	Cost of sales			Closing inventories		
	Tonnes	Cost/tonne £	Total £000	Tonnes	Cost/tonne £	Total £000
3 May	8,000	12	96.0			
2 May	1,000	11	11.0	4,000	11	44.0
1 May				1,000	10	10.0
Cost of sales			107.0	Closing inventories		54.0

Weighted average cost (AVCO)

Using this approach, a weighted average cost will be determined that will be used to derive both the cost of goods sold and the cost of the remaining inventories held. This simply means that the total cost of the opening inventories, the 2 May and 3 May purchases are added together and divided by the total number of tonnes, to obtain the weighted average cost per tonne. Both the cost of sales and closing inventories values are based on that average cost per tonne. Thus, we have:

		Purchases	
	Tonnes	Cost/tonne £	Total £000
1 May	1,000	10	10.0
2 May	5,000	11	55.0
3 May	8,000	12	96.0
	14,000		161.0

Average cost = £161,000/14,000 = £11.5 per tonne

	Cost of sales			Closing inventories	
Tonnes	Cost/tonne £	Total £000	Tonnes	Cost/tonne £	Total £000
9,000	11.5	103.5	5,000	11.5	57.5

Activity 3.10

Suppose the 9,000 tonnes of inventories in Example 3.8 were sold for £15 per tonne.

(a) Calculate the gross profit for the period under each of the three methods.
(b) What observations concerning the portrayal of financial position and performance can you make about each method when prices are rising?

Your answer should be along the following lines:

(a) Gross profit calculation:

	FIFO £000	LIFO £000	AVCO £000
Sales revenue (9,000 @ £15)	135.0	135.0	135.0
Cost of sales	(101.0)	(107.0)	(103.5)
Gross profit	34.0	28.0	31.5
	£000	£000	£000
Closing inventories figure	60.0	54.0	57.5

(b) The above figures reveal that FIFO will give the highest gross profit during a period of rising prices. This is because sales revenue is matched with the earlier (and cheaper) purchases. LIFO will give the lowest gross profit because sales revenue is matched against the more recent (and dearer) purchases. The AVCO method will normally give a figure that is between these two extremes.

  The closing inventories figure in the balance sheet will be highest with the FIFO method. This is because the cost of goods still held will be based on the more recent (and dearer) purchases. LIFO will give the lowest closing inventories figure as the goods held will be based on the earlier (and cheaper) purchases. Once again, the AVCO method will normally give a figure that is between these two extremes.

Activity 3.11

Assume that prices in Activity 3.10 are falling rather than rising. How would your observations concerning the portrayal of financial performance and position be different for the various costing methods?

When prices are falling, the position of FIFO and LIFO is reversed. FIFO will give the lowest gross profit as sales revenue is matched against the earlier (and dearer) goods bought. LIFO will give the highest gross profit as sales revenue is matched against the more recent (and cheaper) goods bought. AVCO will give a cost of sales figure between these two extremes. The closing inventories figure in the balance sheet will be lowest under FIFO as the cost of inventories will be based on the more recent (and cheaper) purchases. LIFO will provide the highest closing inventories figure and AVCO will provide a figure between the two extremes.

The different costing methods will only have an effect on the reported profit from one year to the next. The figure derived for closing inventories will be carried forward and matched with sales revenue in a later period. Thus, if the cheaper purchases of inventories are matched to sales revenue in the current period, it will mean that the dearer purchases will be matched to sales revenue in a later period. Over the life of the business, therefore, the total profit will be the same whichever costing method has been used.

Inventories – some further issues

We saw in Chapter 2 that the convention of prudence requires that inventories be valued at the lower of cost and net realisable value. (The net realisable value of inventories is the estimated selling price less any further costs that may be necessary to complete the goods and any costs involved in selling and distributing the goods.) This rule may mean that the valuation method applied to inventories (cost or net realisable value) will switch each year depending on which of cost and net realisable value is the lower. In practice, however, the cost of the inventories held is usually below the current net realisable value – particularly during a period of rising prices. It is, therefore, the cost figure that will normally appear in the balance sheet.

Activity 3.12

Can you think of any circumstances where the net realisable value will be lower than the cost of inventories held, even during a period of generally rising prices?

The net realisable value may be lower where:

- goods have deteriorated or become obsolete;
- there has been a fall in the market price of the goods;
- the goods are being used as a 'loss leader';
- bad buying decisions have been made.

There is an international financial reporting standard that deals with inventories. It states that the cost of inventories should normally be determined using either FIFO or AVCO. The LIFO approach is not an acceptable method to use. The standard also requires the 'lower of cost or net realisable value' rule to be used.

Real World 3.7 sets out the costing methods of two large businesses.

Real World 3.7

Costing inventories in practice

Tate and Lyle plc, the sugar and other starch-based food processor, reports inventories on either a 'first in, first out' basis or weighted average cost basis.

British-American Tobacco, the cigarette manufacturer, uses weighted average cost only.

Sources: Tate and Lyle plc, Annual Report 2006, p. 75; British-American Tobacco, Directors Report and Accounts 2005, p. 33.

→ Costing inventories and depreciation provide two examples where the **consistency convention** must be applied. This convention holds that once a particular method of accounting is selected, it should be applied consistently over time. Thus, it would not be acceptable to switch from, say, FIFO to AVCO between periods (unless exceptional circumstances make it appropriate). The purpose of this convention is to help users make valid comparisons of performance and position from one period to the next.

Activity 3.13

Reporting inventories in the financial statements provides a further example of the need to apply subjective judgement. For the inventories of a retail business, what are the main areas where judgement is required?

The main areas are:

- the choice of cost method (FIFO, LIFO, AVCO);
- deducing the net realisable value figure for inventories held.

Dealing with trade receivables problems

We have seen that, when businesses sell goods or services on credit, revenue will often be recognised before the customer pays the amounts owing. Recording the dual aspect of a credit sale will involve:

- increasing sales revenue;
- increasing trade receivables (debtors) by the amount of the revenue from the credit sale.

With this type of sale there is always the risk that the customer will not pay the amount due, however reliable they might have appeared to be at the time of the sale. When it becomes reasonably certain that the customer will never pay, the debt owed is considered to be 'bad' and this must be taken into account when preparing the financial statements.

Activity 3.14

When preparing the financial statements, what would be the effect on the income statement and on the balance sheet, of not taking into account the fact that a debt is bad?

The effect would be to overstate the assets (trade receivables) on the balance sheet and to overstate profit in the income statement, as the revenue (which has been recognised) will not result in any future benefit.

To provide a more realistic picture of financial performance and position, the **bad debt** must be 'written off'. This will involve:

- reducing the trade receivables;
- increasing expenses (by creating an expense known as 'bad debts written off') by the amount of the bad debt.

The matching convention requires that the bad debt is written off in the same period as the sale that gave rise to the debt is recognised.

Note that, when a debt is bad, the accounting response is not simply to cancel the original sale. If this were done, the income statement would not be so informative. Reporting the bad debts as an expense can be extremely useful in assessing management performance.

At the end of the accounting period, it may not be possible to identify with reasonable certainty all the bad debts that have been incurred during the period. It may be that some trade receivables appear doubtful, but only at some later point in time will the true position become clear. The uncertainty that exists does not mean that, when preparing the financial statements, we should ignore the possibility that some of the trade receivables outstanding will eventually prove to be bad. It would not be prudent to do so, nor would it comply with the need to match expenses to the period in which the associated sale is recognised. As a result, the business will normally try to identify all those trade receivables that, at the end of the period, can be classified as doubtful (that is, there is a possibility that they may eventually prove to be bad). This can be done by examining individual accounts of trade receivables or by taking a proportion of the total trade receivables outstanding based on past experience.

→ Once a figure has been derived, an expense known as **allowances for trade receivables** can be created. This will be:

● shown as an expense in the income statement; and
● deducted from the total trade receivables figure in the balance sheet.

By doing this, full account is taken, in the appropriate accounting period, of those trade receivables where there is a risk of non-payment. This accounting treatment of these trade receivables will be in addition to the treatment of bad debts described above.

Example 3.9 illustrates the reporting of bad debts and allowances for trade receivables.

Example 3.9

Desai Enterprises had trade receivables of £350,000 outstanding at the end of the accounting year to 30 June 2007. Investigation of these trade receivables revealed that £10,000 would probably be irrecoverable and that a further £30,000 were doubtful of being recoverable.

Relevant extracts from the income statement for that year would be as follows:

Income statement (extracts) for the year ended 30 June 2007

	£
Bad debts written off	10,000
Allowances for trade receivables	30,000

Balance sheet (extracts) as at 30 June 2007

	£
Trade receivables	340,000*
Allowances for trade receivables	(30,000)
	310,000

* That is, £350,000 – £10,000 irrecoverable trade receivables.

The allowances for trade receivables figure is, of course, an estimate, and it is quite likely that the actual amount of trade receivables that prove to be bad will be different from the estimate. Let us say that, during the next accounting period, it was discovered that, in fact, £26,000 of the trade receivables considered doubtful proved to be irrecoverable. These trade receivables must now be written off as follows:

● reduce trade receivables by £26,000; and
● reduce allowances for trade receivables by £26,000.

However, allowances for trade receivables of £4,000 will remain. This amount represents an overestimate made when creating the allowance as at 30 June 2007. As the allowance is no longer needed, it should be eliminated. Remember that the allowance was made by creating an expense in the income statement for the year to 30 June 2007. As the expense was too high, the amount of the overestimate should be 'written back' in the next accounting period. In other words, it will be treated as revenue for the year to 30 June 2008. This will mean:

● reducing the allowances for trade receivables by £4,000; and
● increasing revenue by £4,000.

Ideally, of course, the amount should be written back to the 2007 income statement; however, it is too late to do this. At the end of of the year to 30 June 2008, not only will 2007's overestimate be written back but a new allowance should be created to take account of the trade receivables arising from 2008's credit sales that are considered doubtful.

Activity 3.15

Clayton Conglomerates had trade receivables of £870,000 outstanding at the end of the accounting year to 31 March 2006. The chief accountant believed that £40,000 of those trade receivables were irrecoverable and that a further £60,000 were doubtful of being recoverable. In the subsequent year, it was found that an over-pessimistic estimate of those trade receivables considered doubtful had been made and that only a further £45,000 of trade receivables had actually proved to be bad.

Show the relevant extracts in the income statement for both 2006 and 2007 to report the bad debts written off and the allowances for trade receivables. Also show the relevant balance sheet extract as at 31 March 2006.

Your answer should be as follows:

Income statement (extracts) for the year ended 31 March 2006

	£
Bad debts written off	40,000
Allowances for trade receivables	60,000

Income statement (extracts) for the year ended 31 March 2007

	£
Allowances for trade receivables written back (revenue)	15,000

Note: this figure will usually be netted off against any allowances for trade receivables created in respect of 2007.

Balance sheet (extracts) as at 31 March 2006

	£
Trade receivables	830,000
Allowances for trade receivables	(60,000)
	770,000

Activity 3.16

Bad debts and allowances for trade receivables are two further examples where judgement is needed to derive an appropriate expense figure. What will be the effect of different judgements concerning the appropriate amount of bad debts expense and allowances for trade receivables expense on the profit for a particular period and on the total profit reported over the life of the business?

→

Activity 3.16 continued

Judgement is often required in deriving a figure for bad debts incurred during a period. There may be situations where views will differ concerning whether or not a debt is irrecoverable. The decision concerning whether or not to write off a bad debt will have an effect on the expenses for the period and, hence, the reported profit. However, over the life of the business the total reported profit would not be affected, as incorrect judgements in one period will be adjusted for in a later period.

Suppose that a debt of £100 was written off in a period and that, in a later period, the amount owing was actually received. The increase in expenses of £100 in the period in which the bad debt was written off would be compensated for by an increase in revenue of £100 when the amount outstanding was finally received (bad debt recoverable). If, on the other hand, the amount owing of £100 was never written off in the first place, the profit for the two periods would not be affected by the bad debt adjustment and would, therefore, be different – but the total profit for the two periods would be the same.

A similar situation would apply where there are differences in judgements concerning allowances for trade receivables.

Real World 3.8 shows the effect of bad debts on the banking sector.

Real World 3.8

'Household Debt Adds to Rise in Bank Write-offs'   FT

Banks were forced to write off record amounts of bad debts last year, Bank of England figures are expected to show this week. The figures, to be published on Thursday, are likely to increase concern about soaring levels of consumer debt and, in particular, the willingness of banks to offer large loans to poorer households.

The data are expected to show that write-offs in the fourth quarter of 2004 reached a record level of more than £6 bn for the year as a whole. The previous record for bad debt write-offs occurred in the early 1990s when Britain was mired in a recession.

The banks' write-offs, which have risen sharply since 2001, are largely a result of consumer rather than corporate bad debts.

Credit card lending, in particular, has been a problem, with write-offs more than trebling since 1995 to more than 3 per cent by the end of 2003.

Simon Walker, head of retail banking at accountants KPMG, said most of the rise in write-offs could be attributed to the decision of banks to go 'more downmarket' as they expanded their credit card lending books.

Write-offs of lending to individuals because of increased write-offs of credit card debt have risen from £100 m a decade ago to nearly £2 bn now.

The increase has driven up the percentage of household write-offs accounted for by credit card debt from less than 20 per cent in 1993 to nearly 50 per cent now.

The boom in lending has generally been profitable for the banks despite sharp rises in bad debts.

Write-offs on mortgage debts have declined and remain at modest levels. Secured lending, such as mortgages, is less likely to be written off since banks can possess the property if the loan cannot be repaid.

Rising house prices have also reduced the amount of debt outstanding after a property is repossessed and sold, thereby cutting the amounts a bank would need to write off.

Source: Briscoe, Simon 'Household Debt Adds to Rise in Bank Write-offs', *Financial Times*, 28 March 2005, FT.com.

Let us now try to bring together some of the points that we have raised in this chapter through a self-assessment question.

Self-assessment question 3.1

TT and Co is a new business that started trading on 1 January 2006. The following is a summary of transactions that occurred during the first year of trading:

1 The owners introduced £50,000 of capital, which was paid into a bank account opened in the name of the business.
2 Premises were rented from 1 January 2006 at an annual rental of £20,000. During the year, rent of £25,000 was paid to the owner of the premises.
3 Rates (a tax on business premises) were paid during the year as follows:

   For the period 1 January 2006 to 31 March 2006   £500
   For the period 1 April 2006 to 31 March 2007   £1,200

4 A delivery van was bought on 1 January 2006 for £12,000. This is expected to be used in the business for four years and then to be sold for £2,000.
5 Wages totalling £33,500 were paid during the year. At the end of the year, the business owed £630 of wages for the last week of the year.
6 Electricity bills for the first three quarters of the year were paid totalling £1,650. After 31 December 2006, but before the financial statements had been finalised for the year, the bill for the last quarter arrived showing a charge of £620.
7 Inventories totalling £143,000 were bought on credit.
8 Inventories totalling £12,000 were bought for cash.
9 Sales revenue on credit totalled £152,000 (cost of sales £74,000).
10 Cash sales revenue totalled £35,000 (cost of sales £16,000).
11 Receipts from trade receivables totalled £132,000.
12 Payments to trade payables totalled £121,000.
13 Van running expenses paid totalled £9,400.

At the end of the year it was clear that a trade receivable who owed £400 would not be able to pay any part of the debt. The business uses the straight-line method for depreciating non-current assets.

Required:
Prepare a balance sheet as at 31 December 2006 and an income statement for the year to that date. (Use the outline financial statements produced below to help you.)

TT and Co
Balance sheet as at 31 December 2006

	£
Non-current assets	
Motor van	
Accumulated depreciation	_____
	_____
Current assets	
Inventories	
Trade receivables	
Prepaid expenses	
Cash	_____
	_____
Total assets	_____
Capital (owner's equity)	
Original	
Profit	_____
	_____

→

Self-assessment question 3.1 continued

Current liabilities
Trade payables
Accrued expenses
——

——
Total equity and liabilities ——

Income statement for the year ended 31 December 2006

£

Sales revenue
Cost of goods sold ——
Gross profit
Rent
Rates
Wages
Electricity
Bad debts
Van expenses
Van depreciation ——
Profit for the year ——

The answer to this question can be found at the back of the book on p. 401.

Interpreting the income statement

When an income statement is presented to users it is sometimes the case that the only item that will concern them will be the final profit figure, or *bottom line* as it is sometimes called. Although the profit figure is a primary measure of performance, and its importance is difficult to overstate, the income statement contains other information that should also be of interest. To evaluate business performance effectively, it is important to find out how the final profit figure was derived. Thus, the level of sales revenue, the nature and amount of expenses incurred, and the profit in relation to sales revenue are important factors in understanding the performance of the business over a period. The analysis and interpretation of financial statements is considered in detail in Chapters 7 and 8.

Summary

The main points of this chapter may be summarised as follows:

The income statement (profit and loss account)
- Measures and reports how much profit (loss) has been generated over a period.
- Profit (loss) for the period is the difference between the total revenue and total expenses for the period.
- Links the balance sheets at the beginning and end of an accounting period.

- The income statement of a retail business will first calculate gross profit, then add any additional revenue and then deduct any overheads for the period. The final figure derived is the profit (loss) for the period.
- Gross profit represents the difference between the sales revenue for the period and the cost of sales.

Expenses and revenue

- Cost of sales may be identified by either matching the cost of each sale to the particular sale or by adjusting the goods bought during the period to take account of opening and closing inventories.
- The classification of expenses is often a matter of judgement, although there are rules for businesses that trade as limited companies.
- Revenue is recognised when the amount of revenue can be measured reliably and it is probable that the economic benefits will be received.
- Where there is a sale of goods, there is an additional criterion that ownership and control must pass to the buyer before revenue can be recognised.
- Revenue can be recognised after partial completion provided a particular stage of completion can be measured reliably.
- The matching convention states that expenses should be matched to the revenue that they help generate.
- A particular expense reported in the income statement may not be the same as the cash paid. This will result in some adjustment for accruals or prepayments.
- The materiality convention states that where the amounts are immaterial, we should consider only what is expedient.
- 'Accruals accounting' is preparing the income statement and balance sheet following the accruals convention, which says that profit = revenue − expenses (not cash receipts − cash payments).

Depreciation of non-current assets

- Depreciation requires a consideration of the cost (or fair value), useful life and residual value of an asset. It also requires a consideration of the method of depreciation.
- The straight-line method of depreciation allocates the amount to be depreciated evenly over the useful life of the asset.
- The reducing-balance method applies a fixed percentage rate of depreciation to the written-down value of an asset each year.
- The depreciation method chosen should reflect the pattern of benefits associated with the asset.
- Depreciation is an attempt to allocate the cost (or fair value), less the residual value, of an asset over its useful life. It does not provide funds for replacement of the asset.

Costing inventories

- The way in which we derive the cost of inventories is important in the calculation of profit and the presentation of financial position.
- The first in, first out (FIFO) method approaches matters as if the earliest inventories held are the first to be used.
- The last in, first out (LIFO) method approaches matters as if the latest inventories are the first to be used.

- The weighted average cost (AVCO) method applies an average cost to all inventories used.

- When prices are rising, FIFO gives the lowest cost of sales figure and highest closing inventories figure and LIFO gives the highest cost of sales figure and the lowest closing inventories figure. AVCO gives figures for cost of sales and closing inventories that lie between FIFO and LIFO.

- When prices are falling, the positions of FIFO and LIFO are reversed.

- Inventories are shown at the lower of cost and net realisable value.

- When a particular method of accounting, such as an inventories' costing method, is selected, it should be applied consistently over time.

Bad debts

- Where it is reasonably certain that a credit customer will not pay, the debt is regarded as 'bad' and written off.

- Where it is doubtful that a credit customer will pay, an allowances for trade receivables expense should be created.

→ Key terms

Profit p. 65	**Depreciation** p. 80
Revenue p. 65	**Residual value** p. 82
Expense p. 65	**Straight-line method** p. 82
Income statement p. 65	**Carrying amount** p. 83
Gross profit p. 68	**Written-down value** p. 83
Operating profit p. 68	**Reducing-balance method** p. 83
Net profit p. 68	**First in, first out (FIFO)** p. 90
Cost of sales p. 68	**Last in, first out (LIFO)** p. 90
Matching convention p. 75	**Weighted average cost (AVCO)**
Accrued expenses p. 76	p. 90
Prepaid expenses p. 78	**Consistency convention** p. 94
Materiality convention p. 79	**Bad debt** p. 95
Accruals convention p. 80	**Allowances for trade receivables**
Accruals accounting p. 80	p. 96

Further reading

If you would like to explore the topics covered in this chapter in more depth, we recommend the following books:

KPMG (2006) *KPMG's Practical Guide to International Financial Reporting Standards*, 3rd edn, Thomson, Sections 3.2, 3.3 and 3.8.

Elliott, B. and Elliott, J. (2006) *Financial Accounting and Reporting*, 11th edn, Financial Times Prentice Hall, Chapters 2, 16, 18 and 19.

Kirk, R. J. (2005) *International Financial Reporting Standards in Depth*, CIMA Publishing, Chapters 2 and 3.

Sutton, T. (2004) *Corporate Financial Accounting and Reporting*, 2nd edn, Financial Times Prentice Hall, Chapters 2, 8, 9 and 10.

Review questions

Answers to these questions can be found at the back of the book on p. 411.

3.1 'Although the income statement is a record of past achievement, the calculations required for certain expenses involve estimates of the future.' What is meant by this statement? Can you think of examples where estimates of the future are used?

3.2 'Depreciation is a process of allocation and not valuation.' What do you think is meant by this statement?

3.3 What is the convention of consistency? Does this convention help users in making a more valid comparison between businesses?

3.4 'An asset is similar to an expense.' Do you agree?

Exercises

Exercises 3.6 to 3.8 are more advanced than 3.1 to 3.5. Those with a coloured number have answers at the back of the book starting on p. 421.

If you wish to try more exercises, visit the students' side of the Companion Website.

3.1 You have heard the following statements made. Comment critically on them.

(a) 'Capital only increases or decreases as a result of the owners putting more cash into the business or taking some out.'
(b) 'An accrued expense is one that relates to next year.'
(c) 'Unless we depreciate this asset we shall be unable to provide for its replacement.'
(d) 'There is no point in depreciating the factory building. It is appreciating in value each year.'

3.2 Singh Enterprises has an accounting year to 31 December and uses the straight-line method of depreciation. On 1 January 2004 the business bought a machine for £10,000. The machine had an expected useful life of four years and an estimated residual value of £2,000. On 1 January 2005 the business bought another machine for £15,000. This machine had an expected useful life of five years and an estimated residual value of £2,500. On 31 December 2006 the business sold the first machine bought for £3,000.

Required:
Show the relevant income statement extracts and balance sheet extracts for the years 2004, 2005 and 2006.

3.3 The owner of a business is confused, and comes to you for help. The financial statements for the business, prepared by an accountant, for the last accounting period revealed an increase in profit of £50,000. However, during the accounting period the bank balance declined by £30,000. What reasons might explain this apparent discrepancy?

3.4 Spratley Ltd is a builders' merchant. On 1 September the business had, as part of its inventories, 20 tonnes of sand at a cost of £18 per tonne and at a total cost of £360. During the first week in September, the business bought the following amounts of sand:

September	Tonnes	Cost per tonne £
2	48	20
4	15	24
6	10	25

On 7 September the business sold 60 tonnes of sand to a local builder.

Required:

Calculate the cost of goods sold and the closing inventories from the above information using the following costing methods:

(a) first in, first out;
(b) last in, first out;
(c) weighted average cost.

3.5 Fill in the values (a) to (f) in the following table on the assumption that there were no opening balances involved:

	Relating to period		At end of period	
	Paid/Received	Expense/revenue for period	Prepaid	Accruals/deferred revenues
	£	£	£	£
Rent payable	10,000	a	1,000	
Rates and insurance	5,000	b		1,000
General expenses	c	6,000	1,000	
Loan interest payable	3,000	2,500	d	
Salaries	e	9,000		3,000
Rent receivable	f	1,500		1,500

3.6 The following is the balance sheet of TT and Co at the end of its first year of trading (from Self-assessment question 3.1):

TT and Co
Balance sheet as at 31 December 2006

	£
Non-current assets	
Motor van: Cost	12,000
Depreciation	(2,500)
	9,500
Current assets	
Inventories	65,000
Trade receivables	19,600
Prepaid expenses*	5,300
Cash	750
	90,650
Total assets	100,150
Capital (owner's equity)	
Original	50,000
Profit	26,900
	76,900
Current liabilities	
Trade payables	22,000
Accrued expenses†	1,250
	23,250
Total equity and liabilities	100,150

* The prepaid expenses consisted of rates (£300) and rent (£5,000).
† The accrued expenses consisted of wages (£630) and electricity (£620).

During 2007, the following transactions took place:

1 The owners withdrew capital in the form of cash of £20,000.
2 Premises continued to be rented at an annual rental of £20,000. During the year, rent of £15,000 was paid to the owner of the premises.
3 Rates on the premises were paid during the year as follows: for the period 1 April 2007 to 31 March 2008 £1,300.
4 A second delivery van was bought on 1 January 2007 for £13,000. This is expected to be used in the business for four years and then to be sold for £3,000.
5 Wages totalling £36,700 were paid during the year. At the end of the year, the business owed £860 of wages for the last week of the year.
6 Electricity bills for the first three quarters of the year and £620 for the last quarter of the previous year were paid totalling £1,820. After 31 December 2007, but before the accounts had been finalised for the year, the bill for the last quarter arrived showing a charge of £690.
7 Inventories totalling £67,000 were bought on credit.
8 Inventories totalling £8,000 were bought for cash.
9 Sales revenue on credit totalled £179,000 (cost £89,000).
10 Cash sales revenue totalled £54,000 (cost £25,000).
11 Receipts from trade receivables totalled £178,000.
12 Payments to trade payables totalled £71,000.
13 Van running expenses paid totalled £16,200.

The business uses the straight-line method for depreciating non-current assets.

Required:
Prepare a balance sheet as at 31 December 2007 and an income statement for the year to that date.

3.7   The following is the balance sheet of WW Associates as at 31 December 2005:

Balance sheet as at 31 December 2005

	£
Non-current assets	
Machinery	25,300
Current assets	
Inventories	12,200
Trade receivables	21,300
Prepaid expenses (rates)	400
Cash	8,300
	42,200
Total assets	67,500
Capital	
Original	25,000
Retained profit	23,900
	48,900
Current liabilities	
Trade payables	16,900
Accrued expenses (wages)	1,700
	18,600
Total equity and liabilities	67,500

During 2006, the following transactions took place:

1 The owners withdrew capital in the form of cash of £23,000.
2 Premises were rented at an annual rental of £20,000. During the year, rent of £25,000 was paid to the owner of the premises.
3 Rates on the premises were paid during the year for the period 1 April 2006 to 31 March 2007 and amounted to £2,000.
4 Some machinery (a non-current asset), which was bought on 1 January 2005 for £13,000, has proved to be unsatisfactory. It was part-exchanged for some new machinery on 1 January 2006, and WW Associates paid a cash amount of £6,000. The new machinery would have cost £15,000 had the business bought it without the trade-in.
5 Wages totalling £23,800 were paid during the year. At the end of the year, the business owed £860 of wages.
6 Electricity bills for the four quarters of the year were paid totalling £2,700.
7 Inventories totalling £143,000 were bought on credit.
8 Inventories totalling £12,000 were bought for cash.
9 Sales revenue on credit totalled £211,000 (cost £127,000).
10 Cash sales revenue totalled £42,000 (cost £25,000).
11 Receipts from trade receivables totalled £198,000.
12 Payments to trade payables totalled £156,000.
13 Van running expenses paid totalled £17,500.

The business uses the reducing-balance method of depreciation for non-current assets at the rate of 30 per cent each year.

Required:
Prepare a balance sheet as at 31 December 2006 and an income statement (profit and loss

account) for the year to that date.

3.8   The following is the income statement for Nikov and Co. for the year ended 31 December 2006, along with information relating to the preceding year.

Income statement for the year ended 31 December

	2006	2005
	£000	£000
Sales revenue	420.2	382.5
Cost of sales	(126.1)	(114.8)
Gross profit	294.1	267.7
Salaries and wages	(92.6)	(86.4)
Selling and distribution costs	(98.9)	(75.4)
Rent and rates	(22.0)	(22.0)
Bad debts written off	(19.7)	(4.0)
Telephone and postage	(4.8)	(4.4)
Insurance	(2.9)	(2.8)
Motor vehicle expenses	(10.3)	(8.6)
Depreciation – Delivery van	(3.1)	(3.3)
– Fixtures and fittings	(4.3)	(4.5)
Operating profit	35.5	56.3
Loan interest	(4.6)	(5.4)
Profit for the year	30.9	50.9

Required:

Analyse the performance of the business for the year to 31 December 2006 in so far as the information allows.

4

Accounting for limited companies (1)

Introduction

Most businesses in the UK, except the very smallest, operate in the form of limited companies. More than 2 million limited companies now exist and they account for the majority of UK business activity and employment. The economic significance of this type of business is not confined to the UK; it can be seen in many of the world's developed countries.

In this chapter we consider the nature of limited companies and how they differ from sole proprietorship businesses and partnerships. We examine the ways in which the owners provide finance as well as the rules governing the way in which limited companies must account to their owners and to other interested parties. We shall also see how the financial statements, which were discussed in the previous two chapters, are prepared for this type of business.

Learning outcomes

When you have completed this chapter, you should be able to:

- Discuss the nature of the limited company.

- Explain the role of directors of limited companies.

- Describe the main features of the owners' claim in a limited company.

- Explain how the income statement and balance sheet of a limited company differ in detail from that of sole proprietorships and partnerships.

The main features of limited companies

Legal nature

Let us begin our examination of limited companies by discussing their legal nature. A **limited company** has been described as an artificial person that has been created by law. This means that a company has many of the rights and obligations that 'real' people have. It can, for example, sue or be sued by others and can enter into contracts in its own name. This contrasts sharply with other types of businesses, such as sole proprietorships and partnerships (that is unincorporated businesses), where it is the owner(s) rather than the business that must sue, enter into contracts and so on, because the business has no separate legal identity.

With the rare exceptions of those that are created by Act of Parliament or by Royal Charter, all UK companies are created (or *incorporated*) by registration. To create a company the person or persons (usually known as *promoters*) wishing to create it, fill in a few simple forms and pay a modest registration fee. After having ensured that the necessary formalities have been met, the Registrar of Companies, a government official, enters the name of the new company on the Registry of Companies. Thus, in the UK, companies can be formed very easily and cheaply (for about £100).

Companies may be owned by just one person, but most have more than one owner and some have many owners. The owners are usually known as *members* or *shareholders*. The ownership of a company is normally divided into a number, frequently a large number, of **shares**, each of equal size. Each owner, or shareholder, owns one or more shares in the company. Large companies typically have a very large number of shareholders. For example, at 31 March 2006, BT Group plc, the telecommunications business, had nearly 1.4 million different shareholders.

As a limited company has its own legal identity, it is regarded as being quite separate from those that own and manage it. This fact leads to two important features of the limited company: perpetual life and limited liability. These are explained below.

Just before we leave the topic of the legal separateness of owners and the company, however, it is worth emphasising that this has no connection with the business entity convention of accounting, which we discussed in Chapter 2. This accounting convention applies equally well to all business types, including sole proprietorships and partnerships where there is certainly no legal distinction between the owner(s) and the business.

Perpetual life

A company is normally granted a perpetual existence and so will continue even where an owner of some, or even all, of the shares in the company dies. The shares of the deceased person will simply pass to the beneficiary of his or her estate. The granting of perpetual existence means that the life of a company is quite separate from the lives of those individuals who own or manage it. It is not, therefore, affected by changes in ownership that arise when individuals buy and sell shares in the company.

Though a company may be granted a perpetual existence when it is first formed, it is possible for either the shareholders or the courts to bring this existence to an end. When this is done, the assets of the company are sold off to meet outstanding liabilities. Any surplus arising from the sale will then be used to pay the shareholders.

Shareholders may agree to end the life of a company where it has achieved the purpose for which it was formed or where they feel that the company has no real future. The courts may bring the life of a company to an end where creditors have applied to the courts for this to be done because they have not been paid amounts owing.

Where shareholders agree to end the life of a company, it is referred to as a 'voluntary liquidation'. **Real World 4.1** describes the demise of one company by this method.

Real World 4.1

'Monotub Industries in a Spin as Founder Gets Titan for £1'

FT

Monotub Industries, maker of the Titan washing machine, yesterday passed into corporate history with very little ceremony and with only a whimper of protest from minority shareholders.

At an extraordinary meeting held in a basement room of the group's West End headquarters, shareholders voted to put the company into voluntary liquidation and sell its assets and intellectual property to founder Martin Myerscough for £1. (The shares in the company were at one time worth 650 p each.)

The only significant opposition came from Giuliano Gnagnatti who, along with other shareholders, has seen his investment shrink faster than a wool twin-set on a boil wash.

The not-so-proud owner of 100,000 Monotub shares, Mr Gnagnatti, the managing director of an online retailer . . . described the sale of Monotub as a 'free gift' to Mr Myerscough. This assessment was denied by Ian Green, the chairman of Monotub, who said the closest the beleaguered company had come to a sale was an offer for £60,000 that gave no guarantees against liabilities, which are thought to amount to £750,000.

The quiet passing of the washing machine, eventually dubbed the Titanic, was in strong contrast to its performance in many kitchens.

Originally touted as the 'great white goods hope' of the washing machine industry with its larger capacity and removable drum, the Titan ran into problems when it kept stopping during the spin cycle, causing it to emit a loud bang and leap into the air.

Summing up the demise of the Titan, Mr Green said: 'Clearly the machine had some revolutionary aspects, but you can't get away from the fact that the machine was faulty and should not have been launched with those defects.'

The usually vocal Mr Myerscough, who has promised to pump £250,000 into the company and give Monotub shareholders £4 for every machine sold, refused to comment on his plans for the Titan or reveal who his backers were. But . . . he did say that he intended to 'take the Titan forward'.

Source: Urquhart, Lisa 'Monotub Industries in a Spin as Founder Gets Titan for £1', *Financial Times*, 23 January 2003, FT.com.

Limited liability

Since the company is a legal person in its own right, it must take responsibility for its own debts and losses. This means that once the shareholders have paid what they have agreed to pay for the shares, their obligation to the company, and to the company's creditors, is satisfied. Thus, shareholders can limit their losses to that which they have paid, or agreed to pay, for their shares. This is of great practical importance to potential shareholders, since they know that what they can lose, as part owners of the business, is limited.

Contrast this with the position of sole proprietors or partners. They cannot 'ring fence' assets that they do not want to put into the business. If a sole proprietary or partnership business finds itself in a position where liabilities exceed the business assets, the law gives unsatisfied creditors the right to demand payment out of what the sole proprietor or partner may have regarded as 'non-business' assets. Thus the sole proprietor or partner could lose everything – house, car, the lot. This is because the law sees Jill, the sole proprietor, as being the same as Jill the private individual. The shareholder, by contrast, can lose only the amount committed to that company. Legally, the business operating as a limited company, in which Jack owns shares, is not the same as Jack himself. This is true even if Jack were to own all of the shares in the company.

Real World 4.2 gives an example of a well-known case where the shareholders of a particular company were able to avoid any liability to those that had lost money as a result of dealing with the company.

Real World 4.2

Carlton and Granada 1 - Nationwide Football League 0

Two television broadcasting companies, Carlton and Granada, each owned 50 per cent of a separate company, ITV Digital (formerly ON Digital). ITV Digital signed a contract to pay the Nationwide Football League (in effect the three divisions of English football below the Premiership) more than £89 million on both 1 August 2002 and 1 August 2003 for the rights to broadcast football matches over three seasons. ITV Digital was unable to sell enough subscriptions for the broadcasts and collapsed because it was unable to meet its liabilities. The Nationwide Football League tried to force Carlton and Granada (ITV Digital's only shareholders) to meet the ITV Digital's contractual obligations. It was unable to do so because the shareholders could not be held legally liable for the amounts owing.

Carlton and Granada merged into one business in 2003, but at the time of ITV Digital were two independent companies.

Activity 4.1

The fact that shareholders can limit their losses to that which they have paid, or have agreed to pay, for their shares is of great practical importance to potential shareholders.

Can you think of any practical benefit to a private-sector economy, in general, of this ability of shareholders to limit losses?

Business is a risky venture – in some cases very risky. People with money to invest will usually be happier to do so when they know the limit of their liability. By giving investors limited liability, new businesses are more likely to be formed and existing ones are likely to find it easier to raise more finance. This is good for the private-sector economy and may ultimately lead to the generation of greater wealth for society as a whole.

→ Though **limited liability** has this advantage to the providers of capital (the share-holders), it is not necessarily to the advantage of all others who have a stake in the business, like the Nationwide Football League clubs (see **Real World 4.2**). Limited liability is attractive to shareholders because they can, in effect, walk away from the unpaid debts of the company if their contribution has not been sufficient to meet those debts. This is likely to make any individual, or another business, that is considering entering into a contract, wary of dealing with the limited company. This can be a real problem for smaller, less established companies. Suppliers may insist on cash payment before delivery of goods or the rendering of a service. Alternatively, they may require a personal guarantee from a major shareholder that the debt will be paid before allowing trade credit. In the latter case, the supplier circumvents the company's limited liability status by demanding the personal liability of an individual. Larger, more established companies, on the other hand, tend to have built up the confidence of suppliers.

Legal safeguards

Various safeguards exist to protect individuals and businesses contemplating dealing with a limited company. These include the requirement to indicate limited liability status in the name of the company. By doing this, an alert is issued to prospective suppliers and lenders.

A further safeguard is the restrictions placed on the ability of shareholders to withdraw their investment from the company. These restrictions are designed to prevent shareholders from protecting their own investment and, as a result, leaving lenders and suppliers in an exposed position. We consider this point in more detail later in the chapter.

Finally, limited companies are required to produce annual financial statements (income statement, balance sheet and cash flow statement), and make them publicly available. This means that anyone interested can gain an impression of the financial performance and position of the company. The form and content of these statements are considered in some detail later in the chapter.

Public and private companies

When a company is registered with the Registrar of Companies, it must be registered either as a public or as a private company. The main practical difference between these is that a **public company** can offer its shares for sale to the general public, but a **private company** is restricted from doing so. A public limited company must signal its status to all interested parties by having the words 'public limited company', or its abbreviation 'plc' in its name. For a private limited company, the word 'limited' or 'Ltd' must appear as part of its name.

Private limited companies tend to be smaller businesses where the ownership is divided among relatively few shareholders who are usually fairly close to one another – for example, a family company. Numerically, there are vastly more private limited companies in the UK than there are public ones. Of the 2.1 million UK limited companies now in existence, only 11,500 (representing 0.5 per cent of the total) are public limited companies. Figure 4.1 shows the trend in the numbers of public and private limited companies in recent years.

Since public companies tend to be individually larger, they are often economically more important. In some industry sectors such as banking, insurance, oil refining and grocery retailing they are completely dominant. Although some large private limited companies exist, many are little more than the vehicle through which one-person businesses operate.

Figure 4.1   **Number of private and public limited companies registered 2001 to 2006**

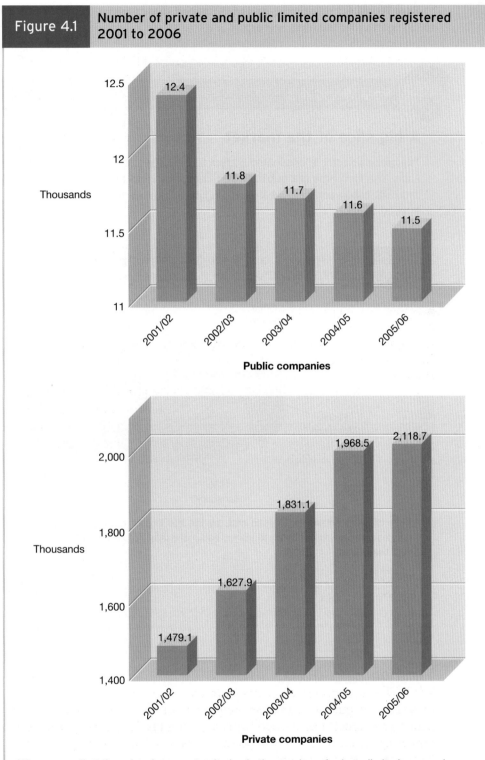

Public companies

Private companies

We can see that there has been a steady rise in the number of private limited companies over the five-year period. This has been matched by a gradual decline in the number of public limited companies.

Source: www.companieshouse.gov.uk

Real World 4.3 reveals the extent of market dominance of public limited companies in one particular business sector.

Real World 4.3

A big slice of the market

The grocery sector is dominated by four large players: Tesco, Sainsbury, Morrisons and Asda. The first three are public limited companies and the fourth, Asda, is owned by a large US public company (Wal-Mart). Figure 4.2 shows the share of the grocery market enjoyed by each.

Figure 4.2	Market share of the four largest grocers: 12 weeks to 16 July 2006

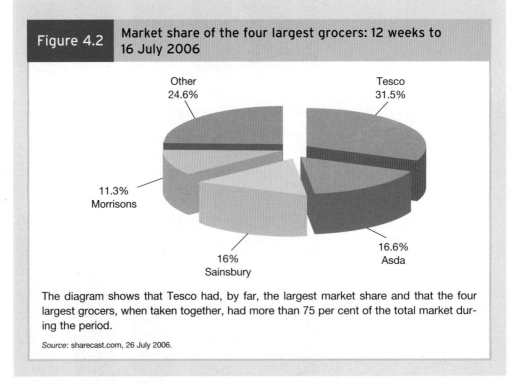

Other
24.6%

Tesco
31.5%

11.3%
Morrisons

16%
Sainsbury

16.6%
Asda

The diagram shows that Tesco had, by far, the largest market share and that the four largest grocers, when taken together, had more than 75 per cent of the total market during the period.

Source: sharecast.com, 26 July 2006.

Taxation

Another consequence of the legal separation of the limited company from its owners is that companies must be accountable to the tax authorities for tax on their profits and gains. This leads to the reporting of tax in the financial statements of limited companies. The charge for tax is shown in the income statement (profit and loss account). The tax charge for a particular year is based on that year's profit. Since only 50 per cent of a company's tax liability is due for payment during the year concerned, the other 50 per cent will appear on the end-of-year balance sheet as a short-term liability. This will be illustrated a little later in the chapter. The tax position of companies contrasts with that of sole proprietorships and partnerships, where tax is levied not on the business but on the owner(s). Thus, tax does not impact on the financial statements of unincorporated businesses, but is an individual matter between the owner(s) and the tax authorities.

Companies are charged **corporation tax** on their profits and gains. The percentage rates of tax tend to vary from year to year, but have recently been 30 per cent for larger companies and nineteen per cent for smaller companies. These rates of tax are levied on the company's taxable profit, which is not necessarily the same as the profit shown on the income statement. This is because tax law does not, in every respect, follow the normal accounting rules. Generally, however, the taxable profit and the company's accounting profit are pretty close to one another.

Transferring share ownership – the role of the Stock Exchange

The point has already been made that shares in a company may be transferred from one owner to another. The desire of some shareholders to sell their shares, coupled with the desire of others to buy those shares, has led to the existence of a formal market in which shares can be bought and sold. The London Stock Exchange, and similar organisations around the world, provide a market place in which shares in public companies may be bought and sold. Share prices are determined by the laws of supply and demand, which are, in turn, determined by investors' perceptions of the future economic prospects of the companies concerned. Only the shares of certain companies (*listed* companies) may be traded on the London Stock Exchange. About 1,300 UK companies are listed. This represents only one in about 1,600 of all UK companies (public and private) and about one in nine public limited companies. However, many of these 1,300 listed companies are massive. Nearly all of the 'household name' UK businesses (for example, Tesco, Boots, BT, Cadbury-Schweppes, Vodafone, BP and so on) are listed companies.

Activity 4.2

If, as has been pointed out earlier, the change in ownership of shares does not directly affect the particular company, why do many public companies actively seek to have their shares traded in a recognised market?

The main reason is that investors are generally very reluctant to pledge their money unless they can see some way in which they can turn their investment back into cash. In theory, the shares of a particular company may be very valuable because it has bright prospects. However, unless this value is capable of being turned into cash, the benefit to the shareholders is dubious. After all, we cannot spend shares; we generally need cash.

This means that potential shareholders are much more likely to be prepared to buy new shares from the company (thereby providing the company with new finance) where they can see a way of liquidating their investment (turning it into cash), as and when they wish. Stock exchanges provide the means of liquidation.

Though the buying and selling of 'second-hand' shares does not provide the company with cash, the fact that the buying and selling facility exists will make it easier for the company to raise new share capital when it needs to do so.

Managing a company

A limited company may have legal personality, but it is not a human being capable of making decisions and plans about the business and exercising control over it. People must undertake these management tasks. The most senior level of management of a company is the board of directors.

→ The shareholders elect **directors** (by law there must be at least one director for a private limited company and two for a public limited company) to manage the company on a day-to-day basis on behalf of those shareholders. In a small company, the board may be the only level of management and consist of all of the shareholders. In larger companies, the board may consist of ten or so directors out of many thousands of shareholders. Indeed, directors are not even required to be shareholders. Below the board of directors of the typical large company could be several layers of management comprising thousands of people.

→ In recent years, the issue of **corporate governance** has generated much debate. The term is used to describe the ways in which companies are directed and controlled. The issue of corporate governance is important because, with larger companies, those who own the company (that is, the shareholders) are usually divorced from the day-to-day control of the business. The shareholders employ the directors to manage the company for them. Given this position, it may seem reasonable to assume that the best interests of shareholders will guide the directors' decisions. However, in practice this does not always occur. The directors may be more concerned with pursuing their own interests, such as increasing their pay and 'perks' (such as expensive motor cars, overseas visits and so on) and improving their job security and status. As a result, a conflict can occur between the interests of shareholders and the interests of directors.

The problems and issues associated with corporate governance will be explored in detail in Chapter 10.

Financing limited companies

The owners' claim

The owner's claim of a sole proprietorship is normally encompassed in one figure on the balance sheet, usually labelled 'capital'. With companies, this is usually a little more complicated, though in essence the same broad principles apply. With a company, the owners' claim is divided between shares (for example, the original invest-
→ ment), on the one hand, and **reserves** (that is, profits and gains subsequently made), on the other. There is also the possibility that there will be more than one type of shares and of reserves. Thus, within the basic divisions of share capital and reserves, there might well be further subdivisions. This might seem quite complicated, but we shall shortly consider the reasons for these subdivisions and all should become clearer.
→ The sum of share capital and reserves is commonly known as **equity**.

The basic division

When a company is first formed, those who take steps to form it (the promoters) will decide how much needs to be raised by the potential shareholders to set the company up with the necessary assets to operate. Example 4.1 acts as a basis for illustration.

Example 4.1

A group of friends get together and decide to form a company to operate an office cleaning business. They estimate that the company will need £50,000 to obtain the necessary assets to operate. Between them, they raise the cash, which they use to buy shares in the company, on 31 March 2006, with a **nominal value** (or **par value**) of £1 each.

At this point the balance sheet of the company would be:

Balance sheet as at 31 March 2006

	£
Net assets (all in cash)	50,000
Equity	
Share capital	
50,000 shares of £1 each	50,000

The company now buys the necessary non-current assets (vacuum cleaners and so on) and inventories (cleaning materials) and starts to trade. During the first year, the company makes a profit of £10,000. This, by definition, means that the owners' claim expands by £10,000. During the year, the shareholders (owners) make no drawings of their claim, so at the end of the year the summarised balance sheet looks like this:

Balance sheet as at 31 March 2007

	£
Net assets (various assets less liabilities*)	60,000
Equity	
Share capital	
50,000 shares of £1 each	50,000
Reserves (revenue reserve)	10,000
Total equity	60,000

* We know from Chapter 2 that Assets = Capital (Equity) + Liabilities. This can be rearranged so that Assets – Liabilities = Capital (Equity).

The profit is shown in a reserve, known as a **revenue reserve**, because it arises from generating revenue (making sales). Note that we do not simply merge the profit with the share capital: we must keep the two amounts separate (to satisfy company law). The reason for this is that there is a legal restriction on the maximum drawings of the shareholders' claim (or payment of a **dividend**) that the owners can make. This is defined by the amount of revenue reserves, and so it is helpful to show these separately. We shall look at why there is this restriction, and how it works, a little later in the chapter.

Share capital

Shares represent the basic units of ownership of a business. All companies issue **ordinary shares**. Ordinary shares are often known as *equities*. The nominal value of such shares is at the discretion of the people that start up the company. For example, if the initial capital is to be £50,000, this could be two shares of £25,000 each, 5 million shares of one penny each or any other combination that gives a total of £50,000. Each share must have equal value.

Activity 4.3

The initial capital requirement for a new company is £50,000. There are to be two equal shareholders. Would you advise them to issue two shares of £25,000 each? Why?

Such large denomination shares tend to be unwieldy. Suppose that one of the shareholders wanted to sell his or her shares. S/he would have to find one buyer. If there were shares of smaller denomination, it would be possible to sell part of the shareholding to various potential buyers. Furthermore, it would be possible to sell just part of the holding and retain a part.

In practice, £1 is the normal maximum nominal value for shares. Shares of 25 pence each and 50 pence each are probably the most common.

Some companies also issue other classes of shares, **preference shares** being the most common. Preference shares guarantee that *if a dividend is paid*, the preference shareholders will be entitled to the first part of it up to a maximum value. This maximum is normally defined as a fixed percentage of the nominal value of the preference shares. If, for example, a company issues 10,000 preference shares of £1 each with a dividend rate of 6 per cent, this means that the preference shareholders are entitled to receive the first £600 (that is, 6 per cent of £10,000) of any dividend that is paid by the company for a year. The excess over £600 goes to the ordinary shareholders. Normally, any undistributed profits and gains also accrue to the ordinary shareholders.

The ordinary shareholders are the primary risk-takers as they are entitled to share in the profits of the company only after other claims have been satisfied, and their potential rewards reflect this risk. There are no upper limits, however, on the amount by which they may benefit. The potential rewards available to ordinary shareholders reflect the risks that they are prepared to take. Since ordinary shareholders take most of the risks, power normally resides in their hands. Usually, only the ordinary shareholders are able to vote on issues that affect the company, such as who the directors should be.

It is open to the company to issue shares of various classes – perhaps with some having unusual and exotic conditions – but in practice it is rare to find other than straightforward ordinary and preference shares. Though a company may have different classes of shares whose holders have different rights, within each class all shares must be treated equally. The rights of the various classes of shareholders, as well as other matters relating to a particular company, are contained in that company's set of rules, known as the 'articles and memorandum of association'. A copy of these rules must be lodged with the Registrar of Companies, who makes it available for inspection by the general public.

Reserves

Reserves are profits and gains that have been made by a company, which still form part of the shareholders' (owners') claim or equity. One reason that past profits and gains may not remain part of equity is that they have been paid out to shareholders (as dividends and so on). Another reason is that reserves will be reduced by the amount of any losses that the company might suffer. In the same way that profits increase equity, losses reduce it.

The shareholders' claim consists of share capital and reserves.

Activity 4.4

Are reserves amounts of cash? Can you think of a reason why this is an odd question?

To deal with the second point first, it is an odd question because reserves are a claim, or part of one, on the assets of the company, whereas cash is an asset. So reserves cannot be cash.

Reserves are classified as either revenue reserves or capital reserves. In Example 4.1 we came across one type of reserve, the revenue reserve. We should recall that this reserve represents the company's retained trading profits and gains on the disposal of non-current assets. It is worth mentioning that retained profits, or earnings as they are often called, represent overwhelmingly the largest source of new finance for UK companies. For most companies they amount to more than share issues and borrowings combined.

→ **Capital reserves** arise for two main reasons:

- issuing shares at above their nominal value (for example, issuing £1 shares at £1.50);
- revaluing (upwards) non-current assets.

Where a company issues shares at above their nominal value, UK law requires that the excess of the issue price over the nominal value be shown separately.

Activity 4.5

Can you think why shares might be issued at above their nominal value? (*Hint*: this would not usually happen when a company is first formed and the initial shares are being issued.)

Once a company has traded and has been successful, the shares would normally be worth more than the nominal value at which they were issued. If additional shares are to be issued to new shareholders to raise finance for further expansion, unless they are issued at a value higher than the nominal value, the new shareholders will be gaining at the expense of the original ones.

Example 4.2 shows how this works.

Example 4.2

Based on future prospects, the net assets of a company are worth £1.5 million. There are currently 1 million ordinary shares in the company, each with a face (nominal) value of £1. The company wishes to raise an additional £0.6 million of cash for expansion and has decided to raise it by issuing new shares. If the shares are issued for £1 each (that is 600,000 shares), the total number of shares will be:

$$1.0 \text{ m} + 0.6 \text{ m} = 1.6 \text{ million}$$

→

Example 4.2 continued

and their total value will be the value of the existing net assets plus the new injection of cash:

$$£1.5 \text{ m} + £0.6 \text{ m} = £2.1 \text{ million}$$

This means that the value of each share after the new issue will be:

$$£2.1 \text{ m}/1.6 \text{ m} = £1.3125$$

The current value of each share is:

$$£1.5 \text{ m}/1.0 \text{ m} = £1.50$$

So the original shareholders will lose:

$$£1.50 - £1.3125 = £0.1875 \text{ a share}$$

and the new shareholders will have gained

$$£1.3125 - £1.0 = £0.3125 \text{ a share}$$

The new shareholders will, no doubt, be delighted with this outcome; the original ones will not.

Things could be made fair between the two sets of shareholders described in Example 4.2 by issuing the new shares at £1.50 each. In this case it would be necessary to issue 400,000 shares to raise the necessary £0.6 million. £1 a share of the £1.50 is the nominal value and will be included with share capital in the balance sheet (£400,000 in total). The remaining £0.50 is a share premium, which will be shown as a capital reserve known as the **share premium account** (£200,000 in total).

It is not clear why UK company law insists on the distinction between nominal share values and the premium. In some other countries (for example, the United States) with similar laws governing the corporate sector, there is not the necessity of distinguishing between share capital and share premium. Instead, the total value at which shares are issued is shown as one comprehensive figure on the company balance sheet. **Real World 4.4** shows the shareholders' claim of one well-known business.

Real World 4.4

How Thorntons is funded

Thorntons plc, the chocolate maker, had the following share capital and reserves as at 24 June 2006:

	£m
Share capital (10 p ordinary shares)	6,724
Share premium account	12,890
Retained earnings	12,340
Total equity	31,954

Note how the nominal share capital figure is nearly half the share premium account figure. This implies that Thorntons has issued shares at higher prices than the 10 p per share nominal value. This reflects its trading success since the company was first formed. Note also how, at balance sheet values, retained earnings (profits) make up nearly 40 per cent of the total for share capital and reserves.

Source: Thorntons plc, Annual Report 2006, p. 22.

Altering the nominal value of shares

The point has already been made that the promoters of a new company may make their own choice of the nominal or par value of the shares. This value need not be permanent. At a later date the shareholders can decide to change it.

Suppose that a company has 1 million ordinary shares of £1 each and a decision is made to change the nominal value of the shares from £1 to £0.50, in other words to halve the value. This would lead the company to issue each shareholder with a new share certificate (the shareholders' evidence of ownership of their shareholding) for exactly twice as many shares, each with half the nominal value. The result would be that each shareholder retains a holding of the same total nominal value. This process is known, not surprisingly, as splitting the shares. The opposite, reducing the number of shares and increasing their nominal value per share to compensate, is known as **consolidating**.

→

Since each shareholder would be left, after a split or consolidation, with exactly the same proportion of ownership of the company's assets as before, the process should not increase the value of the total shares held.

Activity 4.6

Why might the shareholders want to split their shares in the manner described above?

The answer is probably to avoid individual shares becoming too valuable and making them a bit unwieldy, in the way discussed in the answer to Activity 4.3. If a company trades successfully, the value of each share is likely to rise, and in time could increase to a level that makes them less marketable. Splitting would solve this problem.

Real World 4.5 gives an example of a share split by a large UK company.

Real World 4.5

Share split at Pennon

Pennon Group plc owns South West Water Ltd, the business that provides water and sewerage services to the far south-west of England and Viridor Waste Ltd a waste management business.

In July 2006, Pennon Group plc decided to split its ordinary shares. Each share with a nominal value of 122.1 p was subdivided into three new ordinary shares of 40.7 p per share. This meant that each ordinary shareholder became the owner of three times as many new shares, with each share having a market value of one third of each of the old ones. The reason given by the company was as follows:

> In recent years the price of the company's ordinary shares has risen to the point where they are now one of the most highly priced ordinary shares compared with comparator companies quoted on the London Stock Exchange. It is hoped that the share split will lead to increased market liquidity of the company's shares.

Source: www.pennon-group.co.uk, Investor Information.

Bonus shares

It is always open to a company to take reserves of any kind (irrespective of whether they are capital or revenue) and turn them into share capital. This will involve transferring the desired amount from the reserve concerned to share capital and then distributing the appropriate number of new shares to the existing shareholders. New shares arising from such a conversion are known as **bonus shares**. Issues of bonus shares are quite frequently encountered in practice. Example 4.3 illustrates this aspect of share issues.

Example 4.3

The summary balance sheet of a company is as follows:

Balance sheet as at 31 March 2007

	£
Net assets (various assets less liabilities)	128,000
Equity	
Share capital	
50,000 shares of £1 each	50,000
Reserves	78,000
Total equity	128,000

The company decides that it will issue existing shareholders with one new share for every share currently owned by each shareholder. The balance sheet immediately following this will appear as follows:

Balance sheet as at 31 March 2007

	£
Net assets (various assets less liabilities)	128,000
Equity	
Share capital	
100,000 shares of £1 each (50,000 + 50,000)	100,000
Reserves (78,000 − 50,000)	28,000
Total equity	128,000

We can see that the reserves have decreased by £50,000 and share capital has increased by the same amount. Share certificates for the 50,000 ordinary shares of £1 each that have been created from reserves will be issued to the existing shareholders to complete the transaction.

Activity 4.7

A shareholder of the company in Example 4.3 owned 100 shares before the bonus issue. How will things change for this shareholder as regards the number of shares owned and the value of the shareholding?

The answer should be that the number of shares will double, from 100 to 200. Now the shareholder owns one five-hundredth of the company (that is, 200/100,000). Before the bonus issue, the shareholder also owned one five-hundredth of the company (that is, 100/50,000). The company's assets and liabilities have not changed as a result of the bonus issue and so, logically, one five-hundredth of the value of the company should be identical to what it was before. Thus, each share is worth half as much.

A bonus issue simply takes one part of the owners' claim (part of a reserve) and puts it into another part of the owners' claim (share capital). The transaction has no effect on the company's assets or liabilities, so there is no effect on shareholders' wealth.

Note that a bonus issue is not the same as a share split. A split does not affect the reserves.

Activity 4.8

Can you think of any reasons why a company might want to make a bonus issue if it has no economic consequence?

We think that there are three possible reasons:

- *Share price.* To lower the value of each share without reducing the shareholders' collective or individual wealth. This has a similar effect to share splitting.
- *Shareholder confidence.* To provide the shareholders with a 'feel-good factor'. It is believed that shareholders like bonus issues because it seems to make them better off, though in practice it should not affect their wealth.
- *Lender confidence.* Where reserves arising from operating profits and/or realised gains on the sale of non-current assets are used to make the bonus issue, it has the effect of taking part of that portion of the owners' claim that could be drawn by the shareholders, as drawings (or dividends), and locking it up. The amount transferred becomes part of the permanent capital base of the company. (We shall see, a little later in this chapter, that there are severe restrictions on the extent to which shareholders may make drawings from their claim.) An individual or business contemplating lending money to the company may insist that the dividend payment possibilities are restricted as a condition of making the loan. This point will be explained shortly.

Real World 4.6 provides an example of a bonus share issue.

Real World 4.6

Bonus shares

Workspace Group plc provides flexible business accommodation for small and medium-size businesses. In March 2005 it made a 9 for 1 bonus issue of shares following a £15.2 m capitalisation of reserves. The nominal value of a share in the company is 10 p and a total of 151,955,694 new shares was issued. Following the issue, the net asset value per share was divided by 10 so that year-end net asset values were adjusted from £22.40 per share to £2.24 per share.

Source: based on information in 2005 Annual Report and www.workspacegroup.co.uk.

Share capital jargon

Before leaving our detailed discussion of share capital, it might be helpful to clarify some of the jargon relating to shares that is used in company financial statements.

 Share capital that has been issued to shareholders is known as the **issued** (or **allotted**) **share capital**. Sometimes, but not very often, a company may not require shareholders to pay the whole amount that is due to be paid for the shares at the time of issue. This may happen where the company does not need the money all at once.

Some money would normally be paid at the time of issue and the company would 'call' for further instalments until the shares were **fully paid**. That part of the total issue price that has been 'called' is known as the **called-up share capital**. That part that has been called and paid is known as the **paid-up share capital**.

Raising share capital

Once the company has made its initial share issue to start business (usually soon after the company is first formed) it may decide to make further issues of new shares. These may be:

- rights issues, that is issues made to existing shareholders, in proportion to their existing shareholding;
- public issues, that is issues made to the general investing public;
- private placings, that is issues made to selected individuals who are usually approached and asked if they would be interested in taking up new shares.

During its lifetime a company may use all three of these approaches to raising funds through issuing new shares (although only public companies can make appeals to the general public).

Borrowings

Most companies borrow money to supplement that raised from share issues and ploughed-back profits. Company borrowing is often on a long-term basis, perhaps on a ten-year contract. Lenders may be banks and other professional providers of loan finance. Many companies raise loan finance in such a way that small investors, including private individuals, are able to lend small amounts. This is particularly the case with the larger, Stock Exchange listed, companies and involves their making a **loan notes issue**, which, though large in total, can be taken up in small slices by individual investors, both private individuals and investing institutions, such as pension funds and insurance companies. In some cases, these slices of loans can be bought and sold through the Stock Exchange. This means that investors do not have to wait the full term of the loan to obtain repayment, but can sell their slice of the loan to another would-be lender at intermediate points in the term of the loan. Loan notes are often known as *loan stock* or **debentures**.

Some of the features of loan notes financing, particularly the possibility that the loan notes may be traded on the Stock Exchange, can lead to a confusion that loan notes are shares by another name. We should be clear that this is not the case. It is the shareholders who own the company and, therefore, who share in its losses and profits. Holders of loan notes lend money to the company under a legally binding contract that normally specifies the rate of interest, the interest payment dates and the date of repayment of the loan itself. Usually, long-term loans are secured on assets of the company.

Long-term financing of companies can be depicted as in Figure 4.3.

It is important to the prosperity and stability of a company that it strikes a suitable balance between finance provided by the shareholders (equity) and from borrowing. This topic will be explored in Chapter 7.

Real World 4.7 shows the long-term borrowings of Rolls-Royce plc, the engine-building business, at 31 December 2005.

Figure 4.3 | Sources of long-term finance for a typical limited company

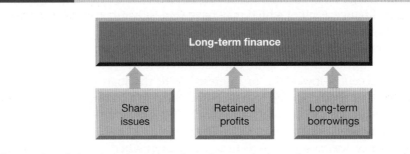

Companies derive their long-term financing needs from three sources: new share issues, retained profit and long-term borrowings. For a typical company, the sum of the first two (jointly known as 'equity finance') exceeds the third. Retained profit usually exceeds either of the other two in terms of the amount of finance raised in most years.

Real World 4.7

Borrowing at Rolls-Royce

The following extract from the annual financial statements of Rolls-Royce plc sets out the sources of the company's long-term borrowing as at 31 December 2005.

	2005 £m
Unsecured	
Bank loans	4
$6^3/8$% Notes 2007	354
$7^3/8$% Notes 2016	200
5.84% Notes 2010	107
6.38% Notes 2013	134
6.55% Notes 2015	49
$4^1/2$% Notes 2011	524
Other loans 2009 (interest rates nil)	1
Secured	
Bank loans	71
Obligations under finance leases payable:	
Between one and two years	5
Between two and five years	8
After five years	1
	1,458
Repayable	
Between one and two years – by instalments	49
– otherwise	–
Between two and five years – by instalments	11
– otherwise	354
After five years – by instalments	29
– otherwise	1,015
	1,458

Source: Rolls-Royce plc Annual Report and Accounts, 2005, Note 18.

Note the large number of sources from which the company borrows. This is typical of most large companies and probably reflects a desire to exploit all available means of raising finance, each of which may have some advantages and disadvantages. 'Secured' in this context means that the lender would have the right, should Rolls-Royce fail to meet its interest and/or capital repayment obligations, to seize a specified asset of the business (probably some land) and use it to raise the sums involved. Normally, a lender would accept a lower rate of interest where the loan is secured as there is less risk involved. It should be said that whether a loan to a company like Rolls-Royce is secured or unsecured is usually pretty academic. It is unlikely that such a large and profitable company would fail to meet its obligations.

'Finance leases' are, in effect, arrangements where Rolls-Royce needs the use of a non-current asset (such as an item of machinery) and, instead of buying the asset itself, it arranges for a financier to buy the asset. The financier then leases it to the business, probably for the entire economic life of the asset. Though legally it is the financier who owns the asset, from an accounting point of view the essence of the arrangement is that, in effect, Rolls-Royce has borrowed cash from the financier to buy the asset. Thus, the asset appears among the business's non-current assets and the financial obligation to the financier is shown here as long-term borrowing. This is a good example of how accounting tries to report the economic *substance* of a transaction, rather than its strict legal *form*. Finance leasing is a fairly popular means of raising long-term funds.

Withdrawing equity

Companies are legally obliged to distinguish between that part of the shareholders' equity which may be withdrawn and that part which may not. The withdrawable part consists of profits arising from trading and from the disposal of non-current assets. It is represented in the balance sheet by *revenue reserves*.

It is important to appreciate that the total revenue reserves appearing in the balance sheet is rarely the total of all trading profits and profits on disposals of non-current assets generated by the company. This total will normally have been reduced by at least one of the following three factors:

● corporation tax paid on those profits;
● any dividends paid;
● any losses from trading and the disposal of non-current assets.

The non-withdrawable part consists of profits arising from shareholders buying shares in the company and from upward revaluations of assets still held. It is represented in the balance sheet by *share capital and capital reserves*.

The law does not specify how large the non-withdrawable part of a particular company's shareholders' equity should be. However, when seeking to impress prospective lenders and credit suppliers, the larger this part, the better. Those considering doing business with the company must be able to see from the company's balance sheet how large it is.

Activity 4.9

Why are limited companies required to distinguish different parts of their shareholders' claim whereas sole proprietorship and partnership businesses are not?

The reason stems from the limited liability that company shareholders enjoy, but which owners of unincorporated businesses do not. If a sole proprietor or partner withdraws all of the owner's claim, or even an amount in excess of this, the position of the lenders and credit suppliers of the business is not weakened since they can legally enforce their claims against the sole proprietor or partner as an individual. With a limited company, the business and the owners are legally separated and such right to enforce claims against individuals does not exist. To protect the company's lenders and credit suppliers, however, the law insists that the shareholders cannot normally withdraw a specific part of their claim.

Let us now look at another example.

Example 4.4

The summary balance sheet of a company at a particular date is as follows:

Balance sheet

	£
Total assets	43,000
Equity	
Share capital	
20,000 shares of £1 each	20,000
Reserves (revenue)	23,000
Total equity	43,000

A bank has been asked to make a £25,000 long-term loan to the company. If the loan were to be made, the balance sheet immediately following would appear as follows:

Balance Sheet (after the loan)

	£
Total assets (£43,000 + £25,000)	68,000
Equity	
Share capital	
20,000 shares of £1 each	20,000
Reserves (revenue)	23,000
	43,000
Non-current liability	
Borrowings – loan	25,000
Total equity and liabilities	68,000

As things stand, there are assets to a total balance sheet value of £68,000 to meet the bank's claim of £25,000. It would be possible and perfectly legal, however, for the company to pay a dividend (withdraw part of their claim) of £23,000. The balance sheet would then appear as follows:

$\rightarrow$

Example 4.4 continued

Balance Sheet

	£
Total assets (£68,000 – £23,000)	45,000
Equity	
Share capital	
20,000 shares of £1 each	20,000
Reserves (revenue (£23,000 – £23,000))	–
	20,000
Non-current liabilities	
Borrowings – loan	25,000
Total equity and liabilities	45,000

This leaves the bank in a very much weaker position, in that there are now total assets with a balance sheet value of £45,000 to meet a claim of £25,000. Note that the difference between the amount of the borrowings (bank loan) and the total assets equals the capital and reserves total. Thus, the capital and reserves represent a **margin of safety** for lenders and suppliers. The larger the amount of the owners' claim withdrawable by the shareholders, the smaller is the potential margin of safety for lenders and suppliers.

As we have already seen, the law says nothing about how large the margin of safety must be. It is up to each company to decide what is appropriate.

As a practical footnote to Example 4.4, it is worth pointing out that long-term lenders would normally seek to secure a loan against an asset of the company, such as land. This, as we have seen, would give the lender the right to seize the asset concerned, sell it and satisfy the repayment obligation, should the company default.

Activity 4.10

Would you expect a company to pay all of its revenue reserves as a dividend? What factors might be involved with a dividend decision?

It would be rare for a company to pay all of its revenue reserves as a dividend: the fact that it is legally possible does not necessarily make it a good idea. Most companies see ploughed-back profits as a major – usually *the* major – source of new finance. The factors that influence the dividend decision are likely to include:

● the availability of cash to pay a dividend; it would not be illegal to borrow to pay a dividend, but it would be unusual and, possibly, imprudent;
● the needs of the business for finance for new investment;
● the expectations of shareholders concerning the amount of dividends to be paid.

You may have thought of others.

The law states, however, that shareholders cannot, under normal circumstances, withdraw that part of their claim that is represented by shares and capital reserves. This means that potential lenders and credit suppliers know the maximum amount of the shareholders' equity that can be withdrawn. Figure 4.4 shows the important division between that part of the shareholders' equity which can be withdrawn as a dividend and that part which cannot.

Figure 4.4	Availability for dividends of various parts of the shareholders' claim

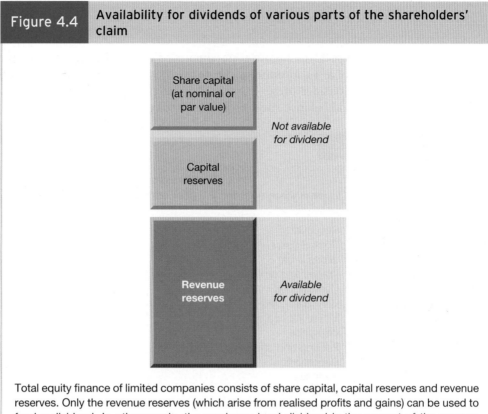

Total equity finance of limited companies consists of share capital, capital reserves and revenue reserves. Only the revenue reserves (which arise from realised profits and gains) can be used to fund a dividend. In other words, the maximum legal dividend is the amount of the revenue reserves.

Earlier in this chapter, the point was made that a potential lender may insist that some revenue reserves are converted to bonus shares (or capitalised) to increase the margin of safety as a condition of granting the loan.

If we refer back to **Real World 4.4**, we can see that Thorntons plc could legally have paid a dividend of £12,340 m on 24 June 2006, which is the amount of its revenue reserves. For several reasons, including the fact that this represented nearly 40 per cent of the balance sheet value of the company's net assets, no such dividend was paid.

Activity 4.11

Can you think of any circumstances where the non-withdrawable part of a company's capital could be reduced, without contravening the law?

It can be reduced as a result of the company sustaining trading losses, or losses on disposal of non-current assets, which exceed the withdrawable amount of shareholders' equity. It cannot be reduced by shareholders making withdrawals.

Though payment of a cash dividend is the standard way for shareholders to withdraw equity from a company, it is not the only way. Provided that certain conditions are met, it is perfectly legal for a company to redeem some of its shares or to buy some of its shares from particular shareholders and cancel them. These conditions are generally not difficult to meet for profitable companies.

The main financial statements

As we might expect, the financial statements of a limited company are, in essence, the same as those of a sole proprietor. There are, however, some differences of detail, and we shall now consider these. Example 4.5 sets out the income statement (profit and loss account) and balance sheet of a limited company:

Example 4.5

Da Silva plc
Income statement for the year ended 31 December 2006

	£m
Revenue	840
Cost of sales	(520)
Gross profit	320
Wages and salaries	(98)
Heat and light	(18)
Rent and rates	(24)
Motor-vehicle expenses	(20)
Insurance	(4)
Printing and stationery	(12)
Depreciation	(45)
Audit fee	(4)
Operating profit	95
Interest payable	(10)
Profit before taxation	85
Taxation	(24)
Profit for the year	61

Balance sheet as at 31 December 2006

	£m
Non-current assets	
Property, plant and equipment	203
Intangible assets	100
	303
Current assets	
Inventories	65
Trade receivables	112
Cash	36
	213
Total assets	516
Equity	
Ordinary shares of £0.50 each	200
Share premium account	30
Other reserves	50
Retained earnings	25
	305
Non-current liabilities	
Borrowings	100
Current liabilities	
Trade payables	99
Taxation	12
	111
Total equity and liabilities	516

Perhaps the most striking thing about these statements is their similarity to those of sole proprietors; the differences are small. Let us now go through and pick up these differences.

The income statement

There are a few features in the income statement that need consideration.

Profit

→ We can see that, following the calculation of **operating profit**, two further measures of profit are shown.

- The first of these is the *profit before taxation*. Interest charges are deducted from the operating profit to derive this figure. In the case of a sole proprietor or partnership business, the income statement would end here.
- The second measure of profit is the *profit for the year*. As the company is a separate legal entity, it is liable to pay tax (known as corporation tax) on the profits generated. (This contrasts with the sole proprietor business where it is the owner rather than the business that is liable for the tax on profits, as we saw earlier in the chapter.) This measure of profit represents the amount that is available for the shareholders.

Audit fee

Companies beyond a certain size are required to have their financial statements audited by an independent firm of accountants, for which a fee is charged. As we shall see in Chapters 5 and 10, the purpose of the audit is to lend credibility to the financial statements. Though it is also open to sole proprietors and partnerships to have their financial statements audited, relatively few do, so this is an expense that is most often seen in the income statement of a company.

The balance sheet

The main points for consideration in the balance sheet are taxation and other reserves.

Taxation

The amount that appears as part of the current liabilities represents 50 per cent of the tax on the profit for the year 2006. It is, therefore, 50 per cent (£12 m) of the charge that appears in the income statement (£24 m); the other 50 per cent (£12 m) will already have been paid. The unpaid 50 per cent will be paid shortly after the balance sheet date. These payment dates are set down by law.

Other reserves

This will include any reserves that are not separately identified on the face of the balance sheet. It may include a *general reserve*, which normally consists of trading profits that have been transferred to this separate reserve for re-investment ('ploughing back') into the operations of the company. In theory, there is no reason to set up a separate reserve for this purpose. The trading profits could remain unallocated and so swell the retained earnings of the company. It is not entirely clear why directors decide to make transfers to general reserves, since the profits concerned remain part of the revenue reserves, and are, therefore, still available for dividend. The most plausible explanation seems to be that directors feel that placing profits in a separate reserve indicates an intention to invest the funds, represented by the reserve, permanently in the company and, therefore, not to use them to pay a dividend. Of course, the retained earnings appearing on the balance sheet is also a reserve, but that fact is not indicated in its title.

Dividends

It has already been mentioned that dividends represent drawings by the shareholders of the company. Dividends are paid out of the revenue reserves of the company and should be deducted from these reserves (usually retained earnings) when preparing the balance sheet. Shareholders are often paid an annual dividend, which may be paid by the company in two parts. An 'interim' dividend may be paid part way through the year and a 'final' dividend shortly after the year end.

Dividends declared by the directors during the year but still unpaid at the year end *may* appear as a liability in the balance sheet. To be recognised as a liability, however, they must be properly authorised before the balance sheet date. This normally means that the dividend must be approved by the shareholders.

Large companies tend to have a clear and consistent policy towards the payment of dividends. Any change in the policy provokes considerable interest and is usually interpreted by shareholders as a signal of the directors' views concerning the future. For example, an increase in dividends may be taken as a signal from the directors' that future prospects are bright: a higher dividend being seen as tangible evidence of their confidence. **Real World 4.8** provides an example of a dividend payment that may well have been interpreted in this way.

Real World 4.8

'MyTravel Set to Resume Its Dividend'   **FT**

MyTravel, the tour operator formerly known as Airtours, has marked a return to financial good health by signalling that it would resume dividend payments for the first time since it fell into financial difficulties in 2001.

The group's improved performance was led by MyTravel's UK business, which has returned to growth after a dismal few years.

The gains in UK performance offset declines at MyTravel's North American operations, which were hit by the effects of Hurricane Wilma.

My Travel came close to collapse four years ago when a series of accounting errors and profit warnings caused the shares to tumble.

But the tour operator has completed a long restructuring, overhauling its management, cutting costs and changing its revenue recognition policies. Yesterday it said that advance bookings for this summer were outperforming the market.

Source: 'MyTravel Set to Resume Its Dividend' FT.com, 14 March 2006.

ws:

cember 2006

	£
ties)	235,000
each	100,000
	30,000
	37,000
	68,000
	235,000

same time, the company made a one-
yable in cash. This means that each
ve already held. All shareholders took
company made a one-for-two bonus
owing the bonus issue, assuming that
dend payment potential for the future.
e directors to choose not to retain the

g the bonus issue, assuming that the
d payment potential for the future.
be paid before and after the events
ent potential is achieved?
nts described in (a). Assuming that the
o their balance sheet value, show how

td, shown above, what four things do
tory that are not specifically stated on

back of the book on p. 402.

ised as follows:

The main features of a limited company

- It is an artificial person that has been created by law.
- It has a separate life to its owners and is granted a perpetual existence.
- It must take responsibility for its own debts and losses but its owners are granted limited liability.
- A public company can offer its shares for sale to the public; a private company cannot.
- It is governed by a board of directors, which is elected by the shareholders.

Financing the limited company

● The share capital of a company can be of two main types – ordinary shares and preference shares.

● Ordinary shares (equities) are the main risk-takers and are given voting rights; they form the backbone of the company.

● Preference shares are given a right to a fixed dividend before ordinary shareholders receive a dividend.

● Reserves are profits and gains made by the company and form part of the ordinary shareholders' claim.

● Borrowings provide another major source of finance.

Share issues

● Bonus shares are issued to existing shareholders when part of the reserves of the company is converted into share capital.

● Rights issues give existing shareholders the right to buy new shares in proportion to their existing holding.

● Public issues are made direct to the investing public generally.

● Private placings are share issues to particular investors.

● The shares of public companies may be bought and sold on a recognised Stock Exchange.

Reserves

● Reserves are of two types – revenue reserves and capital reserves.

● Revenue reserves arise from trading profits and from realised profits on the sale of non-current assets.

● Capital reserves arise from the issue of shares above their nominal value or from the upward revaluation of non-current assets.

● Revenue reserves can be withdrawn as dividends by the shareholders whereas capital reserves, normally, cannot.

Financial statements of limited companies

● The financial statements of limited companies are based on the same principles as those of sole proprietorship and partnership businesses. However, there are some differences in detail.

● The income statement has three measures of profit displayed after the gross profit figure: operating profit, net profit before tax and net profit for the year.

● The income statement also shows audit fees and corporation tax on profits for the year.

● Any unpaid tax and unpaid, but authorised, dividends will appear in the balance sheet as current liabilities.

● The share capital plus the reserves will be shown as 'equity'.

→ Key terms

Limited company p. 109	Capital reserves p. 119
Shares p. 109	Share premium account p. 120
Limited liability p. 111	Consolidating p. 121
Public company p. 112	Bonus shares p. 122
Private company p. 112	Issued share capital p. 123
Corporation tax p. 115	Fully paid shares p. 124
Director p. 116	Called-up share capital p. 124
Corporate governance p. 116	Paid-up share capital p. 124
Reserves p. 116	Loan notes p. 124
Equity p. 116	Rights issue p. 124
Nominal value p. 117	Private placing p. 124
Revenue reserve p. 117	Debentures p. 124
Dividend p. 117	Margin of safety p. 128
Ordinary shares p. 117	Operating profit p. 131
Preference shares p. 118	

Further reading

If you would like to explore the topics covered in this chapter in more depth, we recommend the following books:

Elliott, B. and Elliott, J. (2006) *Financial Accounting and Reporting*, 11th edn, Financial Times Prentice Hall, Chapters 5–6, 8 and 21–3.

KPMG (2006) *KPMG's Practical Guide to International Financial Reporting Standards*, 3rd edn, Thomson, Section 2.5.

Sutton, T. (2004) *Corporate Financial Accounting and Reporting*, 2nd edn, Financial Times Prentice Hall, Chapters 6 and 12.

Review questions

Answers to these questions can be found at the back of the book on p. 412.

4.1 How does the liability of a limited company differ from the liability of a real person, in respect of amounts owed to others?

4.2 Some people are about to form a company, as a vehicle through which to run a new business. What are the advantages to them of forming a private limited company rather than a public one?

4.3 What is a reserve? Distinguish between a revenue reserve and a capital reserve.

4.4 What is a preference share? Compare the main features of a preference share with those of:

(a) an ordinary share; and
(b) loan notes.

Exercises

Exercises 4.6 to 4.8 are more advanced than 4.1 to 4.5. Those with a coloured number have an answer at the back of the book, starting on p. 424.

If you wish to try more exercises, visit the students' side of the Companion Website.

4.1 Comment on the following quote:

> 'Limited companies can set a limit on the amount of debts that they will meet. They tend to have reserves of cash, as well as share capital and they can use these reserves to pay dividends to the shareholders. Many companies have preference as well as ordinary shares. The preference shares give a guaranteed dividend. The shares of many companies can be bought and sold on the Stock Exchange, and shareholders selling their shares can represent a useful source of new capital to the company.'

4.2 Comment on the following quotes:

(a) 'Bonus shares increase the shareholders' wealth because, after the issue, they have more shares, but each one of the same nominal value as they had before.'
(b) 'By law, once shares have been issued at a particular nominal value, they must always be issued at that value in any future share issues.'
(c) 'By law, companies can pay as much as they like by way of dividends on their shares, provided that they have sufficient cash to do so.'
(d) 'Companies do not have to pay tax on their profits because the shareholders have to pay tax on their dividends.'

4.3 Briefly explain each of the following expressions that you have seen in the financial statements of a limited company:

(a) dividend;
(b) audit fee;
(c) share premium account.

4.4 Iqbal Ltd started trading on 1 January 2002. During the first five years of trading, the following occurred:

Year ended 31 December	Trading profit (loss) £	Profit (loss) on sale of non-current assets £	Upward revaluation of non-current assets £
2002	(15,000)	–	–
2003	8,000	–	10,000
2004	15,000	5,000	–
2005	20,000	(6,000)	–
2006	22,000	–	–

Required:
Assume that the company paid the maximum legal dividend each year. Under normal circumstances, how much would each year's dividend be?

4.5 Da Silva plc's outline balance sheet as at a particular date was as follows:

	£m
Net assets (assets less liabilities)	72
Equity	
£1 ordinary shares	40
General reserve	32
	72

The directors made a one-for-four bonus issue, immediately followed by a one-for-four rights issue at a price of £1.80 per share.

Required:
Show the balance sheet of Da Silva plc immediately following the two share issues.

4.6 Presented below is a draft set of simplified financial statements for Pear Limited for the year ended 30 September 2006.

Income statement for the year ended 30 September 2006

	£000
Revenue	1,456
Cost of sales	(768)
Gross profit	688
Salaries	(220)
Depreciation	(249)
Other operating costs	(131)
Operating profit	88
Interest payable	(15)
Profit before taxation	73
Taxation at 30%	(22)
Profit for the year	51

Balance sheet as at 30 September 2006

Non-current assets	
Property, plant and equipment	
Cost	1,570
Depreciation	(690)
	880
Current assets	
Inventories	207
Trade receivables	182
Cash at bank	21
	410
Total assets	1,290
Equity	
Share capital	300
Share premium account	300
Retained earnings at beginning of year	104
Profit for year	51
	755
Non-current liabilities	
Borrowings (10% loan repayable 2009)	300
Current liabilities	
Trade payables	88
Other payables	20
Taxation	22
Borrowings (bank overdraft)	105
	235
Total equity and liabilities	1,290

The following information is available:

(a) Depreciation has not been charged on office equipment with a carrying amount of £100,000. This class of assets is depreciated at 12 per cent a year using the reducing balance method.

(b) A new machine was purchased, on credit, for £30,000 and delivered on 29 September 2006 but has not been included in the financial statements. (Ignore depreciation.)

(c) A sales invoice to the value of £18,000 for September 2006 has been omitted from the financial statements. (The cost of sales figure is stated correctly.)

(d) A dividend of £25,000 had been approved by the shareholders before 30 September 2006, but was unpaid at that date. This is not reflected in the financial statements.

(e) The interest payable on the debenture for the second half-year was not paid until 1 October 2006 and has not been included in the financial statements.

(f) An allowance for receivables is to be made at the level of 2 per cent of receivables.

(g) An invoice for electricity to the value of £2,000 for the quarter ended 30 September 2006 arrived on 4 October and has not been included in the financial statements.

(h) The charge for taxation will have to be amended to take account of the above information. Make the simplifying assumption that tax is payable shortly after the end of the year, at the rate of 30 per cent of the profit before tax.

Required:

Prepare a revised set of financial statements for the year ended 30 September 2006 incorporating the additional information in (a) to (h) above. Note: work to the nearest £1,000.

4.7 Presented below is a draft set of financial statements for Chips Limited.

Chips Limited
Income statement for the year ended 30 June 2006

	£000
Revenue	1,850
Cost of sales	(1,040)
Gross profit	810
Depreciation	(220)
Other operating costs	(375)
Operating profit	215
Interest payable	(35)
Profit before taxation	180
Taxation	(60)
Profit for the year	120

Balance sheet as at 30 June 2006

	Cost £000	Depr'n £000	£000
Non-current assets			
Property, plant and equipment			
Buildings	800	(112)	688
Plant and equipment	650	(367)	283
Motor vehicles	102	(53)	49
	1,552	(532)	1,020
Current assets			
Inventories			950
Trade receivables			420
Cash at bank			16
			1,386
Total assets			2,406
Equity			
Ordinary shares of £1, fully paid			800
Reserves at 1 July 2005			248
Profit for the year			120
			1,168
Non-current liabilities			
Borrowings (Secured 10% loan)			700
Current liabilities			
Trade payables			361
Other payables			117
Taxation			60
			538
Total equity and liabilities			2,406

The following additional information is available:

1 Purchase invoices for goods received on 29 June 2006 amounting to £23,000 have not been included. This means that the cost of sales figure in the income statement has been understated.

2 A motor vehicle costing £8,000 with depreciation amounting to £5,000 was sold on 30 June 2006 for £2,000, paid by cheque. This transaction has not been included in the company's records.

3 No depreciation on motor vehicles has been charged. The annual rate is 20 per cent of cost at the year end.

4 A sale on credit for £16,000 made on 1 July 2006 has been included in the financial statements in error. The cost of sales figure is correct in respect of this item.

5 A half-yearly payment of interest on the secured loan due on 30 June 2006 has not been paid.

6 The tax charge should be 30 per cent of the reported profit before taxation. Assume that it is payable, in full, shortly after the year-end.

Required:

Prepare a revised set of financial statements incorporating the additional information in 1 to 6 above. Note: work to the nearest £1,000.

4.8 Rose Limited operates a small chain of retail shops that sell high-quality teas and coffees. Approximately half of sales are on credit. Abbreviated and unaudited financial statements are given below:

Rose Limited
Income statement for the year ended 31 March 2006

	£000
Revenue	12,080
Cost of sales	(6,282)
Gross profit	5,798
Labour costs	(2,658)
Depreciation	(625)
Other operating costs	(1,003)
Operating profit	1,512
Interest payable	(66)
Net profit before tax	1,446
Taxation	(434)
Net profit for the year	1,012

Balance sheet as at 31 March 2006

	£000
Non-current assets	2,728
Current assets	
Inventories	1,583
Receivables	996
Cash	26
	2,605
Total assets	5,333
Equity	
Share capital (50 p shares, fully paid)	750
Share premium	250
Retained earnings	1,468
	2,468
Non-current liabilities	
Borrowings – Secured loan (2011)	300
Current liabilities	
Trade payables	1,118
Other payables	417
Tax	434
Borrowings – Overdraft	596
	2,565
Total equity and liabilities	5,333

Since the unaudited financial statements for Rose Limited were prepared, the following information has become available:

1 An additional £74,000 of depreciation should have been charged on fixtures and fittings.
2 Invoices for credit sales on 31 March 2006 amounting to £34,000 have not been included; cost of sales is not affected.
3 Allowances for receivables should be provided at a level of 2 per cent of receivables at the year end.
4 Inventories, which had been purchased for £2,000, have been damaged and are unsaleable. This is not reflected in the financial statements.
5 Fixtures and fittings to the value of £16,000 were delivered just before 31 March 2006, but these assets were not included in the financial statements and the purchase invoice had not been processed.
6 Wages for Saturday-only staff, amounting to £1,000, have not been paid for the final Saturday of the year. This is not reflected in the financial statements.
7 Tax is payable at 30 per cent of net profit after tax. Assume that it is payable shortly after the year-end.

Required:
Prepare revised financial statements for Rose Limited for the year ended 31 March 2006, incorporating the information in 1 to 7 above. Note: work to the nearest £1,000.

5

Accounting for limited companies (2)

Introduction

This chapter continues our examination of the financial statements of limited companies. We begin by identifying the legal responsibilities of directors and then go on to discuss the main sources of accounting rules governing published financial statements. Although a detailed consideration of these accounting rules is beyond the scope of this book, the key rules that shape the form and content of the published financial statements are discussed. We also consider the efforts made to ensure that these rules are underpinned by a coherent framework of principles.

The increasing complexity of business and the added demands for information by financial report users have led to the publication of a number of additional financial reports. This chapter considers two of these, namely the segmental financial report and the operating and financial review. These reports aim to provide users with a more complete picture of financial performance and position.

Despite the proliferation of accounting rules and the increasing supply of financial information to users of financial reports, concerns have been expressed over the quality of some of those published reports. This chapter ends by considering some well-publicised accounting scandals and the problem of creative accounting.

Learning outcomes

When you have completed this chapter, you should be able to:

- Describe the responsibilities of directors and auditors concerning the annual financial statements provided to shareholders and others.

- Identify the main sources of regulation affecting the financial statements of limited companies.

- Discuss the framework of principles for accounting.

- Prepare an income statement, balance sheet and statement of changes in equity for a limited company in accordance with international financial reporting standards.

● Explain the purpose of the segmental report and the operating and financial review and describe their main features.

● Discuss the threat posed by creative accounting to the quality of published financial statements.

The directors' duty to account

With most large companies, it is not possible for all shareholders to be involved in the management of the company, nor do most of them wish to be involved. Instead, they appoint directors to act on their behalf. This separation of ownership from day-to-day control creates the need for directors to be accountable for their stewardship (management) of the company's assets. Thus, the law requires that directors:

● maintain appropriate accounting records;
● prepare annual financial statements and a directors' report, and make these available to all shareholders and to the public at large.

The financial statements are made available to the public by submitting a copy to the Companies Registry (Department of Trade and Industry), which allows anyone who wishes to do so to inspect them. In addition, listed companies are required to publish their financial statements on their website.

Activity 5.1

Why does the law require directors to account in this way and who benefits from these requirements?

We thought of the following benefits and beneficiaries:

● *To inform and protect shareholders*. If shareholders do not receive information about the performance and position of their company, they will have problems in appraising their investment. Under these circumstances, they would probably be reluctant to invest and this, in turn, would affect the functioning of the private sector. Any society with a significant private sector needs to encourage equity investment.

● *To inform and protect suppliers of labour, goods, services and finance, particularly those supplying credit (loans) or goods and services on credit*. Individuals and organisations would be reluctant to engage in commercial relationships, such as supplying goods or lending money, where a company does not provide information about its financial health. The fact that a company has limited liability increases the risks involved in dealing with the company. An unwillingness to engage in commercial relationships with limited companies will, once again, affect the functioning of the private sector.

● *To inform and protect society more generally*. Some companies exercise enormous power and influence in society generally, particularly on a geographically local basis. For example, a particular company may be the dominant employer and purchaser of commercial goods and services in a particular town or city. Legislators have tended to take the view that society has the right to information about the company and its activities.

The directors' duty to account is considered in more detail in Chapter 10.

The need for accounting rules

If we accept the need for directors to prepare and publish financial statements, we must also accept the need for a framework of rules concerning how these statements are prepared and presented. Without rules, there is a much greater risk that unscrupulous directors will adopt policies and practices that portray an unrealistic view of financial health. There is also a much greater risk that the financial statements will not be comparable over time or with those of other companies. These risks are likely to undermine the integrity of financial statements in the eyes of users.

Users must, however, be realistic about what can be achieved through regulation. Problems of manipulation and of concealment can still occur even within a highly regulated environment and some examples of both will be considered later in the chapter. The scale of these problems, however, should be reduced. Problems of comparability can also still occur, as accounting is not a precise science. Judgements and estimates must be made when preparing financial statements and these may hinder comparisons. Furthermore, no two companies are identical and the accounting policies adopted may vary between companies for valid reasons.

Sources of accounting rules

In recent years there has been a trend towards the internationalisation of business, which seems set to continue. This trend has led to calls for the international harmonisation of accounting rules to help both users and companies. Harmonisation should help investors and other users of financial statements by making it easier to compare the performance and position of different companies operating in different countries. It should help companies with international operations by reducing the time and cost of producing financial statements: different sets of financial statements would no longer have to be prepared to comply with the rules of different countries.

The International Accounting Standards Board (IASB) is an independent body which is at the forefront of the move towards harmonisation. The Board, which is based in the UK, is dedicated to developing a single set of high quality, global accounting rules that provide transparent and comparable information in financial statements. These rules, which are known as **International Financial Reporting Standards** or International Accounting Standards, deal with key issues such as:

● what information should be disclosed;
● how information should be presented;
● how assets should be valued;
● how profit should be measured.

The overriding requirement for financial statements prepared according to IASB standards is to provide a fair representation of the company's financial position, financial performance and cash flows. There is a presumption that this fair representation will be achieved where the financial statements are drawn up in accordance with the various IASB standards that have been issued.

The authority of the IASB was given a huge boost when the European Commission adopted a regulation requiring nearly all Stock Exchange listed companies of EU member states to prepare their financial statements according to IASB standards for accounting periods commencing on or after 1 January 2005. Although non-listed UK companies are not currently required to adopt IASB standards, they have the option to do so. Many informed observers believe, however, that IASB standards will soon become a requirement for all UK companies.

The EU regulation overrides any laws in force in member states that could either hinder or restrict compliance with IASB standards. The ultimate aim is to achieve a single framework of accounting rules for companies from all member states. The EU recognises that this will only be achieved if individual governments do not add to the requirements imposed by the various IASB standards. Thus, it seems that accounting rules developed within individual EU member countries will eventually disappear. For the time being, however, the EU accepts that the governments of member states may need to impose additional disclosures for some corporate governance matters and regulatory requirements. In the UK, company law requires disclosure relating to various corporate governance issues. There is, for example, a requirement to disclose details of directors' remuneration in the published financial statements, which goes beyond anything required by IASB standards. Furthermore, the Financial Services Authority (FSA), in its role as the UK (Stock Exchange) listing authority, imposes rules on Stock Exchange listed companies. These include the requirement to publish a condensed set of interim (half-year) financial statements in addition to the annual financial statements. (These statements are not required by the IASB, although there is a standard providing guidance on their content and structure.)

Figure 5.1 sets out the main sources of accounting rules for Stock Exchange listed companies discussed above. Whilst company law and the FSA still play an important role, in the longer term, IASB standards seem set to become the sole source of company accounting rules.

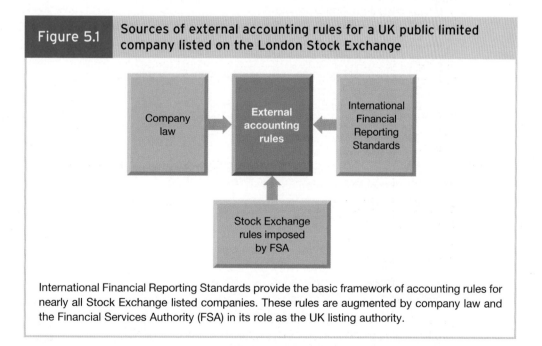

Figure 5.1 Sources of external accounting rules for a UK public limited company listed on the London Stock Exchange

International Financial Reporting Standards provide the basic framework of accounting rules for nearly all Stock Exchange listed companies. These rules are augmented by company law and the Financial Services Authority (FSA) in its role as the UK listing authority.

Real World 5.1 provides a list of standards that have been issued, or adopted, by the IASB to give an idea of the range of topics that are covered.

Real World 5.1

International standards

The following is a list of the International Accounting Standards (IASs) or International Financial Reporting Standards (IFRSs) in issue as at 1 August 2007. (The latter term is used for standards issued from 2003 onwards.) Several standards have been issued and subsequently withdrawn, which explains the numerical gaps in sequence. In addition, several have been revised and re-issued.

IAS 1	Presentation of Financial Statements
IAS 2	Inventories
IAS 7	Cash Flow Statements
IAS 8	Accounting Policies, Changes in Accounting Estimates and Errors
IAS 10	Events after the Balance Sheet Date
IAS 11	Construction Contracts
IAS 12	Income Taxes
IAS 14	Segment Reporting
IAS 15	Information Reflecting the Effects of Changing Prices
IAS 16	Property, Plant and Equipment
IAS 17	Leases
IAS 18	Revenue
IAS 19	Employee Benefits
IAS 20	Accounting for Government Grants and Disclosure of Government Assistance
IAS 21	The Effects of Changes in Foreign Exchange Rates
IAS 23	Borrowing Costs
IAS 24	Related Party Disclosures
IAS 26	Accounting and Reporting by Retirement Benefit Plans
IAS 27	Consolidated and Separate Financial Statements
IAS 28	Investments in Associates
IAS 29	Financial Reporting in Hyperinflationary Economies
IAS 31	Interests in Joint Ventures
IAS 32	Financial Instruments: Presentation
IAS 33	Earnings per Share
IAS 34	Interim Financial Reporting
IAS 36	Impairment of Assets
IAS 37	Provisions, Contingent Liabilities and Contingent Assets
IAS 38	Intangible Assets
IAS 39	Financial Instruments: Recognition and Measurement
IAS 40	Investment Property
IAS 41	Agriculture
IFRS 1	First-time Adoption of International Financial Reporting Standards
IFRS 2	Share-based Payment
IFRS 3	Business Combinations
IFRS 4	Insurance Contracts
IFRS 5	Non-current Assets Held For Sale and Discontinued Operations
IFRS 6	Exploration for and Evaluation of Mineral Resources
IFRS 7	Financial Instruments: Disclosures

The IASB has promised a period of stability over the short-term with no new major standards becoming effective until 2009. This should ease the transition to international standards and allow countries to amend their laws where necessary. The IASB, however, has an ambitious agenda and significant changes are likely to occur over the longer term.

Presenting the financial statements

Now that we have gained an impression of the sources of rules affecting limited companies, let us turn our attention to the main rules to be followed in the presentation of financial statements. We shall focus on the IASB rules and, in particular, those contained in IAS 1 *Presentation of Financial Statements*. This standard is very important as it sets out the structure and content of financial statements and the principles to be followed in preparing these statements.

According to IAS 1, the financial statements consist of:

● an income statement;
● a balance sheet;
● a statement of changes in equity;
● a cash flow statement;
● notes on accounting policies and other explanatory notes.

We shall discuss each of these below but, before doing so, we should be clear as to what is the main consideration when preparing these statements.

Fair representation

The overriding requirement is for the financial statements to provide a fair representation of the company's financial position, financial performance and cash flows. There is a presumption that this will be achieved where the financial statements are drawn up in accordance with the various IASB standards that have been issued. It is only in very rare circumstances that compliance with a standard would not result in a fair representation of the financial health of a company.

Activity 5.2

IAS 1 does not say that the overriding requirement is for the financial statements to show a 'correct' or an 'accurate' presentation of financial health. Why, in your opinion, does it not use those words? (*Hint*: think of depreciation of non-current assets.)

Accounting can never really be said to be 'correct' or 'accurate' as these words imply that there is a precise value that any asset, claim, revenue or expense could have. This is simply not true in many, if not most, cases.

Depreciation provides a good example. The annual depreciation expense is based on judgements about the future concerning the expected useful life and residual value. If all relevant factors are taken into account and reasonable judgements are applied, it may be possible to achieve a fair representation of the amount of the cost or fair value of the asset that is consumed for a particular period. However, a precise figure for depreciation for a period cannot be achieved.

Income statement

Although the format of the income statement is not prescribed, IAS 1 sets out the *minimum* information to be presented on the face of income statement. These items include:

- revenue;
- finance costs;
- gains or losses on the sale of assets or settlement of liabilities arising from discontinued operations;
- tax expense; and
- profit or loss.

The standard makes it clear, however, that further items should be shown on the face of the income statement where they are relevant to an understanding of performance. For example, if a business is badly affected by flooding, and inventories are destroyed as a result, the cost of the flood damage should be shown.

As a further aid to understanding, all material expenses must be separately disclosed. However, they need not be shown on the face of the income statement: they can appear in the notes to the financial statements. The sort of material items that may require separate disclosure include:

- write down of inventories to net realisable value;
- write down or disposal of property, plant and equipment;
- disposal of investments;
- restructuring costs;
- discontinuing operations; and
- litigation settlements.

This is not an exhaustive list and, in practice, other material expenses may require separate disclosure.

The standard suggests two possible ways in which expenses can be presented on the face of the income statement. Expenses can be either presented according to their nature, such as depreciation, employee expenses and so on, or according to business functions, such administrative activities and distribution.

So far in this book, expenses have been broadly set out according to their nature. Example 5.1 below, however, shows how expenses may be presented according to business functions.

Example 5.1

Degas plc
Income statement for the year ended 31 May 2007

	£000
Revenue	690
Cost of sales	(330)
Gross profit	360
Distribution costs	(102)
Administrative expenses	(115)
Other expenses	(14)
Operating profit	129
Finance costs	(20)
Profit before tax	109
Taxation	24
Profit for the period	85

The choice between the two ways of presenting expenses should depend on which the directors believe will provide the more relevant and reliable information. The second of these two ways, which is illustrated above, shows how much of the revenue generated was absorbed by particular functions and may provide a better impression of the efficiency of the business. However, it is not always easy to attribute costs to particular functional areas, particularly where facilities and other resources are being shared. If this second approach is adopted, additional information concerning the nature of the expenses, including depreciation charges and employee costs, must also be shown. This is because this kind of information can be useful in predicting future cash flows.

The balance sheet

Again, IAS 1 does not prescribe the format of this financial statement but does set out the *minimum* information that should be presented on the face of the balance sheet. This includes the following:

- property, plant and equipment;
- investment property;
- intangible assets;
- financial assets (such as shares and loan notes of other companies held);
- inventories;
- trade and other receivables;
- cash and cash equivalents;
- trade and other payables;
- provisions;
- financial liabilities (excluding payables and provisions shown above);
- tax liabilities; and
- issued share capital and reserves (equity).

Additional information should be also shown where it is relevant to an understanding of the financial position of the business.

The standard requires that normally a distinction be made on the balance sheet between current assets and non-current assets and between current liabilities and non-current liabilities. However, where a company considers that more reliable and relevant information will be presented by ordering the items according to their liquidity, it is permitted to do this.

The sub-classification of some of the items shown above may be necessary, either to comply with particular standards or because of their size or nature. For example, sub-classifications are required for certain assets such as property, plant and equipment and inventories as well as for provisions and reserves. In addition, details of share capital, such as the number of issued shares, and their par value must also be shown. However, to avoid cluttering up the balance sheet, this additional information can be shown in the notes.

Statement of changes to equity

The **statement of changes to equity** aims to help users to understand the changes in share capital and reserves that took place during the period. It reconciles the capital and reserves figures at the beginning of the period with those at the end of the period. This is achieved by showing the effect on the capital and reserves of all revenue and expenses, including gains and losses, as well as the effect of share issues and purchases during the period.

To show the effect on capital and reserves of gains and losses, we first need to understand how they are reported in the financial statements. The general rule is that the income statement should show all *realised* gains and losses for the period. Those gains and losses that remain *unrealised* (because the asset is still held) do not pass through the income statement, but, instead, go directly to a reserve. We saw, in an earlier chapter, an example of an unrealised gain, or loss, which is not passed through the income statement.

Activity 5.3

Can you think of this example?

It is where a business revalues its land and buildings, the gain, or loss, arising is not shown in the income statement. It is transferred to a revaluation reserve, which forms part of the equity. The rule does not just relate to land and buildings, but these types of asset are, in practice, the most common examples of unrealised gains.

Another example of an unrealised gain or loss, which has not been mentioned so far, arises from exchange differences when the results of foreign operations are translated into UK currency. Once again, any gain, or loss, bypasses the income statement and is taken directly to a currency translation reserve. In the statement of changes in equity, we need to take account of *all* gains and losses that have arisen during the period. Thus, movements in the revaluation reserve and currency translation reserve must be identified in addition to realised profits (or losses) reported in the income statement.

To see how a statement of changes in equity may be prepared, let us consider Example 5.2.

Example 5.2

At 1 January 2007 Miro plc had the following equity:

Miro plc

	£m
Share capital (£1 ordinary shares)	100
Revaluation reserve	20
Translation reserve	40
Retained earnings	150
Total equity	310

During 2007, the company made a profit after tax from normal business operations of £42 m and reported a revaluation gain on land and buildings of £120 m. A loss on exchange differences on translating the results of foreign operations of £10 m was also reported. To strengthen its balance sheet, the company issued 50 m new shares during the year at a premium of £0.40. Dividends for the year were £27 m.

The above information for 2007 can be set out in a statement of changes in equity as follows:

Statement of changes in equity for the year ended 31 December 2007

	Share capital £m	Share premium £m	Revaluation reserve £m	Translation reserve £m	Retained earnings £m	Total £m
Balance as at 1 January 2007	100	–	20	40	150	310
Changes in equity for 2007						
Gain on revaluation of properties	–	–	120	–	–	120
Exchange differences on translation of foreign operations	–	–	–	(10)	–	(10)
Net income recognised directly to equity	–	–	120	(10)	–	110
Profit for the period	–	–	–	–	42	42
Total recognised income and expense for the period	–	–	120	(10)	42	152
Dividends	–	–	–	–	(27)	(27)
Issue of share capital	50	20	–	–	–	70
Balance at 31 December 2007	150	20	140	30	165	505

We can see from the example that dividends are shown in the statement of changes in equity and are an appropriation of equity.

Cash flow statement

The cash flow statement tries to help users to assess the ability of a company to generate cash and to assess the company's need for cash. The presentation requirements for this statement are set out in IAS 7 *Cash Flow Statements*, which we shall consider in some detail in Chapter 6.

Explanatory notes

The notes play an important role in helping users to understand the financial statements. They will normally contain the following information:

● a statement that the financial statements comply with relevant IFRSs;
● a summary of the measurement bases used and other significant accounting policies applied (for example, the basis of inventories valuation);
● supporting information relating to items appearing on the income statement, balance sheet, statement of changes in equity or cash flow statement; and
● other disclosures such as future contractual commitments that have not been recognised and management's objectives and policies.

General points

The standard requires that the financial statements be prepared annually, as a minimum. It also requires that comparative figures (that is, the equivalent figures for the immediately preceding period) be provided. The comparative figures enable users to assess the current figure for a particular item against its counterpart for the previous period.

The standard provides support for three key accounting conventions when preparing the financial statements. These are:

● going concern;
● accruals (except for the cash flow statement);
● consistency.

These conventions were covered in Chapters 2 and 3.

To improve the transparency of financial statements, the standard states that:

● offsetting liabilities against assets, or expenses against income, is not allowed. Thus, it is not acceptable, for example, to offset a bank overdraft against a positive bank balance (where the company has both); and
● material items must be shown separately.

The framework of principles

In Chapters 2 and 3, we came across various accounting conventions such as prudence, historic cost, going concern and so on. These conventions were developed as a practical response to particular problems that were confronted when preparing financial statements. They have stood the test of time and are still of value to preparers today. However, they do not provide, and were never designed to provide, a framework of principles to guide the development of financial statements. As we grapple with increasingly complex financial reporting problems, the need to have a sound understanding of *why* we account for things in a particular way becomes more and more pressing. Knowing *why* we account, rather than simply *how* we account, is vitally important if we are to improve the quality of financial statements.

In recent years, much effort has been expended in various countries, including the UK, to develop a clear **framework of principles** that will guide us in the development of accounting. Such a framework should provide clear answers to such fundamental questions as:

● Who are the main users of financial statements?
● What is the purpose of financial statements?
● What qualities should financial information possess?
● What are the main elements of financial statements?
● How should these elements be defined, recognised and measured?

If these questions can be answered, accounting rule makers, such as the IASB, will be in a stronger position to identify best practice and to develop more coherent rules. This should, in turn, increase the credibility of financial reports in the eyes of users. It may even help reduce the possible number of rules, because some issues may be resolved by reference to the application of general principles rather than by the generation of further rules.

The IASB framework

The quest for a framework of accounting principles began in earnest in the 1970s when the Financial Accounting Standards Board (FASB) in the US devoted a very large amount of time and resources to this endeavour. This resulted in a broad framework of principles, which other rule-making bodies, including the IASB, have drawn upon when developing their own frameworks.

The IASB has produced a 'Framework for the Preparation and Presentation of Financial Statements', which begins by discussing the main user groups and their needs. This is well-trodden territory and the various groups and needs identified are broadly in line with those set out in the sections on this topic in Chapter 1. The framework goes on to identify the objective of financial statements, which is:

> to provide information about the financial position, performance and changes in financial position of an enterprise that is useful to a wide range of users in making economic decisions.

This reflects the mainstream view and is very similar to the objective of financial statements that others have developed in recent years.

The IASB framework sets out the qualitative characteristics that make financial statements useful. The main characteristics identified are relevance, reliability, comparability, and understandability, all of which were discussed in Chapter 1. The framework also identifies the main elements of financial statements. These are assets, liabilities, equity, income and expense, and definitions for each element are provided. The definitions adopted hold no surprises and are very similar to those adopted by other rule-making bodies and to those discussed earlier, in Chapters 2 and 3.

The IASB framework identifies different valuation bases in use but does not indicate a preference for a particular valuation method. It simply notes that historic cost is the most widely used method of valuation (although fair values are now increasingly used in international financial reporting standards). Finally, the framework discusses the type of capital base that a business should try to maintain. It includes a discussion of the two main types of capital base – financial capital and physical capital – but, again, expresses no preference as to which should be maintained. The IASB framework does not have the same legal status as an IASB standard. Nevertheless, it offers guidance for dealing with accounting issues, particularly where no relevant accounting standard exists.

Overall, the IASB framework has provoked little debate and the principles and definitions adopted appear to enjoy widespread acceptance. There has been some criticism, mainly from academics, that the framework is really a descriptive document and does not provide theoretical underpinning to the financial statements. There has also been some criticism of the definitions of the elements of the financial statements. However, these criticisms have not sparked any major controversies.

The auditors' role

Shareholders are required to elect a qualified and independent person or, more usually, a firm to act as **auditors**. The auditors' main duty is to make a report as to whether, in their opinion, the financial statements do what they are supposed to do, namely to show a true and fair view of the financial performance, position and cash flows of the company by complying with the relevant accounting rules. To be able to form such an opinion, auditors must scrutinise both the annual financial statements and the evidence upon which they are based. The auditors' opinion must be included with the financial statements sent to the shareholders and to the Registrar of Companies.

The relationship between the shareholders, the directors and the auditors is illustrated in Figure 5.2. This shows that the shareholders elect the directors to act on their behalf, in the day-to-day running of the company. The directors are then required to 'account' to the shareholders on the performance, position and cash flows of the company, on an annual basis. The shareholders also elect auditors, whose role it is to give the shareholders an independent view of the truth and fairness of the financial statements prepared by the directors.

| Figure 5.2 | The relationship between the shareholders, the directors and the auditors |

The directors are appointed by the shareholders to manage the company on the shareholders' behalf. The directors are required to report each year to the shareholders, principally by means of financial statements, on the company's performance, position and cash flows. To give greater confidence in the statements, the shareholders also appoint auditors to investigate the reports and to express an opinion on their reliability.

The role of the auditors and the audit process is considered in more detail in Chapter 10.

Directors' report

In addition to preparing the financial statements, the law requires the directors to prepare an annual report to shareholders and other interested parties. This report contains information of both a financial and a non-financial nature and goes beyond that which is contained in the financial statements. The information disclosed covers a variety of topics including details of share ownership, details of directors and their financial interests in the company, employment policies, and charitable and political donations. The auditors do not carry out an audit of the **directors' report**. However, they will check to see that the information in the report is consistent with that contained within the audited financial statements.

Segmental financial reports

Most large businesses are engaged in a variety of activities, with each activity having its own levels of risk, growth and profitability. Information relating to each type of business activity, however, is normally aggregated in the financial statements to provide an overall picture of financial performance and position. This aggregation (that is, adding together) of information makes it difficult to undertake comparisons over time or between businesses. Some idea of the range and scale of the various business activities must be gained for a proper assessment of financial health.

Where a business operates in different geographical markets, the same arguments apply. Markets in different countries or regions may have different levels of risk, profitability and growth which will be obscured by aggregation. The impact on a business of changes in such factors as the political climate, inflation or exchange rates relating to a particular country, or geographical region, cannot be assessed unless the degree of exposure to the country, or region, is known.

To undertake any meaningful analysis of financial performance and position, it is usually necessary to disaggregate the information contained within the financial statements. By breaking down the financial information according to business activities and/or geographical markets, we can evaluate the relative risks and profitability of each segment and make useful comparisons with other businesses or other business segments. We can also see the trend of performance for each segment over time and so determine more accurately the likely growth prospects for the business as a whole. We should also be able to assess more easily the impact on the overall business, of changes in market conditions relating to particular activities.

Disclosure of information relating to the performance of each segment may also help to improve the efficiency of the business by keeping managers on their toes. Business segments that are performing poorly will be revealed and this should put pressure on managers to take corrective action. In addition, where a business segment has been sold, the shareholders will be better placed to assess the wisdom of the managers' decision.

Segmental reporting rules

An IASB standard (IAS 14 *Segment Reporting*) requires listed companies to disclose segmental information according to each business segment *and* to each geographical region. Both forms of segmentation are regarded as important to users. A business segment, for the purposes of the standard, is a part of the business that can be separately identified and which provides an individual product or service, or a group of related products or services. A geographical segment is a part of the business that can be separately identified and which provides products or services within a particular economic environment. The environment may comprise a region within a country, a country or a group of countries. One problem that must be confronted when identifying geographical segments is whether the business should be segmented according to where the *operations* are located or where the *markets* are located. The relevant standard allows either approach to be used but states that the choice should be based on the way in which the business is organised and structured.

To be reported separately, a business or geographical segment must be of significant size. This means that it must account for 10 per cent or more of the business's revenue, or operating results or total revenue. A segment that does not meet this size threshold may be combined with other segments, shown as an allocated item, or separately reported despite its size.

For reporting purposes, it is necessary to establish whether it is

1 the products or services offered; or
2 the geographical regions in which the company operates

that has the bigger impact on the risks and returns of the company.

It is for the directors to decide which has the bigger impact and is, therefore, the primary segment. The way in which a business is organised and structured should provide a useful indicator.

Identifying which is the primary and secondary segments is important because disclosure requirements are greater for the former.

Segmental disclosure

The following are the main items of information that should be disclosed for the primary segments:

- revenue, distinguishing between revenue from external customers and revenue from other segments of the business;
- total assets;
- capital expenditure for the period;
- depreciation, impairments and other non-cash items;
- segment operating result (that is, segment revenue less segment operating expenses); and
- total liabilities.

For secondary segments, only the first three items identified above need be disclosed.

Example 5.3 provides an illustrative **segmental financial report** for a business where the business segments are the primary segments. Following the example, we shall discuss some of the key points that are raised.

Example 5.3

Goya plc
Segmental report for the year ended 30 June 2007

	Publishing £m	Film making £m	Eliminations £m	Consolidation (Total) £m
Revenue				
External sales	150	200		
Inter-segment sales	20	10	(30)	
Total revenue	170	210	(30)	350
Result				
Segment result	15	19	(2)	32
Unallocated expenses				14
Operating profit				18
Interest expense				(6)
Net profit before tax				12
Corporation tax				(3)
Profit for the year				9
Other information				
Segment assets	74	86		160
Unallocated assets				32
Consolidated total assets				192
Segment liabilities	24	21		45
Unallocated liabilities				30
Consolidated total liabilities				75
Capital expenditure	10	8		
Depreciation	15	21		

We can see that information relating to each segment is shown as well as information relating to the business as a whole. Revenue from both external and inter-segment sales for each segment appear separately, however, only the combined external sales revenue for the segments appear in the far right-hand column. This is because the revenue from inter-segment sales will cancel one another out when calculating the revenue for the business as a whole. Similarly, the combined operating profit of each segment *less* the inter-segment profit will appear as the operating profit for the business as a whole.

Unallocated expenses appearing in the above report are those which are not attributable to a particular segment or which cannot be allocated to a segment on any reasonable basis. Note that these expenses have not been apportioned between the two segments but have been deducted from the results of the business as a whole.

Activity 5.4

What kind of items do you think may appear as unallocated expenses?

These items may include:

- head office expenses;
- research and development costs;
- marketing expenses;
- finance charges.

You may have thought of others.

Unallocated assets and liabilities are those which are not attributable to a particular segment or which cannot be allocated to a particular segment on any reasonable basis. Head office buildings may provide an example of such an unallocated asset and loan capital may provide an example of an unallocated liability.

A similar layout to the report shown above can be used to show geographical segments, where they are regarded as the primary segments.

Problems of segmental reporting

There are various problems associated with preparing segmental reports, not least of which is the problem of identifying a segment. The relevant standard mentions some of the factors that should be taken into account when identifying segments; however, a fair amount of judgement by the directors will often be required. Although this may be the only sensible course of action, it does mean that comparisons between businesses may still be difficult because of different judgements being applied within different companies.

Many segments do not operate in a completely independent manner and there may be a significant amount of sales between segments. If this is the case, the **transfer price** of the goods or services between segments can have a substantial impact on the reported profits of each segment. (The transfer price is the price at which sales are made between different segments of the company.) Indeed, it may be possible to manipulate profit figures for each segment through the use of particular transfer pricing policies. For this reason, the international financial reporting standard requires that the basis for inter-segment transfers must be disclosed.

Finally, there may be problems where expenses incurred relate to more than one business segment. The way in which these costs are treated may vary between businesses and so may hinder comparisons.

Self-assessment question 5.1

Segmental information relating to J. Baxter plc, which has operations in three different countries, for the year to 30 April 2007 is shown below.

	UK £m	France £m	Italy £m	Eliminations £m	Consolidation £m
Revenue					
External sales	230	180	360		
Inter-segment sales	40	20	30	(90)	
Total revenue	270	200	390	(90)	770
Result					
Segment result	34	30	8	(6)	66
Unallocated expenses					18
Operating profit					48
Interest expense					(16)
Corporation tax					(6)
Profit for the year					26
Other information					
Segment assets	129	150	116		395
Unallocated assets					36
Consolidated total assets					431
Segment liabilities	35	28	22		85
Unallocated liabilities					40
Consolidated total liabilities					125
Capital expenditure	20	15	35		
Depreciation	28	35	11		

Required:
Analyse the performance of each of the business segments for the year and comment on your results.

The answer to this question can be found at the back of the book on p. 403.

Narrative reporting

A business, particularly a large business, may have extremely complex organisational arrangements, financing methods and operating characteristics. To portray financial performance and position faithfully, the published financial statements must reflect this complexity. As a result, these statements may well be difficult to understand and to interpret. To help users gain a clearer picture, a narrative report may be produced to accompany the financial statements. This report will provide a commentary on the business and its financial results.

The UK Accounting Standards Board (ASB) has issued a reporting statement (RS1), mainly aimed at listed companies, for an **operating and financial review** (OFR). The OFR is a narrative report which aims to provide a balanced and comprehensive examination of:

- the performance of the business during the year and its position at the end of the year;
- the key trends and factors affecting performance and position during the year as well as those which are likely to affect future performance and position.

The OFR is meant to reflect the directors' views of the business and should complement as well as supplement the financial statements.

Activity 5.5

What are the main characteristics concerning quality that information contained within the OFR should possess? (*Hint*: think back to Chapter 1.)

To be useful, the information should contain the characteristics for accounting information in general, which we identified in Chapter 1. Thus, the information should be relevant, understandable, reliable and comparable. The fact that we are dealing with narrative information does not alter the need for these characteristics to be present.

A further requirement of the OFR is comprehensiveness. This means that it should include all significant information that will help assess business performance. Thus, information that places the business in an unfavourable light should not be omitted.

The OFR framework

The framework for an OFR, rests on the disclosure of four key elements of a business. Each of these elements is discussed below.

1. The nature of the business

This element will include a description of the environment within which the business operates. It is a potentially wide area and may include a commentary on products sold, business processes, business structure, and competitive position. A commentary on the legal, economic and social environment may also be included.

The objectives of the business and the strategy adopted to achieve those objectives should also be discussed. **Real World 5.2** below reveals how one well-known business describes in its OFR the strategy that has been adopted.

Real World 5.2

Tesco's strategy

The 2006 annual report of Tesco plc includes a 17-page OFR, which provides a lot of information about its business and its financial results. The strategy of the business is described in the OFR as follows:

Tesco has a well-established and consistent strategy for growth, which is strengthening the core business and driving our expansion into new markets. This four-part strategy was laid down in 1997 and it has been the foundation of Tesco's success in recent years. Its objectives are:

- to grow the core business;
- to become a successful international retailer;
- to be as strong in non-food as in food; and
- to develop retailing services – such as Tesco Personal Finance, Telecoms and tesco.com.

Source: 2006 Annual Report Tesco plc, p. 1.

Key performance indicators (KPIs) used by the directors to assess whether the strategy is effective should be included in the OFR. These KPIs quantify the factors that are critical to the success of the business and are often a mixture of financial and non-financial measures. Key financial measures may relate to sales revenue growth, profit, total shareholder return, dividends and so on. Key non-financial measures may relate to market share, employee satisfaction, product quality, supplier satisfaction and so on.

2. Business performance

This element will examine the development and performance of the business for both the year under review and the future. It should include any factors affecting performance, such as changes in market conditions or the launch of new products or services. It should also examine trends and factors that may affect future prospects. **Real World 5.3** provides an extract from Tesco's OFR, which describes plans that have potentially a significant effect on future prospects.

Real World 5.3

Foreign parts

In line with the strategy mentioned above, Tesco plc has become increasingly international in its focus. Future growth in international activities is planned to be significant, as stated in the following extract from Tesco's 2006 OFR:

> At the end of February (2006), our international operations were trading from 814 stores, including 341 hypermarkets, with a total of 32.8 m sq. ft. of selling space. Almost 56% of Group sales area is now in International . . . We plan to open 396 new stores in the current year (2006/2007), adding 6.6 m sq. ft. of selling area.

Source: 2006 Annual Report Tesco plc, p. 8.

3. Resources, risks and relationships

The OFR should describe the resources of the business and how they are managed. The resources identified should include any items not reflected in the balance sheet. These items will, of course, vary between businesses but may include corporate reputation, patents, trademarks, brand names, market position and the quality of employees.

The OFR should also include a description of the main risks and uncertainties facing the business and the ways in which the directors deal with them. **Real World 5.4** reveals how Tesco plc comments on one important risk in its OFR.

Real World 5.4

Risky business

In its 2006 OFR, Tesco plc identifies more than twenty forms of risk that the business must consider. These cover a wide range and include competition, financial, environmental, product safety, terrorism and currency risks. The risk posed by competitors is described as follows:

> The retail industry is highly competitive. The Group competes with a wide variety of retailers of varying sizes, and faces increased competition from UK retailers, as well as international operators, here

and overseas. Failure to compete with competitors on areas including price, product range, quality and service could have an adverse effect on the Group's financial results.

We aim to have a broad appeal in price, range and store format in a way that allows us to compete in different markets. We track performance against a range of measures that customers tell us are critical to their shopping trip experience. We constantly monitor customer perceptions of ourselves and our competitors to ensure that we can respond quickly if we need to.

Source: 2006 Annual Report Tesco plc, p. 14.

This element also requires a commentary on key relationships with stakeholders, apart from shareholders, that may affect the performance of the business and its value. The stakeholders may include customers, suppliers, employees, contractors, lenders as well as other businesses with which the business has strategic alliances. **Real World 5.5** reveals how, in the 2006 OFR, Tesco plc describes the relationship with its customers.

Real World 5.5

Every little helps

Our customers have told us what they want from an 'every little helps' shopping trip and this year 12,000 of them attended our Customer Question Times to offer ideas on how we can improve. Clubcard also helps us to understand what our customers want, whilst allowing us to thank them for shopping with us – this year we gave away £320 m in Clubcard vouchers.

We don't always get it right but we try to make their shopping trip as easy as possible, reduce prices where we can to help them spend less and give them the convenience of shopping where and when they want – in small stores, large stores or on-line.

Source: 2006 Annual Report Tesco plc, p. 14.

4. Financial position

This final element of the OFR framework should describe events that have influenced the financial position of the business during the year and those that are likely to affect the business in the future. It should also include a discussion of the capital structure, cash flows and liquidity of the company. **Real World 5.6** reveals how Tesco plc comments on its cash flows.

Real World 5.6

Tesco's cash

Tesco's 2006 OFR contains the following comment concerning its cash flows.

The Group generated net cash of £165 m during the year, benefiting from strong cash flow from operating activities of £3.4 bn and the net proceeds of £346 m from our property joint venture with Concensus. Within this, £239 m of cash was released from working capital, which was £199 m lower than last year. This was mainly due to a smaller rise in trade creditors (payables) than last year (last year's increase was exceptionally large and the change in International year end reduced trade creditors), higher non-food stocks (linked to global sourcing) and increased debtors (resulting from advance rent on new leasehold stores in Korea).

Source: 2006 Annual Report Tesco plc, p. 4.

This final element should also comment on the treasury policy of the business. Treasury policy is concerned with such matters as managing cash, obtaining finance and managing relationships with financial institutions. Possible areas for discussion may include major financing transactions and the effects of interest charges or interest rate changes on current or future results. **Real World 5.7** shows how Tesco plc comments on major new funding arrangements during the year and its debt position at the end of the year in its 2006 OFR.

Real World 5.7

Funding Tesco

Tesco plc finances its operations by a combination of retained profits, share issues, leases and borrowing of different forms. The 2006 OFR includes the following:

> New funding of £529 m was arranged during the year, including a net £484 m from property joint ventures and £45 m from medium-term notes (MTNs). We renewed our €10 bn MTN programme on 28 February 2006. At the year end, net debt was £4.5 bn (last year £3.9 bn) and the average debt maturity was six years (last year eight years).

Source: 2006 Annual Report Tesco plc, p. 16.

The Business Review and RS1

Recent legislation requires all companies (except small companies) to include a Business Review as part of the Directors Report. This is a narrative report, which for listed companies in particular, covers much of the ground discussed above. As the form that a Business Review should take is not clearly specified, directors of larger companies are likely to look to RS1 for guidance.

Summary financial statements

We saw earlier that the directors must provide each shareholder with a copy of the annual financial statements. For large companies, these financial statements can be extremely detailed and complicated: along with the accompanying notes they may extend over many pages. It is possible, however, for the directors to provide a summarised version of the full financial statements as an alternative. The main advantages of providing summarised financial statements are that:

● many shareholders do not wish to receive the full version, because they may not have the time, interest or skill necessary to be able to gain much from it;
● directors could improve their communication with their shareholders by providing something closer to the needs of many shareholders;
● reproducing and posting copies of the full version is expensive and a waste of resources where particular shareholders do not wish to receive it.

→   Many large companies send all of their private shareholders a copy of the **summary financial statements,** with a clear message that the full versions are available on request. The full version is, however, required for filing with the Registrar of Companies.

Creative accounting

Despite the proliferation of accounting rules and the independent checks that are imposed, concerns over the quality of published financial statements surface from time to time. Some directors apply particular accounting policies or structure particular transactions in such a way as to portray a picture of financial health that is in line with what they would like users to see rather than what is a true and fair view of financial position and performance. This practice is referred to as **creative accounting** and it poses a major problem for accounting rule makers and for society generally.

Activity 5.6

Why might the directors of a company engage in creative accounting?

There are many reasons and these include:

- to get around restrictions (for example, to report sufficient profit to pay a dividend);
- to avoid government action (for example, the taxation of excessive profits);
- to hide poor management decisions;
- to achieve sales revenue or profit targets, thereby ensuring that performance bonuses are paid to the directors;
- to attract new share capital or loan capital by showing a healthy financial position;
- to satisfy the demands of major investors concerning levels of return.

Creative accounting methods

The ways in which unscrupulous directors can manipulate the financial statements are many and varied. However, they usually involve adopting unorthodox practices for reporting key elements of the financial statements such as revenue, expenses, assets and liabilities. They may also involve the use of complicated or obscure transactions in an attempt to hide the underlying economic reality. The manipulation carried out may be designed to 'bend' the rules or may be designed to break the rules. Below we consider some of the more important ways in which rules may be bent or broken.

Overstating revenue

Some creative accounting methods are designed to overstate the revenue for a period. These methods often involve the early recognition of sales revenue or the reporting of sales transactions that have no real substance. **Real World 5.8** below, which is an extract from an article that appeared in *The Times*, provides examples of both types of revenue manipulation.

Real World 5.8

Overstating revenue

Hollow swaps: telecoms companies sell useless fibre optic capacity to each other in order to generate revenues on their income statements. Example: Global Crossing.

Channel stuffing: a company floods the market with more products than its distributors can sell, artificially boosting its sales. SSL, the condom maker, shifted £60 million in excess inventories on to trade customers. Also known as 'trade loading'.

Round tripping: also known as 'in-and-out trading'. Used to notorious effect by Enron. Two or more traders buy and sell energy among themselves for the same price and at the same time. Inflates trading volumes and makes participants appear to be doing more business than they really are.

Pre-dispatching: goods such as carpets are marked as 'sold' as soon as an order is placed . . . This inflates sales and profits.

Note that some of the techniques used, such as round tripping, may inflate the sales revenue for a period but will not inflate reported profits. Nevertheless, this may still benefit the business. Sales revenue growth has become an important yardstick of performance for some investors and can affect the value they place on the business.

Source: (2002) 'Dirty Laundry: How Companies Fudge the Numbers', *The Times* Business, 22 September.

The manipulation of revenue has been at the heart of many of the accounting scandals recently exposed. Given its critical role in the measurement of performance, this is, perhaps, not surprising. **Real World 5.9** provides an example of the impact of the early recognition of revenue on the financial results of one well-known business.

Real World 5.9

Not to be copied

One case of overstating revenue is alleged to have been carried out by the Xerox Corporation, a large US company and a leading player in the photocopying business. It is alleged that the company brought forward revenues in order to improve reported profits as its fortunes declined in the late 1990s. These revenues related to copier equipment sales, particularly in Latin America. To correct for the overstatement of revenues, Xerox had to restate its equipment sales revenue figures for a five-year period. The result was a reversal in reported revenues of a staggering $6.4 billion, although $5.1 billion was reallocated to other revenues as a result. This restatement was one of the largest in US corporate history.

In June 2002 the company paid a fine of $10 m but denied any wrongdoing.

Sources: based on information in (2003) 'Can't Tell the Scandals without a Scorecard', *The Wall Street Journal Europe*, October, p. A5; 'Xerox Acts to Put Itself on a Firmer Footing', FT.com, 28 June 2002.

Massaging expenses

Some creative accounting methods focus on the manipulation of expenses. Those expenses that rely on directors' estimates of the future or their choice of accounting policy are particularly vulnerable to manipulation.

Activity 5.7

Can you identify the kind of expenses where the directors make estimates or choices in the ways described?

These include certain expenses that we discussed in Chapter 3, such as:

- depreciation of property, plant and equipment;
- amortisation of intangible assets, such as goodwill;
- inventory costing methods; and
- allowances for receivables.

By changing estimates about the future (for example, the useful life or residual value of an asset), or by changing accounting policies (for example, switching from FIFO to AVCO), it may be possible to derive an expense figure, and consequently a profit figure, that suits the directors.

The incorrect capitalisation of expenses may also be used as a means of manipulation. This involves treating expenses as if they were amounts incurred to acquire or develop non-current assets, rather than amounts consumed during the period. Businesses that build their own assets are often best placed to undertake this form of malpractice.

Activity 5.8

What would be the effect on the profits and total assets of a business of incorrectly capitalising expenses?

Both would be artificially inflated. Reported profits would increase because expenses would be reduced. Total assets would be increased because the expenses would be incorrectly treated as non-current assets.

Real World 5.10 provides an example of one business that capitalised expenses on a huge scale.

Real World 5.10

Sorry - wrong numbers

One particularly notorious case of capitalising expenses is alleged to have occurred in the financial statements of WorldCom (now renamed MCI). This company, which is a large US telecommunications business, is alleged to have overstated profits by treating certain operating expenses, such as basic network maintenance, as capital expenditure. This happened over a fifteen-month period during 2001 and 2002. To correct for this over-statement, profits had to be reduced by a massive $3.8 bn.

Source: based on two personal views on WorldCom: FT.com site, 27 June 2002.

Concealing 'bad news'

Some creative accounting methods focus on the concealment of losses or liabilities. The financial statements can look much healthier if these can somehow be eliminated.

One way of doing this is to create a 'separate' entity that will take over the losses or liabilities.

Real World 5.11 describes how one large business concealed losses and liabilities.

Real World 5.11

For a very special purpose

Perhaps the most well-known case of concealment of losses and liabilities concerned the Enron Corporation. This was a large US energy business that used 'special purpose entities' (SPEs) as a means of concealment. SPEs were used by Enron to rid itself of problem assets that were falling in value, such as its broadband operations. In addition, liabilities were transferred to these entities to help Enron's balance sheet look healthier. The company had to keep its gearing ratios (the relationship between borrowing and equity) within particular limits to satisfy credit-rating agencies and SPEs were used to achieve this. The SPEs used for concealment purposes were not independent of the company and should have been consolidated in the balance sheet of Enron, along with their losses and liabilities.

When these, and other accounting irregularities, were discovered in 2001, there was a restatement of Enron's financial performance and position to reflect the consolidation of the SPEs, which had previously been omitted. As a result of this restatement, the company recognised $591 m in losses over the preceding four years and an additional $628 m worth of liabilities at the end of 2000.

The company collapsed at the end of 2001.

Source: Thomas, C. W. (2002) 'The Rise and Fall of Enron', *Journal of Accountancy*, 194(3), April. This article represents the opinion of the author and necessarily that of the Texas Society of Certified Public Accountants.

Overstating assets

Finally, creative accounting may involve the overstatement of asset values. This may involve revaluing the assets, using figures that are higher than their fair market values. It may also involve the capitalising of costs that should have been written off as expenses, as described earlier.

Real World 5.12 describes how one large business went much further by reporting assets that simply did not exist.

Real World 5.12

When things go sour

Parmalat, a large, family-controlled, Italian dairy-and-food business, announced in December 2003 that a bank account held in the Cayman Islands did not, as had been previously reported, have a balance of $3.95 billion. The fake balance turned out to be part of a web of deception: it had simply been 'invented' in order to help offset more than $16 billion of outstanding borrowings. According to Italian prosecutors, the business had borrowed heavily on the strength of fictitious sales revenues.

A Cayman Islands subsidiary, which was supposed to hold the fake bank balance, engaged in fictitious trading in an attempt to conceal the true nature of the deception. This included the supply of 300,000 tones of milk powder from a fake Singapore-based business to a Cuban business through the subsidiary.

Source: Based on information in 'How it all went so sour' P. Gumbel *Time Europe Magazine* 21 November 2004.

Checking for creative accounting

When examining the financial statements of a business, a number of checks may be carried out on the financial statements to help gain a 'feel' for their reliability. These can include checks to see whether:

- the reported profits are significantly higher than the operating cash flows for the period, which may suggest that profits have been overstated;
- the corporation tax charge is low in relation to reported profits, which may suggest, again, that profits are overstated, although there may be other, more innocent explanations;
- the valuation methods used for assets held are based on historic cost or fair values, and if the latter approach has been used why and how the fair values were determined;
- there have been any changes in accounting policies over the period, particularly in key areas such as revenue recognition, inventories valuation and depreciation;
- the accounting policies adopted are in line with those adopted by the rest of the industry;
- the auditors' report gives a 'clean bill of health' to the financial statements; and
- the 'small print', that is the notes to the financial statements, is not being used to hide significant events or changes.

Real World 5.13 describes the emphasis that one analyst places on this last check.

Real World 5.13

Taking note

FT

Alistair Hodgson, investment manager at private client stockbroker Pilling and Co says:

> I almost look at the notes more than I look at the main figures at first. The notes tend to hold the key to anything that looks strange. I look to pick out things that the auditor has told the company to declare – the kind of thing they might not want to declare, but they have got to do so in order to make the accounts honest.

Source: 'It Pays to Read Between the Lines', FT.com, 17 September 2005.

Some further checks may be carried out to provide confirmation of positive financial health. These may include checks to see whether:

- the business is paying increased dividends;
- the directors are buying shares in the business.

Although the various checks described are useful, they cannot be used to guarantee the reliability of the financial statements. Some creative accounting practices may be very deeply seated and may go undetected for years.

Creative accounting and economic growth

A few years ago there was a wave of creative accounting scandals, particularly in the USA, but also in Europe; however, it seems that this wave has now subsided. The quality of financial statements is improving and, it is to be hoped, trust among investors and others is being restored. As a result of the actions taken by various regulatory bodies and by accounting rule makers, creative accounting has become a more risky and difficult process for those who attempt it. However, it will never disappear completely and a further wave of creative accounting scandals may occur in the future.

The recent wave coincided with a period of strong economic growth, and during good economic times, investors and auditors become less vigilant. Thus, the opportunity to manipulate the figures becomes easier. We must not, therefore, become too complacent. Things may change again when we next experience a period of strong growth.

Summary

The main points of this chapter may be summarised as follows:

The directors' have a duty to:

- Maintain appropriate accounting records.
- Prepare and publish financial statements and a directors' report.

Accounting rules are necessary to:

- Avoid unacceptable accounting practices.
- Improve the comparability of financial statements.

Accounting rules

- The International Accounting Standards Board (IASB) has become an important source of rules.
- Company law and the London Stock Exchange are also a source of rules for UK companies.

Presenting financial statements

- IAS 1 sets out the structure and content of financial statements.
- It identifies five financial statements – the income statement, balance sheet, statement of changes in equity, cash flow statement and explanatory notes.
- The overriding consideration is to provide a fair representation of the financial health of a company and this will normally be achieved by adherence to relevant IASB standards.
- IAS 1 identifies information to be shown in the various financial statements.
- It also identifies some of the principles to be followed in preparing the statements.

Framework of principles

- This helps to underpin accounting rules.
- The IASB framework identifies and discusses, the users of financial statements, the objective of financial statements, the qualitative characteristics of financial statements, the elements of financial statements, different valuation bases, and different capital maintenance bases.
- The IASB framework draws on earlier work by other rule-making bodies.

Other statutory reports

- The auditors' report provides an opinion by an independent auditor concerning whether the financial statements provide a true and fair view of the financial health of a business.

- The directors' report contains information of a financial and a non-financial nature, which goes beyond that contained in the financial statements.

Additional financial reports

- Segmental reports disaggregate information on the financial statements to help achieve a better understanding of financial health.
- Companies can be segmented according to products or services and according to geographical operations.
- An IASB standard requires certain information relating to each segment to be shown.
- Identifying a segment and allocating costs between segments can raise problems.
- An operating and financial review (OFR) discusses the nature and objectives of the business, the development and performance of the business both in the period and in the future, the resources, risks and key relationships of the business and the financial position of the business both during the period and in the future.
- In the UK, the ASB has issued a reporting standard on the preparation of an OFR.
- Summary financial statements are available to investors who do not require the full set of financial statements.

Creative accounting

- Despite the accounting rules in place there have been examples of creative accounting by directors.
- This involves using accounting practices to show what the directors would like users to see rather than what is a fair representation of reality.
- There are various checks that can be carried out to the financial statements to see whether creative accounting practices may have been used.

→ **Key terms**

International Financial Reporting standards p. 144	Segmental financial report p. 156
	Transfer price p. 157
Statement of changes to equity p. 149	Operating and financial review (OFR) p. 158
Framework of principles p. 152	
Auditor p. 153	Summary financial statements p. 162
Directors' report p. 154	Creative accounting p. 163

Further reading

If you would like to explore the topics covered in this chapter in more depth, we recommend the following books:

Sutton, T. (2004) *Corporate Financial Accounting and Reporting*, 2nd edn, Financial Times Prentice Hall, Chapters 6 and 7.

Elliott, B. and Elliott, J. (2006) *Financial Accounting and Reporting*, 11th edn, Financial Times Prentice Hall, Chapters 5, 6, 7 and 8.

KPMG Thomson (2006) *Insights into IFRS*, 3rd edn, Sections 3.1, 4.1 and 5.2.

Accounting Standards Board (2005) *Operating and Financial Review*, ASB, May.

Review questions

Answers to these questions can be found at the back of the book on pp. 412–13.

5.1 'Searching for an agreed framework of principles for accounting rules is likely to be a journey without an ending.' Discuss.

5.2 The size of annual financial reports published by limited companies has increased steadily over the years. Can you think of any reasons, apart from the increasing volume of accounting regulation, why this has occurred?

5.3 What problems does a user of segmental financial statements face when seeking to make comparisons between businesses?

5.4 'An OFR should not be prepared by accountants but should be prepared by the board of directors.' Why should this be the case?

Exercises

Exercises 5.6 to 5.8 are more advanced than 5.1 to 5.5. Those with a coloured number have an answer at the back of the book, starting on p. 426.

If you wish to try more exercises, visit the students' side of the Companion Website.

5.1 It has been suggested that too much information might be as bad as too little information for users of annual reports. Explain.

5.2 What problems are likely to be encountered when preparing summary financial statements for shareholders?

5.3 The following information was extracted from the financial statements of I. Ching (Booksellers) plc for the year to 31 December 2006:

	£m
Interest payable	40
Cost of sales	460
Distribution costs	110
Revenue	943
Administration expenses	212
Other expenses	25

Note: Corporation tax is calculated at 25% of the profit available to shareholders.

Required:
Prepare an income statement for the year ended 31 December 2006 that is set out in accordance with the requirements of IAS 1 *Presentation of Financial Statements*.

5.4   Manet plc had the following share capital and reserves as at 30 June 2006:

	£m
Share capital (£0.25 ordinary shares)	250
Share premium account	50
Revaluation reserve	120
Currency translation reserve	15
Retained earnings	380
Total equity	815

During the year to 30 June 2007, the company revalued its freehold land upwards by £30 m and made a loss on foreign exchange translation of £5 m. The company made a profit after tax from operations of £160 m during the year and the dividend payout was 50% of the profit available to shareholders.

Required:

Prepare a statement of changes in equity in accordance with the requirements of IAS 1 *Presentation of Financial Statements*.

5.5   Professor Myddleton argues that accounting standards should be limited to disclosure requirements and should not impose rules on companies as to how to measure particular items in the financial statements. He states:

> The volume of accounting instructions is already high. If things go on like this, where will we be in 20 or 30 years time? On balance I conclude we would be better off without any standards on accounting measurement. There could still be some disclosure requirements for listed companies, though probably less than now.

Do you agree with this idea? Discuss. (*Note*: this issue has not been directly covered in the chapter, but you should be able to use your knowledge to try to come up with some points on both sides of the argument.)

5.6   The following is the segment reports of Tora plc, which manufactures and sells three main classes of product, for the year ended 31 December 2006.

	Paper £m	Plastic £m	Metal £m	Eliminations £m	Consolidation £m
Revenue					
External sales	420	280	140		
Inter-segment sales	20	10	15	(45)	
Total revenue	440	290	155	(45)	840
Result					
Segment result	80	65	45	(6)	184
Unallocated expenses					38
					146
Interest expense					(14)
Corporation tax					(26)
Profit for the year					106
Other information					
Segment assets	350	650	226		1,226
Unallocated assets					146
Consolidated total assets					1,372
Segment liabilities	55	150	42		247
Unallocated liabilities					60
Consolidated total liabilities					307
Capital expenditure	10	–	15		25
Depreciation	72	130	70		272

Required:

Analyse the performance of each of the business segments for the year and comment on your results.

5.7   Obtain a copy of an operating and financial review of two companies within the same industry. Compare the usefulness of each. In answering this question, you should consider the extent to which the OFRs incorporate the recommendations made by the Accounting Standards Board.

5.8   The following information has been extracted from the segmental report for 2006 for Carpetright plc, a leading carpet retailer.

Segmental analysis

The Group's primary reporting segment is geographic, as this is the basis on which the Group is organised and managed. The Group does not report a secondary segment on the basis of business operations because business operations throughout the Group are the same. The geographical sectors are: United Kingdom & Republic of Ireland ('UK & RoI'), and Poland, Belgium and The Netherlands ('Rest of Europe'). Central costs are incurred principally in the UK and are immaterial. As such these costs are included within the UK & RoI segment. Segment revenue, expense, result, assets and liabilities include transfers between geographical segments. Such transfers are priced at arm's length and are eliminated on consolidation.

Analysis by geography

	2006			2005		
	UK & RoI	Rest of Europe	Group	UK & RoI	Rest of Europe	Group
	£m	£m	£m	£m	£m	£m
Gross Revenue	400.7	53.7	454.4	411.8	53.3	465.1
Inter-segment revenue	(3.0)	–	(3.0)	(2.6)	–	(2.6)
Segment revenue						
(by origin and destination)	397.7	53.7	451.4	409.2	53.3	462.5
Gross profit	241.2	29.7	270.9	245.2	27.8	273.0
Operating profit						
before exceptional items	55.1	3.6	58.7	60.4	3.0	63.4
Segment result: operating	62.6	3.6	66.2	71.4	3.0	74.4
profit after exceptional items						
Net interest payable			(2.0)			(1.9)
Profit before taxation			64.2			72.5
Taxation			(20.1)			(23.2)
Profit for the financial period			44.1			49.3
Other non-cash expenses:						
Depreciation of property, plant and equipment	9.9	2.2	12.1	9.5	2.3	11.8
Depreciation of investment property	0.1	0.3	0.4	–	–	–
Amortisation of intangible assets	1.1	–	1.1	0.4	–	0.4
Impairment of goodwill	–	–	–	0.5	–	0.5
Share-based payments	0.4	–	0.4	0.2	–	0.2
Segment assets:						
Gross assets						
(by origin and destination)	163.1	74.8	237.9	151.9	64.2	216.1
Inter-segment balances	(0.4)	–	(0.4)	(4.0)	–	(4.0)
Total segment assets	162.7	74.8	237.5	147.9	64.2	212.1
Segment liabilities:						
Gross liabilities						
(by origin and destination)	110.0	15.0	125.0	100.9	15.8	116.7
Inter-segment balances	–	(0.4)	(0.4)	–	(4.0)	(4.0)
Total segment liabilities	110.0	14.6	124.6	100.9	11.8	112.7
Capital expenditure:						
Capital expenditure						
(by origin and destination)	30.8	4.3	35.1	23.6	9.5	33.1

Source: Carpetright plc Annual Report and Accounts 2006.

Required:

Analyse the performance of each of the major segments in so far as the information allows.

6

Measuring and reporting cash flows

Introduction

This chapter is devoted to the third major financial statement identified in Chapter 2 – the cash flow statement. This statement reveals the movements of cash over a period and the effect of these movements on the cash position of the business. It is an important financial statement because cash is vital to the survival of a business. Without cash, no business can operate.

In this chapter, we shall see how the cash flow statement is prepared and how the information that it contains may be interpreted. We shall also see why the deficiencies of the income statement in revealing cash flows over time make a separate cash flow statement necessary.

The cash flow statement is being considered after the chapter on limited companies because the format of the statement requires an understanding of this type of business. Limited companies are required to provide a cash flow statement, as well as the more traditional income statement and balance sheet, for shareholders and other interested parties.

Learning outcomes

When you have completed this chapter, you should be able to:

- Discuss the crucial importance of cash to a business.

- Explain the nature of the cash flow statement and discuss how it can be helpful in identifying cash flow problems.

- Prepare a cash flow statement.

- Interpret a cash flow statement.

The cash flow statement (or statement of cash flows)

The cash flow statement is a fairly recent addition to the set of financial statements sent to shareholders and to others. There used to be no regulation requiring companies to produce more than an income statement and a balance sheet. The prevailing view seems to have been that any financial information required would be contained within these two statements. This view may have been based partly on the assumption that if a business were profitable, it would also have plenty of cash. Though in the very long run this is likely to be true, it is not necessarily true in the short to medium term.

We have already seen in Chapter 3 that the income statement sets out the revenue and expenses, rather than the cash receipts and cash payments, for the period. Thus, profit (loss), which represents the difference between the revenue and expenses for the period, may have little or no relation to the cash generated for the period. To illustrate this point, let us take the example of a business making a sale (a revenue). This may well lead to an increase in wealth and will be reflected in the income statement. However, if the sale is made on credit, no cash changes hands – not at the time of sale at least. Instead, the increase in wealth is reflected in another asset – an increase in trade receivables. Furthermore, if an item of inventories is the subject of the sale, wealth is lost to the business through the reduction in the inventories. This means an expense is incurred in making the sale, which will be shown in the income statement. Once again, however, no cash has changed hands at the time of sale. For such reasons, the profit and the cash generated for a period will rarely go hand in hand.

The following activity helps to underline how profit and cash for a period may be affected differently by particular transactions or events.

Activity 6.1

The following is a list of business/accounting events. In each case, state the effect (increase, decrease or no effect) on both profit and cash:

		Effect	
		on profit	*on cash*
1	Repayment of borrowings	_____	_____
2	Making a sale on credit	_____	_____
3	Buying a current asset on credit	_____	_____
4	Receiving cash from a credit customer (trade receivable)	_____	_____
5	Depreciating a non-current asset	_____	_____
6	Buying some inventories for cash	_____	_____
7	Making a share issue for cash	_____	_____

You should have come up with the following:

		Effect	
		on profit	*on cash*
1	Repayment of borrowings	none	decrease
2	Making a sale on credit	increase	none
3	Buying a current asset on credit	none	none
4	Receiving cash from a credit customer (trade receivable)	none	increase
5	Depreciating a non-current asset	decrease	none
6	Buying some inventories for cash	none	decrease
7	Making a share issue for cash	none	increase

The reasons for these answers are as follows:

1 Repaying borrowings requires that cash be paid to the lender. Thus two figures in the balance sheet will be affected, but not the income statement.
2 Making a sale on credit will increase the sales revenue figure (and a profit or a loss – unless the sale was made for a price that precisely equalled the expenses involved). No cash will change hands at this point, however.
3 Buying a current asset on credit affects neither the cash balance nor the profit figure.
4 Receiving cash from a receivable increases the cash balance and reduces the credit customer's balance. Both of these figures are on the balance sheet. The income statement is unaffected.
5 Depreciating a non-current asset means that an expense is recognised. This causes the value of the asset, as it is recorded on the balance sheet, to fall by an amount equal to the amount of the expense. No cash is paid or received.
6 Buying some inventories for cash means that the value of the inventories will increase and the cash balance will decrease by a similar amount. Profit is not affected.
7 Making a share issue for cash increases the owners' claim and increases the cash balance; profit is unaffected.

It is clear from the above that if we are to gain an insight to cash movements over time, the income statement is not the answer. Instead we need a separate financial statement. This fact has become widely recognised in recent years and in 1991 a UK financial reporting standard, FRS 1, emerged that required all but the smallest companies to produce and publish a cash flow statement. This standard has been superseded for many companies from 2005 by the International Accounting Standard IAS 7. The two standards have broadly similar requirements. This chapter follows the provisions of IAS 7.

Why is cash so important?

It is worth asking why cash is so important. After all, cash is just an asset that the business needs to help it to function. In that sense, it is no different from inventories or non-current assets.

The reason for the importance of cash is that people and organisations will not normally accept other than cash in settlement of their claims against the business. If a business wants to employ people it must pay them in cash. If it wants to buy a new non-current asset to exploit a business opportunity, the seller of the asset will normally insist on being paid in cash, probably after a short period of credit. When businesses fail, it is their inability to find the cash to pay the amounts owed that really pushes them under.

These factors lead to cash being the pre-eminent business asset. It is the one that analysts tend to watch most carefully when trying to assess the ability of businesses to survive and/or to take advantage of commercial opportunities as they arise. The fact that cash and profits do not always go hand in hand is illustrated in **Real World 6.1**. This explains how Eurotunnel, the cross-channel business between England and France continues to struggle to achieve profit, yet generates positive cash flows.

Real World 6.1

Cash flows under the channel

FT

Richard Shirrefs [Eurotunnel's chief executive] called for a shift from 'a stable equilibrium of failure to a stable equilibrium of success'.

The company, which last restructured its long term debt in 2003, proposes to shift to a lower price, higher volume model for tunnel usage. Access rates for train operators would be reduced to entice them to introduce more services to more destinations, such as Amsterdam, and to encourage greater freight traffic.

Eurotunnel progressed its own plans for freight on Monday, announcing it expected to start a traction business in 2005 and that a platform designed to accept continental gauge freight trains would begin operations at Folkestone at the same time.

Mr Shirrefs said taxpayers had invested £10 bn and industry £15 bn in the tunnel and associated infrastructure and: 'We need to get all that infrastructure working . . . neither investor nor taxpayer is getting value'.

Last year was a difficult one for Eurotunnel with reduced cross channel passenger flows bringing fare competition from ferry operators.

The company's operating revenue was down 5 per cent at £566 m and its operating profit down 18 per cent at £170 m. With interest payments of £318 m, the underlying loss was up 40 per cent at £148 m. However, it maintained a positive cash flow of £290 m, down from £307 m in 2002.

Source: Shelley, Toby, extracts from 'Eurotunnel Takes £1.3 bn Impairment Charge', FT.com, 9 February 2004.

The main features of the cash flow statement

The cash flow statement is a summary of the cash receipts and payments over the period concerned. All payments of a particular type, for example cash payments to acquire additional non-current assets or other investments, are added together to give just one figure that appears in the statement. The net total of the statement is the net increase or decrease of the cash (and cash equivalents) of the business over the period. The statement is basically an analysis of the business's cash (and cash equivalents) movements for the period.

A definition of cash and cash equivalents

IAS 7 defines cash as notes and coins in hand and deposits in banks and similar institutions that are accessible to the business on demand. Cash equivalents are short-term, highly liquid investments that are readily convertible to known amounts of cash and which are subject to an insignificant risk of changes of value. Cash equivalents are held for the purpose of meeting short-term cash commitments rather than for investment or other purposes.

Activity 6.2 should clarify the types of items that fall within the definition of 'cash equivalents'.

Activity 6.2

At the end of its accounting period, Zeneb plc's balance sheet included the following items:

1 *A bank deposit account where one month's notice of withdrawal is required.* This deposit was made because the business has a temporary cash surplus that it will need to use in the short term for operating purposes.
2 *Ordinary shares in Jones plc (a Stock Exchange listed business).* These were acquired because the business has a temporary cash surplus and Zeneb plc's directors believed that the share represented a good short-term investment. The funds invested will need to be used in the short term for operating purposes.
3 *A bank deposit account that is withdrawable instantly.* This represents an investment of surplus funds that are not seen as being needed in the short term.
4 *An overdraft on the business's bank current account.*

Which (if any) of these four items would be included in the figure for cash and cash equivalents?

Your response should have been as follows:

1 A cash equivalent, because the deposit is part of the business's normal cash management activities and there is little doubt about how much cash will be obtained when the deposit is withdrawn.
2 Not a cash equivalent. Although the investment was made as part of normal cash management, there is a significant risk that the amount expected (hoped for!) when the shares are sold may not actually be forthcoming.
3 Not a cash equivalent, because this represents an investment, rather than a short-term surplus amount of cash.
4 This is cash itself, though a negative amount of it. The only exception to this classification would be where the business is financed in the longer term by an overdraft, when it would be part of the financing of the business.

As can be seen from the responses to Activity 6.2, whether a particular item falls within the definition of cash and cash equivalent depends on two factors:

● the nature of the item;
● why it has arisen.

In practice, it is not usually difficult to decide whether an item is a cash equivalent.

The relationship between the primary financial statements

The cash flow statement is now accepted, along with the income statement, the statement of changes in equity and the balance sheet, as a primary financial statement. The relationship between the four statements is shown in Figure 6.1. The balance sheet reflects the combination of assets (including cash) and claims (including the owners' claim) of the business *at a particular point in time*. The cash flow statement, the income statement and the statement of changes in equity explain the *changes over a period* to two of the items in the balance sheet. The cash flow statement explains the changes to cash. The income statement, together with the statement of changes in equity, explains changes to the owners' claim (equity).

Figure 6.1	The relationship between the balance sheet, the income statement, the statement of changes in equity and the cash flow statement

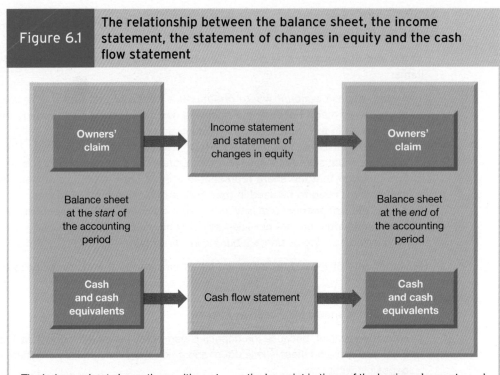

The balance sheet shows the position, at a particular point in time, of the business's assets and claims. The income statement explains how, over a period between two balance sheets, the owners' claim figure in the first balance sheet has altered as a result of trading operations. The statement of changes in equity explains how the owners' claim has altered, through non-trading actions, to become the owners' claim (equity) figure in the second balance sheet. The cash flow statement also looks at changes over the accounting period, but this statement explains the alteration in the cash (and cash equivalent) balances from the first to the second of the two consecutive balance sheets.

The form of the cash flow statement

The standard layout of the cash flow statement is summarised in Figure 6.2. Explanations of the terms used in the cash flow statement are given below.

Cash flows from operating activities

This is the net inflow or outflow from trading operations, after tax and financing costs. It is equal to the sum of cash receipts from trade receivables, and cash receipts from cash sales where relevant, less the sums paid to buy inventories, to pay rent, to pay wages and so on. From this are also deducted payments for interest on the business's borrowings, corporation tax and dividends paid.

Note that it is the amounts of cash received and paid during the period that feature in the cash flow statement, not the revenue and expenses for that period. It is, of course, the income statement that deals with the revenue and expenses. Similarly the tax and

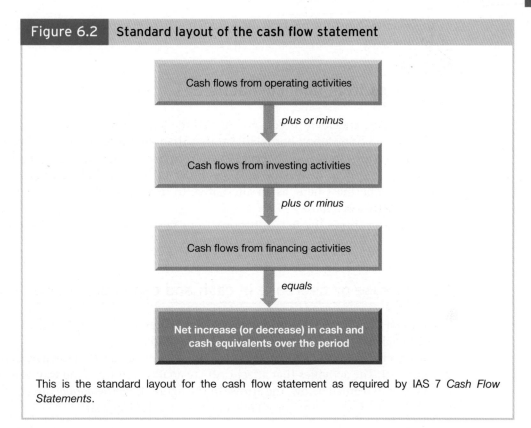

Figure 6.2 Standard layout of the cash flow statement

Cash flows from operating activities

plus or minus

Cash flows from investing activities

plus or minus

Cash flows from financing activities

equals

Net increase (or decrease) in cash and cash equivalents over the period

This is the standard layout for the cash flow statement as required by IAS 7 *Cash Flow Statements*.

dividend payments that appear in the cash flow statement are those made in the period of the statement. Companies normally pay tax on their profits in four equal instalments. Two of these are during the year concerned, and the other two are during the following year. Thus by the end of each accounting year, one half of the tax will have been paid and the remainder will be a current liability at the end of the year, to be paid off during the following year. During any particular year, therefore, the tax payment would normally equal 50 per cent of the previous year's tax charge and 50 per cent of that of the current year.

The net figure for this section is intended to indicate the net cash flows for the period that arose from normal day-to-day trading activities after taking account of the tax that has to be paid on them and the cost of servicing the finance (equity and borrowings) needed to support them.

Cash flows from investing activities

This section of the statement is concerned with cash payments made to acquire additional non-current assets and with cash receipts from the disposal of non-current assets. These non-current assets will tend to be the usual items such as buildings and machinery. They might also be loans made by the business or shares in another business bought by the business.

This section also includes receipts from investments (loans and equity investments) made outside the business. These receipts are interest on loans made by the business and dividends from shares in other businesses that are owned by the business.

This section shows the net cash flows from making new investments and/or disposing of existing ones.

Cash flows from financing activities

This part of the statement is concerned with the long-term financing of the business. So here we are considering borrowings (other than very short term) and finance from share issues. This category is concerned with repayment/redemption of finance as well as with the raising of it. It is permissible under IAS 7 to include dividend payments made by the business here, as an alternative to including them in 'Cash flows from operating activities' (above).

This section shows the net cash flows from raising and/or paying back long-term finance.

Net increase or decrease in cash and cash equivalents

The total of the statement must, of course, be the net increase or decrease in cash and cash equivalents over the period covered by the statement.

The effect on a business's cash and cash equivalents of its various activities is shown in Figure 6.3. The activities that affect cash are analysed in the same way as is required by IAS 7. As explained below, the arrows in the figure show the *normal* direction of cash flow for the typical healthy, profitable business in a typical year.

Figure 6.3	Diagrammatical representation of the cash flow statement

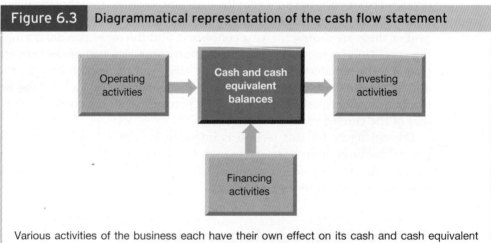

Various activities of the business each have their own effect on its cash and cash equivalent balances, either positive (increasing them) or negative (reducing them). The net increase or decrease in the cash and cash equivalent balances over a period will be the sum of these individual effects, taking account of the direction (cash in or cash out) of each activity.

Note that the direction of the arrow shows the *normal* direction of the cash flow in respect of each activity. In certain circumstances, each of these arrows could be reversed in direction.

The normal direction of cash flows

Normally 'operating activities' provide positive cash flows: that is, they help to increase the business's cash resources. In fact, for most UK businesses in most time periods, cash generated from day-to-day trading, even after deducting tax, interest and dividends, is overwhelmingly the most important source of new finance.

Activity 6.3

Last year's cash flow statement for Angus plc showed a negative cash flow from operating activities. What could be the reason for this, and should the business's management be alarmed by it? (*Hint*: we think that there are two broad possible reasons for a negative cash flow.)

The two reasons are:

- The business is unprofitable. This leads to more cash being paid out to employees, suppliers of goods and services, interest and so on, than is received from receivables in respect of sales. This would be particularly alarming, because a major expense for most businesses is depreciation of non-current assets. Since depreciation does not lead to a cash flow, it is not considered in 'net cash inflows from operating activities'. Thus, a negative operating cash flow might well indicate a very much larger trading loss – in other words, a significant loss of the business's wealth; something to concern management.
- The other reason might be less alarming. A business that is expanding its activities (level of sales revenue) would tend to spend quite a lot of cash, relative to the amount of cash coming in from sales. This is because it will probably be expanding its assets (non-current and current) to accommodate the increased demand. For example, a business may well need to have inventories in place before additional sales can be made. Even when the additional sales are made, these sales would normally be made on credit, with the cash inflow lagging behind the sale. All of this means that in the first instance, in cash flow terms, the business would not necessarily benefit from the additional sales revenue. This would be particularly likely to be true of a new business, which would be expanding inventories and other assets from zero. Expansion typically causes cash flow strains for the reasons just explained. This can be a particular problem because the business's increased profitability might encourage a feeling of optimism, which could lead to lack of attention being paid to the cash flow problem.

Investing activities typically cause net negative cash flows. This is because many types of non-current asset wear out, and many that do not wear out become obsolete. Also, businesses tend to seek to expand their asset base. When a business sells some non-current assets, the sale will give rise to positive cash flows, but in net terms the cash flows are normally negative with cash spent on new assets outweighing that received from disposal of old ones.

Financing can go in either direction, depending on the financing strategy at the time. Since businesses seek to expand, there is a general tendency for this area to lead to cash coming into the business rather than leaving it.

Real World 6.2 shows the summarised cash flow statement of Tesco plc, the UK-based supermarket.

Real World 6.2

Cashing in

The published, summarised cash flow statement for Tesco plc (the UK-based super-market) for the six months to 26 August 2006, shows the cash flows of the business under each of the headings described above:

Summarised cash flow statement for the half year to 26 August 2006

	£m
Net cash from operating activities	1,319
Net cash used in investing activities	(1,109)
Net cash used in financing activities	(124)
Net increase in cash and cash equivalents	86
Cash and cash equivalents at beginning of period	1,325
Effects of foreign exchange rate changes*	(21)
Cash and cash equivalents at end of period	1,390

[* This adjustment is required because transactions are undertaken by the business in different curren-cies and movements in exchange rates can lead to gains or losses.]

Source: adapted from www.tescocorporate.com.

As we shall see shortly, more detailed information under each of the main headings is provided when a cash flow statement for a full year is prepared.

Preparing the cash flow statement

Deducing net cash flows from operating activities

The first section of the cash flow statement is the 'cash flows from operating activities'. There are two methods that can be used to derive this figure: the direct method and the indirect method.

The direct method

→ The **direct method** involves an analysis of the cash records of the business for the period, picking out all payments and receipts relating to operating activities. These are summarised to give the total figures for inclusion in the cash flow statement. Done on the computer, this would be a simple matter, but not many businesses adopt this approach.

The indirect method

→ The **indirect method** is the more popular method. It relies on the fact that, broadly, sales revenue gives rise to cash inflows, and expenses give rise to outflows. This means that the profit for the year figure will be closely linked to the net cash inflows from operating activities. Since businesses have to produce an income statement in any case, information from it can be used as a starting point to deduce the cash flows from operating activities.

Of course, within a particular accounting period, profit for the year will not normally equal the net cash inflows from operating activities. We saw in Chapter 3 that, when sales are made on credit, the cash receipt occurs some time after the sale. This means that sales revenue made towards the end of an accounting year will be included in that year's income statement, but most of the cash from those sales will flow into the business, and should be included in the cash flow statement, in the following year. Fortunately it is easy to deduce the cash received from sales if we have the relevant income statement and balance sheets, as we shall see in Activity 6.4.

Activity 6.4

How can we deduce the cash inflows from sales using the income statement and balance sheet for the business?

The balance sheet will tell us how much was owed in respect of credit sales at the beginning and end of the year (trade receivables). The income statement tells us the sales revenue figure. If we adjust the sales revenue figure by the increase or decrease in trade receivables over the year, we deduce the cash from sales for the year.

Example 6.1

The sales revenue figure for a business for the year was £34 m. The trade receivables totalled £4 m at the beginning of the year, but had increased to £5 m by the end of the year.

Basically, the trade receivables figure is affected by sales revenue and cash receipts. It is increased when a sale is made and decreased when cash is received from a credit customer. If, over the year, the sales revenue and the cash receipts had been equal, the beginning-of-year and end-of-year trade receivables figures would have been equal. Since the trade receivables figure increased, it must mean that less cash was received than sales revenues were made. Thus, the cash receipts from sales must be £33 m (that is, 34 − (5 − 4)).

Put slightly differently, we can say that as a result of sales, assets of £34 m flowed into the business during the year. If £1 m of this went to increasing the asset of trade receivables, this leaves only £33 m that went to increase cash.

The same general point is true in respect of nearly all of the other items that are taken into account in deducing the operating profit figure. The exception is depreciation. This is not necessarily associated with any movement in cash during the accounting period.

All of this means that we can take the profit before taxation (that is, the profit after interest but before taxation) for the year, add back the depreciation and interest expense charged in arriving at that profit, and adjust this total by movements in inventories, trade receivables and payables. If we then go on to deduct payments made during the accounting period for taxation, interest on borrowings and dividends, we have the net cash from operating activities.

Example 6.2

The relevant information from the financial statements of Dido plc for last year is as follows:

	£m
Profit before taxation (after interest)	122
Depreciation charged in arriving at profit before taxation	34
Interest expense	6
At the beginning of the year	
Inventories	15
Trade receivables	24
Trade payables	18
At the end of the year	
Inventories	17
Trade receivables	21
Trade payables	19

The following further information is available about payments during last year:

	£m
Taxation paid	32
Interest paid	5
Dividends paid	9

The cash flow from operating activities is derived as follows:

	£m	£m
Profit before taxation (after interest)		122
Add Depreciation	34	
Interest expense	6	40
		162
Less Increase in inventories (17 – 15)		(2)
Add Decrease in trade receivables (21 – 24)	3	
Increase in trade payables (19 – 18)	1	4
Cash generated from operations		164
Less Interest paid	5	
Taxation paid	32	
Dividends paid	9	46
Net cash from operating activities		118

Thus, the net increase in working capital, as a result of trading, was £162 million. Of this, £2 million went into increased inventories. More cash was received from trade receivables than sales revenues were made, and less cash was paid to trade payables than purchases of goods and services on credit. Both of these had a favourable effect on cash, which increased by £164 million. When account was taken of the payments for interest, tax and dividends, the net cash flow from operating activities was £118 million (inflow).

Note that we needed to adjust the profit before taxation (after interest) by the depreciation and interest expenses to derive the profit before depreciation, interest and taxation.

The indirect method of deducing the net cash flow from operating activities is summarised in Figure 6.4.

Figure 6.4	The indirect method of deducing the net cash flows from operating activities

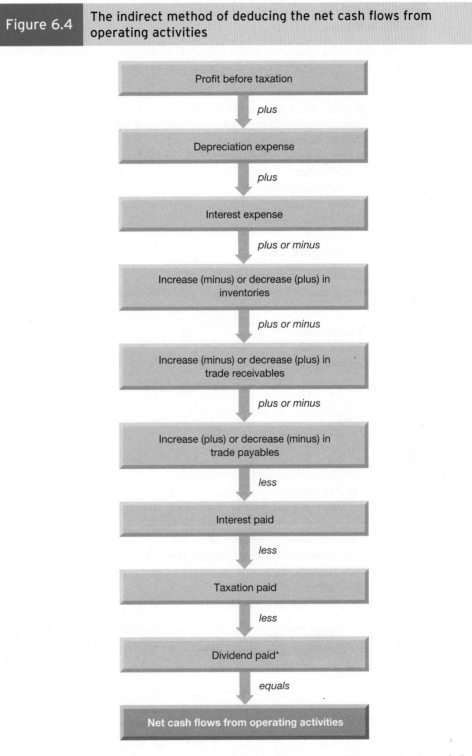

Determining the net cash from operating activities firstly involves adding back the depreciation and the interest expense to the profit before taxation. Next, adjustment is made for increases or decreases in inventories, trade receivables and trade payables. Lastly, cash paid for interest, taxation and dividends is deducted.

* Note that dividends could alternatively be included under the heading 'Cash flows from financing activities'.

Activity 6.5

The relevant information from the financial statements of Pluto plc for last year is as follows:

	£m
Profit before taxation (after interest)	165
Depreciation charged in arriving at operating profit	41
Interest expense	21
At the beginning of the year:	
Inventories	22
Trade receivables	18
Trade payables	15
At the end of the year:	
Inventories	23
Trade receivables	21
Trade payables	17

The following further information is available about payments during last year:

	£m
Taxation paid	49
Interest paid	25
Dividends paid	28

What figure should appear in the cash flow statement for 'Cash flows from operating activities'?

Net cash inflows from operating activities:

	£m	£m
Profit before taxation (after interest)		165
Add Depreciation	41	
Interest expense	21	62
		227
Less Increase in inventories (23 − 22)	1	
Increase in trade receivables (21 − 18)	3	(4)
Add Increase in trade payables (17 − 15)		2
Cash generated from operations		225
Less Interest paid	25	
Taxation paid	49	
Dividends paid	28	(102)
Net cash from operating activities		123

Figure 6.4 shows how the net cash flow from operating activities is derived.

Deducing the other areas of the cash flow statement

We can now go on to take a look at the preparation of a complete cash flow statement through Example 6.3.

Example 6.3

Torbryan plc's income statement for the year ended 31 December 2007 and the balance sheets as at 31 December 2006 and 2007 are as follows:

Income statement for the year ended 31 December 2007

	£m
Revenue	576
Cost of sales	(307)
Gross profit	269
Distribution expenses	(65)
Administrative expenses	(26)
	178
Other operating income	21
Operating profit	199
Interest receivable	17
	216
Interest payable	(23)
Profit before taxation	193
Taxation	(46)
Profit for the year	147

Balance sheets as at 31 December 2006 and 2007

	2006 £m	2007 £m
Non-current assets		
Property, plant and equipment		
Land and buildings	241	241
Plant and machinery	309	325
	550	566
Current assets		
Inventories	44	41
Trade receivables	121	139
	165	180
Total assets	715	746
Equity		
Called-up ordinary share capital	150	200
Share premium account	–	40
Retained earnings	26	123
	176	363
Non-current liabilities		
Borrowings – Loan notes	400	250
Current liabilities		
Borrowings (all bank overdraft)	68	56
Trade payables	55	54
Taxation	16	23
	139	133
Total equity and liabilities	715	746

→

Example 6.3 continued

During 2007, the business spent £95 million on additional plant and machinery. There were no other non-current-asset acquisitions or disposals. A dividend of £50 million was paid on ordinary shares during the year. The interest receivable revenue and the interest payable expenses for the year were equal to the cash inflow and outflow respectively.

The cash flow statement would be as follows:

Torbryan plc
Cash flow statement for the year ended 31 December 2007

	£m	£m
Cash flows from operating activities		
Profit before taxation (after interest) (see Note 1 below)		193
Adjustments for:		
Depreciation (Note 2)		79
Interest receivable (Note 3)		(17)
Interest payable (Note 4)		23
		278
Increase in trade receivables (139 – 121)		(18)
Decrease in trade payables (55 – 54)		(1)
Decrease in inventories (44 – 41)		3
Cash generated from operations		262
Interest paid		(23)
Taxation paid (Note 5)		(39)
Dividend paid		(50)
Net cash from operating activities		150
Cash flows from investing activities		
Payments to acquire tangible non-current assets	(95)	
Interest received (Note 3)	17	
Net cash used in investing activities		(78)
Cash flows from financing activities		
Repayments of loan notes (Note 6)	(150)	
Issue of ordinary shares (Note 7)	90	
Net cash used in financing activities		(60)
Net increase in cash and cash equivalents		12
Cash and cash equivalents at 1 January 2007 (Note 8)		(68)
Cash and cash equivalents at 31 December 2007		(56)

To see how this relates to the cash of the business at the beginning and end of the year it can be useful to provide a reconciliation as follows:

Analysis of cash and cash equivalents during the year ended 31 December 2007

	£m
Overdraft balance at 1 January 2007	(68)
Net cash inflow	12
Overdraft balance at 31 December 2007	(56)

Notes
1 This is simply taken from the income statement for the year.
2 Since there were no disposals, the depreciation charges must be the difference between the start and end of the year's plant and machinery (non-current assets) values, adjusted by the cost of any additions.

	£m
Carrying amount at 1 January 2007	309
Additions	95
	404
Depreciation (balancing figure)	(79)
Carrying amount at 31 December 2007	325

3 Interest receivable must be taken away to work towards the profit before crediting it, because it is not part of operations, but of investing activities. The cash inflow from this source appears under the 'Cash flows from investing activities' heading.

4 Interest payable expense must be taken out, by adding it back to the profit figure. We subsequently deduct the cash paid for interest payable during the year. In this case the two figures are identical.

5 Taxation is paid by companies 50 per cent during their accounting year and 50 per cent in the following year. Thus, the 2007 payment would have been half the tax on the 2006 profit (that is, the figure that would have appeared in the current liabilities at the end of 2006), plus half of the 2007 taxation charge (that is, $16 + (^1/_2 \times 46) = 39$). Probably the easiest way to deduce the amount paid during the year to 31 December 2007 is by following this approach:

	£m
Taxation owed at start of the year (from the balance sheet as at 31 December 2006)	16
Taxation charge for the year (from the income statement)	46
	62
Less Taxation owed at the end of the year (from the balance sheet as at 31 December 2007)	(23)
Taxation paid during the year	39

This follows the logic that if we start with what the business owed at the beginning of the year, add the increase in what was owed as a result of the current year's taxation charge and then deduct what was owed at the end, the resulting figure must be what was paid during the year.

6 It has been assumed that the loan notes were redeemed for their balance sheet value. This is not, however, always the case.

7 The share issue raised £90 million, of which £50 million went into the share capital total on the balance sheet and £40 million into share premium.

8 There were no 'cash equivalents', just cash (though negative).

What does the cash flow statement tell us?

The cash flow statement tells us how the business has generated cash during the period and where that cash has gone. Since cash is properly regarded as the lifeblood of just about any business, this is potentially very useful information.

Tracking the sources and uses of cash over several years could show financing trends that a reader of the statements could use to help to make judgements about the likely future behaviour of the business.

Looking specifically at the cash flow statement for Torbryan plc, in Example 6.3, we can see the following:

● Net cash flow from operations was strong, much larger than the profit for the year figure, after taking account of the dividend paid. This would be expected because depreciation is deducted in arriving at profit. There was a general tendency for working capital to absorb some cash. This would not be surprising had there been an expansion of activity (sales revenue) over the year. From the information supplied, we do not know whether there was an expansion or not. (We have only one year's income statement.)

- There were net outflows of cash for investing activities, but this would not be unusual. Many items of property, plant and equipment have limited lives and need to be replaced with new ones. The expenditure during the year was not out of line with the depreciation expense for the year, which is what we might expect.
- There was a fairly major outflow of cash to redeem some borrowings, partly offset by the proceeds of a share issue. This presumably represents a change of financing strategy. Together with the ploughed-back profit from trading, there has been a significant shift in the equity/borrowings balance.

Real World 6.3 indicates the importance of the cash flow statement in analysing the health of one well-known business.

Real World 6.3

Watching the cash flows   **FT**

When WaterfordWedgwood reports its annual results today, brokers will be focused not just on the income statement of the crystal and porcelain manufacturer, or the balance sheet – the traditional windows on the health of a company – but on the cash flow statement.

Brokers, in particular, are looking for signs of improvement in the working capital position – the company's ability to squeeze more cash from suppliers, to get paid earlier by its customers and reduce the amount of costly product held in its warehouses or elsewhere in the supply chain.

The signs are mixed. The company this month warned that profits for the period to March 31 would be €12m (£8 m) or 15 per cent shy of what it had been predicting in January.

It cited difficulties at its German porcelain subsidiary. It was also hit when US stores did not restock after the Christmas sales.

The poorer trading means inventories levels should be lower. On the other hand, there is less cash generated to pay down the debt . . .

Going forward, the big challenge is to extract more cash from the businesses. Accenture, the consultant, has been asked to look at the issue.

John Sheehan, at NCB stockbrokers, anticipates big inventories write-offs. 'The real issue is can they do this without saturating the market and hurting the brand?' he asks.

On the manufacturing side, the company is adopting a twin approach, outsourcing the manufacturing to cheaper locations while harnessing big-name designers to appeal to a younger consumer.

Source: 'WaterfordWedgwood Faces Some Intense Questions Over Its Cash Flow', *Financial Times*, 17 June 2004, FT.com.

Real World 6.4 looks at the cash flow statement of an emerging business, LiDCO Group plc, that is experiencing negative cash flows as it seeks to establish a profitable market for its products.

Real World 6.4

Not losing heart

LiDCO Group plc is a smaller business whose shares are listed on the Alternative Investment Market (AIM). AIM is a section of the London Stock Exchange that specialises in providing a market for the shares of smaller up and coming businesses.

LiDCO makes highly sophisticated equipment for monitoring the hearts of cardiac patients, typically in hospitals and clinics. The business was started by four doctors and scientists. It has spent £6.8 million over 10 years developing its products, obtaining registration for their use from both the UK and US authorities and creating manufacturing facilities.

LiDCO's cash flow statement for the year to 31 Janua

Cash flows from operating activities
Profit before taxation
Depreciation
Decrease in inventories
Increase in trade receivables
Decrease in trade payables

Cash flows from investing activities

Payments to acquire tangible non-current assets	(55)	
Payments to acquire intangible non-current assets	(362)	
Interest received	42	
Net cash inflow from investing activities		(375)
Cash flows from financing activities		
Issue of ordinary share capital	203	
Convertible loan	1,355	
Net cash inflow from financing activities		1,558
Net decrease in cash and cash equivalents		(656)

To put these figures into context, the sales revenue for the year was £3,421,000. This means that the net cash outflow from operating activities was equal to over 50 per cent of the revenue figure. Such cash flow profiles are fairly typical of 'high-tech' businesses that have enormous start-up costs to bring their products to the market in sufficient quantities to yield a profit. Of course, not all such businesses achieve this, but LiDCO seems confident of success.

Source: information taken from LiDCO Group plc Annual Report 2006; and AIM company profile, www.londonstockexchange.com.

Self-assessment question 6.1

Touchstone plc's income statements for the years ended 31 December 2006 and 2007 and the balance sheets as at 31 December 2006 and 2007 are as follows:

Income statements for the years ended 2006 and 2007

	2006	2007
	£m	£m
Revenue	173	207
Cost of sales	(96)	(101)
Gross profit	77	106
Distribution expenses	(18)	(20)
Administrative expenses	(24)	(26)
	35	60
Other operating income	3	4
Operating profit	38	64
Interest payable	(2)	(4)
Profit before taxation	36	60
Taxation	(8)	(16)
Profit for the year	28	44

→

Balance sheets as at 31 December 2006 and 2007

	2005 £m	2006 £m
Non-current assets		
Property, plant and equipment		
Land and buildings	94	110
Plant and machinery	53	62
	147	172
Current assets		
Inventories	25	24
Treasury bills (short-term investments)	–	15
Trade receivables	16	26
Cash at bank and in hand	4	4
	45	69
Total assets	192	241
Equity		
Called-up ordinary share capital	100	100
Retained earnings	30	56
	130	156
Non-current liabilities		
Borrowings – Loan notes (10%)	20	40
Current liabilities		
Trade payables	38	37
Taxation	4	8
	42	45
Total equity and liabilities	192	241

Included in 'cost of sales', 'distribution costs' and 'administration expenses', depreciation was as follows:

	2006 £m	2007 £m
Land and buildings	5	6
Plant and machinery	6	10

There were no non-current asset disposals in either year.

The interest payable expense equalled the cash payment made during the year.

Dividends were paid on ordinary shares of £14 million during 2006 and £18 million during 2007.

The Treasury bills represent a short-term investment of funds that will be used shortly in operations. There is insignificant risk that this investment will lose value.

Required:

Prepare a cash flow statement for the business for 2007.

The answer to this question can be found at the back of the book on p. 404.

Summary

The main points of this chapter may be summarised as follows:

The need for a cash flow statement

- Cash is important because no business can operate without it.
- The cash flow statement is specifically designed to reveal movements in cash over a period.
- Cash movements cannot be readily detected from the income statement, which focuses on revenue and expenses rather than on cash receipts and cash payments.
- Profit (loss) and cash generated for the period are rarely equal.
- The cash flow statement is a primary financial statement, along with the income statement, the balance sheet and the statement of changes in equity.

Preparing the cash flow statement

- The layout of the statement contains three categories of cash movement:
  - cash flows from operating activities;
  - cash flows from investing activities;
  - cash flows from financing activities.
- The total of the cash movements under these three categories will provide the net increase or decrease in cash and cash equivalents for the period.
- A reconciliation can be undertaken to check that the opening balance of cash and cash equivalents plus the net increase (decrease) for the period equals the closing balance.

Calculating the cash generated from operations

- The net cash flows from operating activities can be derived by either the direct method or the indirect method.
- The direct method is based on an analysis of the cash records for the period, whereas the indirect method uses information contained within the income statement and balance sheets of the business.
- The indirect method takes the net operating profit for the period, adds back any depreciation charge and then adjusts for changes in inventories, receivables and payables during the period.

Interpreting the cash flow statement

- The cash flow statement shows the main sources and uses of cash.
- Tracking the cash movements over several periods may reveal financing and investing patterns and may help predict future management action.

→ Key terms

Direct method   p. 182
Indirect method   p. 182

Further reading

If you would like to explore the topics covered in this chapter in more depth, we recommend the following books:

KPMG (2006) *KPMG's Practical Guide to International Financial Reporting Standards*, 3rd edn, Thomson, Section 2.4.

Elliott, B. and Elliott, J. (2006) *Financial Accounting and Reporting*, 11th edn, Financial Times Prentice Hall, Chapter 27.

Sutton, T. (2004) *Corporate Financial Accounting and Reporting*, 2nd edn, Financial Times Prentice Hall, Chapters 6 and 18.

Review questions

Answers to these questions can be found at the back of the book on pp. 413–14.

6.1 The typical business outside the service sector has about 50 per cent more of its resources tied up in inventories than in cash, yet there is no call for an 'inventories flow statement' to be prepared. Why is cash regarded as more important than inventories?

6.2 What is the difference between the direct and indirect methods of deducing cash generated from operations?

6.3 Taking each of the categories of the cash flow statement in turn, in which direction would you normally expect the cash flow to be? Explain your answer.

(a) Cash flows from operating activities.
(b) Cash flows from investing activities.
(c) Cash flows from financing activities.

6.4 What causes the profit for the year not to equal the net cash inflow?

Exercises

Exercises 6.3 to 6.8 are more advanced than 6.1 and 6.2. Those with a coloured number have answers at the back of the book starting on p. 430.

If you wish to try more exercises, visit the students' side of the Companion Website.

6.1 How will each of the following events ultimately affect the amount of cash?

(a) An increase in the level of inventories.
(b) A rights issue of ordinary shares.
(c) A bonus issue of ordinary shares.
(d) Writing off part of the value of some inventories.
(e) The disposal of a large number of the business's shares by a major shareholder.
(f) Depreciating a non-current asset.

6.2 The following information has been taken from the financial statements of Juno plc for last year and the year before last:

	Year before last £m	Last year £m
Operating profit	156	187
Depreciation charged in arriving at operating profit	47	55
Inventories held at the end of:	27	31
Receivables at the end of:	24	23
Payables at the end of:	15	17

Required:
What is the cash generated from operations figure for Juno plc for last year?

6.3   Torrent plc's income statement for the year ended 31 December 2007 and the balance sheets as at 31 December 2006 and 2007 are as follows:

Income statement

	£m
Revenue	623
Cost of sales	(353)
Gross profit	270
Distribution expenses	(71)
Administrative expenses	(30)
	169
Rental income	27
Operating profit	196
Interest payable	(26)
Profit before taxation	170
Taxation	(36)
Profit for the year	134

Balance sheets as at 31 December 2006 and 2007

	2006 £m	2007 £m
Non-current assets		
Property, plant and equipment		
Land and buildings	310	310
Plant and machinery	325	314
	635	624
Current assets		
Inventories	41	35
Trade receivables	139	145
	180	180
Total assets	815	804
Equity		
Called-up ordinary share capital	200	300
Share premium account	40	–
Revaluation reserve	69	9
Retained earnings	123	197
	432	506
Non-current liabilities		
Borrowings – Loan notes	250	150
Current liabilities		
Borrowings (all bank overdraft)	56	89
Trade payables	54	41
Taxation	23	18
	133	148
Total equity and liabilities	815	804

During 2007, the business spent £67 million on additional plant and machinery. There were no other non-current asset acquisitions or disposals.

There was no share issue for cash during the year. The interest payable expense was equal in amount to the cash outflow. A dividend of £60 million was paid.

***Required*:**
Prepare the cash flow statement for Torrent plc for the year ended 31 December 2007.

6.4 Chen plc's income statements for the years ended 31 December 2006 and 2007 and the balance sheets as at 31 December 2006 and 2007 are as follows:

Income statement

	2006	2007
	£m	£m
Revenue	207	153
Cost of sales	(101)	(76)
Gross profit	106	77
Distribution expenses	(22)	(20)
Administrative expenses	(20)	(28)
Operating profit	64	29
Interest payable	(4)	(4)
Profit before taxation	60	25
Taxation	(16)	(6)
Profit for the year	44	19

Balance sheets as at 31 December 2006 and 2007

	2006	2007
	£m	£m
Non-current assets		
Property, plant and equipment		
Land and buildings	110	130
Plant and machinery	62	56
	172	186
Current assets		
Inventories	24	25
Trade receivables	26	25
Cash at bank and in hand	19	–
	69	50
Total assets	241	236
Equity		
Called-up ordinary share capital	100	100
Retained earnings	56	57
	156	157
Non-current liabilities		
Borrowings – Loan notes (10%)	40	40
Current liabilities		
Borrowings (all bank overdraft)	–	2
Trade payables	37	34
Taxation	8	3
	45	39
Total equity and liabilities	241	236

Included in 'cost of sales', 'distribution costs' and 'administrative expenses', depreciation was as follows:

	2006	2007
	£m	£m
Land and buildings	6	10
Plant and machinery	10	12

There were no non-current asset disposals in either year. The amount of cash paid for interest equalled the expense in both years. Dividends were paid totalling £18 million in each year.

Required:
Prepare a cash flow statement for the business for 2007.

6.5 The following are the financial statements for Nailsea plc for the years ended 30 June 2006 and 2007:

Income statement for years ended 30 June

	2006 £m	2007 £m
Revenue	1,230	2,280
Operating expenses	(722)	(1,618)
Depreciation	(270)	(320)
Operating profit	238	342
Interest payable	–	(27)
Profit before taxation	238	315
Taxation	(110)	(140)
Profit for the year	128	175

Balance sheets as at 30 June

	2006 £m	2007 £m
Non-current assets		
Property, plant and equipment (at carrying amount)		
Land and buildings	1,500	1,900
Plant and machinery	810	740
	2,310	2,640
Current assets		
Inventories	275	450
Trade receivables	100	250
Bank	–	118
	375	818
Total assets	2,685	3,458
Equity		
Share capital (fully paid £1 shares)	1,400	1,600
Share premium account	200	300
Retained profits	828	958
	2,428	2,858
Non-current liabilities		
Borrowings – 9% Loan notes (repayable 2011)	–	300
Current liabilities		
Borrowings (all bank overdraft)	32	–
Trade payables	170	230
Taxation	55	70
	257	300
Total equity and liabilities	2,685	3,458

There were no disposals of non-current assets in either year.

Dividends were paid in 2006 and 2007 of £40 million and £45 million, respectively.

Required:

Prepare a cash flow statement for Nailsea plc for the year ended 30 June 2007.

6.6 The following financial statements for Blackstone plc are a slightly simplified set of published accounts. Blackstone plc is an engineering business that developed a new range of products in 2005; these products now account for 60 per cent of its turnover.

Income statement for the years ended 31 March

	Notes	2006 £m	2007 £m
Revenue		7,003	11,205
Cost of sales		(3,748)	(5,809)
Gross profit		3,255	5,396
Operating expenses		(2,205)	(3,087)
Operating profit		1,050	2,309
Interest payable	1	(216)	(456)
Profit before taxation		834	1,853
Taxation		(210)	(390)
Profit for the year		624	1,463

Balance sheets as at 31 March

	Notes	2005 £m	2006 £m
Non-current assets			
Property, plant and equipment	2	4,300	7,535
Intangible assets	3	–	700
		4,300	8,235
Current assets			
Inventories		1,209	2,410
Trade receivables		641	1,173
Cash at bank		123	–
		1,973	3,583
Total assets		6,273	11,818
Equity			
Share capital		1,800	1,800
Share premium		600	600
Capital reserves		352	352
Retained profits		685	1,748
		3,437	4,500
Non-current liabilities			
Borrowings – Bank loan (repayable 2011)		1,800	3,800
Current liabilities			
Trade payables		931	1,507
Taxation		105	195
Borrowings (all bank overdraft)			
		–	1,816
		1,036	3,518
Total equity and liabilities		6,273	11,818

Notes
1 The expense and the cash outflow for interest payable are equal.
2 The movements in property, plant and equipment during the year are set out below.
3 Intangible assets represent the amounts paid for the goodwill of another engineering business acquired during the year.

	Land and buildings £m	Plant and machinery £m	Fixtures and fittings £m	Total £m
Cost				
At 1 April 2006	4,500	3,850	2,120	10,470
Additions	–	2,970	1,608	4,578
Disposals	–	(365)	(216)	(581)
At 31 March 2007	4,500	6,455	3,512	14,467
Depreciation				
At 1 April 2006	1,275	3,080	1,815	6,170
Charge for year	225	745	281	1,251
Disposals	–	(305)	(184)	(489)
At 31 March 2007	1,500	3,520	1,912)	6,932
Carrying amount				
At 31 March 2007	3,000	2,935	1,600	7,535

Proceeds from the sale of non-current assets in the year ended 31 March 2007 amounted to £54 million.

4 Dividends were paid on ordinary shares of £300 million in 2006 and £400 million in 2007.

Required:

Prepare a cash flow statement for Blackstone plc for the year ended 31 March 2007. (*Hint*: a loss (deficit) on disposal of non-current assets is simply an additional amount of depreciation and should be dealt with as such in preparing the cash flow statement.)

6.7   Simplified financial statements for York plc are as follows:

York plc
Income statement for the year ended 30 September 2007

	£m
Revenue	290.0
Cost of sales	(215.0)
Gross profit	75.0
Operating expenses (Note 1)	(62.0)
Operating profit	13.0
Interest payable (Note 2)	(3.0)
Profit before taxation	10.0
Taxation	(2.6)
Profit for the year	7.4

Balance sheet at 30 September

	2006 £m	2007 £m
Non-current assets (Note 4)	80.0	85.0
Current assets		
Inventories and trade receivables	119.8	122.1
Cash at bank	9.2	16.6
	129.0	138.7
Total assets	209.0	223.7
Equity		
Share capital	35.0	40.0
Share premium account	30.0	30.0
Reserves	31.0	34.9
	96.0	104.9
Non-current liabilities		
Borrowings	32.0	35.0
Current liabilities		
Trade payables	80.0	82.5
Taxation	1.0	1.3
	81.0	83.8
Total equity and liabilities	209.0	223.7

Notes

1 Operating expenses include depreciation of £13 m and a surplus of £3.2 m on the sale of non-current assets.

2 The expense and the cash outflow for interest payable are equal.

3 A dividend of £3.5 million was paid during 2007.

4 Non-current asset costs and depreciation:

	Cost	Accumulated depreciation	Carrying amount
	£m	£m	£m
At 1 October 2006	120.0	40.0	80.0
Disposals	(10.0)	(8.0)	(2.0)
Additions	20.0		20.0
Depreciation		13.0	(13.0)
At 30 September 2007	130.0	45.0	85.0

Required:

Prepare a cash flow statement for York plc for the year ended 30 September 2007.

6.8 The balance sheets of Axis plc as at 31 December 2006 and 2007 and the income statement for the year ended 31 December 2007 were as follows:

Balance sheet as at 31 December

	2006		2007	
	£m	£m	£m	£m
Non-current assets				
Property, plant and equipment				
Land and building at cost	130		130	
Accumulated depreciation	(30)	100	(32)	98
Plant and machinery at cost	70		80	
Accumulated depreciation	(17)	53	(23)	57
		153		155
Current assets				
Inventories		25		24
Trade receivables		16		26
Short-term investments		–		12
Cash at bank and in hand		–		7
		41		69
Total assets		194		224
Equity				
Share capital		100		100
Retained earnings		36		40
		136		140
Non-current liabilities				
Borrowings – 10% loan notes		20		40
Current liabilities				
Trade payables		31		36
Taxation		7		8
		38		44
Total equity and liabilities		194		224

Income statement for the year ended 31 December 2007

	£m
Revenue	173
Cost of sales	(96)
Gross profit	77
Interest receivable	2
	79
Sundry operating expenses	(24)
Deficit on sale of non-current asset	(1)
Depreciation – buildings	(2)
– plant	(16)
Operating profit	36
Interest payable	(2)
Profit before taxation	34
Taxation	(16)
Profit for the year	18

During the year, plant (a non-current asset) costing £15 m and with accumulated depreciation of £10 m was sold.

The short-term investments were government securities, where there was little or no risk of loss of value.

The expense and the cash outflow for interest payable were equal.

During 2007 a dividend of £14 million was paid.

Required:

Prepare a cash flow statement for Axis plc for the year ended 31 December 2007.

7

Analysing and interpreting financial statements (1)

Introduction

In this chapter we consider the analysis and interpretation of the financial statements discussed in earlier chapters. We shall see how financial (or accounting) ratios can help in developing a financial profile of a business and in assessing its financial health. Ratios can be used to examine various aspects of financial position and performance and are widely used for planning and control purposes.

The analysis and interpretation of financial statements is an important area that we shall continue to examine in Chapter 8.

Learning outcomes

When you have completed this chapter, you should be able to:

- Explain how ratios can be used to assess the position and performance of a business.

- Identify the major categories of ratios that can be used for analysis purposes.

- Calculate key ratios for assessing the profitability, efficiency, liquidity and gearing of a business.

- Explain the significance of the ratios calculated.

Financial ratios

Financial ratios provide a quick and relatively simple means of assessing the financial health of a business. A ratio simply relates one figure appearing in the financial statements to some other figure appearing there (for example, operating profit in relation to capital employed) or, perhaps, to some resource of the business (for example, operating profit per employee, sales revenue per square metre of selling space and so on).

Ratios can be very helpful when comparing the financial health of different businesses. Differences may exist between businesses in the scale of operations, and so a direct comparison of, say, the operating profit generated by each business may be misleading. By expressing operating profit in relation to some other measure (for example, capital (or funds) employed), the problem of scale is eliminated. A business with an operating profit of, say, £10,000 and capital employed of £100,000 can be compared with a much larger business with an operating profit of, say, £80,000 and sales revenue of £1,000,000 by the use of a simple ratio. The operating profit to capital employed ratio for the smaller business is 10 per cent ([10,000/100,000] × 100%) and the same ratio for the larger business is 8 per cent ([80,000/1,000,000] × 100%). These ratios can be directly compared whereas comparison of the absolute operating profit figures would be less meaningful. The need to eliminate differences in scale through the use of ratios can also apply when comparing the performance of the same business over time.

By calculating a relatively small number of ratios, it is often possible to build up a good picture of the position and performance of a business. It is not surprising, therefore, that ratios are widely used by those who have an interest in businesses and business performance. Though ratios are not difficult to calculate, they can be difficult to interpret and so it is important to appreciate that they are really only the starting point for further analysis.

Ratios help to highlight the financial strengths and weaknesses of a business, but they cannot, by themselves, explain why those strengths or weaknesses exist, or why certain changes have occurred. Only a detailed investigation will reveal these underlying reasons. Ratios tend to enable us to know which questions to ask, rather than providing the answers.

Ratios can be expressed in various forms, for example as a percentage or as a proportion. The way that a particular ratio is presented will depend on the needs of those who will use the information. Although it is possible to calculate a large number of ratios, only a relatively few, based on key relationships, tend to be helpful to a particular user. Many ratios that could be calculated from the financial statements (for example, rent payable in relation to current assets) may not be considered because there is no clear or meaningful relationship between the two items.

There is no generally accepted list of ratios that can be applied to the financial statements, nor is there a standard method of calculating many ratios. Variations in both the choice of ratios and their calculation will be found in practice. However, it is important to be consistent in the way in which ratios are calculated for comparison purposes. The ratios that we shall now go on to discuss are those that are widely used. They are popular because many consider them to be among the more important for decision-making purposes.

Financial ratio classifications

Ratios can be grouped into categories, each of which relates to a particular aspect of financial performance or position. The following broad categories provide a useful basis for explaining the nature of the financial ratios to be dealt with. There are five of them:

- *Profitability*. Businesses generally exist with the primary purpose of creating wealth for their owners. Profitability ratios provide an insight to the degree of success in achieving this purpose. They express the profit made (or figures bearing on profit, such as sales revenue or overheads) in relation to other key figures in the financial statements or to some business resource.
- *Efficiency*. Ratios may be used to measure the efficiency with which particular resources have been used within the business. These ratios are also referred to as *activity* ratios.
- *Liquidity*. It is vital to the survival of a business that there are sufficient liquid resources available to meet maturing obligations (that is, amounts owing that must be paid in the relatively near future). Some liquidity ratios examine the relationship between liquid resources held and amounts due for payment in the near future.
- *Financial gearing*. This is the relationship between the contribution to financing the business made by the owners of the business and the amount contributed by others, in the form of loans. The level of gearing has an important effect on the degree of risk associated with a business, as we shall see. Gearing is, therefore, something that managers must consider when making financing decisions.
- *Investment*. Certain ratios are concerned with assessing the returns and performance of shares held in a particular business, from the perspective of shareholders who are not involved with the management of the business.

When analysing financial statements, the analysts must be clear about *who* the target users are and *why* they need the information. Different users are likely to have different information needs, which will in turn determine the ratios that they find useful. For example, shareholders are likely to be interested in their returns in relation to the level of risk associated with their investment. Profitability, investment and gearing ratios will, therefore, be of particular interest. Long-term lenders are concerned with the long-term viability of the business and to help them to assess this, the profitability and gearing ratios of the business are also likely to be of particular interest. Short-term lenders, such as suppliers of goods and services on credit, may be interested in the ability of the business to repay the amounts owing in the short term. As a result, the liquidity ratios should be of interest.

We shall consider ratios falling into the first four of these five categories (profitability, efficiency, liquidity and gearing) a little later in the chapter. The remaining category (investment) takes a rather different perspective and will be considered in Chapter 8, along with other interpretation issues.

The need for comparison

Merely calculating a ratio will not tell us very much about the position or performance of a business. For example, if a ratio revealed that the business was generating £100 in sales revenue per square metre of selling space, it would not be possible to deduce from this information alone whether this particular level of performance was good, bad or indifferent. It is only when we compare this ratio with some 'benchmark' that the information can be interpreted and evaluated.

Activity 7.1

Can you think of any bases that could be used to compare a ratio you have calculated from the financial statements of a particular period?
We feel that there are three sensible possibilities.

You may have thought of the following bases:

- past periods for the same business;
- similar businesses for the same or past periods; and
- planned performance for the business.

We shall now take a closer look at these three in turn.

Past periods

By comparing the ratio we have calculated with the same ratio, but for a previous period, it is possible to detect whether there has been an improvement or deterioration in performance. Indeed, it is often useful to track particular ratios over time (say, five or ten years) to see whether it is possible to detect trends. The comparison of ratios from different time periods brings certain problems, however. In particular, there is always the possibility that trading conditions may have been quite different in the periods being compared. There is the further problem that, when comparing the performance of a single business over time, operating inefficiencies may not be clearly exposed. For example, the fact that sales revenue per employee has risen by 10 per cent over the previous period may at first sight appear to be satisfactory. This may not be the case, however, if similar businesses have shown an improvement of 50 per cent for the same period. Finally, there is the problem that inflation may have distorted the figures on which the ratios are based. Inflation can lead to an overstatement of profit and an understatement of asset values.

Similar businesses

In a competitive environment, a business must consider its performance in relation to that of other businesses operating in the same industry. Survival may depend on the ability to achieve comparable levels of performance. A very useful basis for comparing a particular ratio, therefore, is the ratio achieved by similar businesses during the same period. This basis is not, however, without its problems. Competitors may have different year ends, and therefore trading conditions may not be identical. They may also have different accounting policies, which can have a significant effect on reported profits and asset values (for example, different methods of calculating depreciation or valuing inventories). Finally, it may be difficult to obtain the financial statements of competitor businesses. Sole proprietorships and partnerships, for example, are not obliged to make their financial statements available to the public. In the case of limited companies, there is a legal obligation to do so. However, a diversified business may not provide a breakdown of activities that is sufficiently detailed to enable analysts to compare the activities with those of other businesses.

Planned performance

Ratios may be compared with the targets that management developed before the start of the period under review. The comparison of planned performance with actual performance may therefore be a useful way of revealing the level of achievement attained. However, the planned levels of performance must be based on realistic assumptions if they are to be useful for comparison purposes.

Planned performance is likely to be the most valuable benchmark for the managers to assess their own business. Businesses tend to develop planned ratios for each aspect of their activities. When formulating its plans, a business may usefully take account of its own past performance and that of other businesses. There is no reason, however, why a particular business should seek to achieve either its own previous performance or that of other businesses. Neither of these may be seen as an appropriate target.

Analysts outside the business do not normally have access to the business's plans. For these people, past performance and the performances of other, similar, businesses may be the only practical benchmarks.

Calculating the ratios

Probably the best way to explain financial ratios is through an example. Example 7.1 provides a set of financial statements from which we can calculate important ratios.

Example 7.1

The following financial statements relate to Alexis plc, which operates a wholesale carpet business:

Balance sheets as at 31 March

	2006	2007
	£m	£m
Non-current assets		
Property, plant and equipment (at cost less depreciation)		
Land and buildings	381	427
Fixtures and fittings	129	160
	510	587
Current assets		
Inventories at cost	300	406
Trade receivables	240	273
Cash at bank	4	–
	544	679
Total assets	1,054	1,266
Equity		
£0.50 ordinary shares (Note 1)	300	300
Retained earnings	263	234
	563	534
Non-current liabilities		
Borrowings – 9% loan notes (secured)	200	300
Current liabilities		
Trade payables	261	354
Taxation	30	2
Short-term borrowings (all bank overdraft)	–	76
	291	432
Total equity and liabilities	1,054	1,266

→

Example 7.1 continued

Income statements for the year ended 31 March

	2006 £m	2007 £m
Revenue (Note 2)	2,240	2,681
Cost of sales (Note 3)	(1,745)	(2,272)
Gross profit	495	409
Operating expenses	(252)	(362)
Operating profit	243	47
Interest payable	(18)	(32)
Profit before taxation	225	15
Taxation	(60)	(4)
Profit for the year	165	11

Cash flow statement for the year ended 31 March

	2006 £m	2006 £m	2007 £m	2007 £m
Cash flows from operating activities				
Net profit, after interest, before taxation	225		15	
Adjustments for:				
Depreciation	26		33	
Interest expense	18		32	
	269		80	
Increase in inventories	(59)		(106)	
Increase in trade receivables	(17)		(33)	
Increase in trade payables	58		93	
Cash generated from operations	251		34	
Interest paid	(18)		(32)	
Taxation paid	(63)		(32)	
Dividend paid	(40)		(40)	
Net cash from/(used in) operating activities		130		(70)
Cash flows from investing activities				
Payments to acquire property, plant and equipment	(77)		(110)	
Net cash used in investing activities		(77)		(110)
Cash flows from financing activities				
Issue of loan notes	–		100	
Net cash from financing activities		–		100
Net increase in cash and cash equivalents		53		(80)
Cash and cash equivalents at start of year				
Cash/(overdraft)		(49)		4
Cash and cash equivalents at end of year				
Cash/(overdraft)		4		(76)

Notes

1 The market value of the shares of the business at the end of the year was £2.50 for 2006 and £1.50 for 2007.
2 All sales and purchases are made on credit.
3 The cost of sales figure can be analysed as follows:

	2006 £m	2007 £m
Opening inventories	241	300
Purchases (Note 2)	1,804	2,378
	2,045	2,678
Closing inventories	(300)	(406)
Cost of sales	1,745	2,272

4 A dividend of £40 million had been paid to the shareholders in respect of each of the years.

5 The business employed 13,995 staff at 31 March 2006 and 18,623 at 31 March 2007.

6 The business expanded its capacity during 2007 by setting up a new warehouse and distribution centre in the north of England.

7 At 1 April 2005, the total of equity stood at £438 million and the total of equity and non-current liabilities stood at £638 million.

A brief overview

Before we start our detailed look at the ratios for Alexis plc (in Example 7.1), it is useful to take a quick look at what information is obvious from the financial statements. This may help us to identify issues that the ratios would not pick up. It may also highlight points that could help us in our interpretation of the ratios. Starting at the top of the balance sheet, the following can be noted:

- *Expansion of non-current assets*. These have increased by about 15 per cent (from £510 million to £587 million). Note 5 mentions a new warehouse and distribution centre, which may account for much of the additional investment in non-current assets. We are not told when this new facility was established, but it is quite possible that it was well into the year. This could mean that not much benefit was reflected in terms of additional sales revenue or cost saving during 2007. Sales revenue, in fact, expanded by about 20 per cent (from £2,240 million to £2,681 million), greater than the expansion in non-current assets.

- *Major expansion in the elements of working capital*. Inventories increased by about 35 per cent, trade receivables by about 14 per cent and trade payables by about 36 per cent between 2006 and 2007. These are major increases, particularly in inventories and payables (which are linked because the inventories are all bought on credit – see Note 2).

- *Reduction in the cash balance*. The cash balance fell from £4 million (in funds) to a £76 million overdraft, between 2006 and 2007. The bank may be putting the business under pressure to reverse this, which could raise difficulties.

- *Apparent debt capacity*. Comparing the non-current assets with the long-term borrowings implies that the business may well be able to offer security on further borrowing. This is because potential lenders usually look at the value of assets that can be offered as security when assessing loan requests. Lenders seem particularly attracted to land and, to a lesser extent, buildings as security. For example, at 31 March 2007, non-current assets had a balance sheet value of £587 million, but long-term borrowing was only £300 million (though there was also an overdraft of £76 million). Balance sheet values are not normally, of course, market values. On the other hand, land and buildings tend to have a market value higher than their balance sheet value due to inflation in property values.

- *Lower operating profit*. Though sales revenue expanded by 20 per cent between 2006 and 2007, both cost of sales and operating expenses rose by a greater percentage, leaving both gross profit and, particularly, operating profit massively reduced. The level of staffing, which increased by about 33 per cent (from 13,995 to 18,623 employees), may have greatly affected the operating expenses. (Without knowing when the additional employees were recruited during 2007, we cannot be sure of the effect on operating expenses.) Increasing staffing by 33 per cent must put an enormous strain on management, at least in the short term. It is not surprising, therefore that 2007 was not successful for the business.

Having had a quick look at what is fairly obvious, without calculating any financial ratios, we shall now go on to calculate and interpret those relating to profitability and efficiency, liquidity and gearing.

Profitability

The following ratios may be used to evaluate the profitability of the business:

● return on ordinary shareholders' funds;
● return on capital employed;
● operating profit margin; and
● gross profit margin.

We shall now look at each of these in turn.

Return on ordinary shareholders' funds (ROSF)

→ The **return on ordinary shareholders' funds ratio** compares the amount of profit for the period available to the owners, with the owners' average stake in the business during that same period. The ratio (which is normally expressed in percentage terms) is as follows:

$$\text{ROSF} = \frac{\text{Profit for the year (net profit) less any preference dividend}}{\text{Ordinary share capital plus reserves}} \times 100$$

The profit for the year (less preference dividend (if any)) is used in calculating the ratio, as this figure represents the amount of profit that is left for the owners.

In the case of Alexis plc, the ratio for the year ended 31 March 2006 is:

$$\text{ROSF} = \frac{165}{(438 + 563)/2} \times 100$$

$$= 33.0\%$$

Note that, when calculating the ROSF, the average of the figures for ordinary shareholders' funds as at the beginning and at the end of the year has been used. It is preferable to use an average figure, as this is likely to be more representative. This is because the shareholders' funds did not have the same total throughout the year, yet we want to compare it with the profit earned during the whole period. We know, from Note 7, that the total of the shareholders' funds at 1 April 2005 was £438 million. By a year later, however, it had risen to £563 million, according to the balance sheet as at 31 March 2006.

The easiest approach to calculating the average amount of shareholders' funds is to take a simple average based on the opening and closing figures for the year. This is often the only information available, as is the case with Example 7.1. Averaging in this way is generally valid for all ratios that combine a figure for a period (such as profit for the year) with one taken at a point in time (such as shareholders' funds).

Where not even the beginning-of-year figure is available, it is usually acceptable to use just the year-end figure, provided that this approach is consistently adopted.

Activity 7.2

Calculate the ROSF for Alexis plc for the year to 31 March 2007.

The ratio for 2007 is:

$$\text{ROSF} = \frac{11}{(563 + 534)/2} \times 100 = 2.0\%$$

Broadly, businesses seek to generate as high a value as possible for this ratio, provided that it is not achieved at the expense of potential future returns by, for example, taking on more risky activities. In view of this, the 2007 ratio is very poor by any standards; a bank deposit account will yield a better return than this. We need to try to find out why things went so badly wrong in 2007. As we look at other ratios, we should find some clues.

Return on capital employed (ROCE)

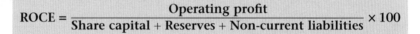 The **return on capital employed ratio** is a fundamental measure of business performance. This ratio expresses the relationship between the operating profit generated during a period and the average long-term capital invested in the business during that period.

The ratio is expressed in percentage terms and is as follows:

$$\text{ROCE} = \frac{\text{Operating profit}}{\text{Share capital} + \text{Reserves} + \text{Non-current liabilities}} \times 100$$

Note, in this case, that the profit figure used is the operating profit (that is, the net profit *before* interest and taxation), because the ratio attempts to measure the returns to all suppliers of long-term finance before any deductions for interest payable on borrowings, or payments of dividends to shareholders, are made.

For the year to 31 March 2006, the ratio for Alexis plc is:

$$\text{ROCE} = \frac{243}{(638 + 763)/2} \times 100 = 34.7\%$$

ROCE is considered by many to be a primary measure of profitability. It compares inputs (capital invested) with outputs (operating profit). This comparison is vital in assessing the effectiveness with which funds have been deployed. Once again, an average figure for capital employed may be used where the information is available.

Activity 7.3

Calculate the ROCE for Alexis plc for the year to 31 March 2007.

For 2007, the ratio is:

$$\text{ROCE} = \frac{47}{(763 + 834)/2} \times 100 = 5.9\%$$

This ratio tells much the same story as ROSF; namely a poor performance, with the return on the assets being less than the rate that the business has to pay for most of its borrowed funds (that is, 10 per cent for the loan notes).

Real World 7.1 shows how ROCE may be used by businesses as a basis for setting profitability targets.

Real World 7.1

Targeting profitability

The ROCE ratio is widely used by businesses when establishing targets for profitability. These targets are sometimes made public and here are some examples:

De Vere Hotels and Leisure Ltd, the UK hotels business has a target for a 10 per cent ROCE by 2006/7.

BSkyB plc, the satelite broadcaster has a target ROCE of 15 per cent by 2011 for its broadband operation.

Sources: information from Garrahan, M. 'De Vere Is Prepared to Sell More Assets', *Financial Times*, 12 July 2004; 'BskyB/Triple Play', www.ft.com, 12 July 2006.

Real World 7.2 provides some insight to the levels of ROCE achieved by UK businesses.

Real World 7.2

Achieving profitability

UK businesses reported an average ROCE of 14.4 per cent for the first quarter of 2006, equalling the 2005 rate. This was the highest level of ROCE since the Office of National Statistics first kept records.

Service-sector businesses were much the more successful with an average ROCE of 19.9 per cent, compared with 6.6 per cent among manufacturers. In fact manufacturers' average ROCE had fallen from 9.9 per cent in 2005.

Source: information taken from Giles, Chris 'Services Companies See Record Return on Capital but Manufacturing Struggles', *Financial Times*, 5 July 2006.

Operating profit margin

→ The **operating profit margin ratio** relates the operating profit for the period to the sales revenue during that period. The ratio is expressed as follows:

$$\text{Operating net profit margin} = \frac{\text{Operating profit}}{\text{Sales revenue}} \times 100$$

The operating profit (that is, net profit before interest and taxation) is used in this ratio as it represents the profit from trading operations before the interest payable expense is taken into account. This is often regarded as the most appropriate measure of operational performance, when used as a basis of comparison, because differences arising from the way in which the business is financed will not influence the measure.

For the year ended 31 March 2006, Alexis plc's operating profit margin ratio is:

$$\text{Operating profit margin} = \frac{243}{2,240} \times 100 = 10.8\%$$

This ratio compares one output of the business (operating profit) with another output (sales revenue). The ratio can vary considerably between types of business. For example, supermarkets tend to operate on low prices and, therefore, low operating profit margins. This is done in an attempt to stimulate sales and thereby increase the total amount of operating profit generated. Jewellers, on the other hand, tend to have high operating profit margins, but have much lower levels of sales volume. Factors such as the degree of competition, the type of customer, the economic climate and industry characteristics (such as the level of risk) will influence the operating profit margin of a business. This point is picked up again later in the chapter.

Activity 7.4

Calculate the operating profit margin for Alexis plc for the year to 31 March 2007.

The ratio for 2007 is:

$$\text{Operating profit margin} = \frac{47}{2,681} \times 100 = 1.8\%$$

Once again a very weak performance compared with that of 2006. Whereas in 2006 for every £1 of sales revenue an average of 10.8 p (that is, 10.8 per cent) was left as operating profit, after paying the cost of the carpets sold and other expenses of operating the business, for 2007 this had fallen to only 1.8 p for every £1. It seems that the reason for the poor ROSF and ROCE ratios was partially, perhaps wholly, a high level of expenses relative to sales revenue. The next ratio should provide us with a clue as to how the sharp decline in this ratio occurred.

Real World 7.3 describes how one well-known business uses the operating profit margin as a performance target.

Real World 7.3

Increasing the operating profit margin   **FT**

Toyota, the Japanese car maker, soon to overtake General Motors of the USA as the world's leader, is determined to increase its operating profit margin and has set a target return of 10 per cent.

Source: Sanchanta, M. 'Nissan's Empty Products Pipeline', *Financial Times*, 6 November 2006.

Gross profit margin

The **gross profit margin ratio** relates the gross profit of the business to the sales revenue generated for the same period. Gross profit represents the difference between sales revenue and the cost of sales. The ratio is therefore a measure of profitability in buying (or producing) and selling goods before any other expenses are taken into account. As cost of sales represents a major expense for many businesses, a change in this ratio can have a significant effect on the 'bottom line' (that is, the profit for the year). The gross profit margin ratio is calculated as follows:

$$\text{Gross profit margin} = \frac{\text{Gross profit}}{\text{Sales revenue}} \times 100$$

For the year to 31 March 2006, the ratio for Alexis plc is:

$$\text{Gross profit margin} = \frac{495}{2{,}240} \times 100 = 22.1\%$$

Activity 7.5

Calculate the gross profit margin for Alexis plc for the year to 31 March 2007.

The ratio for 2007 is:

$$\text{Gross profit margin} = \frac{409}{2{,}681} \times 100 = 15.3\%$$

The decline in this ratio means that gross profit was lower *relative* to sales revenue in 2007 than it had been in 2006. Bearing in mind that:

Gross profit = Sales revenue − Cost of sales (or cost of goods sold)

this means that cost of sales was higher *relative* to sales revenue in 2007, than in 2006. This may be due to lower sales prices and/or an increase in cost of goods sold. There are, however, other possible explanations. Both sales prices and the cost of goods sold may have reduced, but the former at a greater rate than the latter. Alternatively, both may have increased, but with sales prices at a lesser rate than the cost of the goods sold.

Clearly, part of the decline in the operating profit margin ratio is linked to the dramatic decline in the gross profit margin ratio. Whereas, after paying for the carpets sold, for each £1 of sales revenue 22.1 p was left to cover other operating expenses and leave an operating profit in 2006, this was only 15.3 p in 2007.

The profitability ratios for the business over the two years can be set out as follows:

	2006 %	2007 %
ROSF	33.0	2.0
ROCE	34.7	5.9
Operating profit margin	10.8	1.8
Gross profit margin	22.1	15.3

Activity 7.6

What do you deduce from a comparison of the declines in the operating profit and gross profit margin ratios?

It occurs to us that the decline in the operating profit margin was 9 per cent (that is, 10.8 per cent to 1.8 per cent), whereas that of the gross profit margin was only 6.8 per cent (that is, from 22.1 per cent to 15.3 per cent). This can only mean that operating expenses were greater, compared with sales revenue in 2007, than they had been in 2006. The declines in both ROSF and ROCE were caused partly, therefore, by the business incurring higher inventories purchasing costs relative to sales revenue and partly through higher operating expenses to sales revenue. We would need to compare these ratios with the planned levels for them before we could usefully assess the business's success.

The analyst must now carry out some investigation to discover what caused the increases in both cost of sales and operating expenses, relative to sales revenue, from 2006 to 2007. This will involve checking on what has happened with sales and inventories prices over the two years. Similarly, it will involve looking at each of the individual areas that make up operating expenses to discover which ones were responsible for the increase, relative to sales revenue. Here further ratios, for example, staff expenses (wages and salaries) to sales revenue, could be calculated in an attempt to isolate the cause of the change from 2006 to 2007. In fact, as we discussed when we took an overview of the financial statements, the increase in staffing may well account for most of the increase in operating expenses.

Real World 7.4 shows how one well-known international business is seeking to improve its ROCE.

Real World 7.4

Lazy assets raise the ROCE at Shell

During 2003 Shell, the oil business (The 'Shell' Transport and Trading Company plc) disposed of $4 billion of what it called 'lazy assets'. These are assets that the business felt were not earning their keep and were holding the ROCE below the target range of 13 to 15 per cent. The business had also identified a further $3 billion of assets that could be 'improved', so that they could also boost the business's ROCE.

Source: based on information in Shelly, Toby 'Shell Disposals of $4 Billion Double Initial Estimate', FT.com, 22 December 2003.

Efficiency

Efficiency ratios examine the ways in which various resources of the business are managed. The following ratios consider some of the more important aspects of resource management:

- average inventories turnover period;
- average settlement period for trade receivables;
- average settlement period for trade payables;
- sales revenue to capital employed; and
- sales revenue per employee.

We shall now look at each of these in turn.

Average inventories turnover period

Inventories often represent a significant investment for a business. For some types of business (for example, manufacturers), inventories may account for a substantial proportion of the total assets held (see **Real World 8.5**, p. 256). The **average inventories turnover period ratio** measures the average period for which inventories are being held and is calculated as follows:

$$\text{Average inventories turnover period} = \frac{\text{Average inventories held}}{\text{Cost of sales}} \times 365$$

The average inventories for the period can be calculated as a simple average of the opening and closing inventories levels for the year. However, in the case of a highly seasonal business, where inventories levels may vary considerably over the year, a monthly average may be more appropriate.

In the case of Alexis plc, the inventories turnover period for the year ended 31 March 2006 is:

$$\text{Average inventories turnover period} = \frac{(241 + 300)/2}{1,745} \times 365 = 56.6 \text{ days}$$

This means that, on average, the inventories held are being 'turned over' every 56.6 days. So, a carpet bought by the business on a particular day would, on average, have been sold about eight weeks later. A business will normally prefer a short inventories turnover period to a long one, because holding inventories has a cost, such as the opportunity cost of the funds tied up. When judging the amount of inventories to carry, the business must consider such things as the likely demand for the inventories, the possibility of supply shortages, the likelihood of price rises, the amount of storage space available and the perishability/susceptibility to obsolescence of the inventories.

This ratio is sometimes expressed in terms of months rather than days. Multiplying by 12 rather than 365 will achieve this.

Activity 7.7

Calculate the average inventories turnover period for Alexis plc for the year ended 31 March 2007.

The ratio for 2007 is:

$$\text{Average inventories turnover period} = \frac{(300 + 406)/2}{2,272} \times 365 = 56.7 \text{ days}$$

The inventories turnover period is virtually the same in both years.

Average settlement period for trade receivables

A business will usually be concerned with the amount of funds tied up in trade receivables and trying to keep this to a minimum. The speed of payment can have a significant effect on the business's cash flow. The **average settlement period for trade receivables ratio** calculates how long, on average, credit customers take to pay the amounts that they owe to the business. It is calculated as follows:

$$\text{Average settlement period of trade receivables} = \frac{\text{Trade receivables}}{\text{Credit sales revenue}} \times 365$$

A business will normally prefer a shorter average settlement period to a longer one as, once again, funds are being tied up that may be used for more profitable purposes. Though this ratio can be useful, it is important to remember that it produces an *average* figure for the number of days for which debts are outstanding. This average may be badly distorted by, for example, a few large customers who are very slow or very fast payers.

Since all sales made by Alexis plc are on credit, the average settlement period for trade receivables for the year ended 31 March 2006 is:

$$\text{Average settlement period for trade receivables} = \frac{240}{2,240} \times 365 = 39.1 \text{ days}$$

As no figure for opening trade receivables is available, only the year-end figure is used. This is common practice for calculating any ratio where averaging would be desirable, but impossible through lack of the opening value.

Activity 7.8

Calculate the average settlement period for Alexis plc's trade receivables for the year ended 31 March 2007. (To be consistent with the 2006 calculation, use the year-end trade receivables figure rather than an average figure.)

The ratio for 2007 is:

$$\text{Average settlement period for trade receivables} = \frac{273}{2,681} \times 365 = 37.2 \text{ days}$$

On the face of it, this reduction in the settlement period is welcome. It means that less cash was tied up in trade receivables for each £1 of sales revenue in 2007 than in 2006. Only if the reduction were achieved at the expense of customer goodwill, or at a high financial cost, might its desirability be questioned. Thus, chasing credit customers too vigorously or incurring higher expenses, such as discounts for prompt payment, might offset the benefit of any reduction.

Average settlement period for trade payables

→ The **average settlement period for trade payables ratio** measures how long, on average, the business takes to pay those who have supplied goods and services on credit. The ratio is calculated as follows:

$$\text{Average settlement period for trade payables} = \frac{\text{Trade payables}}{\text{Credit purchases}} \times 365$$

This ratio provides an average figure, which, like the average settlement period for trade receivables ratio, can be distorted by the payment period for one or two large suppliers.

As trade payables provide a free source of finance for the business, it is not surprising that some businesses attempt to increase their average settlement period for trade payables. However, such a policy can be taken too far and result in a loss of goodwill of suppliers.

For the year ended 31 March 2006, Alexis plc's average settlement period for trade payables is:

$$\text{Average settlement period for trade payables} = \frac{261}{1,804} \times 365 = 52.8 \text{ days}$$

Once again, the year-end figure rather than an average figure for trade payables has been used in the calculations.

Activity 7.9

Calculate the average settlement period for trade payables for Alexis plc for the year ended 31 March 2007. (For the sake of consistency, use a year-end figure for trade payables.)

The ratio for 2007 is:

$$\text{Average settlement period for trade payables} = \frac{354}{2{,}378} \times 365 = 54.3 \text{ days}$$

There was an increase, between 2006 and 2007, in the average length of time that elapsed between buying inventories and services and paying for them. On the face of it, this is beneficial because the business is using free finance provided by suppliers. If, however, a longer payment period leads to a loss of supplier goodwill, there could be adverse consequences for Alexis plc.

Sales revenue to capital employed

→ The **sales revenue to capital employed ratio** (or asset turnover ratio) examines how effectively the assets of the business are being used to generate sales revenue. It is calculated as follows:

$$\frac{\text{Sales revenue to}}{\text{capital employed ratio}} = \frac{\text{Sales revenue}}{\text{Share capital + Reserves + Non-current liabilities}}$$

Generally speaking, a higher asset turnover ratio is preferred to a lower one. A higher ratio will normally suggest that assets are being used more productively in the generation of revenue. However, a very high ratio may suggest that the business is 'overtrading on its assets', that is, it has insufficient assets to sustain the level of sales revenue achieved. (Overtrading will be discussed in more detail in Chapter 8.) When comparing this ratio for different businesses, factors such as the age and condition of assets held, the valuation bases for assets and whether assets are leased or owned outright can complicate interpretation.

A variation of this formula is to use the total assets less current liabilities (which is equivalent to long-term capital employed) in the denominator (lower part of the fraction) – the identical result is obtained.

For the year ended 31 March 2006 this ratio for Alexis plc is:

$$\text{Sales revenue to capital employed} = \frac{2{,}240}{(638 + 763)/2} = 3.20 \text{ times}$$

Activity 7.10

Calculate the sales revenue to capital employed ratio for Alexis plc for the year ended 31 March 2007.

The sales revenue to capital employed ratio for the 2007 is:

$$\text{Sales revenue to capital employed} = \frac{2{,}681}{(763 + 834)/2} = 3.36 \text{ times}$$

This seems to be an improvement, since in 2007 more sales revenue was being generated for each £1 of capital employed (£3.36) than was the case in 2006 (£3.20). Provided that overtrading is not an issue and that the additional sales are generating an acceptable profit, this is to be welcomed.

Sales revenue per employee

→ The **sales revenue per employee ratio** relates sales revenue generated to a particular business resource, that is, labour. It provides a measure of the productivity of the workforce. The ratio is:

$$\text{Sales revenue per employee} = \frac{\text{Sales revenue}}{\text{Number of employees}}$$

Generally, businesses would prefer to have a high value for this ratio, implying that they are using their staff efficiently.

For the year ended 31 March 2006, the ratio for Alexis plc is:

$$\text{Sales revenue per employee} = \frac{£2,240 \text{ m}}{13,995}$$

$$= £160,057$$

Activity 7.11

Calculate the sales revenue per employee for Alexis plc for the year ended 31 March 2007.

The ratio for 2007 is:

$$\text{Sales revenue per employee} = \frac{£2,681 \text{ m}}{18,623}$$

$$= £143,962$$

This represents a fairly significant decline and probably one that merits further investigation. As we discussed previously, the number of employees had increased significantly (by about 33 per cent) during 2007 and it would be useful to know why this has not generated sufficient additional sales revenue to maintain the ratio at its 2006 level. It could be that the additional employees were not appointed until late in the year ended 31 March 2007.

The efficiency, or activity, ratios may be summarised as follows:

	2006	2007
Average inventories turnover period	56.6 days	56.7 days
Average settlement period for trade receivables	39.1 days	37.2 days
Average settlement period for trade payables	52.8 days	54.3 days
Sales revenue to capital employed (asset turnover)	3.20 times	3.36 times
Sales revenue per employee	£160,057	£143,962

Activity 7.12

What do you deduce from a comparison of the efficiency ratios over the two years?

Maintaining the inventories turnover period at the 2006 level might be reasonable, although this can only really be assessed by looking at the business's planned inventories period. The inventories holding period for other businesses operating in carpet retailing, particularly those regarded as the market leaders, may have been helpful in formulating the plans. On the face of things, a shorter receivables collection period and a longer payables payment period are both desirable. On the other hand, these may have been achieved at the cost of a loss of the goodwill of customers and suppliers, respectively. The increased asset turnover ratio seems beneficial, provided that the business can manage this increase. The decline in the sales revenue per employee ratio is undesirable but, as we have already seen, is probably related to the dramatic increase in the level of staffing. As with the inventories turnover period, these other ratios need to be compared with the planned levels of performance.

The relationship between profitability and efficiency

In our earlier discussions concerning profitability ratios on p. 211, we saw that return on capital employed (ROCE) is regarded as a key ratio by many businesses. The ratio is:

$$\text{ROCE} = \frac{\text{Operating profit}}{\text{Long-term capital employed}} \times 100$$

(where long-term capital comprises share capital plus reserves plus long-term borrowings). This ratio can be broken down into two elements, as shown in Figure 7.1.

Figure 7.1   The main elements comprising the ROCE ratio

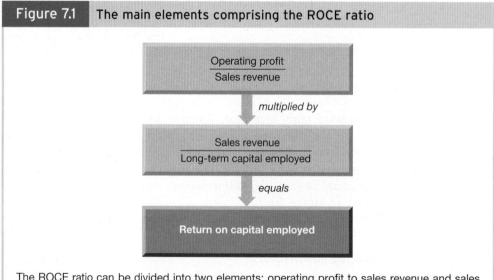

The ROCE ratio can be divided into two elements: operating profit to sales revenue and sales revenue to capital employed. By analysing ROCE in this way, we can see the influence of both profitability and efficiency on this important ratio.

The first ratio is the operating profit margin ratio, and the second is the sales revenue to capital employed (asset turnover) ratio, both of which we discussed earlier.

By breaking down the ROCE ratio in this manner, we highlight the fact that the overall return on funds employed within the business will be determined both by the profitability of sales and by efficiency in the use of capital.

Example 7.2

Consider the following information, for last year, concerning two different businesses operating within the same industry:

	Antler plc	Baker plc
Operating profit	£20 m	£15 m
Average long-term capital employed	£100 m	£75 m
Sales revenue	£200 m	£300 m

The ROCE for each business is identical (20 per cent). However, the manner in which that return was achieved by each business was quite different. In the case of Antler plc, the operating profit margin is 10 per cent and the sales revenue to capital employed ratio is 2 times (so, ROCE = 10% × 2 = 20%). In the case of Baker plc, the operating profit margin is 5 per cent and the sales revenue to capital employed ratio is 4 times (and so, ROCE = 5% × 4 = 20%).

Example 7.2 demonstrates that a relatively high sales revenue to capital employed ratio can compensate for a relatively low operating profit margin. Similarly, a relatively low sales revenue to capital employed ratio can be overcome by a relatively high operating profit margin. In many areas of retail and distribution (for example, supermarkets and delivery services) the operating profit margins are quite low but the ROCE can be high, provided that the assets are used productively (that is, low margin, high turnover).

Activity 7.13

Show how the ROCE ratio for Alexis plc can be analysed into the two elements for each of the years 2006 and 2007.
What conclusions can we draw from your figures?

	ROCE	=	Operating profit margin	×	Sales revenue to capital employed
2006	34.7%		10.8%		3.20
2007	5.9%		1.8%		3.36

As we can see, the relationship between the three ratios holds for Alexis plc, for both years. The small apparent differences arise because the three ratios are stated above only to one or two decimal places.

Though the business was more effective at generating sales revenue (sales revenue to capital employed ratio increased) in 2007 than in 2006, in 2007 it fell well below the level necessary to compensate for the sharp decline in the effectiveness of each sale (operating profit margin). As a result, the 2007 ROCE was well below the 2006 value.

Liquidity

Liquidity ratios are concerned with the ability of the business to meet its short-term financial obligations. The following ratios are widely used:

● current ratio;
● acid test ratio; and
● operating cash flows to maturing obligations.

These three will now be considered.

Current ratio

→ The **current ratio** compares the 'liquid' assets (that is, cash and those assets held that will soon be turned into cash) of the business with the current liabilities. The ratio is calculated as follows:

$$\text{Current ratio} = \frac{\text{Current assets}}{\text{Current liabilities}}$$

Some people seem to believe that there is an 'ideal' current ratio (usually 2 times or 2:1) for all businesses. However, this fails to take into account the fact that different types of business require different current ratios. For example, a manufacturing business will often have a relatively high current ratio because it is necessary to hold inventories of finished goods, raw materials and work in progress. It will also normally sell goods on credit, thereby giving rise to trade receivables. A supermarket chain, on the other hand, will have a relatively low ratio, as it will hold only fast-moving inventories of finished goods and all of its sales will be made for cash (no credit sales). (See **Real World 8.5** on p. 256.)

The higher the ratio, the more liquid the business is considered to be. As liquidity is vital to the survival of a business, a higher current ratio might be thought to be preferable to a lower one. If a business has a very high ratio, however, it may be that funds are tied up in cash or other liquid assets and are not, therefore, being used as productively as they might otherwise be.

As at 31 March 2006, the current ratio of Alexis plc is:

$$\text{Current ratio} = \frac{544}{291} = 1.9 \text{ times (or 1.9:1)}$$

Activity 7.14

Calculate the current ratio for Alexis plc as at 31 March 2007.

The ratio as at 31 March 2007 is:

$$\text{Current ratio} = \frac{679}{432} = 1.6 \text{ times (or 1.6:1)}$$

Though this is a decline from 2006 to 2007, it is not necessarily a matter of concern. The next ratio may provide a clue as to whether there seems to be a problem.

Acid test ratio

→ The **acid test ratio** is very similar to the current ratio, but represents a more stringent test of liquidity. It can be argued that, for many businesses, inventories cannot be converted into cash quickly. (Note that, in the case of Alexis plc, the inventories turnover period was about 57 days in both years (see page 216).) As a result, it may be better to exclude this particular asset from any measure of liquidity. The acid test ratio does precisely this.

The acid test ratio is calculated as follows:

$$\text{Acid test ratio} = \frac{\text{Current assets (excluding inventories)}}{\text{Current liabilities}}$$

The acid test ratio for Alexis plc as at 31 March 2006 is:

$$\text{Acid test ratio} = \frac{544 - 300}{291} = 0.8 \text{ times (or 0.8:1)}$$

We can see that the 'liquid' current assets do not quite cover the current liabilities, so the business may be experiencing some liquidity problems.

Activity 7.15

Calculate the acid test ratio for Alexis plc as at 31 March 2007.

The ratio as at 31 March 2006 is:

$$\text{Acid test ratio} = \frac{679 - 406}{432} = 0.6 \text{ times}$$

The 2007 ratio is significantly below that for 2006. The 2007 level may well be a cause for concern. The rapid decline in this ratio should lead to steps being taken, at least, to stop further decline.

It is sometimes suggested that the minimum level for this ratio should be 1.0 times (or 1:1 – that is, current assets (excluding inventories) equals current liabilities). In many highly successful businesses, it is not unusual, however, for the acid test ratio to be below 1.0 without causing liquidity problems. (See **Real World 8.5** on p. 256.)

Cash generated from operations to maturing obligations

→ The **cash generated from operations to maturing obligations ratio** compares the cash generated from operations (taken from the cash flow statement) to the current liabilities of the business. It provides a further indication of the ability of the business to meet its maturing obligations. The ratio is expressed as:

$$\frac{\textbf{Cash generated from}}{\textbf{operations to maturing obligations}} = \frac{\textbf{Cash generated from operations}}{\textbf{Current liabilities}}$$

The higher this ratio, the better is the liquidity of the business. As the ratio uses operating cash flows generated over a period, it can provide a more reliable guide to liquidity than the current ratio, which uses current assets held at the balance sheet date. Alexis plc's ratio for the year ended 31 March 2006 is:

$$\text{Cash generated from operations to maturing obligations ratio} = \frac{251}{291} = 0.9 \text{ times}$$

This ratio reveals that the operating cash flows for the period are not quite sufficient to cover the current liabilities at the end of the period.

Activity 7.16

Calculate the cash generated from operations to maturing obligations ratio for Alexis plc for the year ended 31 March 2007.

$$\text{Cash generated from operations to maturing obligations ratio} = \frac{34}{432} = 0.1 \text{ times}$$

This ratio shows an alarming decline in the ability of the business to meet its maturing obligations from its operating cash flows. Thus, liquidity should be a real cause for concern for the business.

The liquidity ratios for the two-year period may be summarised as follows:

	2006	2007
Current ratio	1.9	1.6
Acid test ratio	0.8	0.6
Cash generated from operations to maturing obligations	0.9	0.1

Activity 7.17

What do you deduce from the liquidity ratios set out above?

Though it is not possible to make a full judgement without knowing the planned ratios, there seems to be a worrying decline in liquidity. This is indicated by all three of these ratios. The last ratio, which shows the decline in the ability of the business to generate cash from operations to cover short-term debts, gives the greatest concern. The apparent liquidity problem may, however, be planned, short term and linked to the expansion in non-current assets and staffing. It may be that when the benefits of the expansion come on stream, liquidity will improve. On the other hand, short-term claimants may become anxious when they see signs of poor liquidity. This anxiety could lead to steps being taken to press for payment, which could in turn cause problems for Alexis plc.

Operating cash cycle (OCC)

When assessing the liquidity of a business, it is important to be aware of the **operating cash cycle (OCC)**. In the case of a business that purchases goods on credit for subsequent resale on credit (for example, a wholesaler), this may be defined as the time period between the outlay of cash necessary for the purchase of inventories and the ultimate receipt of cash from the credit customer. For such a business, the OCC is as shown in Figure 7.2

Figure 7.2 shows that payment for inventories acquired on credit occurs some time after those inventories have been purchased and, therefore, no immediate cash outflow arises from the purchase. Similarly, cash receipts from credit customers will occur some time after the sale is made, and so there will be no immediate cash inflow as a result of

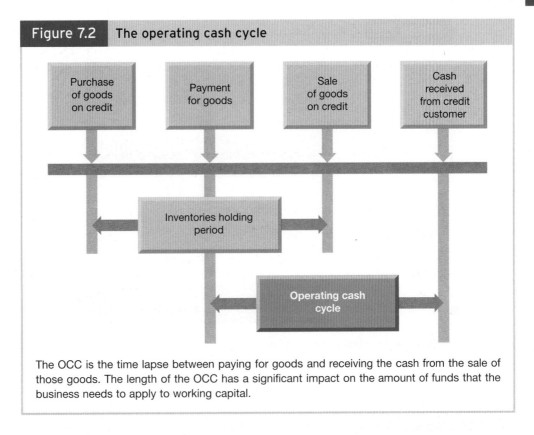

Figure 7.2 The operating cash cycle

The OCC is the time lapse between paying for goods and receiving the cash from the sale of those goods. The length of the OCC has a significant impact on the amount of funds that the business needs to apply to working capital.

the sale. The OCC is the time period between the payment made to the supplier for goods concerned and the cash received from the credit customer. Though Figure 7.2 depicts the position for a wholesaling business, the definition of the OCC can easily be adapted for other types of businesses, such as retailers and manufacturers.

The OCC is important because it has a significant influence on the financing requirements of the business. Broadly speaking, the longer the cycle, the greater the financing requirements of the business and the greater the financial risks. For this reason, a business may wish to reduce the OCC to the minimum possible period.

For the type of business that buys inventories and then sells them on credit, the OCC can be calculated from the financial statements by using certain ratios. The calculation is as shown in Figure 7.3.

Activity 7.18

Calculate the length of the OCC for Alexis plc for the year ended 31 March 2007, using the values that you calculated in the relevant Activities earlier in this chapter.

The OCC for the year ended 31 March 2007 is follows:

	Number of days
Average inventories holding period (from Activity 7.7)	56.7
Average settlement period for trade receivables (from Activity 7.8)	37.2
	93.9
Less: Average settlement period for trade payables (from Activity 7.9)	54.3
OCC	39.6

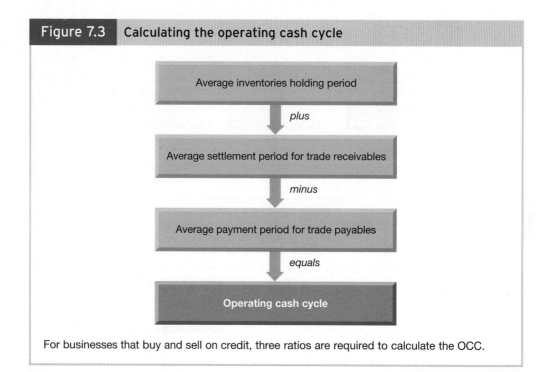

Figure 7.3 Calculating the operating cash cycle

For businesses that buy and sell on credit, three ratios are required to calculate the OCC.

Financial gearing

→ **Financial gearing** occurs when a business is financed, at least in part, by borrowing, instead of by finance provided by the owners (the shareholders) as equity. A business's level of gearing (that is, the extent to which it is financed from sources that require a fixed return) is an important factor in assessing risk. Where a business borrows, it takes on a commitment to pay interest charges and make capital repayments. Where the borrowing is heavy, this can be a significant financial burden and can increase the risk of insolvency. Nevertheless, most businesses are geared to some extent.

Given the risks involved, we may wonder why a business would want to take on gearing (that is, borrowing). One reason may be that the owners have insufficient funds, so the only way to finance the business adequately is to borrow from others. Another reason is that gearing can be used to increase the returns to owners. This is possible provided the returns generated from borrowed funds exceed the cost of paying interest. Example 7.3 illustrates this point.

Example 7.3

The long-term capital structures of two new businesses, Lee Ltd and Nova Ltd, are as follows:

	Lee Ltd £	Nova Ltd £
£1 ordinary shares	100,000	200,000
10% loan notes	200,000	100,000
	300,000	300,000

In their first year of operations, they each make an operating profit (that is, profit before interest and taxation) of £50,000. The tax rate is 30 per cent of the profit after interest and before taxation.

Lee Ltd would probably be considered relatively highly geared, as it has a high proportion of borrowed funds in its long-term capital structure. Nova Ltd is much lower geared. The profit available to the shareholders of each business in the first year of operations will be:

	Lee Ltd £	Nova Ltd £
Operating profit	50,000	50,000
Interest payable	(20,000)	(10,000)
Profit before taxation	30,000	40,000
Taxation (30%)	(9,000)	(12,000)
Profit for the year (available to ordinary shareholders)	21,000	28,000

The return on ordinary shareholders' funds (ROSF) for each business will be:

Lee Ltd

$$\frac{21,000}{100,000} \times 100 = 21\%$$

Nova Ltd

$$\frac{28,000}{200,000} \times 100 = 14\%$$

We can see that Lee Ltd, the more highly geared business, has generated a better ROSF than Nova Ltd. This is despite the fact that the ROCE (return on capital employed) is identical for both businesses (that is ($£50,000/£300,000) \times 100 = 16.7\%$).

Note that at the £50,000 level of operating profit, the shareholders of both Lee Ltd and Nova Ltd benefit from gearing. Were the two businesses totally reliant on equity financing, the profit for the year (after taxation profit) would be £35,000 (that is, £50,000 less 30 per cent taxation), giving a ROSF of 11.7 per cent (that is £35,000/£300,000). Both businesses generate higher ROSFs than this as a result of financial gearing.

An effect of gearing is that returns to shareholders become more sensitive to changes in operating profits. For a highly geared business, a change in operating profits will lead to a proportionately greater change in the ROSF ratio.

Activity 7.19

Assume that the operating profit was 20 per cent higher for each business than stated above (that is, an operating profit of £60,000). What would be the effect of this on ROSF?

The revised profit available to the shareholders of each business in the first year of operations will be:

	Lee Ltd £	Nova Ltd £
Operating profit	60,000	60,000
Interest payable	(20,000)	(10,000)
Profit before taxation	40,000	50,000
Taxation (30%)	(12,000)	(15,000)
Profit for the year (available to ordinary shareholders)	28,000	35,000

The ROSF for each business will now be:

Lee Ltd

$$\frac{28,000}{100,000} \times 100 = 28\%$$

Nova Ltd

$$\frac{35,000}{200,000} \times 100 = 17.5\%$$

We can see that for Lee Ltd, the higher-geared business, the returns to shareholders have increased by a third (from 21 per cent to 28 per cent), whereas for the lower-geared business, Nova Ltd, the benefits of gearing are less pronounced, increasing by only a quarter (from 14 per cent to 17.5 per cent). The effect of gearing, of course, can work in both directions. So, for a highly geared business, a small decline in operating profit will bring about a much greater decline in the returns to shareholders.

Gearing tends to benefit shareholders because interest rates on borrowings are low compared with the returns that the typical business can earn. On top of this, interest expenses are tax deductible, in the way shown in Example 7.3 and Activity 7.19, making the effective cost of borrowing quite cheap. It is debatable whether the apparent low interest rates really are beneficial to the shareholders. Some argue that since borrowing increases the risk to shareholders, there is a hidden cost of borrowing. What are not illusory, however, are the benefits to the shareholders of the tax deductibility of loan interest.

The effect of gearing is like that of two intermeshing cogwheels of unequal size (see Figure 7.4). The movement in the larger cog (operating profit) causes a more than proportionate movement in the smaller cog (returns to ordinary shareholders).

Figure 7.4	The effect of financial gearing

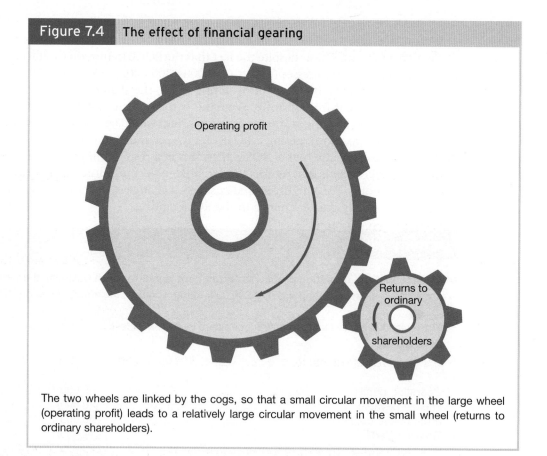

The two wheels are linked by the cogs, so that a small circular movement in the large wheel (operating profit) leads to a relatively large circular movement in the small wheel (returns to ordinary shareholders).

Two ratios are widely used to assess gearing:

● gearing ratio;
● interest cover ratio.

Gearing ratio

 The **gearing ratio** measures the contribution of long-term lenders to the long-term capital structure of a business:

$$\text{Gearing ratio} = \frac{\text{Long-term (non-current) liabilities}}{\text{Share capital + Reserves} + \substack{\text{Long-term (non-current)} \\ \text{liabilities}}} \times 100$$

The gearing ratio for Alexis plc, as at 31 March 2006, is:

$$\text{Gearing ratio} = \frac{200}{(563 + 200)} \times 100 = 26.2\%$$

This ratio reveals a level of gearing that would not normally be considered to be very high.

Activity 7.20

Calculate the gearing ratio of Alexis plc as at 31 March 2007.

The ratio as at 31 March 2007 is:

$$\text{Gearing ratio} = \frac{300}{(534 + 300)} \times 100$$

$$= 36.0\%$$

This ratio reveals a substantial increase in the level of gearing over the year.

Interest cover ratio

 The **interest cover ratio** measures the amount of operating profit available to cover interest payable. The ratio may be calculated as follows:

$$\text{Interest cover ratio} = \frac{\text{Operating profit}}{\text{Interest payable}}$$

The ratio for Alexis plc for the year ended 31 March 2006 is:

$$\text{Interest cover ratio} = \frac{243}{18}$$

$$= 13.5 \text{ times}$$

This ratio shows that the level of operating profit is considerably higher than the level of interest payable. This means that a significant fall in operating profit could occur before operating profit levels failed to cover interest payable. The lower the level of operating profit coverage, the greater the risk to lenders that interest payments will not be met, and the greater the risk to the shareholders that the lenders will take action against the business to recover the interest due.

Calculate the interest cover ratio of Alexis plc for the year ended 31 March 2007.

The ratio for the year ended 31 March 2007 will be:

$$\text{Interest cover ratio} = \frac{47}{32} = 1.5 \text{ times}$$

Real World 7.5 shows how Tesco plc, the supermarket chain, was able to use financial gearing to boost ROSF in the early 2000s.

Real World 7.5

Changing gear at Tesco

Figure 7.5 plots the ROSF, ROCE and interest cover ratios over the period 2000 to 2006.

Figure 7.5 The effect of financial gearing at Tesco plc 2000 to 2006

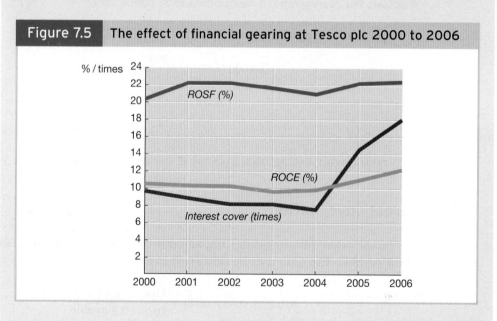

Tesco was able to boost returns to shareholders (ROSF), despite the business not producing a better ROCE (which reduced slightly between 1999 and 2003). This was achieved as a result of increasing financial gearing (as measured by interest cover) over that period. After 2004, Tesco started to reduce gearing again. Now ROSF continued to increase, but as a result of increasing ROCE.

Source: based on information contained in Tesco plc Annual Reports from 2003 to 2006.

Alexis plc's gearing ratios are:

	2006	2007
Gearing ratio	26.2%	36.0%
Interest cover ratio	13.5 times	1.5 times

Activity 7.22

What do you deduce from a comparison of Alexis plc's gearing ratios over the two years?

The gearing ratio altered significantly. This is mainly due to the substantial increase in long-term lenders to the financing of the business.

The interest cover ratio has declined dramatically from a position where operating profit covered interest 13.5 times in 2006, to one where operating profit covered interest only 1.5 times in 2007. This was partly caused by the increase in borrowings in 2007, but mainly caused by the dramatic decline in profitability in that year. The later situation looks hazardous; only a small decline in future profitability in 2007 would leave the business with insufficient operating profit to cover the interest payments. The gearing ratio at 31 March 2007 would not necessarily be considered to be very high for a business that was trading successfully. It is the low profitability that is the problem.

Without knowing what the business planned these ratios to be, it is not possible to reach a final conclusion on Alexis plc's gearing.

Real World 7.6 below provides some evidence concerning the gearing of listed businesses.

Real World 7.6

The gearing of listed businesses

Larger listed businesses tend to have higher levels of gearing than smaller ones. A Bank of England report on the financing of small businesses found that the average level of gearing among smaller listed businesses was 27 per cent compared with 37 per cent for the top 350 listed businesses. Over recent years the level of borrowing by larger listed businesses has risen steadily (Tesco plc – see Real World 7.5 – provides an example of this) whereas the level of borrowing for smaller listed businesses has remained fairly stable. This difference in gearing levels between larger and smaller businesses flies in the face of conventional wisdom.

Recent government investigations have found that smaller listed businesses often find it hard to attract investors. Many large institutional investors, who dominate the stock market, are not interested in the shares of smaller listed businesses because the amount of investment required is too small. As a result, shares in smaller businesses are less marketable. In such circumstances, it may be imagined that smaller businesses would become more reliant on borrowing and so would have higher levels of gearing than larger businesses. However, this is clearly not the case.

Although smaller businesses increase the level of shareholder funds by paying relatively low dividends and retaining more profits, they tend to be less profitable than larger businesses. So, higher retained profits do not seem to explain satisfactorily this phenomenon.

The only obvious factors that could explain this difference between smaller and larger businesses are the level of tax relief on interest on borrowings and borrowing capacity. Broadly, larger businesses pay tax at a higher rate than their smaller counterparts. This means that the tax benefits of borrowing tend to be greater per £ of interest paid for larger businesses than for smaller ones. It may well be that larger businesses can borrow at lower interest rates than smaller ones, if only because they tend to borrow larger sums and so the economies of scale may apply. Also larger businesses tend to be less likely to get into financial difficulties than smaller ones, so they may be able to borrow at lower interest rates.

Source: Adapted from 'Small Companies Surprise on Lending', *Financial Times*, 25 April 2003.

Self-assessment question 7.1

Both Ali plc and Bhaskar plc operate electrical stores throughout the UK. The financial statements of each business for the year ended 30 June 2007 are as follows:

Balance sheets as at 30 June 2007

	Ali plc £000	Bhaskar plc £000
Non-current assets		
Property, plant and equipment (cost less depreciation)		
Land and buildings	360.0	510.0
Fixtures and fittings	87.0	91.2
	447.0	601.2
Current assets		
Inventories	592.0	403.0
Trade receivables	176.4	321.9
Cash at bank	84.6	91.6
	853.0	816.5
Total assets	1,300.0	1,417.7
Equity		
£1 ordinary shares	320.0	250.0
Retained profit	367.6	624.6
	687.6	874.6
Non-current liabilities		
Borrowings – Loan notes	190.0	250.0
Current liabilities		
Trade payables	406.4	275.7
Taxation	16.0	17.4
	422.4	293.1
Total equity and liabilities	1,300.0	1,417.7

Income statements for the year ended 30 June 2007

	Ali plc £000	Bhaskar plc £000
Revenue	1,478.1	1,790.4
Cost of sales	(1,018.3)	(1,214.9)
Gross profit	459.8	575.5
Operating expenses	(308.5)	(408.6)
Operating profit	151.3	166.9
Interest payable	(19.4)	(27.5)
Profit before taxation	131.9	139.4
Taxation	(32.0)	(34.8)
Profit for the year	99.9	104.6

All purchases and sales were on credit.

Required:
For each business, calculate two ratios that are concerned with each of the following aspects:

* profitability;
* efficiency;
* liquidity; and
* gearing (eight ratios in total).

What can you conclude from the ratios that you have calculated?

The answer to this question can be found at the back of the book on p. 405.

Summary

The main points of this chapter may be summarised as follows:

Ratio analysis

- A ratio compares two related figures, usually both from the same set of financial statements.
- Ratio analysis is an aid to understanding what the financial statements really mean.
- It is an inexact science and so results must be interpreted cautiously.
- Past periods, the performance of similar businesses and planned performance are often used to provide benchmark ratios.
- A brief overview of the financial statements can often provide insights that may not be revealed by ratios and/or may help in the interpretation of them.

Profitability ratios – concerned with effectiveness at generating profit

- Return on ordinary shareholders' funds (ROSF).
- Return on capital employed (ROCE).
- Operating profit margin.
- Gross profit margin.

Efficiency ratios – concerned with efficiency of using assets/resources

- Average inventories turnover period.
- Average settlement period for trade receivables.
- Average settlement period for trade payables.
- Sales revenue to capital employed.
- Sales revenue per employee.

Liquidity ratios – concerned with the ability to meet short-term obligations

- Current ratio.
- Acid test ratio.
- Cash generated from operations to maturing obligations.

Operating cash cycle (for a wholesaler) $=$ length of time from buying inventories to receiving cash from receivables less payables' payment period (in days).

Gearing ratios – concerned with relationship between equity and debt financing

- Gearing ratio.
- Interest cover ratio.

→ **Key terms**

Return on ordinary shareholders' funds (ROSF) ratio p. 210
Return on capital employed (ROCE) ratio p. 211
Operating profit margin ratio p. 212
Gross profit margin ratio p. 213
Average inventories turnover period ratio p. 215
Average settlement period for trade receivables ratio p. 216
Average settlement period for trade payables ratio p. 217

Sales revenue to capital employed ratio p. 218
Sales revenue per employee ratio p. 219
Current ratio p. 222
Acid test ratio p. 223
Cash generated from operations to maturing obligations ratio p. 223
Operating cash cycle (OCC) p. 224
Financial gearing p. 226
Gearing ratio p. 229
Interest cover ratio p. 229

Further reading

If you would like to explore the topics covered in this chapter in more depth, we recommend the following books:

Elliott, B. and Elliott, J. (2006) *Financial Accounting and Reporting*, 11th edn, Financial Times Prentice Hall, Chapters 28 and 29.

Revsine, L., Collins, D. and Bruce Johnson, W. (2005) *Financial Reporting and Analysis*, 3rd edn, Prentice Hall, Chapter 5.

Sutton, T. (2004) *Corporate Financial Accounting and Reporting*, 2nd edn, Financial Times Prentice Hall, Chapter 19.

Wild, J., Subramanyam, K. and Halsey, R. (2006) *Financial Statement Analysis*, 9th edn, McGraw-Hill, Chapters 8, 9 and 11.

Review questions

Answers to these questions can be found at the back of the book on pp. 414–15.

7.1 Some businesses operate on a low operating profit margin (for example, a supermarket chain). Does this mean that the return on capital employed from the business will also be low?

7.2 What problems might a business encounter when it attempts to minimise its operating cash cycle?

7.3 Two businesses operate in the same industry. One has an inventories turnover period that is longer than the industry average. The other has an inventories turnover period that is shorter than the industry average. Give three possible explanations for each business's inventories turnover period ratio.

7.4 In the chapter it was mentioned that ratios help to eliminate some of the problems of comparing businesses of different sizes. Does this mean that size is irrelevant when interpreting and analysing the position and performance of different businesses?

Exercises

Exercises 7.4 to 7.8 are more advanced than 7.1 to 7.3. Those with a coloured number have an answer at the back of the book, starting on p. 434.

If you wish to try more exercises, visit the students' side of the Companion Website.

7.1 Jiang Ltd has recently produced its financial statements for the current year. The directors are concerned that the return on capital employed (ROCE) had decreased from 14 per cent last year to 12 per cent for the current year.

The following reasons were suggested as to why this reduction in ROCE had occurred:

1 an increase in the gross profit margin;
2 a reduction in sales revenue;
3 an increase in overhead expenses;
4 an increase in amount of inventories held;
5 the repayment of some borrowings at the year end; and
6 an increase in the time taken for credit customers (trade receivables) to pay.

Required:
Taking each of these six suggested reasons in turn, state, with reasons, whether each of them could lead to a reduction in ROCE.

7.2 Amsterdam Ltd and Berlin Ltd are both engaged in retailing, but they seem to take a different approach to it according to the following information:

Ratio	Amsterdam Ltd	Berlin Ltd
Return on capital employed (ROCE)	20%	17%
Return on ordinary shareholders' funds (ROSF)	30%	18%
Average settlement period for trade receivables	63 days	21 days
Average settlement period for trade payables	50 days	45 days
Gross profit margin	40%	15%
Operating profit margin	10%	10%
Average inventories turnover period	52 days	25 days

Required:

Describe what this information indicates about the differences in approach between the two businesses. If one of them prides itself on personal service and one of them on competitive prices, which do you think is which and why?

7.3 The directors of Helena Beauty Products Ltd have been presented with the following abridged financial statements:

Helena Beauty Products Ltd
Income statement for the year ended 30 September

	2006		2007	
	£000	£000	£000	£000
Sales revenue		3,600		3,840
Cost of sales				
Opening inventories	320		400	
Purchases	2,240		2,350	
	2,560		2,750	
Closing inventories	(400)	(2,160)	(500)	(2,250)
Gross profit		1,440		1,590
Expenses		(1,360)		(1,500)
Profit		80		90

Balance sheet as at 30 September

	2006	2007
	£000	£000
Non-current assets		
Property, plant and equipment	1,900	1,860
Current assets		
Inventories	400	500
Trade receivables	750	960
Cash at bank	8	4
	1,158	1,464
Total assets	3,058	3,324
Equity		
£1 ordinary shares	1,650	1,766
Reserves	1,018	1,108
	2,668	2,874
Current liabilities	390	450
Total equity and liabilities	3,058	3,324

Required:

Using six ratios, comment on the profitability (three ratios) and efficiency (three ratios) of the business as revealed by the statements shown above.

7.4 Conday and Co. Ltd has been in operation for three years and produces antique reproduction furniture for the export market. The most recent set of financial statements for the business is set out as follows:

Balance sheet as at 30 November

	£000
Non-current assets	
Property, plant and equipment (Cost less depr'n)	
Land and buildings	228
Plant and machinery	762
	990
Current assets	
Inventories	600
Trade receivables	820
	1,420
Total assets	2,410
Equity	
Ordinary shares of £1 each	700
Retained earnings	365
	1,065
Non-current liabilities	
Borrowings – 9% loan notes (Note 1)	200
Current liabilities	
Trade payables	665
Taxation	48
Short-term borrowings (all bank overdraft)	432
	1,145
Total equity and liabilities	2,410

Income statement for the year ended 30 November

	£000
Revenue	2,600
Cost of sales	(1,620)
Gross profit	980
Selling and distribution expenses (Note 2)	(408)
Administration expenses	(194)
Operating profit	378
Finance expenses	(58)
Profit before taxation	320
Taxation	(95)
Profit for the year	225

Notes

1　The loan notes are secured on the freehold land and buildings.
2　Selling and distribution expenses include £170,000 in respect of bad debts.
3　A dividend of £160,000 was paid on the ordinary shares during the year.
4　The directors have invited an investor to take up a new issue of ordinary shares in the business at £6.40 each making a total investment of £200,000. The directors wish to use the funds to finance a programme of further expansion.

Required:

(a) Analyse the financial position and performance of the business and comment on any features that you consider to be significant.

(b) State, with reasons, whether or not the investor should invest in the business on the terms outlined.

7.5 Threads Limited manufactures nuts and bolts, which are sold to industrial users. The abbreviated financial statements for 2006 and 2007 are as follows:

Income statements for the year ended 30 June

	2006	2007
	£000	£000
Revenue	1,180	1,200
Cost of sales	(680)	(750)
Gross profit	500	450
Operating expenses	(200)	(208)
Depreciation	(66)	(75)
Operating profit	234	167
Interest	(–)	(8)
Profit before taxation	234	159
Taxation	(80)	(48)
Profit for the year	154	111

Balance sheets as at 30 June

	2006	2007
	£000	£000
Non-current assets		
Property, plant and equipment	702	687
Current assets		
Inventories	148	236
Trade receivables	102	156
Cash	3	4
	253	396
Total assets	955	1,083
Equity		
Ordinary share capital of £1 (fully paid)	500	500
Retained earnings	256	295
	756	795
Non-current liabilities		
Borrowings – Bank loan	–	50
Current liabilities		
Trade payables	60	76
Other payables and accruals	18	16
Taxation	40	24
Short-term borrowings (all bank overdraft)	81	122
	199	238
Total equity and liabilities	955	1,083

Required:

(a) Calculate the following financial ratios for *both* 2006 and 2007 (using year-end figures for balance sheet items):
- return on capital employed;
- operating profit margin;
- gross profit margin;
- current ratio;
- acid test ratio;
- settlement period for trade receivables;
- settlement period for trade payables; and
- inventories turnover period.

(b) Comment on the performance of Threads Limited from the viewpoint of a business considering supplying a substantial amount of goods to Threads Limited on usual trade credit terms.

7.6 Bradbury Ltd is a family-owned clothes manufacturer based in the south-west of England. For a number of years the chairman and managing director was David Bradbury. During his period of office, sales revenue had grown steadily at a rate of 2 to 3 per cent each year. David Bradbury retired on 30 November 2006 and was succeeded by his son Simon. Soon after taking office, Simon decided to expand the business. Within weeks he had successfully negotiated a five-year contract with a large clothes retailer to make a range of sports and leisurewear items. The contract will result in an additional £2 million in sales revenue during each year of the contract. To fulfil the contract, Bradbury Ltd acquired new equipment and premises.

Financial information concerning the business is given below:

Income statements for the year ended 30 November

	2006 £000	2007 £000
Revenue	9,482	11,365
Operating profit	914	1,042
Interest charges	(22)	(81)
Profit before taxation	892	961
Taxation	(358)	(386)
Profit for the year	534	575

Balance sheets as at 30 November

	2006 £000	2007 £000
Non-current assets		
Property, plant and equipment		
Premises at cost	5,240	7,360
Plant and equipment (net)	2,375	4,057
	7,615	11,417
Current assets		
Inventories	2,386	3,420
Trade receivables	2,540	4,280
	4,926	7,700
Total assets	12,541	19,117
Equity		
Share capital	2,000	2,000
Reserves	7,813	8,268
	9,813	10,268
Non-current liabilities		
Borrowing – Loans	1,220	3,675
Current liabilities		
Trade payables	1,157	2,245
Taxation	179	193
Short-term borrowings (all bank overdraft)	172	2,736
	1,508	5,174
Total equity and liabilities	12,541	19,117

Required:

(a) Calculate, for each year (using year-end figures for balance sheet items), the following ratios:
   1 operating profit margin;
   2 return on capital employed;
   3 current ratio;

4 gearing ratio;

5 days trade receivables (settlement period); and

6 sales revenue to capital employed.

(b) Using the above ratios, and any other ratios or information you consider relevant, comment on the results of the expansion programme.

7.7 The financial statements for Harridges Limited are given below for the two years ended 30 June 2006 and 2007. Harridges Limited operates a department store in the centre of a small town.

Harridges Limited
Income statement for the years ended 30 June

	2006 £000	2007 £000
Sales revenue	2,600	3,500
Cost of sales	(1,560)	(2,350)
Gross profit	1,040	1,150
Wages and salaries	(320)	(350)
Overheads	(260)	(200)
Depreciation	(150)	(250)
Operating profit	310	350
Interest payable	(50)	(50)
Profit before taxation	260	300
Taxation	(105)	(125)
Profit for the year	155	175

Balance sheet as at 30 June

	2006 £000	2007 £000
Non-current assets		
Property, plant and equipment	1,265	1,525
Current assets		
Inventories	250	400
Trade receivables	105	145
Cash at bank	380	115
	735	660
Total assets	2,000	2,185
Equity		
Share capital: £1 shares fully paid	490	490
Share premium	260	260
Retained earnings	350	450
	1,100	1,200
Non-current liabilities		
Borrowings – 10% loan notes	500	500
Current liabilities		
Trade payables	300	375
Other payables	100	110
	400	485
Total equity and liabilities	2,000	2,185

Required:

(a) Choose and calculate eight ratios that would be helpful in assessing the performance of Harridges Limited. Use end-of-year values and calculate ratios for both 2006 and 2007.

(b) Using the ratios calculated in (a) and any others you consider helpful, comment on the business's performance from the viewpoint of a prospective purchaser of a majority of shares.

7.8 The financial statements of Freezeqwik Ltd, a distributor of frozen foods, are set out below for the year ended 31 December last year.

Income statement for the year ended 31 December last year

	£000	£000
Sales revenue		820
Cost of sales		
Opening inventories	142	
Purchases	568	
	710	
Closing inventories	166	544
Gross profit		276
Administration expenses		(120)
Distribution expenses		(95)
Operating profit		61
Financial expenses		(32)
Profit before taxation		29
Taxation		(7)
Profit for the period		22

Balance sheet as at 31 December last year

		£000
Non-current assets		
Property, plant and equipment		
Freehold premises at valuation	180	
Fixtures and fittings at cost less depreciation	82	
Motor vans at cost less depreciation	102	364
Current assets		
Inventories	166	
Trade receivables	264	
Cash	24	454
Total assets		818
Equity		
Ordinary share capital	300	
Share premium account	200	
Retained earnings	152	652
Current liabilities		
Trade payables	159	
Taxation	7	166
Total equity and liabilities		818

All purchases and sales are on credit. There has been no change in the level of trade receivables or payables over the period.

Required:

Calculate the length of the OCC for the business and go on to suggest how the business may seek to reduce this period.

8

Analysing and interpreting financial statements (2)

Introduction

In this chapter we shall continue our examination of the analysis and interpretation of financial statements. We start by taking a detailed look at investment ratios, that is those which consider business performance from the perspective of a shareholder. We then go on to consider common-size financial statements. This technique presents the financial statements themselves as ratios and can offer useful insights to performance and position.

We shall also consider the value of ratios in predicting the future. In particular, we shall examine the extent to which ratios can help predict financial collapse. Finally, we consider problems that are encountered when undertaking ratio analysis. Although ratios can be extremely useful in assessing financial health, it is important to be aware of their limitations when making decisions.

Learning outcomes

When you have completed this chapter, you should be able to:

● Calculate and interpret key investment ratios.

● Prepare and interpret common-size financial statements.

● Evaluate the use of ratios in helping to predict financial failure.

● Discuss the limitations of ratios as a tool of financial analysis.

Alexis plc

To demonstrate how particular ratios are calculated and interpreted, we shall continue to refer to Alexis plc, whose financial statements and other information are set out in Example 7.1 on p. 207.

Investment ratios

There are various ratios available that are designed to help investors assess the returns on their investment. The following are widely used:

- dividend payout ratio;
- dividend yield ratio;
- earnings per share;
- operating cash flow per share; and
- price/earnings ratio.

Dividend payout ratio

→ The **dividend payout ratio** measures the proportion of earnings that a business pays out to shareholders in the form of dividends. The ratio is calculated as follows:

$$\text{Dividend payout ratio} = \frac{\text{Dividends announced for the year}}{\text{Earnings for the year available for dividends}} \times 100$$

In the case of ordinary shares, the earnings available for dividend will normally be the profit for the year (that is, the net profit after taxation) less any preference dividends relating to the year. This ratio is normally expressed as a percentage.

The dividend payout ratio for Alexis plc for the year ended 31 March 2006 is:

$$\text{Dividend payout ratio} = \frac{40}{165} \times 100$$

$$= 24.2\%$$

Activity 8.1

Calculate the dividend payout ratio of Alexis plc for the year ended 31 March 2007.

The ratio for 2007 is:

$$\frac{40}{11} = 363.6\%$$

This would normally be considered to be a very alarming increase in the ratio over the two years. Paying a dividend of £40 m in 2007 would probably be regarded as very imprudent.

The information provided by the dividend payout ratio is often expressed slightly
differently as the **dividend cover ratio**. Here the calculation is:

$$\text{Dividend cover ratio} = \frac{\text{Earnings for the year available for dividend}}{\text{Dividend announced for the year}}$$

In the case of Alexis plc, (for 2006) it would be 165/40 = 4.1 times. That is to say, the
earnings available for dividend cover the actual dividend by just over four times.

Dividend yield ratio

The **dividend yield ratio** relates the cash return from a share to its current market value.
This can help investors to assess the cash return on their investment in the business.
The ratio, expressed as a percentage is:

$$\text{Dividend yield} = \frac{\text{Dividend per share}/(1 - t)}{\text{Market value per share}} \times 100$$

Where t is the appropriate rate of income tax.

This requires some explanation. In the UK, investors who receive a dividend from a
business also receive a tax credit. This tax credit is equal to 10 per cent of the dividend,
plus the tax credit (or one ninth of the amount of the dividend paid). This tax credit
can be offset against any Income Tax liability arising from the dividends received. If
the dividend is received by a non-tax-paying shareholder, such as a pension fund or a
registered charity, there is no right to reclaim the tax credit.

Investors may wish to compare the returns from shares with the returns from other
forms of investment. As these other forms of investment are often quoted on a 'gross'
(that is, pre-tax) basis it is useful to 'gross up' the dividend to make comparison easier.
We can achieve this by dividing the **dividend per share** by $(1 - t)$, where t is the
dividend income tax credit rate.

Assuming a dividend income tax credit rate of 10 per cent, the dividend yield for
Alexis plc for the year ended 31 March 2006 is:

$$\text{Dividend yield} = \frac{0.067^*/(1 - 0.10)}{2.50} \times 100 = 3.0\%$$

* Dividend proposed/number of shares = 40/(300 × 2) = £0.067 dividend per share (the 300 is multi-
plied by 2 because they are £0.50 shares).

Activity 8.2

Calculate the dividend yield for Alexis plc for the year ended 31 March 2007.

The ratio for 2007 is:

$$\text{Dividend yield} = \frac{0.067^*/(1 - 0.10)}{1.50} \times 100 = 4.9\%$$

* 40/(300 × 2) = £0.067

Earnings per share

→ The **earnings per share (EPS) ratio** relates the earnings generated by the business, and available to shareholders, during a period to the number of shares in issue. For equity (ordinary) shareholders, the amount available will be represented by the profit for the year (net profit after taxation) less any preference dividend, where applicable. The ratio for equity shareholders is calculated as follows:

$$\text{Earnings per share} = \frac{\text{Earnings available to ordinary shareholders}}{\text{Number of ordinary shares in issue}}$$

In the case of Alexis plc, the earnings per share for the year ended 31 March 2006 is:

$$\text{EPS} = \frac{£165 \text{ m}}{600 \text{ m}} = 27.5 \text{ p}$$

Many investment analysts regard the EPS ratio as a fundamental measure of share performance. The trend in earnings per share over time is used to help assess the investment potential of a business's shares. Though it is possible to make total profit rise through ordinary shareholders investing more in the business, this will not necessarily mean that the profitability *per share* will rise as a result.

It is not usually very helpful to compare the earnings per share of one business with those of another. Differences in capital structure (for example, in the nominal value of shares issued) can render any such comparison meaningless. However, it can be very useful to monitor the changes that occur in this ratio for a particular business over time.

Activity 8.3

Calculate the earnings per share of Alexis plc for the year ended 31 March 2007.

The ratio for 2007 is:

$$\text{EPS} = \frac{£11 \text{ m}}{600 \text{ m}} = 1.8 \text{ p}$$

Cash generated from operations per share

It can be argued that, in the short term at least, cash generated from operations (found in the cash flow statement) provides a better guide to the ability of a business to pay dividends and to undertake planned expenditures than the earnings per share figure.

→ The **cash generated from operations (CGO) per ordinary share ratio** is calculated as follows:

$$\text{Cash generated from operations per share} = \frac{\text{Cash generated from operations less preference dividend (if any)}}{\text{Number of ordinary shares in issue}}$$

The ratio for Alexis plc for the year ended 31 March 2006 is as follows:

$$\text{CGO per share} = \frac{£251 \text{ m}}{600 \text{ m}} = 41.8 \text{ p}$$

Activity 8.4

Calculate the CGO per ordinary share for Alexis plc for the year ended 31 March 2007.

The ratio for 2007 is:

$$\text{CGO per share} = \frac{£34 \text{ m}}{600 \text{ m}} = 5.7 \text{ p}$$

There has been a dramatic decrease in this ratio over the two-year period.

Note that, for both years, the CGO per share for Alexis plc is higher than the earnings per share. This is not unusual. The effect of adding back depreciation to derive the CGO figures will often ensure that a higher figure is derived.

Price/earnings (P/E) ratio

→ The **price/earnings ratio** relates the market value of a share to the earnings per share. This ratio can be calculated as follows:

$$\text{P/E ratio} = \frac{\text{Market value per share}}{\text{Earnings per share}}$$

The P/E ratio for Alexis plc as at 31 March 2006 is:

$$\text{P/E ratio} = \frac{£2.50}{27.5 \text{ p}^*}$$
$$= 9.1 \text{ times}$$

* The EPS figure (27.5 p) was calculated on p. 245.

This ratio reveals that the capital value of the share is 9.1 times higher than its current level of earnings. The ratio is a measure of market confidence in the future of a business. The higher the P/E ratio, the greater the confidence in the future earning power of the business and, consequently, the more investors are prepared to pay in relation to the earnings stream of the business.

P/E ratios provide a useful guide to market confidence concerning the future and they can, therefore, be helpful when comparing different businesses. However, differences in accounting policies between businesses can lead to different profit and earnings per share figures, and this can distort comparisons.

Activity 8.5

Calculate the P/E ratio of Alexis plc as at 31 March 2007.

The ratio for 2007 is:

$$\text{P/E ratio} = \frac{£1.50}{1.8 \text{ p}} = 83.3 \text{ times}$$

The investment ratios for Alexis plc over the two-year period are as follows:

	2006	2007
Dividend payout ratio	24.2%	363.6%
Dividend yield ratio	3.0%	4.9%
Earnings per share	27.5 p	1.8 p
Cash generated from operations per share	41.8 p	5.7 p
P/E ratio	9.1 times	83.3 times

Activity 8.6

What do you deduce from the investment ratios set out above?

Can you offer an explanation why the share price has not fallen as much as it might have done, bearing in mind the very poor (relative to 2006) trading performance in 2007?

We thought that, though the EPS has fallen dramatically and the dividend payment for 2007 seems very imprudent, the share price seems to have held up remarkably well (fallen from £2.50 to £1.50, see Chapter 7, p. 208). This means that dividend yield and P/E value for 2007 look better than those for 2006. This is an anomaly of these two ratios, which stems from using a forward-looking value (the share price) in conjunction with historic data (dividends and earnings). Share prices are based on investors' assessments of the business's future. It seems with Alexis plc that, at the end of 2007, the 'market' was not happy with the business, relative to 2006. This is evidenced by the fact that the share price had fallen by £1 a share. On the other hand, the share price has not fallen as much as profit for the year. It appears that investors believe that the business will perform better in the future than it did in 2007. This may well be because they believe that the large expansion in assets and employee numbers that occurred in 2007 will yield benefits in the future; benefits that the business was not able to generate during 2007.

Real World 8.1 gives some information about the shares of several large, well-known UK businesses. This type of information is provided on a daily basis by several newspapers, notably the *Financial Times*.

Real World 8.1

Market statistics for some well-known businesses   **FT**

The following data were extracted from the *Financial Times* on 11 November 2006, relating to the previous day's trading of the shares of some well-known businesses on the London Stock Exchange:

Share	Price	Chng	2006		Y'ld	P/E	Volume
			High	Low			000s
BP	598	−3.5	723.08	558.5	3.6	11.2	101,930
JD Wetherspoon	646.5	+19	646.5	317	0.7	27.3	419
BSkyB	551	−3	578	471.19	2.2	18.3	7,677
Marks and Spencer	702	–	716.50	477.19	2	19.9	19,533
Rolls-Royce	461.25	+2.75	496.75	373	1.6	9.4	3,823
Vodafone	134.50	+0.50	138.38	107.37	4.5	9.8	353,257

→

Real World 8.1 continued

The column headings are as follows:

Price   Mid-market price in pence (that is, the price midway between buying and selling price) of the shares at the end of 10 November 2006.

Chng   Gain or loss in mid-market price during 10 November 2006.

High/Low   Highest and lowest prices reached by the share during the year.

Y'ld   Gross dividend yield, based on the most recent year's dividend and the current share price.

P/E   Price/earnings ratio, based on the most recent year's (after-taxation) profit for the year and the current share price.

Volume   The number of shares (in thousands) that were bought/sold on 10 November 2006.

So, for example for BP (the oil business):

- the shares had a mid-market price of £5.98 each at the close of Stock Exchange trading on 10 November 2006;
- the shares had decreased in price by 3.5 pence during trading on 10 November;
- the shares had highest and lowest prices during 2006 of £7.2308 and £5.585, repectively;
- the shares had a dividend yield, based on the 10 November price (and the dividend for the most recent year) of 3.6 per cent;
- the shares had a P/E ratio, based on the 10 November price (and the after taxation earnings per share for the most recent year) of 11.2;
- During trading in the shares on 10 November, 101,930,000 of the business's shares had changed hands from one investor to another.

Real World 8.2 shows how investment ratios can vary between different industry sectors.

Real World 8.2

How investment ratios vary between industries

Investment ratios can vary significantly between businesses and between industries. To give some indication of the range of variations that occur, the average dividend yield ratios and average P/E ratios for listed businesses in 12 different industries are shown in Figures 8.1 and 8.2 respectively.

These dividend yield ratios are calculated from the current market value of the shares and the most recent year's dividend paid.

Some industries tend to pay out lower dividends than others, leading to lower dividend yield ratios. The average for all Stock Exchange listed businesses was (as is shown in Figure 8.1) 2.93, but there is a wide variation with Real Estate at 1.74 and Banks at 4.14.

Pharmaceutical businesses tend to invest heavily in developing new drugs, hence their tendency to pay low dividends compared with their share prices. Some of the inter-industry differences in the dividend yield ratio can be explained by the nature of the calculation of the ratio. The prices of shares at any given moment are based on expectations of their economic futures; dividends are actual past events. A business that had a good trading year recently may have paid a dividend that, in the light of investors' assessment on the business's economic future, may be high (a high dividend yield).

These P/E ratios are calculated from the current market value of the shares and the most recent year's earnings per share.

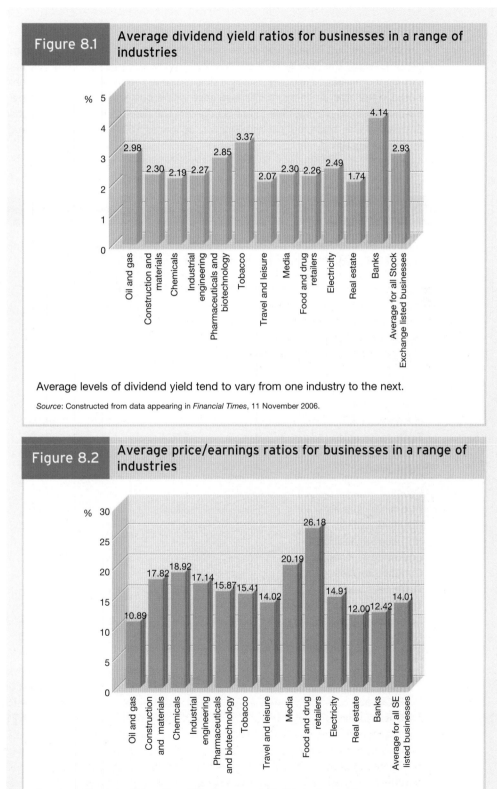

Figure 8.1 Average dividend yield ratios for businesses in a range of industries

Average levels of dividend yield tend to vary from one industry to the next.

Source: Constructed from data appearing in *Financial Times*, 11 November 2006.

Figure 8.2 Average price/earnings ratios for businesses in a range of industries

Average price/earnings ratios differ from one industry to the next.

Source: Constructed from data appearing in *Financial Times*, 11 November 2006.

Real World 8.2 continued

Businesses that have a high share price relative to their recent historic earnings have high P/E ratios. This may be because their future is regarded as economically bright, which may be the result of investing heavily in the future at the expense of recent profits (earnings). On the other hand, high P/Es also arise where businesses have recent low earnings, but investors believe that their future is brighter. The average for all Stock Exchange listed businesses was 14.01, but Oil and Gas was as low as 10.89 and Food and Drug Retailers as high as 26.18.

Self-assessment question 8.1

Both Ali plc and Bhaskar plc operate electrical stores throughout the UK. The financial statements of each business for the year ended 30 June 2007 are as follows:

Balance sheets as at 30 June 2007

	Ali plc		Bhaskar plc	
	£000	£000	£000	£000
Non-current assets				
Property, plant and equipment (cost less depreciation)				
Land and buildings	360.0		510.0	
Fixtures and fittings	87.0	447.0	91.2	601.2
Current assets				
Inventories	592.0		403.0	
Trade receivables	176.4		321.9	
Cash at bank	84.6	853.0	91.6	816.5
Total assets		1,300.0		1,417.7
Equity				
£1 ordinary shares	320.0		250.0	
Retained profit	367.6	687.6	624.6	874.6
Non-current liabilities				
Borrowings – Loan notes		190.0		250.0
Current liabilities				
Trade payables	406.4		275.7	
Taxation	16.0	422.4	17.4	293.1
Total equity and liabilities		1,300.0		1,417.7

Income statements for the year ended 30 June 2007

	Ali plc	Bhaskar plc
	£000	£000
Revenue	1,478.1	1,790.4
Cost of sales	(1,018.3)	(1,214.9)
Gross profit	459.8	575.5
Operating expenses	(308.5)	(408.6)
Operating profit	151.3	166.9
Interest payable	(19.4)	(27.5)
Profit before taxation	131.9	139.4
Taxation	(32.0)	(34.8)
Profit for the year	99.9	104.6

All purchases and sales were on credit. Ali plc had announced its intention to pay a dividend of £135,000 and Bhaskar plc £95,000 in respect of the year. The market values of a share in Ali plc and Bhaskar plc at the end of the year were £6.50 and £8.20 respectively. The dividend income tax credit rate can be taken to be 10 per cent.

Required:
For each business, calculate the following ratios:

● dividend payout ratio;
● dividend yield ratio;
● earnings per share;
● P/E ratio.

What can you conclude from the ratios that you have calculated?

The answer to this question can be found at the back of the book on p. 406.

Financial ratios and the problem of overtrading

→ **Overtrading** occurs where a business is operating at a level of activity that cannot be supported by the amount of finance that has been committed. For example, the business has inadequate finance to fund the level of trade receivables and inventories necessary for the level of sales revenue that it is achieving. This situation usually reflects a poor level of financial control over the business. The reasons for overtrading are varied. It may occur:

● in young, expanding businesses that fail to prepare adequately for the rapid increase in demand for their goods or services;
● in businesses where the managers may have miscalculated the level of expected sales demand or have failed to control escalating project costs;
● as a result of a fall in the value of money (inflation), causing more finance to be committed to inventories and trade receivables, even where there is no expansion in the real volume of trade;
● where the owners are unable both to inject further funds into the business and cannot persuade others to invest in the business.

Whatever the reason, the problems that it brings must be dealt with if the business is to survive over the longer term.

Overtrading results in liquidity problems such as exceeding borrowing limits, or slow repayment of lenders and trade payables. It can also result in suppliers withholding supplies, thereby making it difficult to meet customer needs. The managers of the business might be forced to direct all their efforts to dealing with immediate and pressing problems, such as finding cash to meet interest charges due or paying wages. Longer-term planning becomes difficult and managers may spend their time going from crisis to crisis. At the extreme, a business may fail because it cannot meet its maturing obligations.

Activity 8.7

If a business is overtrading, do you think the following ratios would be higher or lower than normally expected?

(a) Current ratio.
(b) Average inventories turnover period.
(c) Average settlement period for trade receivables.
(d) Average settlement period for trade payables.

Your answer should be as follows:

(a) The current ratio would be lower than normally expected. This is a measure of liquidity, and lack of liquidity is an important symptom of overtrading.
(b) The average inventories turnover period would be lower than normally expected. Where a business is overtrading, the level of inventories held will be low because of the problems of financing them. In the short term, sales revenue may not be badly affected by the low inventories levels and therefore they will be turned over more quickly.
(c) The average settlement period for trade receivables may be lower than normally expected. Where a business is suffering from liquidity problems it may chase credit customers more vigorously so as to improve cash flows.
(d) The average settlement period for trade payables may be higher than normally expected. The business may try to delay payments to its suppliers because of the liquidity problems arising.

To deal with the overtrading problem, a business must ensure that the finance available is consistent with the level of operations. Thus, if a business that is overtrading is unable to raise new finance, it should cut back its level of operations in line with the finance available. Although this may mean lost sales and lost profits in the short term, it may be necessary to ensure survival over the longer term.

Trend analysis

It is often helpful to see whether ratios are indicating trends. Key ratios can be plotted on a graph to provide a simple visual display of changes occurring over time. The trends occurring within a business may, for example, be plotted against trends for rival businesses or for the industry as a whole for comparison purposes. An example of trend analysis is shown in **Real World 8.3**.

Real World 8.3

Trend setting

In Figure 8.3 (below) the current ratio of Tesco plc is plotted against the same ratio for two other businesses within the same industry – J. Sainsbury plc and Wm Morrison plc – over a seven-year period. We can see that the current ratio of Tesco plc has risen slightly over the period but it is, nevertheless, consistently lower than that of its main rivals, until 2005, when it overtook Morrision.

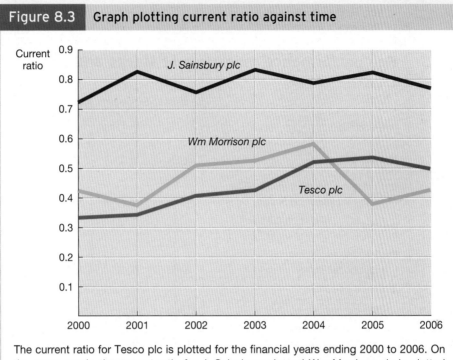

Figure 8.3   Graph plotting current ratio against time

The current ratio for Tesco plc is plotted for the financial years ending 2000 to 2006. On the same graph, the current ratio for J. Sainsbury plc and Wm Morrison plc is plotted for the same financial years, enabling comparison to be made between the ratio for Tesco plc and those of its rivals.

Many larger businesses publish certain key financial ratios as part of their annual reports to help users identify significant trends. These ratios typically cover several years' activities. **Real World 8.4** shows part of the table of 'key performance measures' of Marks and Spencer plc (M&S), the well-known UK high street store.

After many years of profitable growth, M&S suffered a decline in its fortunes during the late 1990s. This was seen by the directors, and by many independent commentators, as arising from the business allowing itself to be drawn away from its traditional areas of strength. Steps were taken to deal with the problem and the business seems to have 'turned the corner'.

M&S reached its low point in the year ended March 2001 when it incurred a significant overall loss, with an operating profit well below that achieved in 1998. The improvements in every year since 2002 are very clear. The return on equity (return on ordinary shareholders' funds) in 2006 is significantly better than for any others of the five years. Though in 2005, both the gross profit and net (operating profit) margins are lower than in 2004, they both recovered strongly in 2006. The return on equity was boosted in 2005 by the profit on disposal of the business's financial services division and a lower equity base due to M&S buying and cancelling some of its own shares.

Real World 8.4

Key performance measures of Marks and Spencer plc

		2006 52 weeks	2005 52 weeks	2004 53 weeks	2003 52 weeks	2002 52 weeks
Gross margin	$\dfrac{\text{Gross profit}}{\text{Turnover}}$	38.3%	34.7%	35.4%	34.8%	34.4%
Net margin	$\dfrac{\text{Operating profit}}{\text{Turnover}}$	10.9%	8.0%	9.9%	8.6%	7.7%
Net margin excluding exceptional items and asset disposals		11.0%	8.7%	10.2%	9.2%	7.1%
Profitability	$\dfrac{\text{Profit before tax}}{\text{Turnover}}$	9.6%	6.7%	9.4%	8.4%	8.5%
Profitability excluding exceptional items		9.6%	7.4%	9.7%	9.0%	7.9%
Earnings per share $\dfrac{\text{Standard earnings}}{\substack{\text{Weighted average ordinary}\\ \text{shares in issue}}}$		31.4 p	29.1 p	24.2 p	21.8 p	5.4 p
Earnings per share adjusted for exceptional items		31.5 p	20.8 p	24.7 p	23.3 p	16.3 p
Dividend per share declared in respect of the year		14.0 p	12.1 p	11.5 p	10.5 p	9.5 p
Dividend cover $\dfrac{\text{Profit attributable to shareholders}}{\text{Dividends payable}}$		2.2x	2.9x	2.1x	2.1x	2.2x
Return on equity $\dfrac{\text{Profit attributable to shareholders}}{\text{Average equity shareholders' funds}}$		52.3%	35.0%	25.2%	22.4%	11.5%

Source: Marks and Spencer plc Annual Report 2006. Reproduced by kind permission of Marks and Spencer plc. The results for 2002 have not been restated following the adoption of a number of accounting standards in 2004. Similarly, the 2002 to 2004 results have not been restated following the adoption of IFRS in 2005. This means that the results over the five years are not strictly comparable.

Common-size financial statements

→ **Common-size financial statements** are normal financial statements (such as the income statement, balance sheet and cash flow statement), which are expressed in terms of some base figure. The objective of presenting financial statements in this way is to help make better comparisons. The detection of differences and trends is often more obvious than may be the case when examining the original statements, which are expressed in financial values.

Vertical analysis

One approach to common-size statements is to express all the figures in a particular statement in terms of one of the figures in that statement. This 'base' figure is typically one that is seen as a key figure in the statement, such as sales revenue in an income statement, total long-term funds in a balance sheet and the cash flow from operating activities in the cash flow statement.

Example 8.1 is a common-size income statement that uses sales revenue as the base figure. Note the base figure is set at 100 and all other figures are expressed as a percentage of this.

Example 8.1

The common-size income statement of Alexis plc (see Example 7.1 on pp. 207–09) for 2006 in abbreviated form, and using revenue as the base figure, will be as follows:

Common-size income statement for the year ended 31 March 2006

		Calculation of figures
Revenue	100.0	Base figure
Cost of sales	(77.9)	(1,745/2,240) × 100%
Gross profit	22.1	(495/2,240) × 100%
Operating expenses	(11.3)	(252/2,240) × 100%
Operating profit	10.8	(243/2,240) × 100%
Interest payable	(0.8)	(18/2,240) × 100%
Profit before taxation	10.0	(225/2,240) × 100%
Taxation	(2.7)	(60/2,240) × 100%
Profit for the year	7.3	(165/2,240) × 100%

Each of the figures in the income statement is simply the original financial figure divided by the revenue figure and then expressed as a percentage.

Of course, not much can be discerned from looking at just one common-size statement. We need some benchmark for comparison, and this could be other accounting periods for the same business.

Activity 8.8

The following is a set of common-size income statements for a major high street department store for five consecutive accounting periods:

	Year 1	Year 2	Year 3	Year 4	Year 5
Revenue	100.0	100.0	100.0	100.0	100.0
Cost of sales	(68.9)	(68.5)	(67.2)	(66.5)	(66.3)
Gross profit	31.1	31.5	32.8	33.5	33.7
Operating expenses	(28.1)	(28.4)	(27.6)	(29.2)	(30.2)
Operating profit	3.0	3.1	5.2	4.3	3.5
Interest payable	(1.1)	(1.2)	(1.6)	(2.1)	(1.3)
Profit before taxation	1.9	1.9	3.6	2.2	2.2

What significant features are revealed by the common-size income statements?

Operating profit, relative to revenue, rose in Year 3 but fell back again in Years 4 and 5 to end the five-year period at a higher level than it had been in Years 1 and 2. Although the gross profit margin rose steadily over the five-year period, so did the operating expenses, with the exception of Year 3. Clearly, the fall in operating expenses to revenue in Year 3 led to the improvement in operating profit to revenue.

The common-size financial statements being compared do not have to be for the same business. They can be for different businesses. **Real World 8.5** gives common-size balance sheets for five UK businesses that are either very well known by name, or whose products are everyday commodities for most of us. These businesses were randomly selected, except that each one is high profile and from a different industry. For each business, the major balance sheet items are expressed as a percentage of the total investment by the providers of long-term finance (equity and non-current liabilities).

Real World 8.5

A summary of the balance sheets of five UK businesses

Business	Next plc	British Airways plc	Rolls-Royce plc	Tesco plc	Severn Trent plc
Balance sheet date	28.1.06	31.3.06	31.12.05	25.2.06	31.3.06
Non-current (fixed) assets	78	97	62	124	114
Current assets					
Inventories	45	1	22	10	–
Trade receivables	72	8	34	6	5
Other receivables	–	5	8	–	–
Cash and near cash	10	28	29	9	–
	127	42	93	25	5
Total assets	205	139	155	149	119
Equity and non-current liabilities	100	100	100	100	100
Current liabilities					
Trade payables	79	32	45	34	–
Taxation	8	1	3	3	1
Other short-term liabilities	–	–	2	–	7
Overdrafts and short-term loans	18	6	5	12	11
	105	39	55	49	19
Total equity and liabilities	205	139	155	149	119

Source: the table was constructed from information appearing in the annual reports of the five businesses concerned.

The non-current assets, current assets and current liabilities are expressed as a percentage of the total net long-term investment (equity plus non-current liabilities) of the business concerned. The businesses were randomly selected, except that they were deliberately taken from different industries. Next is a major retail and home shopping business. British Airways (BA) is a major airline. Rolls-Royce (RR) makes aero and other engines. Tesco is one of the major UK supermarkets. Severn Trent (ST) is a major supplier of water, sewerage services and waste management, mainly in the UK.

It is quite striking, in **Real World 8.5**, how different is the makeup of the balance sheet from one business to the next. Take the current assets and current liabilities for example. Though the totals for current assets are pretty large when compared with the total long-term investment, these percentages vary considerably from one type of business to the next. When we look at the nature of current assets held we can see that Next, RR and Tesco, which produce and/or sell goods, are the only ones that hold significant amounts of inventories. The other two businesses are service providers and so inventories are not a significant item. We can see from the table that Tesco does not sell a lot on credit and very few of BA's and ST's sales are on credit as these businesses have little or nothing invested in trade receivables. It is interesting to note that Tesco's trade payables are much higher than its inventories. Since most of these payables will be suppliers of inventories, it means that the business is able, on average, to have the cash from a particular sale in the bank before it needs to pay for the goods concerned.

→ So far we have been considering what is known as **vertical analysis**. That is, we have been treating all of the figures in each statement as a percentage of a figure in that statement, the sales revenue figure, in the case of the income statement, and the total long-term investment with the balance sheet. Note that common-size statements do not have to be expressed in terms of any particular factor; it is up to the individual carrying out the analysis. It seems, however, that revenue and long-term investment are popular bases for vertically analysed common-size income statements and balance sheets, respectively.

Horizontal analysis

→ **Horizontal analysis** is an alternative to the vertical analysis that we have seen so far. Here the figures appearing in a particular financial statement are expressed as a base figure (that is 100) and the equivalent figures appearing in similar statements are expressed as a percentage of this base figure. So, for example, the inventories figure appearing in a particular balance sheet may be set as the base figure (that is, set at 100) and then the inventories figures appearing in successive balance sheets could each be expressed as a percentage of this base inventories figure. The 'base' statement would normally be the earliest (or latest) of a set of statements for the same business. Where the analysis was between businesses, as in **Real World 8.5** (above), selecting which business should be the base one is not so obvious, unless one of the businesses is the one of most interest, perhaps because the objective is to compare a particular business with each of the others in turn.

Example 8.2 shows a horizontally analysed common-size income statement for the business, a department store, which was the subject of Activity 8.8.

Example 8.2

The following is a set of common-size income statements for a major high street department store for five consecutive accounting periods, using horizontal analysis and making Year 1 the base year:

	Year 1	Year 2	Year 3	Year 4	Year 5
Revenue	100.0	104.3	108.4	106.5	108.9
Cost of sales	(100.0)	(103.7)	(105.7)	(102.9)	(104.8)
Gross profit	100.0	105.5	114.4	114.5	118.0
Operating expenses	(100.0)	(105.4)	(106.7)	(110.4)	(117.2)
Operating profit	100.0	106.6	185.9	153.3	125.6
Interest payable	(100.0)	(111.9)	(157.1)	(202.4)	(127.4)
Profit before taxation	100.0	103.5	202.8	124.5	124.5

Year 1 is the base year so all of the figures in the Year 1 income statement are 100.0. All of the figures for the other years are that year's figure divided by the

Example 8.2 continued

Year 1 figure for the same item and then expressed as a percentage. For example, the Year 4 profit before taxation, divided by the profit before taxation for Year 1 was 124.5 or the profit was 24.5 per cent greater in Year 4 than it had been for Year 1. (By coincidence, the profits before taxation for Years 4 and 5 were identical.)

Activity 8.9

What are the significant features revealed by the common-size income statement in Example 8.2?

Revenue did not show much of an increase over the five years, particularly if these figures are not adjusted for inflation. Years 2 and 3 saw increases, but Years 4 and 5 were less impressive. The rate of increase in the cost of sales was less than that for revenue, and, therefore, the gross profit growth was greater, than the rate of increase of revenue. Operating expenses showed growth over the years. Interest payable increased strongly during the first four years of the period, but then fell back significantly in Year 5.

Activity 8.10

The vertical approach to common-size financial statements has the advantage of enabling the analyst to see each figure expressed in terms of the same item (revenue, long-term finance and so on).

● What are the disadvantages of this approach?
● How do horizontally analysed common-sized statements overcome any problems?
● What problems do they bring?

The problem with the horizontal approach is that it is not possible to see, for example, that revenue values are different from one year or business to the next. Normally a vertically analysed common-size income statement shows the revenue figure as 100 for all years or businesses. This is, of course, a problem of all approaches to ratio analysis.

Horizontally analysed common-sized statements overcome this problem because, say, revenue figures are expressed in terms of one year or one particular business. This makes differences in revenue levels crystal clear. Unfortunately, such an approach makes comparison within each year's, or within a particular business's, statement rather difficult.

Perhaps the answer is to produce two sets of common-size statements, one analysed vertically and the other horizontally.

Using ratios to predict financial failure

Financial ratios, based on current or past performance, are often used to help predict the future. However, both the choice of ratios and the interpretation of results are normally dependent on the judgement and opinion of the analyst. In recent years, however, attempts have been made to develop a more rigorous and systematic approach to the use of ratios for prediction purposes. In particular, researchers have shown an interest in the ability of ratios to predict the financial failure of a business.

By financial failure, we mean a business either being forced out of business or being severely adversely affected by its inability to meet its financial obligations. It is often referred to as 'going bust' or 'going bankrupt'. This, of course, is an area with which all those connected with the business are likely to be concerned.

Using single ratios

Many approaches that attempt to use ratios to predict future financial failure have been developed. Early research focused on the examination of ratios on an individual basis to see whether they were good or bad predictors of financial failure. Here a particular ratio (for example the current ratio), for a business that had failed, was tracked over several years leading up to the date of the failure. This was to see whether it was possible to say that the ratio had shown a trend that could have been taken as a warning sign.

Beaver (see reference 1 at the end of the chapter) carried out the first research in this area. He identified 79 different businesses that had failed. He then calculated the average (mean) of various ratios for these 79 businesses, going back over the financial statements of each business for each of the ten years leading up to each one's failure. Beaver then compared these average ratios with similarly derived ratios for a sample of 79 businesses that did not fail over this period. (The research used a matched-pair design, where each failed business was matched with a non-failed business of similar size and industry type.) Beaver found that some ratios exhibited a marked difference between the failed and non-failed businesses for up to five years prior to failure. This is shown in Figure 8.4.

To explain Figure 8.4, let us take a closer look at graph (a). This plots the ratio, cash flow (presumably the operating cash flow figure, taken from the cash flow statement) divided by total debt (borrowings). For the non-failed businesses this stayed fairly steady at just below +0.45 over the period. For the failed businesses, however, this was already well below the non-failed businesses at about +0.15 even five years before those businesses eventually failed. It then declined steadily until, by one year before the failure, it was less than –0.15. Note that the scale of the horizontal axis shows the most recent year before actual failure (Year 1) on the left and the earliest one (Year 5) on the right. The other graphs ((b) to (f)) show a similar picture for five other ratios. In each case there is a deteriorating average ratio for the failed businesses, as the time of failure approaches.

What is shown in Figure 8.4 implied that failure could be predicted by careful assessment of the trend shown by particular key ratios.

Research by Zmijewski (see reference 2 at the end of the chapter), using a sample of 72 failed and 3,573 non-failed businesses over a six-year period, found that failed businesses were characterised by lower rates of return, higher levels of gearing, lower levels of coverage for their fixed interest payments and more variable returns on shares. Whilst we may not find these results very surprising, it is interesting to note that Zmijewski, like a number of other researchers in this area, did not find liquidity ratios particularly useful in predicting financial failure. Intuition might have led us (wrongly it seems) to believe that the liquidity ratios would have been particularly helpful in this context.

→ The approach adopted by Beaver and Zmijewski is referred to as **univariate analysis** because it looks at one ratio at a time. Though this approach can produce interesting results, there are practical problems associated with its use. Let us say, for example, that past research has identified two ratios as being good predictors of financial failure. When applied to a particular business, however, it may be found that one ratio predicts financial failure whereas the other does not. Given these conflicting signals, how should the decision maker interpret the results?

Figure 8.4   Average (mean) ratios of failed and non-failed businesses plotted against the number of years before failure

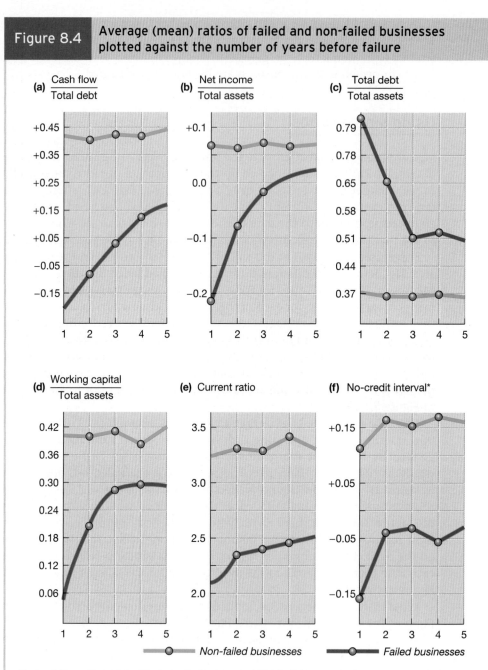

Each of the ratios (a) to (f) above indicates a marked difference in the average ratio between the sample of failed businesses and a matched sample of non-failed businesses. The vertical scale of each graph is the average value of the particular ratio for each group of businesses (failed and non-failed). The horizontal axis is the number of years before failure. Thus, Year 1 is the most recent year and Year 5 the earliest of the years. For each of the six ratios, the difference between the average for the failed and the non-failed businesses can be detected five years prior to the failure of the former group.

* The no-credit interval is the same as the cash generated from operations to maturing obligations ratio discussed in Chapter 7.

Source: Beaver (see reference 1 at the end of the chapter).

Using combinations of ratios

The weaknesses of univariate analysis have led researchers to develop models that combine ratios in such a way as to produce a single index that can be interpreted more clearly. One approach to model development, much favoured by researchers, applies **multiple discriminate analysis (MDA)**. This is, in essence, a statistical technique that is similar to regression analysis and which can be used to draw a boundary between those businesses that fail and those businesses that do not. This boundary is referred to as the **discriminate function**. In this context, MDA attempts to identify those factors likely to influence financial failure. However, unlike regression analysis, MDA assumes that the observations come from two different populations (for example, failed and non-failed businesses) rather than from a single population.

To illustrate this approach, let us assume that we wish to test whether two ratios (say, the current ratio and the return on capital employed) can help to predict failure. To do this, we can calculate these ratios, first for a sample of failed businesses and then for a matched sample of non-failed businesses. From these two sets of data we can produce a scatter diagram that plots each business according to these two ratios to produce a single coordinate. Figure 8.5 illustrates this approach.

Using the observations plotted on the diagram, we try to identify the boundary between the failed and the non-failed businesses. This is the diagonal line in Figure 8.5.

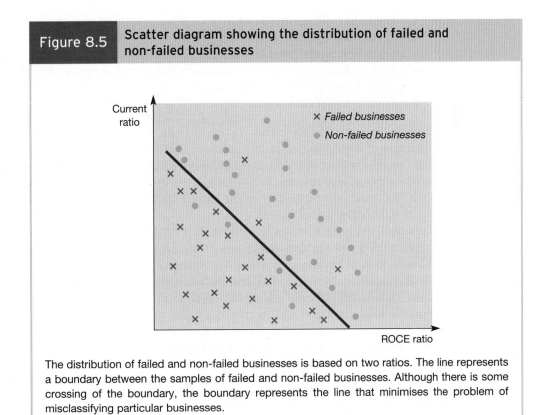

| Figure 8.5 | Scatter diagram showing the distribution of failed and non-failed businesses |

The distribution of failed and non-failed businesses is based on two ratios. The line represents a boundary between the samples of failed and non-failed businesses. Although there is some crossing of the boundary, the boundary represents the line that minimises the problem of misclassifying particular businesses.

We can see that those businesses that fall below and to the left of the line are predominantly failed and those that fall to the right are predominantly non-failed ones. Note that there is some overlap between the two populations. The boundary produced is unlikely, in practice, to eliminate all errors. Some businesses that fail may fall on the side of the boundary with non-failed businesses, and the other way round as well. However, the analysis will *minimise* the misclassification errors.

The boundary shown in Figure 8.5 can be expressed in the form:

$$Z = a + (b \times \text{Current ratio}) + (c \times \text{ROCE})$$

where a is a constant and b and c are weights to be attached to each ratio. A weighted average or total score (Z) is then derived. The weights given to the two ratios will depend on the slope of the line and its absolute position.

Z score models

Altman (see reference 3 at the end of the chapter) was the first to develop a model (in 1968), using financial ratios, that was able to predict financial failure. In 2000 he revised that model. In fact the revisions necessary to make the model effective in present times were quite minor. Altman's revised (2000) model, the Z score model, is based on five financial ratios and is as follows:

$$Z = 0.717a + 0.847b + 3.107c + 0.420d + 0.998e$$

Where a = Working capital/Total assets

b = Accumulated retained profits/Total assets

c = Operating profit/Total assets

d = Book (balance sheet) value of ordinary and preference shares/Total liabilities at book (balance sheet) value

e = Sales revenue/Total assets

In developing, and revising, this model, Altman carried out experiments using a paired sample of failed businesses and non-failed businesses and collected relevant data for each business for five years prior to failure. He found that the model represented by the formula above was able to predict failure for up to two years before it occurred. However, the predictive accuracy of the model became weaker the longer the time before the date of the actual failure.

The ratios used in this model were identified by Altman through a process of trial and error, as there is no underlying theory of financial failure to help guide researchers in their selection of appropriate ratios. According to Altman, those businesses with a Z score of less than 1.23 tend to fail, and the lower the score the greater the probability of failure. Those with a Z score greater than 4.14 tend not to fail. Those businesses with a Z score between 1.23 and 4.14 occupied a 'zone of ignorance' and were difficult to classify. However, the model was able overall to classify 91 per cent of the businesses correctly. Altman based his model on US businesses.

In recent years, other models, using a similar approach, have been developed throughout the world. In the UK, Taffler has developed separate Z score models for different types of business. (See reference 4 at the end of the chapter for a discussion of the work of Taffler and others.)

The prediction of financial failure is not the only area where research into the predictive ability of ratios has taken place. Researchers have also developed ratio-based models that claim to assess the vulnerability of a business to takeover by another. This is another area that is of vital importance to all those connected with the business.

Limitations of ratio analysis

Though ratios offer a quick and useful method of analysing the position and performance of a business, they are not without their problems and limitations. Some of the more important limitations are as follows:

- *Quality of financial statements.* It must always be remembered that ratios are based on financial statements, and the results of ratio analysis are dependent on the quality of these underlying statements. Ratios will inherit the limitations of the financial statements on which they are based. A significant example of this arises from the application of the prudence convention to internally generated intangible non-current assets (as compared with purchased ones). This convention tends to lead to assets of considerable value, like goodwill and brand names, being excluded from the balance sheet. This can mean that ratios, like ROSF, ROCE and the gearing ratio, fail to take account of these assets. There is also the problem of deliberate attempts to make the financial statements misleading. We discussed this problem of *creative accounting* in Chapter 5.

- *Inflation.* A persistent, though recently less severe, problem, in most western countries is that the financial results of businesses can be distorted as a result of inflation. One effect of inflation is that the balance sheet values of assets held for any length of time may bear little relation to current values. Generally speaking, the balance sheet value of assets will be understated in current terms during a period of inflation as they are usually recorded at their original cost (less any amounts written off for depreciation). This means that comparisons, either between businesses or between periods, will be hindered. A difference in, say, return on capital employed may simply be owing to the fact that assets in one of the balance sheets being compared were acquired more recently (ignoring the effect of depreciation on the asset values). Another effect of inflation is to distort the measurement of profit. Sales revenue for a period is often matched against costs from an earlier period, because there is often a time lag between acquiring a particular resource and using it to help generate sales revenue. For example, inventories may be acquired in one period and sold in a later period. During a period of inflation, this will mean that the expense does not reflect current prices. The cost of sales figure is usually based on the historic cost of the inventories concerned. As a result, expenses will be understated in the income statement and this, in turn, means that profit will be overstated. One effect of this will be to distort the profitability ratios discussed earlier.

- *The restricted vision of ratios.* It is important not to rely exclusively on ratios, thereby losing sight of information contained in the underlying financial statements. As we saw in Chapter 7 (p. 209), some items reported in these statements can be vital in assessing position and performance. For example, the total sales revenue, capital employed and profit figures may be useful in assessing changes in absolute size that occur over time, or differences in scale between businesses. Ratios do not provide such information. When comparing one figure with another, ratios measure *relative* performance and position, and therefore provide only part of the picture. When comparing two businesses, therefore, it will often be useful to assess the absolute size of profits, as well as the relative profitability of each business. For example, Business A may generate £1 m operating profit and have a ROCE of 15 per cent, and Business B may generate £100,000 operating profit and have a ROCE of 20 per cent. Although Business B has a higher level of *profitability*, as measured by ROCE, it generates lower total operating profits.

- *The basis for comparison.* We saw earlier that for ratios to be useful they require a basis for comparison. Moreover, it is important that the analyst compares like with like. When comparing businesses, however, no two businesses will be identical, and the greater the differences between the businesses being compared, the greater the limitations of ratio analysis. Also, when comparing businesses, differences in such matters as accounting policies, financing methods (gearing levels) and financial year ends will add to the problems of evaluation.

- *Balance sheet ratios.* Because the balance sheet is only a 'snapshot' of the business at a particular moment in time, any ratios based on balance sheet figures, such as the liquidity ratios, may not be representative of the financial position of the business for the year as a whole. For example, it is common for a seasonal business to have a financial year end that coincides with a low point in business activity. As a result, inventories and trade receivables may be low at the balance sheet date, and so the liquidity ratios may also be low. A more representative picture of liquidity can only really be gained by taking additional measurements at other points in the year.

Real World 8.6 points out another way in which ratios are limited.

Real World 8.6

Remember, it's people that really count . . .

Lord Weinstock (1924–2002) was an influential industrialist whose management style and philosophy helped to shape management practice in many UK businesses. During his long and successful reign at GEC plc, a major engineering business, Lord Weinstock relied heavily on financial ratios to assess performance and to exercise control. In particular, he relied on ratios relating to sales revenue, expenses, trade receivables, profit margins and inventories turnover. However, he was keenly aware of the limitations of ratios and recognised that, ultimately, people produce profits.

In a memo written to GEC managers he pointed out that ratios are an aid to good management, rather than a substitute for it. He wrote:

The operating ratios are of great value as measures of efficiency but they are only the measures and not efficiency itself. Statistics will not design a product better, make it for a lower cost or increase sales. If ill-used, they may so guide action as to diminish resources for the sake of apparent but false signs of improvement.

Management remains a matter of judgement, of knowledge of products and processes and of understanding and skill in dealing with people. The ratios will indicate how well all these things are being done and will show comparison with how they are done elsewhere. But they will tell us nothing about how to do them. That is what you are meant to do.

Source: Extract from Aris, S. (1998) *Arnold Weinstock and the Making of GEC*. Aurum Press, published in *The Sunday Times*, 22 February 1998, p. 3.

Summary

The main points of this chapter may be summarised as follows:

Investment ratios – concerned with returns to shareholders

- Dividend payout ratio.
- Dividend yield ratio.
- Earnings per share.
- Cash generated from operations per share.
- Price/earnings ratio.

Individual ratios can be tracked to detect trends

- For example, plotted on a graph.

Ratios can be used to predict financial failure

- Univariate analysis – looking at just one ratio over time in an attempt to predict financial failure.
- Multiple discriminate analysis – looking at several ratios, put together in a model, over time in an attempt to predict financial failure – Z scores.

Limitations of ratio analysis

- Ratios are only as reliable as the financial statements from which they derive.
- Inflation can distort the information.
- Ratios have restricted vision.
- It can be difficult to find a suitable benchmark (for example, another business) to compare with.
- Some ratios could mislead due to the 'snapshot' nature of the balance sheet.

→ **Key terms**

References

1 Beaver, W. H. (1966) 'Financial Ratios as Predictors of Failure', in *Empirical Research in Accounting: Selected Studies*, pp. 71–111.

2 Zmijewski, M. E. (1983) 'Predicting Corporate Bankruptcy: An Empirical Comparison of the Extent of Financial Distress Models', Research Paper, State University of New York.

3 Altman, E. I. (2000) 'Predicting Financial Distress of Companies: Revisiting the Z-score and Zeta Models', New York University Working Paper, June.

4 Neophytou, E., Charitou, A. and Charalamnous, C. (2001) 'Predicting Corporate Failure: Empirical Evidence for the UK', University of Southampton Department of Accounting and Management Science Working Paper 01-173.

Further reading

If you would like to explore the topics covered in this chapter in more depth, we recommend the following books:

Elliott, B. and Elliott, J. (2006) *Financial Accounting and Reporting*, 11th edn. Financial Times Prentice Hall, Chapters 28 and 29.

Revsine, L., Collins, D. and Bruce Johnson, W. (2005) *Financial Reporting and Analysis*, 3rd edn, Prentice Hall, Chapter 5.

Sutton, T. (2004) *Corporate Financial Accounting and Reporting*, 2nd edn, Financial Times Prentice Hall, Chapter 19.

Wild, J., Subramanyam, K. and Halsey, R. (2006) *Financial Statement Analysis*, 9th edn, McGraw-Hill, Chapters 8, 9 and 11.

Review questions

Answers to these questions can be found at the back of the book on pp. 415–16.

8.1 What potential problems arise for the external analyst from the use of balance sheet figures in the calculation of financial ratios?

8.2 Identify and discuss three factors (apart from those mentioned in the chapter) that might influence the level of dividend per share a company decides to pay.

8.3 Identify and discuss three reasons why the P/E ratio of two businesses operating within the same industry may differ.

8.4 Identify and discuss three ratios (apart from those already mentioned in the chapter) that are likely to be affected by a business overtrading.

Exercises

Exercises 8.5 to 8.8 are more advanced than 8.1 to 8.4. Those with a coloured number have answers at the back of the book, starting on p. 438.

If you wish to try more exercises, visit the students' side of the Companion Website.

8.1 At the close of share trading on 16 March 2007, the market investor ratios for Next plc, the UK fashion and textiles retailer and the averages for the 'general retailers' section were as follows:

	Next plc	General retailers section
Dividend yield (%)	2.2	2.4
P/E ratio (times)	16.2	24.4
Dividend cover (times)	3.43	1.7

Source: Financial Times, 17 March 2007.

Required:
Comment on what can be deduced about Next plc, relative to the general retailers sector, from an equity investor's point of view.

8.2 Telford Industrial Services plc is a medium-sized business.
Extracts from the business's financial statements appear below:

Summary of balance sheet at 31 December

	2004 £m	2005 £m	2006 £m	2007 £m
Non-current assets	48	51	65	64
Current assets				
Inventories	21	22	23	26
Trade receivables	34	42	34	29
Cash	–	3	–	–
	55	67	57	55
Total assets	103	118	122	119

Equity	48	61	61	63
Non-current liabilities	30	30	30	30
Current liabilities				
Trade payables	20	27	25	18
Short-term borrowings	5	–	6	8
	25	27	31	26
Total equity and liabilities	103	118	122	119

Summary of income statements for years ended 31 December

	2004	2005	2006	2007
	£m	£m	£m	£m
Sales revenue	152	170	110	145
Operating profit	28	40	7	15
Interest payable	(4)	(3)	(4)	(5)
Profit before taxation	24	37	3	10
Taxation	(12)	(16)	–	(4)
Profit for the year	12	21	3	6

Required:

Prepare a set of common sized balance sheets and common size income statements, on a vertical basis using equity as the base figure for the balance sheets and sales revenue as the base figure for the for income statements.

8.3　Required:

(a) Calculate the Z-score for Ali plc and Bhaskar plc (see SAQ 8.1 on p. 250), using the Altman model set out on p. 262.

(b) Comment on the Z-scores for the two businesses and the validity of using this particular model to assess these particular businesses.

8.4　Diversified Industries plc (DI) is a business that has interests in engineering, caravan manufacturing and a chain of shops selling car accessories. DI has recently been approached by the directors of Automobile Care plc (AC), a smaller chain of accessory shops, who wish to negotiate the sale of their business to DI. The following information, which has been extracted from AC's financial statements, is available:

	Years ended 31 December		
	2005	2006	2007
	£m	£m	£m
Revenue	18.1	28.2	36.9
Profit before taxation	3.2	4.1	7.3
Taxation	1.0	1.7	3.1
Profit for the year	2.2	2.4	4.2
Dividend paid for the year	0.9	1.1	1.3
Issued share capital			
16 million shares of 25 p each	4.0	4.0	4.0
Reserves	8.0	9.1	13.4

AC's market price per share at 31 December 2007 was £3.15.

Required:

(a) Calculate the following items for AC for 2007 and explain the use of each one:

1　earnings per share;

2　price earnings ratio;

3　dividend yield (assuming a 10 per cent dividend income tax credit rate);

4 dividend payout ratio;

5 net assets per share;

(b) Write some short notes on the factors the directors of DI should take into account when considering the possible purchase of AC. You should use the income statement details together with the figures that you calculated in your answer to part (a).

8.5 One of the main suppliers to your business is Green Ltd, a family-owned business. It is the only available supplier and your business buys 60 per cent of the Green Ltd's output. Recently, Green Ltd has run into a severe cash shortage and it requires extra finance to re-equip its factory with modern machinery that is expected to cost £8 million. The machinery's life is expected to be ten years and savings, before depreciation, arising from its installation, are expected to be £ million a year. Green Ltd has approached your business to see if you are able to help with finance. The directors of Green Ltd have pointed out that, if it could acquire the new machinery, your business will be able to share in the benefits through reduced prices for supplies. Extracts from Green Ltd's recent financial statements are as follows:

Income statement data

| | Years ended 31 December | | |
	2005	2006	2007
	£m	£m	£m
Revenue	11.5	8.0	9.5
Operating profit (loss)	(0.2)	(2.0)	1.9
Interest payable	(1.2)	(2.4)	(1.5)
Profit (loss) before taxation	(1.4)	(4.4)	0.4

There was no charge for taxation and no dividends were paid in respect of any of these three years.

Balance sheets

| | As at 31 December | | |
	2005	2006	2007
	£m	£m	£m
Non-current assets			
Property, plant and equipment, at cost	22.1	23.9	24.0
Depreciation	(10.2)	(12.0)	(14.0)
	11.9	11.9	10.0
Current assets			
Inventories	4.3	3.5	3.8
Trade receivables	2.8	2.6	4.1
	7.1	6.1	7.9
Total assets	19.0	18.0	17.9
Equity			
Ordinary shares	1.0	1.0	1.0
Reserves	7.4	3.0	3.4
	8.4	4.0	4.4
Non-current liabilities			
Borrowings – Loan notes	6.5	8.2	7.4
Current liabilities			
Trade payables	1.4	1.7	1.9
Short-term borrowings (all bank overdraft)	2.7	4.1	4.2
	4.1	5.8	6.1
Total equity and liabilities	19.0	18.0	17.9

Required:

(a) Calculate for each year and comment on each the following ratios for Green Ltd:
   1 return on capital employed ratio;
   2 acid test ratio;
   3 trade receivables collection period (months) ratio;
   4 interest cover ratio;
   5 gearing ratio.

(b) Write some short notes suggesting the level and nature of the financial assistance that your business might be prepared to provide for Green Ltd. Your notes should also suggest what terms and conditions you would seek to impose.

8.6 Russell Ltd installs and services heating and ventilation systems for commercial premises. The business's most recent balance sheet and income statement are as follows:

Balance sheet

	£000	£000
Non-current assets		
Property, plant and equipment		
Machinery and equipment at cost	883.6	
Less Accumulated depreciation	328.4	555.2
Motor vehicles at cost	268.8	
Less Accumulated depreciation	82.2	186.6
		741.8
Current assets		
Inventories at cost	293.2	
Trade receivables	510.3	803.5
		1,545.3
Equity		
£1 ordinary shares	400.0	
General reserve	50.2	
Retained profit	380.2	832.4
Non-current liabilities		
12% loan notes (repayable Year 10/11)		250.0
Current liabilities		
Trade payables	199.7	
Taxation	128.0	
Bank overdraft	135.2	462.9
		1,545.3

Income statement for the year

Sales revenue	5,207.8
Operating profit	542.0
Interest payable	(30.0)
Net profit before taxation	512.0
Taxation (25%)	(128.0)
Profit for the year	384.0
Dividend paid during the year	153.6

The business wishes to invest in more machinery and equipment in order to cope with an upsurge in demand for its services. An additional operating profit of £120,000 a year is expected if an investment of £600,000 is made in machinery.

The directors are considering an offer from venture capitalists to finance the expansion programme. The finance will be made available immediately through either:

(i)   an issue of £1 ordinary shares at a premium on par of £3 a share; or

(ii) an issue of £600,000 10 per cent loan notes at par.

The directors wish to maintain the same dividend payout ratio in future years as in past years whichever method of finance is chosen.

Required:

(a) For each of the financing schemes:
   1   prepare a projected income statement for next year;
   2   calculate the projected earnings per share for next year;
   3   calculate the projected level of gearing as at the end of next year.

(b) Briefly assess both of the financing schemes under consideration from the viewpoint of the existing shareholders.

8.7   The following is the balance sheet (in abbreviated form) of Projections Ltd as at the end of this year:

Balance sheet as at 31 December

	£000	£000
Non-current assets		
Cost	290	
Accumulated depreciation	(110)	180
Current assets		
Inventories	26	
Trade receivables	35	
Cash	5	66
Total assets		246
Equity		
Share capital	150	
Retained profit	48	198
Current liabilities		
Trade payables	21	
Taxation (payable during next year)	27	48
Total equity and liabilities		246

The following plans have been made for next year:

(i)   Sales revenue is expected to total £350,000, all on credit. Sales will be made at a steady rate over the year and two months' credit will be allowed to customers.

(ii)   £200,000 worth of inventories will be bought during the year, all on credit. Purchases will be made at a steady rate over the year and suppliers will allow one month's credit.

(iii) New non-current assets will be bought, and paid for, during the year at a cost of £30,000. No disposals of non-current assets are planned. The depreciation expense for the year will be 10 per cent of the cost of the non-current assets owned at the end of the year.

(iv)   Inventories at the end of the year are expected to be have a value double that which applied at the beginning of the year.

(v)   Operating expenses, other than depreciation, are expected to total £52,000, of which £5,000 will remain unpaid at the end of the year.

(vi)   During the year, the tax noted in the start of the year balance sheet will be paid.

(vii) The tax rate can be assumed to be 25 per cent of operating profit. The tax will not be paid during the year.

(viii) A dividend of £10,000 will be paid during the year.

Required:

Prepare a projected income statement for next year and a balance sheet as at the end of next year, to the nearest £1,000.

8.8 Genesis Ltd was incorporated in 2004 and has grown rapidly over the past three years. The rapid rate of growth has created problems for the business, which the directors have found difficult to deal with. Recently, a firm of management consultants has been asked to help the directors to overcome these problems.

In a preliminary report to the board of directors, the management consultants state: 'Most of the difficulties faced by the business are symptoms of an underlying problem of overtrading.'

The most recent financial statements of the business are set out below:

Balance sheet as at 31 October 2007

	£000	£000
Non-current assets		
Property, plant and equipment		
Land and buildings at cost	530	
Accumulated depreciation	(88)	442
Fixtures and fittings at cost	168	
Accumulated depreciation	(52)	116
Motor vans at cost	118	
Accumulated depreciation	(54)	64
		622
Current assets		
Inventories		128
Trade receivables		104
		232
Total assets		854
Equity		
Ordinary £0.50 shares		60
General reserve		50
Retained earnings		74
		184
Non-current liabilities		
Borrowings – 10% loan notes (secured)		120
Current liabilities		
Trade payables		184
Taxation		8
Short-term borrowings (all bank overdraft)		358
		550
Total equity and liabilities		854

Income statement for the year ended 31 October 2007

	£000	£000
Revenue		1,640
Cost of sales		
Opening inventories	116	
Purchases	1,260	
	1,376	
Closing inventories	(128)	(1,248)
Gross profit		392
Selling and distribution expenses		(204)
Administration expenses		(92)
Operating profit		96
Interest payable		(44)
Profit before taxation		52
Taxation		(16)
Profit for the year		36

All purchases and sales were on credit.
A dividend was paid during the year on ordinary shares of £4,000.

Required:

(a) Explain the term 'overtrading' and state how overtrading might arise for a business.
(b) Discuss the kinds of problem that overtrading can create for a business.
(c) Calculate and discuss *five* financial ratios that might be used to establish whether or not the business is overtrading.
(d) State the ways in which a business may overcome the problem of overtrading.

9

Reporting the financial results of groups of companies

Introduction

Many larger businesses, including virtually all of those that are household names in the UK, consist not just of one single company but of a group of companies. Here one company (the parent company) controls one or more other companies (the subsidiary companies). This usually arises because the parent owns the majority of the shares of the subsidiaries.

In this chapter we shall look at groups and, more particularly, at the accounting treatment that they usually receive. This will draw heavily on what we have already covered so far, particularly in Chapters 2 to 6. We shall also briefly consider associate companies.

Learning outcomes

When you have completed this chapter, you should be able to:

● Discuss the nature of groups, and explain why they exist and how they are formed.

● Prepare a group balance sheet and income statement.

● Explain the nature of associate company status and its accounting implications.

● Explain and interpret the contents of a set of group financial statements.

What is a group of companies?

It is quite common for one company to be able to exercise control over the activities of another. Control typically arises because the first company (the **parent company**) owns a majority of the ordinary (voting) shares of the second company (the **subsidiary company**). This means that the directors of the parent company are able to appoint the directors of the subsidiary company and, therefore, dictate its policies. Where this relationship arises, a **'group' of companies** is said to exist. Where there is a group, the relevant international financial reporting standards (IAS 27 – Consolidated and separate financial statements and IFRS 3 – Business combinations) normally require that a set of financial statements is drawn up annually not only for each individual company, but also for the group taken as a whole. Before we go on to consider how the **group financial statements** (that is, the financial statements of a group of companies) are prepared, we shall look at the reasons why groups exist at all and at the types of group relationships that can exist.

Why do groups exist?

Companies have subsidiaries where:

1 The parent company creates a new company to operate some part of its business, perhaps a new activity.
2 The parent company buys a majority, perhaps all, of the shares of some other existing company; that is, a 'takeover'.

Many companies have subsidiaries as a result of both of these reasons.

Newly created companies

It is very common for large businesses to be made up of, and to operate through, a number, often a large number, of individual companies. All of these subsidiaries are controlled, often wholly owned, by the parent company, sometimes known as the **'holding' company**. In some cases, the only assets of the parent company are the shares that it owns in the subsidiary companies. It is the subsidiary companies that strictly own the land, buildings, machinery, inventories, and so on, which are used to generate profit. However, since the parent owns the subsidiaries, in effect, it owns the individual 'real' assets of those companies. **Real World 9.1** looks at Associated British Foods plc, the major UK food manufacturer and retailer.

Real World 9.1

Food for thought

Under the heading 'Non-current assets' in the balance sheet of Associated British Foods plc (ABF), there is no property, plant and equipment, just 'goodwill' and 'investment in subsidiary undertakings'. The tangible assets of the group are owned by the more than 80 subsidiary companies. These include such well-known names as:

● British Sugar plc;
● R Twinings and Company Limited (tea producers);
● Primart Stores Limited.

Source: Associated British Foods plc Annual Report and Accounts 2006.

An obvious question to ask is why do businesses operate through subsidiaries? To put it another way, why do the parent companies not own all of the assets of the business directly, instead of them being owned by the subsidiaries? The answers to these questions are probably:

● *Limited liability*. Each individual company has individual limited liability. This means that if there is a financial failure of one subsidiary, neither the assets of other subsidiaries nor of the parent could be legally demanded by any unsatisfied claimants (lenders, trade payables and so on) against the failed company. Thus the group can 'ring fence' each part of the business by having separate companies, each with its own limited liability.

● *Individual identity*. A sense of independence and autonomy may be created that could, in turn, increase levels of commitment among staff. It may also help to develop, or perpetuate, a market image of a smaller, independent business. Customers, as well as staff, may prefer to deal with, what they see as a smaller, specialist business than with a division of a large diversified business.

To create a subsidiary, the would-be parent may simply form a new company in the normal way. The new company would then issue shares to the parent, in exchange for some asset or assets of the parent. Where the new subsidiary has been formed to undertake a completely new activity, the asset may well be cash. If the subsidiary is to carry on some activity, which the parent had undertaken directly up to that point, the assets are likely to be such things as the non-current and current assets associated with the particular activity.

Example 9.1

The summarised balance sheet of Baxter plc is as follows:

Balance sheet as at 31 December

	£m	£m
Non-current assets		
Property, plant and equipment		
Land	43	
Plant	15	
Vehicles	8	66
Current assets		
Inventories	15	
Trade receivables	23	
Cash	13	51
Total assets		117
Equity		
Called-up share capital:		
ordinary shares of £1 each, fully paid	50	
Retained earnings	16	66
Non-current liabilities		
Borrowings – Loan notes		40
Current liabilities		
Trade payables		11
Total equity and liabilities		117

Baxter plc has recently formed a new company, Nova Ltd, which is to undertake the work that has previously been done by the industrial fibres division of Baxter plc. The following assets are to be transferred to Nova Ltd at the values that currently are shown in the balance sheet of Baxter plc:

	£m
Land	10
Plant	5
Vehicles	3
Inventories	6
Cash	3
	27

Nova Ltd is to issue £1 ordinary shares at the nominal or par value (that is, £1) to Baxter plc in exchange for these assets.

Baxter plc's balance sheet immediately after these transfers will be:

Balance sheet as at 31 December

	£m	£m
Non-current assets		
Property, plant and equipment		
Land (43 – 10)	33	
Plant (15 – 5)	10	
Vehicles (8 – 3)	5	48
Investments		
27 million ordinary £1 shares of Nova Ltd		27
		75
Current assets		
Inventories (15 – 6)	9	
Trade receivables	23	
Cash (13 – 3)	10	42
Total assets		117
Equity		
Called-up share capital:		
ordinary shares of £1 each, fully paid	50	
Retained earnings	16	66
Non-current liabilities		
Borrowings – Loan notes		40
Current liabilities		
Trade payables		11
Total equity and liabilities		117

As you have probably noted, the individual assets have simply been replaced by the asset, shares in Nova Ltd.

Activity 9.1

Try to prepare the balance sheet of Nova Ltd, immediately following the transfers of the assets and the shares being issued.

It should look something like this:

Balance sheet as at 31 December

	£m	£m
Non-current assets		
Property, plant and equipment (at transfer value)		
Land	10	
Plant	5	
Vehicles	3	18
Current assets		
Inventories	6	
Cash	3	9
Total assets		27
Equity		
Called-up share capital: ordinary shares of £1 each, fully paid		27

Takeovers

A would-be parent company may also create a subsidiary by taking over an existing company. Here it buys enough of the shares of a hitherto unconnected **target company** to enable it to exercise control over the target company, thereby making the target a new subsidiary company. The shares are, of course, bought from the existing shareholders of the target company.

The shares may be bought through the Stock Exchange or an approach may be made directly to the individual shareholders of the target company. This second course is feasible because all companies are required by law to provide the names and addresses of their shareholders to any interested party. In many takeovers, the parent offers to the target company shareholders shares in the parent as all, or part of, the bid consideration. This means the target company shareholders who accept the offer will exchange their shares in the target for shares in the parent. Thus, they cease to be shareholders of the target company and become shareholders in the parent. The parent company simply replaces them as shareholders in the target.

Example 9.2

The summarised balance sheet of Adams plc is as follows:

Balance sheet as at 31 March

	£m	£m
Non-current assets		
Property, plant and equipment		
Land	35	
Plant	21	
Vehicles	12	68
Current assets		
Inventories	25	
Trade receivables	28	
Cash	22	75
Total assets		143

Equity		
Called-up share capital:		
ordinary shares of £1 each, fully paid	50	
Share premium account	5	
Retained earnings	5	70
Non-current liabilities		
Borrowings – Loan notes		50
Current liabilities		
Trade payables		23
Total equity and liabilities		143

Adams plc has recently made an offer of £1 a share for all the share capital of Beta Ltd. Beta Ltd's issued share capital is 20 million shares of 50p each. Adams plc was to 'pay' for this by issuing the appropriate number of new ordinary shares of Adams plc at an issue value of £2 a share.

All the Beta Ltd shareholders accepted the offer. This means that to meet the required consideration, Adams plc will need to issue shares to the value of £20 million (that is, 20 million × £1). Since the Adams plc shares are to be issued at £2 each, 10 million shares will need to be issued, at a share premium of £1 each.

Following the takeover, the balance sheet of Adams plc will look as follows:

Balance sheet as at 31 March

	£m	£m
Non-current assets		
Property, plant and equipment		
Land	35	
Plant	21	
Vehicles	12	68
Investments		
Shares in Beta Ltd		20
		88
Current assets		
Inventories	25	
Trade receivables	28	
Cash	22	75
Total assets		163
Equity		
Called-up share capital:		
ordinary shares of £1 each, fully paid	60	
Share premium account	15	
Retained earnings	15	90
Non-current liabilities		
Borrowings – Loan notes		50
Current liabilities		
Trade payables		23
Total equity and liabilities		163

Note that the assets have increased by £20 million and that this is balanced by the value of the shares issued (£10 million share capital and £10 million share premium).

Activity 9.2

If, instead of the consideration offered being all in shares, the offer had been 50 per cent in cash and 50 per cent in Adams plc shares, what would the balance sheet of Adams plc have looked like after the takeover?

The total offer value would still be £20 million, but this would be met by paying cheques totalling £10 million and by issuing shares worth £10 million (£5 million share capital and £5 million share premium). So the balance sheet would be:

Balance sheet as at 31 March

	£m	£m
Non-current assets		
Property, plant and equipment		
Land	35	
Plant	21	
Vehicles	12	68
Investments		
Shares in Beta Ltd		20
		88
Current assets		
Inventories	25	
Trade receivables	28	
Cash	12	65
Total assets		153
Equity		
Called-up share capital:		
ordinary shares of £1 each, fully paid	55	
Share premium account	10	
Retained earnings	15	80
Non-current liabilities		
Borrowings – Loan notes		50
Current liabilities		
Trade payables		23
Total equity and liabilities		153

Activity 9.3

How would the takeover affect the balance sheet of Beta Ltd?

The balance sheet of Beta Ltd would not be affected at all. A change of shareholders does not affect the financial statements of a company.

It is not necessary that the parent company should retain the target/subsidiary as a separate company, following the takeover. The latter could be wound up and its assets owned directly by the parent. Normally this would not happen, however, for the reasons that we considered above; namely limited liability and individual identity. The latter may be particularly important in the case of a takeover. The new parent company may be very keen to retain the name and identity of its new subsidiary, where the subsidiary has a good marketing image.

Types of group relationship

So far we have considered a situation where there is the simple relationship between a parent and its subsidiary or subsidiaries that is shown in Figure 9.1.

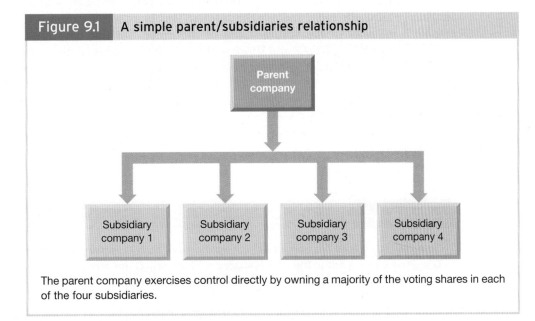

Figure 9.1   A simple parent/subsidiaries relationship

The parent company exercises control directly by owning a majority of the voting shares in each of the four subsidiaries.

A slightly more complex relationship is shown in Figure 9.2.

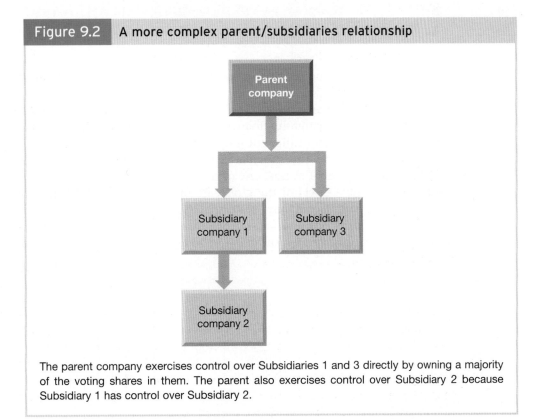

Figure 9.2   A more complex parent/subsidiaries relationship

The parent company exercises control over Subsidiaries 1 and 3 directly by owning a majority of the voting shares in them. The parent also exercises control over Subsidiary 2 because Subsidiary 1 has control over Subsidiary 2.

Here Subsidiary 2 is a subsidiary by virtue of being controlled by another company (Subsidiary 1), that is, in turn, a subsidiary of the parent. In these circumstances, Subsidiary 2 is usually called a 'sub-subsidiary' of the parent. Subsidiary 3 is a straightforward subsidiary. The parent company here is sometimes known as the 'ultimate' parent company of Subsidiary 2.

Earlier in this chapter, it was pointed out that one company is a subsidiary of another because the latter *controls* the former. This is usually as a result of the latter owning a majority of the voting shares of the other, but this does not need to be the case. Consider Figure 9.2 and suppose that the parent owns 60 per cent of the voting shares of Subsidiary 1 and that Subsidiary 1 owns 60 per cent of the shares of Subsidiary 2. In effect, the parent only owns 36 per cent of the shares of Subsidiary 2 (that is, 60 per cent of 60 per cent), yet the latter is a subsidiary of the former. This is because the parent has complete control over (though not total ownership of) Subsidiary 1, which in turn has complete control over (though again not total ownership of) Subsidiary 2.

Activity 9.4

Company A owns 40 per cent of the voting shares of both Company B and Company C. The other 60 per cent of the voting shares of Company C are owned by Company B.
  Is Company C a subsidiary of Company A?

The answer is no. This is despite the fact that company A can be seen to own 64 per cent of the shares of company C; 40 per cent directly and 24 per cent (that is, 40 per cent × 60 per cent) through company B. Since A does not control B, it cannot control B's shares in C.

Though ownership and control do not necessarily go hand-in-hand, in practice this tends to be the case.

The reason that we are concerned as to whether one company is a subsidiary of another is, of course, that group financial statements must be prepared where there is a parent/subsidiary relationship, but not otherwise.

Real World 9.2 shows the subsidiaries of the Go-Ahead Group plc. Most of us in the UK use the services of at least one of the subsidiaries, many of us on a daily basis. Most of the tangible assets of the group are owned by the subsidiaries, rather than directly by the parent company. Note that Go-Ahead uses the word 'group' in its official name. This is not unusual, but is not a legal requirement. Many companies, which operate mainly through subsidiaries, do not indicate this in the company name.

Real World 9.2

Going ahead with subsidiaries

Go-Ahead Group plc

Principal subsidiary undertakings as at 1 July 2006

Name	Principal activity
Brighton & Hove Bus and Coach Company Limited	Bus and coach operator
City of Oxford Motor Services Limited	Bus and coach operator
Go Gateshead Limited	Bus operator
London Central Bus Company Limited	Bus and coach operator
London General Transport Services Limited	Bus and coach operator
Go Northern Limited	Bus and coach operator
Go Wear Buses Limited	Bus operator
Metrobus Limited	Bus operator
New Southern Railway Limited	Train operator
London and South Eastern Railway Limited	Train operator
GOVIA Limited	Intermediate holding co.
Abingdon Bus Company Limited	Intermediate holding co.
Aviance UK Limited	Aviation services
Reed Aviation Limited	Aviation services
Meteor Parking Limited	Aviation services
Wilts and Dorset Bus Company Limited	Bus operator
Chauffeured Parking Services Ltd	Aviation services
Plane Handling Limited	Aviation services
Solent Blue Line Limited	Bus operator
The Southern Vectis Omnibus Company Limited	Bus operator
Southern Vectis Transport Limited	Bus operator
Birmingham Passenger Transport Limited	Bus and coach operator
Hants and Dorset Trim Limited	Services to bus and coach operators

Source: Go-Ahead Group plc Annual Review 2006.

Preparation of a group balance sheet

→ We are now going to look at the preparation of a **group balance sheet**. We shall do this by considering a series of examples, starting with the simplest possible case and gradually building on more and more of the complexities found in real life.

Each company within the group will prepare its own balance sheet, which considers things from the perspective of that particular company. As well as this, the parent company will produce a balance sheet that reflects the assets and claims of the group as a whole. In effect, the group balance sheet looks at the group as if the parent company owned the assets and, therefore, was responsible for the outside liabilities of all the group members. This means, among other things, that whereas the *parent company* balance sheet will include the assets of investments in the shares of the subsidiary companies, in the *group* balance sheet, this will be replaced by the net assets (assets less claims of non-group liabilities). In other words, the group balance sheet looks behind the subsidiary company shares to see what they represent, in terms of assets and liabilities.

→ The assets and liabilities of subsidiaries are '**consolidated**' into the balance sheet of the parent company. This point should become clearer as we look at some examples.

Example 9.3

The balance sheets of Parent plc and of Subsidiary Ltd, on the date that the former bought all the shares in the latter, were as follows:

Balance sheets as at 31 May

	Parent plc		Subsidiary Ltd	
	£m	£m	£m	£m
Non-current assets				
Property, plant and equipment				
Land	40		5	
Plant	30		2	
Vehicles	20		2	
	90		9	
Investment				
5 million shares of Subsidiary Ltd	10	100	–	9
Current assets				
Inventories	20		3	
Trade receivables	30		2	
Cash	10	60	2	7
Total assets		160		16
Equity				
Called-up share capital:				
ordinary shares of £1 each, fully paid	70		5	
Share premium account	10		–	
Retained earnings	30	110	5	10
Non-current liabilities				
Borrowings – Loan notes		30		–
Current liabilities				
Trade payables		20		6
Total equity and liabilities		160		16

To deduce the group balance sheet, we simply combine each of the like items by adding them together. For example, the group investment in land is £45 million, representing £40 million invested by Parent plc and £5 million invested by Subsidiary Ltd.

The only exceptions to the rule that we simply add like items together, lies with the investment in the shares of Subsidiary Ltd, in the balance sheet of Parent plc, and with the equity (share capital plus reserves) in the balance sheet of Subsidiary Ltd. In effect, these are two sides of the same coin, since Parent plc is the owner of Subsidiary Ltd. For this reason, it is logical simply to add these two items together and since one is an asset and the other is a claim and they are equal in amount, they will cancel each other out.

The group balance sheet will be as follows:

Balance sheet as at 31 May

	£m	£m
Non-current assets		
Property, plant and equipment		
Land (40 + 5)	45	
Plant (30 + 2)	32	
Vehicles (20 + 2)	22	99
Current assets		
Inventories (20 + 3)	23	
Trade receivables (30 + 2)	32	
Cash (10 + 2)	12	67
Total assets		166

Equity		
Called-up share capital:		
ordinary shares of £1 each, fully paid	70	
Share premium account	10	
Retained earnings	30	110
Non-current liabilities		
Borrowings – Loan notes (30 + 0)		30
Current liabilities		
Trade payables (20 + 6)		26
Total equity and liabilities		166

The 'Equity' section of the group balance sheet is simply that of Parent plc. The £10 m Equity for Subsidiary Ltd cancels out with the £10 m '5 million shares of Subsidiary Ltd' in the non-current assets section of the parent company's balance sheet.

Activity 9.5

The balance sheets of Large plc and of Small plc, on the date that Large plc bought all the shares in Small plc, were as follows:

Balance sheets as at 30 June

	Large plc		Small plc	
	£m	£m	£m	£m
Non-current assets				
Property, plant and equipment				
Land	55		–	
Plant	43		21	
Vehicles	25	123	17	38
Investment				
20 million shares of Small plc		32		–
		155		38
Current assets				
Inventories	42		18	
Trade receivables	18		13	
Cash	24	84	13	44
Total assets		239		82
Equity				
Called-up share capital:				
ordinary shares of £1 each, fully paid	100		20	
Share premium account	–		5	
Retained earnings	64	164	7	32
Non-current liabilities				
Borrowings – Loan notes		50		30
Current liabilities				
Trade payables		25		20
Total equity and liabilities		239		82

Have a try at deducing the group balance sheet.

Activity 9.5 continued

The group balance sheet will be as follows:

Balance sheet as at 30 June

	£m	£m
Non-current assets		
Property, plant and equipment		
Land (55 + 0)	55	
Plant (43 + 21)	64	
Vehicles (25 + 17)	42	161
Current assets		
Inventories (42 + 18)	60	
Trade receivables (18 + 13)	31	
Cash (24 + 13)	37	128
Total assets		289
Equity		
Called-up share capital:		
ordinary shares of £1 each, fully paid	100	
Retained earnings	64	164
Non-current liabilities		
Borrowings – Loan notes (50 + 30)		80
Current liabilities		
Trade payables (25 + 20)		45
Total equity and liabilities		289

The 'equity' section of the group balance sheet is simply that of Large plc. The £32 m for the equity (share capital and reserves) of Small plc cancels out with the £32 m 'Investment in 20 million shares of Small plc' in the Non-current assets section of the balance sheet of Large plc.

The example and the activity represent the simplest case because:

1 the parent owns all of the shares of the subsidiary;
2 the price paid for the shares (£10 million and £32 million, respectively) exactly equals the 'book' or balance sheet value of the net assets of the subsidiary; and
3 no trading has taken place since the shares were acquired.

In practice, these three 'simplifications' frequently do not all exist; often none of them exists.

We shall now go on to look at the 'complications', firstly, one by one and then together.

Complication 1: less than 100 per cent ownership of the subsidiary by the parent

The problem here is that when we come to set the asset of 'shares of subsidiary', in the balance sheet of the parent, against the 'equity' (owners' claim) in the balance sheet of the subsidiary, they do not completely cancel one another.

Example 9.4

The balance sheets of Parent plc and of Subsidiary Ltd, on the date that the former bought the shares in the latter, are the same as in the previous example (Example 9.3) except that Parent plc owns only 4 million (of the 5 million) shares of Subsidiary Ltd. Thus the investment is only £8 million, instead of £10 million. As a result, Parent plc's cash balance is £2 million greater than in the previous example.

The two balance sheets were as follows:

Balance sheets as at 30 September

	Parent plc		Subsidiary Ltd	
	£m	£m	£m	£m
Non-current assets				
Property, plant and equipment				
Land	40		5	
Plant	30		2	
Vehicles	20	90	2	9
Investment				
4 million shares of Subsidiary Ltd		8		–
		98		9
Current assets				
Inventories	20		3	
Trade receivables	30		2	
Cash	12	62	2	7
Total assets		160		16
Equity				
Called-up share capital:				
ordinary shares of £1 each, fully paid	70		5	
Share premium account	10		–	
Retained earnings	30	110	5	10
Non-current liabilities				
Borrowings – Loan notes		30		–
Current liabilities				
Trade payables		20		6
Total equity and liabilities		160		16

As before, to prepare the group balance sheet, we simply add like items together. The problem is that when we come to set the £8 million investment made by Parent plc against the £10 million equity of Subsidiary Ltd, they do not cancel. There is an owners' claim of £2 million in the balance sheet of Subsidiary Ltd that has not been cancelled out.

→

Activity 9.6

Can you puzzle out what the £2 million represents?

It represents the extent to which Parent plc does not own all of the shares of Subsidiary Ltd. Parent plc only owns 80 per cent of the shares and, therefore, others must own the rest. Since we are including all of the assets and liabilities of Subsidiary Ltd as being those of the group, the group balance sheet needs to acknowledge that there is another source of equity finance, as well as Parent plc.

→ This £2 million owners' claim is known as '**minority interests**' or 'outsiders' interests'. It is shown in the group balance sheet as an addition to, but not part of, the equity.

Example 9.4 continued

The group balance sheet will be as follows:

Balance sheet as at 30 September

	£m	£m
Non-current assets		
Property, plant and equipment		
Land (40 + 5)	45	
Plant (30 + 2)	32	
Vehicles (20 + 2)	22	99
Current assets		
Inventories (20 + 3)	23	
Trade receivables (30 + 2)	32	
Cash (12 + 2)	14	69
Total assets		168
Equity		
Called-up share capital: ordinary shares of £1 each, fully paid	70	
Share premium account	10	
Retained earnings	30	110
Minority or outsiders' interests		2
		112
Non-current liabilities		
Borrowings – Loan notes (30 + 0)		30
Current liabilities		
Trade payables (20 + 6)		26
		168

This balance sheet reflects the fact that the group has control over net assets totalling £112 million (at balance sheet values). Of this, £110 million is financed by the shareholders of the parent company and £2 million by others.

It may have occurred to you that an alternative approach to dealing with less than 100 per cent ownership is to scale down the assets and liabilities, to reflect this, before carrying out the 'consolidation' of the two sets of financial statements. Since Parent plc only owns 80 per cent of Subsidiary Ltd, we could multiply all of the figures in Subsidiary Ltd's balance sheet by 0.8 before preparing the group financial statements. If we did this, the owners' claim would be reduced to £8 million, which would exactly cancel with the asset (shares of Subsidiary Ltd) in the balance sheet of Parent plc.

Activity 9.7

Can you think of the (logical) reason why we do not 'scale down' for less than 100 per cent owned subsidiaries when preparing the group balance sheet?

The reason that all of the assets and liabilities of the subsidiary are included in the group balance sheet, in these circumstances, is that the parent company *controls* all of the subsidiary's assets, even though it may not strictly own them all. Control is the key issue in group financial statements.

Activity 9.8

The balance sheets of Large plc and of Small plc, on the date that Large plc bought the shares in Small plc, were as follows:

Balance sheets as at 30 June

	Large plc		Small plc	
	£m	£m	£m	£m
Non-current assets				
Property, plant and equipment				
Land	55		–	
Plant	43		21	
Vehicles	25	123	17	38
Investment				
15 million shares of Small plc		24		–
		147		38
Current assets				
Inventories	42		18	
Trade receivables	18		13	
Cash	32	92	13	44
Total assets		239		82
Equity				
Called-up share capital:				
ordinary shares of £1 each, fully paid	100		20	
Share premium account	–		5	
Retained earnings	64	164	7	32
Non-current liabilities				
Borrowings – Loan notes		50		30
Current liabilities				
Trade payables		25		20
Total equity and liabilities		239		82

Have a go at preparing the group balance sheet.

Activity 9.8 continued

The group balance sheet will be as follows:

Balance sheet as at 30 June

	£m	£m
Non-current assets		
Property, plant and equipment		
Land (55 + 0)	55	
Plant (43 + 21)	64	
Vehicles (25 + 17)	42	161
Current assets		
Inventories (42 + 18)	60	
Trade receivables (18 + 13)	31	
Cash (32 + 13)	45	136
Total assets		297
Equity		
Called-up share capital:		
ordinary shares of £1 each, fully paid	100	
Retained earnings	64	164
Minority interests		8
		172
Non-current liabilities		
Borrowings – Loan notes (50 + 30)		80
Current liabilities		
Trade payables (25 + 20)		45
Total equity and liabilities		297

The £8 million for minority interests represents the 25 per cent of the Small plc shares owned by the 'outside' shareholders (that is, 25 per cent of £32 million).

Complication 2: paying more or less than the underlying net asset value for the shares

Here the problem is that, even where the subsidiary is 100 per cent owned, the asset of 'shares of the subsidiary', in the balance sheet of the parent, will not exactly cancel against the equity figure in the balance sheet of the subsidiary. Anything paid in excess of the underlying net asset value of the subsidiary's shares must represent an undis-
closed asset, which is normally referred to as '**goodwill arising on consolidation**'. Any amount paid below the underlying net asset value is normally referred to as '**negative goodwill arising on consolidation**'.

This situation tends only to arise where there is a takeover of an existing business. Where a would-be parent creates a new subsidiary, goodwill (positive or negative) will not usually arise.

For the sake of simplicity, we shall assume that the balance sheet of a subsidiary reflects all of its assets and liabilities and that these are recorded at their fair values. We shall, however, consider the situation where this is not the case later in the chapter.

Example 9.5

We are returning to the original balance sheets of Parent plc and Subsidiary Ltd (Example 9.3, p. 284), on the date that the former bought the shares in the latter. So Parent plc owns all of the shares in Subsidiary Ltd, but we shall assume that they were bought for £15 m rather than £10 m. Parent plc's cash balance reflects the higher amount paid. The balance sheets are as follows:

Balance sheets as at 30 September

	Parent plc		Subsidiary Ltd	
	£m	£m	£m	£m
Non-current assets				
Property, plant and equipment				
Land	40		5	
Plant	30		2	
Vehicles	20	90	2	9
Investment				
5 million shares of Subsidiary Ltd		15		–
		105		9
Current assets				
Inventories	20		3	
Trade receivables	30		2	
Cash	5	55	2	7
Total assets		160		16
Equity				
Called-up share capital:				
ordinary shares of £1 each, fully paid	70		5	
Share premium account	10		–	
Retained earnings	30	110	5	10
Non-current liabilities				
Borrowings – Loan notes		30		–
Current liabilities				
Trade payables		20		6
Total equity and liabilities		160		16

The normal routine of adding like items together and cancelling the investment in Subsidiary Ltd shares against the equity of that company is followed, except that the last two do not exactly cancel. The difference is, of course, goodwill arising on consolidation.

The group balance sheet will be as follows:

Example 9.5 continued

Balance sheet as at 30 September

	£m	£m
Non-current assets		
Property, plant and equipment		
Land (40 + 5)	45	
Plant (30 + 2)	32	
Vehicles (20 + 2)	22	99
Intangible asset		
Goodwill arising on consolidation (15 – 10)		5
		104
Current assets		
Inventories (20 + 3)	23	
Trade receivables (30 + 2)	32	
Cash (5 + 2)	7	62
Total assets		166
Equity		
Called-up share capital:		
ordinary shares of £1 each, fully paid	70	
Share premium account	10	
Retained earnings	30	110
Non-current liabilities		
Borrowings – Loan notes (30 + 0)		30
Current liabilities		
Trade payables (20 + 6)		26
Total equity and liabilities		166

The goodwill represents the excess of what was paid by Parent plc for the shares over the fair value of their underlying net assets, at the time of the takeover.

Activity 9.9

The balance sheets of Large plc and of Small plc, on the date that Large plc bought all the shares in Small plc, were as follows:

Balance sheets at 30 June

	Large plc £m	Large plc £m	Small plc £m	Small plc £m
Non-current assets				
Property, plant and equipment				
Land	48		–	
Plant	43		21	
Vehicles	25	116	17	38
Investment				
20 million shares of Small plc		35		–
		151		38
Current assets				
Inventories	42		18	
Trade receivables	18		13	
Cash	28	88	13	44
Total assets		239		82

Equity				
Called-up share capital:				
ordinary shares of £1 each, fully paid	100		20	
Share premium account	–		5	
Retained earnings	<u>64</u>	164	<u>7</u>	32
Non-current liabilities				
Borrowings – Loan notes		50		30
Current liabilities				
Trade payables		<u>25</u>		<u>20</u>
		<u><u>239</u></u>		<u><u>82</u></u>

Have a go at preparing the group balance sheet.

The group balance sheet will be as follows:

Balance sheet as at 30 June

	£m	£m
Non-current assets		
Property, plant and equipment		
Land (48 + 0)	48	
Plant (43 + 21)	64	
Vehicles (25 + 17)	<u>42</u>	154
Intangible asset		
Goodwill arising on consolidation (35 – 32)		<u>3</u>
		157
Current assets		
Inventories (42 + 18)	60	
Trade receivables (18 + 13)	31	
Cash (28 + 13)	<u>41</u>	132
		<u>289</u>
Equity		
Called-up share capital:		
ordinary shares of £1 each, fully paid	100	
Retained earnings	<u>64</u>	164
Non-current liabilities		
Borrowings – Loan notes (50 + 30)		80
Current liabilities		
Trade payables (25 + 20)		45
Total equity and liabilities		<u>289</u>

Complications 1 and 2 taken together

We shall now take a look at how we cope with a situation where the parent owns less than all of the shares of its subsidiary, *and* it has paid more or less than the underlying net asset value of the shares.

Example 9.6

Again we shall look at Parent plc and of Subsidiary Ltd, on the date that the former bought the shares in the latter. This time we shall combine both of the 'complications' that we have already met. Here, Parent plc now only owns 80 per cent of the shares of Subsidiary Ltd, for which it paid £3 a share, that is, £1 above their underlying net asset value.

Balance sheets as at 30 September

	Parent plc		Subsidiary Ltd	
	£m	£m	£m	£m
Non-current assets				
Property, plant and equipment				
Land	40		5	
Plant	30		2	
Vehicles	20	90	2	9
Investment				
4 million shares of Subsidiary Ltd		12		–
		102		9
Current assets				
Inventories	20		3	
Trade receivables	30		2	
Cash	8	58	2	7
Total assets		160		16
Equity				
Called-up share capital:				
ordinary shares of £1 each, fully paid	70		5	
Share premium account	10		–	
Retained earnings	30	110	5	10
Non-current liabilities				
Borrowings – Loan notes		30		–
Current liabilities				
Trade payables		20		6
Total equity and liabilities		160		16

The normal routine still applies. This means adding like items together and cancelling the investment in Subsidiary Ltd shares against the equity of that company. Again they will not cancel, but this time for a combination of two reasons; minority interests *and* goodwill arising on consolidation.

We need to separate out the two issues before we go on to prepare the group financial statements.

To establish the minority interests element, we need simply to calculate the part of the owners' claim of Subsidiary Ltd that is not owned by Parent plc. Parent plc owns 80 per cent of the shares, so others own the remaining 20 per cent. Twenty per cent of the equity of Subsidiary Ltd is £2 million (that is, 20 per cent × £10 million).

To discover the appropriate goodwill figure, we need to compare what Parent plc paid and what it got, in terms of the fair values reflected in the balance sheet. It paid £12 million and got net assets with a fair value of £8 million (that is, 80 per cent × £10 million). Thus, goodwill is £4 million (that is, 12 – 8).

The group balance sheet will be as follows:

Balance sheet as at 30 September

	£m	£m
Non-current assets		
Property, plant and equipment		
Land (40 + 5)	45	
Plant (30 + 2)	32	
Vehicles (20 + 2)	22	99
Intangible asset		
Goodwill arising on consolidation		
(12 − (80% × 10))		4
		103
Current assets		
Inventories (20 + 3)	23	
Trade receivables (30 + 2)	32	
Cash (8 + 2)	10	65
Total assets		168
Equity		
Called-up share capital:		
ordinary shares of £1 each, fully paid	70	
Share premium account	10	
Retained earnings	30	110
Minority interests		2
		112
Non-current liabilities		
Borrowings – Loan notes (30 + 0)		30
Current liabilities		
Trade payables (20 + 6)		26
Total equity and liabilities		168

Activity 9.10

The balance sheets of Large plc and Small plc, on the date that Large plc bought the shares in Small plc, were as follows:

Balance sheets as at 30 June

	Large plc £m	Large plc £m	Small plc £m	Small plc £m
Non-current assets				
Property, plant and equipment				
Land	49		–	
Plant	43		21	
Vehicles	25	117	17	38
Investment				
15 million shares of Small plc		27		–
		144		38
Current assets				
Inventories	42		18	
Trade receivables	18		13	
Cash	35	95	13	44
Total assets		239		82

→

Activity 9.10 continued

Equity

Called-up share capital:				
ordinary shares of £1 each, fully paid	100		20	
Share premium account	–		5	
Retained earnings	64	164	7	32
Non current liabilities				
Borrowings – Loan notes		50		30
Current liabilities				
Trade payables		25		20
Total equity and liabilities		239		82

Have a try at preparing the group balance sheet.

The minority interest will be £8 million (that is, 25 per cent of £32 million).

To discover goodwill, we need to compare what was paid (£27 million) with what was obtained (75 per cent of £32 million = £24 million). Thus, we have goodwill of £3 million.

The group balance sheet will be as follows:

Balance sheet as at 30 June

	£m	£m
Non-current assets		
Property, plant and equipment		
Land (49 + 0)	49	
Plant (43 + 21)	64	
Vehicles (25 + 17)	42	155
Intangible asset		
Goodwill arising on consolidation		3
		158
Current assets		
Inventories (42 + 18)	60	
Trade receivables (18 + 13)	31	
Cash (35 + 13)	48	139
Total assets		297
Equity		
Called-up share capital:		
ordinary shares of £1 each, fully paid	100	
Retained earnings	64	164
Minority interests (25% × 32)		8
		172
Non-current liabilities		
Borrowings – Loan notes (50 + 30)		80
Current liabilities		
Trade payables (25 + 20)		45
Total equity and liabilities		297

Complication 3: trading has taken place since the shares were acquired

Except very rarely, most group balance sheets will be prepared some time after the parent company acquired the shares in the subsidiary. This does not in any way raise major difficulties, but we need to backtrack to the position at the time of the acquisition to establish the goodwill figure.

We shall look at another example, this time a new one will be introduced, just to provide a little variety.

Example 9.7

The balance sheets of Mega plc and Micro plc, as at 31 December, are set out below. Mega plc bought its shares in Micro plc some time ago at which time the latter's share capital was exactly as shown below and the retained earnings balance stood at £30 million.

Balance sheets as at 31 December

	Mega plc		Micro plc	
	£m	£m	£m	£m
Non-current assets				
Property, plant and equipment				
Land	53		18	
Plant	34		11	
Vehicles	24	111	9	38
Investment				
6 million shares of Micro plc		33		–
		144		38
Current assets				
Inventories	27		10	
Trade receivables	29		11	
Cash	11	67	1	22
Total assets		211		60
Equity				
Called-up share capital:				
ordinary shares of £1 each, fully paid	100		10	
Retained earnings	38	138	35	45
Non-current liabilities				
Borrowings – Loan notes		50		10
Current liabilities				
Trade payables		23		5
Total equity and liabilities		211		60

We can see that the investment in the balance sheet of Mega plc (£33 million) comes nowhere near cancelling with the £45 million owners' claim of Micro plc. We need to separate out the elements.

Let us start with minority interests. Here we are not concerned at all with the position at the date of the takeover. If the equity of Micro plc totals £45 million at the balance sheet date and the minorities own 4 million of the 10 million shares, their contribution to the financing of the group's assets must be £18 million (that is, 40 per cent × £45 million).

Next let us ask ourselves what Mega plc got when it paid £33 million for the shares. At that time, the equity part of Micro plc's balance sheet looked like this:

	£m
Called-up share capital:	
Ordinary shares of £1 each, fully paid	10
Retained earnings	30
	40

Example 9.7 continued

This means that the net assets of Micro plc must have also been worth (in terms of fair values reflected in the balance sheet) £40 million; otherwise the balance sheet would not have balanced. Since Mega plc bought 6 million of 10 million shares, it paid £33 million for net assets worth £24 million (that is, 60 per cent of £40 million). Thus, there is goodwill arising on consolidation of £9 million (that is, 33 – 24).

We shall assume that no steps have been taken since the takeover to alter this goodwill figure. We shall consider why such steps may have been taken a little later in this chapter.

In dealing with minority interests and goodwill we have, in effect, picked up the following parts of the owners' claim of Micro plc at 31 December:

- The minorities' share of both the equity (as minority interests).
- Mega plc's share of the share capital and its share of the reserves as they stood at the date of the takeover (in the calculation of the goodwill figure).

The only remaining part of the owners' claim of Micro plc at 31 December is Mega plc's share of Micro plc's reserves that have built up since the takeover, that is, its share of £35 million – £30 million = £5 million. This share is £3 million (that is, 60 per cent of £5 million). This is Mega plc's share of the profits that have been earned by its subsidiary since the takeover, to the extent that profits have not already been paid out as dividends. As such, it is logical for this £3 million to be added to the retained earnings balance of the parent company in arriving at the group reserves.

This treatment of the equity of Micro plc can be represented in a tabular form as shown in Figure 9.3.

Figure 9.3	The treatment of the share equity of Micro plc in producing the group balance sheet

	Total £m	Minorities 40% £m	Mega plc 60% £m	
Share capital	10	4	6	Compare with the cost of the shares to deduce goodwill on consolidation
Retained profit:				
Pre-acquisition	30	12	18	
Post-acquisition	5	2	3	
	45	18	27	Add to the retained profit balance of Mega plc to deduce group revenue reserves

Minority interests

The minority interest total is simply the appropriate percentage of the subsidiary's total equity, without reference to when the reserves arose. The parent's share of the subsidiary's total of equity, at the date of the takeover, is compared with the price paid by the parent to deduce the goodwill arising on consolidation. The parent's share of the subsidiary's post-acquisition reserves is added to the parent's reserves to find the total reserves.

The group balance sheet will be as follows:

Balance sheet as at 31 December

Non-current assets	£m	£m
Property, plant and equipment		
Land (53 + 18)	71	
Plant (34 + 11)	45	
Vehicles (24 + 9)	33	149
Intangible asset		
Goodwill arising on consolidation (33 − (6 + 18))		9
		158
Current assets		
Inventories (27 + 10)	37	
Trade receivables (29 + 11)	40	
Cash (11 + 1)	12	89
Total assets		247
Equity		
Called-up share capital:		
ordinary shares of £1 each, fully paid	100	
Retained earnings (38 + 3)	41	141
Minority interests (40% × 45)		18
		159
Non-current liabilities		
Borrowings – Loan notes (50 + 10)		60
Current liabilities		
Trade payables (23 + 5)		28
Total equity and liabilities		247

Activity 9.11

The balance sheets of Grand plc and Petit Ltd, as at 30 June, are set out below. Grand plc bought its shares in Petit Ltd some time ago at which time the latter's share capital was the same as it is currently and the retained earnings balance stood at £14 million.

Balance sheets as at 30 June

	Grand plc		Petit Ltd	
Non-current assets	£m	£m	£m	£m
Property, plant and equipment				
Land	12		10	
Plant	14		8	
Vehicles	3	29	6	24
Investment				
7.5 million shares of Petit Ltd		21		–
		50		24
Current assets				
Inventories	10		5	
Trade receivables	9		4	
Cash	2	21	2	11
Total assets		71		35

Activity 9.11 continued

Equity
   Called-up share capital:
      ordinary shares of £1 each, fully paid   30   10
      Retained earnings   14   44   22   32
Non-current liabilities
   Borrowings – Loan notes   20   –
Current liabilities
   Trade payables   7   3
Total equity and liabilities   71   35

Prepare the balance sheet for the group as at 30 June.

Your answer should be something like this:

Minority interests

$$25\% \times £32 \text{ million} = £8 \text{ million}$$

Goodwill arising on consolidation

$$£21 \text{ million} - [75\% \times (£10 \text{ million} + £14 \text{ million})] = £3 \text{ million}$$

Grand plc's share of Petit Ltd's post-acquisition reserves

$$75\% \times (£22 \text{ million} - £14 \text{ million}) = £6 \text{ million}$$

Assuming that no steps have been taken since the takeover to alter the goodwill figure, the group balance sheet will be as follows:

Balance sheet as at 30 June

	£m	£m
Non-current assets		
Property, plant and equipment		
Land (12 + 10)	22	
Plant (14 + 8)	22	
Vehicles (3 + 6)	9	53
Intangible asset		
Goodwill arising on consolidation		3
		56
Current assets		
Inventories (10 + 5)	15	
Trade receivables (9 + 4)	13	
Cash (2 + 2)	4	32
Total assets		88
Equity		
Called-up share capital:		
ordinary shares of £1 each, fully paid	30	
Retained earnings (14 + 6)	20	50
Minority interests		8
		58
Non-current liabilities		
Borrowings – Loan notes (20 + 0)		20
Current liabilities		
Trade payables (7 + 3)		10
Total equity and liabilities		88

Goodwill arising on consolidation and balance sheet values

Goodwill on consolidation represents the difference between the cost of acquiring the shares in a subsidiary and the **fair values** of the net assets acquired. In the examples that we have considered so far, we have assumed that the balance sheet values are the same as the fair values of the assets of the subsidiary company. Thus, it has been possible to deduce goodwill by making a comparison of the cost of acquiring the subsidiary with the balance sheet values of the subsidiary. Unfortunately, things are not usually that simple!

Balance sheet values often differ from the fair values of assets. Generally speaking, balance sheet values are lower because accounting conventions, such as prudence and historic cost, conspire to produce a conservative bias. As a result, not only do assets tend to be shown on the balance sheet at less than their fair value, but some assets are completely omitted from the normal balance sheet. This is particularly true of intangible assets, such as brand values. This means that, to calculate goodwill on consolidation, we cannot rely on balance sheet values. We must find out what the fair values of the assets acquired really are. This must include both those on the balance sheet of the subsidiary and those omitted (such as brand values).

Example 9.8 seeks to illustrate this point.

Example 9.8

The balance sheets of Parent plc and of Subsidiary Ltd (which we last met in Example 9.6) on the date that the former bought the shares in the latter, were as follows:

Balance sheets as at 30 September

	Parent plc £m	Parent plc £m	Subsidiary Ltd £m	Subsidiary Ltd £m
Non-current assets				
Property, plant and equipment				
Land	40		5	
Plant	30		2	
Vehicles	20	90	2	9
Investment				
5 million shares of Subsidiary Ltd		15		–
		105		9
Current assets				
Inventories	20		3	
Trade receivables	30		2	
Cash	5	55	2	7
Total assets		160		16
Equity				
Called-up share capital:				
ordinary shares of £1 each, fully paid	70		5	
Share premium account	10		–	
Retained earnings	30	110	5	10
Non-current liabilities				
Borrowings – Loan notes		30		–
Current liabilities				
Trade payables		20		6
Total equity and liabilities		160		16

Example 9.8 continued

When Parent plc was valuing the shares of Subsidiary Ltd, it was judged that most of the balance sheet values were in line with the fair values, but that the following values should be applied to the three categories of property, plant and equipment:

	£m
Land	7
Plant	3
Vehicles	3

In addition it was recognised that the subsidiary has a product with a brand valued at £1 million. When these fair values are incorporated into the group balance sheet, it will be as follows:

Balance sheet as at 30 September

Non-current assets	£m	£m
Property, plant and equipment		
Land (40 + 7)	47	
Plant (30 + 3)	33	
Vehicles (20 + 3)	23	103
Intangible asset		
Brand		1
		104
Current assets		
Inventories (20 + 3)	23	
Trade receivables (30 + 2)	32	
Cash (5 + 2)	7	62
Total assets		166
Equity		
Called-up share capital:		
ordinary shares of £1 each, fully paid	70	
Share premium account	10	
Retained earnings	30	110
Non-current liabilities		
Borrowings – Loan notes (30 + 0)		30
Current liabilities		
Trade payables (20 + 6)		26
Total equity and liabilities		166

This example takes the simple case of no minority interests (that is, a 100 per cent subsidiary) and no post-acquisition trading (the balance sheets are at the date of acquisition), but these 'complications' would not alter the principles.

It should be noted that there is no need for the balance sheet of the subsidiary to be adjusted for fair values, just the group balance sheet. As far as the subsidiary is concerned, no change occurs with the takeover except a change in the names on the list of shareholders.

The financial reporting standard that deals with this area of group financial statements (IRFS 3) is clear that intangible assets of the subsidiary, at the date of the takeover, like brand values and patent rights, must be separately identified at their fair value. These assets must then be incorporated at those values in the group balance sheet.

The non-current assets of the subsidiary that have finite lives should have a depreciation (or amortisation) charge, based on their fair values, in the group income statement. This charge may well be different in amount to that which arises in the financial statements of the subsidiary.

Goodwill arising on consolidation is simply the excess of what the parent company paid for the subsidiary company's shares over their fair value, based on all of the identifiable assets (tangible and intangible) of the subsidiary. This means that what is identified as goodwill tends to represent only the value of:

● having a workforce in place;
● cost synergies – arising from the fact that the combined business can make cost saving by, say, having just one head offices instead of two; and
● sales synergies – arising, for example, from group members trading with one another.

These attributes that represent goodwill could well be enduring, but they can also be lost, either partially or completely. IFRS 3 recognises this and states that the value of goodwill should be reviewed annually, or even more frequently if circumstances dictate. Where its value has been impaired, it must be reduced accordingly in the group financial statements. It should be noted that goodwill arising on consolidation does not appear in the balance sheets either of the parent or the subsidiary. It only appears on the group balance sheet.

Despite the requirement of IFRS 3 that all subsidiary company assets, whether they appear on the subsidiary's balance sheet or not, whether they are tangible or intangible, should be reflected at their fair value in the group balance sheet, this seems not always to happen in reality. **Real World 9.3** relates an investigation into how some large, well-known businesses seem not to be following the spirit of IFRS 3.

Real World 9.3

Where there's goodwill . . .

During the first year that IFRS 3 applied (2005), the largest 100 businesses listed on the London Stock Exchange between them spent £40 billion on taking over other businesses. This acquisition cost was treated as follows in the subsequent group balance sheets:

	£ billion	%
Tangible assets	6.8	17
Intangible assets	12.0	30
Goodwill arising on consolidation	21.2	53

This information is contained in a report by Thane Forbes. He concludes that this treatment was counter to the spirit of IFRS 3. It seemed implausible that such a large proportion of the total should be treated as goodwill, when IFRS 3 limits what should be treated as goodwill quite severely.

He identifies some examples. Included is the takeover of RAC plc (the UK motoring organisation) by Aviva plc (the UK-based insurance business) in March 2005. Aviva paid £1.1 billion, of which the majority was treated as goodwill. RAC had 7 million customers and is one of the most trusted brands in the UK, yet these were valued at only £260 million and £132 million respectively.

→

Real World 9.3 continued

He also identifies four possible reasons for these apparent misapplications of IFRS 3:

1 *To reduce depreciation charges and increase profits.* Since goodwill cannot be depreciated and intangible assets with finite lives should be, reported profit will tend to be enhanced by treating as much of the purchase price as possible as goodwill.

2 *To minimise impairment charges.* Though both intangible assets without finite lives and goodwill are subject to tests of impairment of value and a possible accounting charge as a result, the tests for goodwill are less stringent. So an intangible asset is more likely to lead to an impairment charge than is goodwill.

3 *Lack of skills.* Having to value intangibles following a takeover is a new requirement, so the skills to do so may not be so readily available.

4 *Failure to see the big picture.* Businesses may get so bogged down with the regulations that they fail to consider the key issues and effects of the takeover.

Forbes goes on to say:

The implications of this inadequate reporting are far reaching. It renders annual reports more useless than they currently are, it makes a standard ineffective when applied and the financial bodies that govern them, it sets a dangerous precedent for future years and it opens a new era of creative accounting that distances shareholders and investors further from reality.

Source: Forbes, T. (2007) 'Technical Update – Inadequate IFRS 3', *Finance Week*, 30 January, www.financeweek.co.uk.

Where negative goodwill on consolidation arises, IFRS 3 says that fair values of all assets and liabilities of the subsidiary concerned should be reassessed. This reassessment is to try to ensure that no assets have been overstated or liabilities understated or omitted. If this reassessment still results in negative goodwill, the amount of this negative goodwill should be credited immediately to the group income statement of the year of the acquisition of the subsidiary. In practice negative goodwill would be pretty rare.

Inter-company assets and claims

Though members of a group are separate legal entities, the element of control exercised by the parent, and generally close relations between them, tends to lead to inter-company trading and other inter-company transactions. This, in turn, means that a particular asset in one company's balance sheet could relate to an equal-sized liability in the balance sheet of another member of the same group.

The principle underlying the group balance sheet is that it should represent the situation as if all the assets and claims of individual group members were directly the assets and claims of the parent company. Since the parent company cannot owe itself money, where there are inter-company balances these must be eliminated when preparing the group balance sheet.

Example 9.9

Delta plc and its subsidiary Gamma plc are the only members of a group. Delta plc sells goods on credit to Gamma plc. At the balance sheet date the following balances existed in the books of the companies:

	Trade receivables £m	Trade payables £m
Delta plc	34	26
Gamma plc	23	18

Included in the trade receivables of Delta plc, and the trade payables of Gamma plc, is £5 million in respect of some recent intercompany trading.

In deducing the figures to be included in the group balance sheet, we have to eliminate the intercompany balance, as follows:

Trade receivables = 34 − 5 + 23 = £52 million

Trade payables = 26 + 18 − 5 = £39 million

Note that these consolidated trade receivables and trade payables figures represent what is, respectively, owed by and owed to individuals and organisations outside of the group. This is what they are intended to represent, according to the principles of group accounting.

Preparing the group income statement

→ The **group income statement** follows very similar principles to those that apply to the balance sheet. These are:

- Like items are added together. For example, the revenue of each subsidiary is added to that of the parent company to discover group revenue.
- All the amounts appearing under each heading in the income statements of subsidiaries are included in the total, even where it is not a wholly owned subsidiary. For example, the revenue of a subsidiary, say 60 per cent owned by the parent, is included in full.
- The interests of minorities are separately identified towards the bottom of the income statement.

Example 9.10

Holder plc owns 75 per cent of the ordinary shares of Sub Ltd. The outline income statements of the two companies for the year ended on 31 December are as follows:

Income statements for the year ended 31 December

	Holder plc £m	Holder plc £m	Sub Ltd £m	Sub Ltd £m
Revenue		83		40
Cost of sales		(41)		(15)
Gross profit		42		25
Administration expenses	(16)		(9)	
Distribution expenses	(6)	(22)	(3)	(12)
Operating profit		20		13
Interest payable		(2)		(1)
Profit before taxation		18		12
Taxation		(8)		(4)
Profit for the year		13		8

→

Example 9.10 continued

Preparing the group income statement is a very simple matter of adding like items together, except that not all of the profit for the year of the subsidiary 'belongs' to the group. Twenty-five per cent (£2 million) of it belongs to the minorities. We recognise this in the group income statement by deducting the 25 per cent of the profit for the year of the subsidiary from the combined profit for the year.

The group income statement will be as follows:

Income statement for the year ended 31 December

	£m	£m
Revenue (83 + 40)		123
Cost of sales (41 + 15)		(56)
Gross profit		67
Administration expenses (16 + 9)	(25)	
Distribution expenses (6 + 3)	(9)	(34)
Operating profit		33
Interest payable (2 + 1)		(3)
Profit before taxation		30
Taxation (8 + 4)		(12)
Profit for the year		18
Attributable to minorities		(2)
Profit for the year attributable to Holder plc shareholders		16

This statement says that the assets under the control of the group generated profit for the year of £18 million. Of this, £2 million is the share of the 'outside' shareholders of Sub Ltd. This follows the normal approach of group financial statements of treating all assets, claims, revenues and expenses of group companies as if they were those of the group. Where the subsidiaries are not 100 per cent owned by the parent, this fact is acknowledged by making an adjustment to reflect the minority interests.

Activity 9.12

Ajax plc owns 60 per cent of the ordinary shares of Exeter plc. The outline income statements of the two companies for the year ended on 31 December are as follows:

Income statements for the year ended 31 December

	Ajax plc		Exeter plc	
	£m	£m	£m	£m
Revenue		120		80
Cost of sales		(60)		(40)
Gross profit		60		40
Administration expenses	(17)		(4)	
Distribution expenses	(10)	(27)	(15)	(19)
Operating profit		33		21
Interest payable		(3)		(1)
Profit before taxation		30		20
Taxation		(12)		(10)
Profit for the year		18		10

Have a try at preparing a consolidated (group) income statement.

Your answer should look something like this:

Group income statement for the year ended 31 December

	£m	£m
Revenue (120 + 80)		200
Cost of sales (60 + 40)		(100)
Gross profit		100
Administration expenses (17 + 4)	(21)	
Distribution expenses (10 + 15)	(25)	(46)
Operating profit		54
Interest payable (3 + 1)		(4)
Profit before taxation		50
Taxation (12 + 10)		22
Profit for the year		28
Attributable to minorities (40% × 10)		4
Profit for the year attributable to Ajax plc shareholders		24

Inter-company trading

As we saw earlier in the chapter, it is very common for members of the group to trade with one another. As far as each member of the group is concerned such trading should be dealt with in the accounting records, including the income statement, in exactly the same way as trading with any other party. When we come to the group income statement, however, inter-company trading between group members must be eliminated. It is in the spirit of group accounting that the group income statement should only recognise trading with parties outside of the group, as if the group were one single business. Only sales to outsiders should be reflected in the group sales revenue figure; only purchases of goods and services from parties outside of the group should be reflected.

Group cash flow statements

Groups must normally prepare a cash flow statement that follows the same logic as the balance sheet and income statement. That is, to show the movements in all of the cash that is in the control of the group, for the period under review.

→ The preparation of a **group cash flow statement** follows the same rules as apply to the preparation of the statement for individual companies. In view of this we need not spend time looking separately at cash flow statements in a group context.

Similarly to the balance sheet and income statement, cash transfers between group members should not be reflected in the group cash flow statement.

Self-assessment question 9.1

The balance sheets, as at 31 December last year, and income statements, for the year ended last 31 December, of Great plc and Small plc are set out below. Great plc bought its shares in Small plc on 1 January last year at which time the latter's share capital was the same as it is currently and the retained earnings balance stood at £35 million.

Self-assessment question 9.1 continued

At the time of the acquisition, the fair value of all the assets of Small plc was thought to be the same as that shown in their balance sheets, except for land whose fair value was thought to be £5 million more than the balance sheet value. It is believed that there has been no impairment in the value of the goodwill arising on consolidation since 1 January last year.

Balance sheets as at 31 December last year

	Great plc £m	Great plc £m	Small plc £m	Small plc £m
Non-current assets				
Property, plant and equipment				
Land	80		14	
Plant	33		20	
Vehicles	20	133	11	45
Investment				
16 million shares of Small plc		53		–
		186		45
Current assets				
Inventories	20		9	
Trade receivables	21		6	
Cash	17	58	5	20
Total assets		244		65
Equity				
Called-up share capital:				
ordinary shares of £1 each, fully paid	100		20	
Retained earnings	77	177	40	60
Non-current liabilities				
Borrowings – Loan notes		50		–
Current liabilities				
Trade payables		17		5
Total equity and liabilities		244		65

Income statements for the year ended 31 December last year

	Great plc £m	Great plc £m	Small plc £m	Small plc £m
Revenue		91		27
Cost of sales		(46)		(13)
Gross profit		45		14
Administration expenses	(8)		(3)	
Distribution expenses	(6)	(14)	(2)	(5)
Operating profit		31		9
Interest payable		(3)		–
Profit before taxation		28		9
Taxation		(12)		(4)
Profit for the year		16		5

Required:
Prepare the balance sheet and income statement for the group.

The answer to this question can be found at the back of the book at p. 407.

Accounting for less than a controlling interest – associate companies

What happens when one company makes a substantial investment in another company but this does not provide the investing company with a controlling interest? In other words, the company whose shares have been acquired does not become a subsidiary of the investing company. One approach would simply include the investment of shares in the company at cost in the investing company's balance sheet. Assuming that the shares are held on a long-term basis, they would be treated as a non-current asset. Any dividends received from the investment would be treated as income in the investing company's income statement.

The problem with this approach, however, is that companies normally pay dividends of much less than the profits earned for the period. The profits that are not distributed, but are ploughed back, help to generate more profits for the future, still belong to the shareholders. From the perspective of the investing company, the accounting treatment described would not, therefore, reflect fully the investment made. Where the investment made by the investing group does not involve the purchase of a substantial shareholding in the company, this problem is overlooked and so the treatment of the investment described above (that is, showing the investment, at cost, as a non-current asset and taking account only of any dividends received) is applied. Where, however, the investment involves the purchase of a significant number of voting shares in the company, a different kind of accounting treatment seems more appropriate.

Associate companies

To deal with the problem identified above, a particular type of relationship between the two companies has been defined. An **associate company** is one in which an investing company or group has a substantial, but not a controlling interest in it. To be more precise, it is a company over which another company can exercise significant influence regarding its operating and financial policies. If a company holds 20 per cent or more of the voting shares of another company it is presumed to be able to exercise significant influence. This influence is usually demonstrated by representation on the board of directors of the company or by participation in policy making. The relevant international accounting standard (IAS 28, Investments in associates) provides the detailed guidelines concerning what constitutes an associate company.

The accounting treatment of an associate company falls somewhere between consolidation, as with group financial statements, and the treatment of small share investments, as described at the beginning of this section. Let us assume that a company invests in another company, so that the latter becomes an associate of the former. The accounting treatment will be as follows:

- The investing company will be required to produce consolidated financial statements that reflect, not only its own performance and position, but also those of its associate company.
- In the consolidated income statement, the investing company's share of the operating profit of the associate company (companies) will be shown and will be added to

the operating profit of the investing company. As operating profit represents the profit before interest and taxation, the investing company's share of any interest payable and tax relating to the associate company will also be shown. These will be deducted in deriving the profit for the year for the investing company and its associate company.

- In the consolidated balance sheet, the investment made in the associate company will be shown and the investing company's share of any post-acquisition reserves will be added to the investment. This will have the effect of showing more fully the investment made in the associate company.
- Dividends received by the investing company from the associate company will not be included in the consolidated income statement. This is because the investing company's share of the associate company's profit will already be fully reflected in the financial statements.
- If the investing company also has subsidiaries, their financial statements will also have to be incorporated, in the manner that we saw for groups earlier in the chapter. Thus, a company that has both subsidiary companies and associate companies will prepare consolidated financial statements reflecting all of these.

To illustrate these points, let us take a simple example.

Example 9.11

A plc owns 25 per cent of the ordinary shares of B plc. The price paid for the shares was £26m. A plc bought its shares in B plc, when the latter's reserves stood at £24m. The reserves of B plc have increased to £40m by 31 March last year.

The income statement for A plc and B plc for the year ended 31 March this year are as follows:

Income statements for the year ended 31 March this year

	A plc £m	B plc £m
Revenues	800	100
Cost of sales	(500)	(60)
Gross profit	300	40
Operating expenses	(120)	(12)
Operating profit	180	28
Interest payable	(30)	(8)
Profit before taxation	150	20
Taxation	(40)	(4)
Profit for the year	110	16

To comply with the relevant standard (IAS 28), A plc's share of the operating profit of B plc as well as its share of interest payable and taxation relating to B plc will be incorporated within A plc's consolidated income statement. A plc's consolidated income statement will, therefore, be as follows:

A plc
Consolidated income statement

	£m	£m	
Revenues		800	
Cost of sales		(500)	
Gross profit		300	
Operating expenses		(120)	
		180	
Share of operating profit of associate – B plc		7	(25% × £28 m)
Operating profit		187	
Interest payable:			
A plc	(30)		
Associate – B plc	(2)	(32)	(25% × £8 m)
Profit before taxation		155	
Taxation:			
A plc	(40)		
Associate – B plc	(1)	(41)	(25% × £4 m)
Profit for the year		114	

The consolidated balance sheet of A plc, treating B plc as an associate company, would include an amount for the investment in B plc that is calculated as follows:

Extract from A plc's consolidated balance sheet as at 31 March (this year)

	£m	
Cost of investment in associated company	26	
Share of post-acquisition reserves	4	(that is, 25% × (40 – 24))
	30	

Activity 9.13

What is the crucial difference between the approach taken when consolidating subsidiary company results and incorporating the results of associate companies, as far as the balance sheet and income statement are concerned?

In preparing group financial statements, all of the items in the statements are added together, as if the parent owned them all, even when the subsidiary is less than 100 per cent owned. For example, the revenue figure in the consolidated income statement is the sum of all the revenues made by group companies, the inventories figure in the balance sheet is the sum of all the inventories held by all members of the group.

When dealing with associate companies, we only deal with the shareholding company's share of the profit of the associate and its effect on the value of the shareholding.

Real World 9.4 is the list of the associate companies of Cadbury Schweppes plc, the confectionery and drinks manufacturer. Most of its associate companies are overseas ones that are involved in some aspect of confectionary and beverages, but they also include a stake in Camelot Group plc, the business that operates the UK national lottery.

Real World 9.4

A bit of a lottery

Details of principal associate undertakings

	Activities	Country of incorporation and operation	Proportion of issued share capital held
Camelot Group plc	(c)	Great Britain	20%
L'Europeenne D'Embouteillage SAS	(b)	France	50%
Dr Pepper/Seven Up Bottling Group, Inc	(b)	US	45.4%
Cadbury Nigeria PLC (listed)	(a)	Nigeria	46.4%
Crystal Candy (Private) Ltd	(a)	Zimbabwe	49%
Meito Adams Company Ltd	(a)	Japan	50%

The nature of the activities of the individual companies is designated as follows:

(a) Confectionery
(b) Beverages
(c) Other.

Source: Cadbury Schweppes plc Report and Accounts 2005.

The argument against consolidation

There seems to be a compelling logic for consolidating the results of subsidiaries controlled by a parent company, to reflect the fact that the shareholders of the parent company effectively control all of the assets of all of the companies in the group. There is also, however, a fairly strong argument against doing so.

Anyone reading the consolidated financial statements of a group of companies could be misled into believing that trading with any member of the group would, in effect, be the same as trading with the group as a whole. The person might imagine that all of the group's assets could be called upon to meet any amounts owed by any member of the group. This would be untrue, however. Only the assets owned by the particular group member would be accessible to any creditor of that group member. The reason for this is, of course, the legal separateness of the limited company from its shareholder(s), which in turn leads to limited liability of individual group members. There would be absolutely no legal obligation on a parent company, or a fellow subsidiary, to meet the financial obligations of a struggling subsidiary. In fact, this is a reason why some businesses operate through a series of subsidiaries, a point that was made early in this chapter.

Despite this criticism of consolidation, the requirement to prepare group financial statements is a very popular legal requirement throughout the world.

Summary

The main points of this chapter may be summarised as follows:

Groups

- A group exists where one company (parent) can exercise control over another (subsidiary), usually by owning more than 50 per cent of the voting shares.
- Groups arise by a parent setting up a new company or taking over an existing one.
- Businesses operate as groups:
  - to have limited liability for each part of the business; and
  - to give each part of the business an individual identity.
- Normally parent companies are required to produce financial statements for the group as a whole, as if the parent company itself has all of the group members' assets, liabilities, revenues, expenses and cash flows.

Group balance sheets

- Derived by adding like items (assets and liabilities) together and setting the equity of each subsidiary (in the subsidiary's balance sheet) against the investment in subsidiary figure (in the parent's balance sheet).
- Where the equity of the subsidiary does not cancel the investment in subsidiary it will be for three possible reasons:
  - more (or less) was paid for the subsidiary shares than their 'fair value' leading to 'goodwill on consolidation' (an intangible non-current asset) (or negative goodwill arising on consolidation) in the group balance sheet; and/or
  - the parent does not own all of the shares of the subsidiary, leading to 'minority (or outsiders') interests' (similar to equity in the group balance sheet) reflecting the fact that the parent's shareholders do not supply all of the equity finance for the group's assets;
  - the subsidiary has made profits or losses since it became a subsidiary.
- 'Goodwill arising on consolidation' represents the value of the ability of the subsidiary to generate additional profits as a result of an established workforce and economically valuable cost and/or sales synergies.
- Goodwill remains on the group balance sheet, but is subject to an 'impairment review' annually and written down in value if it is established that its value has diminished.
- Negative goodwill should be immediately credited to the group income statement.
- Inter-group company balances (receivables and payables) must be eliminated from the group balance sheet.

Group income statement

- Derived by adding like items (revenues and expenses).
- The minority shareholders' share of the after tax profit are deducted from the group total to reflect the fact that not all of the subsidiary's profit belongs to the group.
- Inter-group company trading transactions (revenues and expenses) must be eliminated from the group income statement.

Group cash flow statement

● Derived by adding like items (cash flows).

● Inter-group company cash transfers must be eliminated from the group cash flow statement.

Associate companies

● An 'associate company' is one where there is a company that has less than a controlling interest, but yet is able to exert significant influence over it, often indicated by representation on the board of directors.

● The investing company will be required to produce consolidated financial statements that reflect, not only its own performance and position, but those of its associate company (companies) as well.

● In the consolidated income statement, the investing company's share of the operating profit of the associate company is added to the operating profit of the investing company. Any interest payable and tax relating to the associate company will also be shown.

● In the consolidated balance sheet, the investment made in the associate company will be shown and the investing company's share of any post-acquisition reserves will be added to the investment.

● Dividends received by the investing company from the associate company are not included in the consolidated income statement.

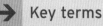 Key terms

---

Further reading

If you would like to explore the topics covered in this chapter in more depth, we recommend the following books:

Alexander, D. and Britton, A. (2004), *Financial Reporting*, 7th edn, Thomson Learning, Chapter 24.

Elliott, B. and Elliott, J. (2006), *Financial Accounting and Reporting*, 11th edn, Financial Times/ Prentice Hall, Chapters 21 to 24.

Sutton, T. (2003), *Corporate Financial Accounting and Reporting*, 2nd edn, Financial Times/Prentice Hall, Chapter 14.

Review questions

Answers to these questions can be found at the back of the book on pp. 416–17.

9.1 When does a group relationship arise and what are its consequences for accounting?

9.2 What does a group balance sheet show?

9.3 Quite often, when an existing company wishes to start a new venture, perhaps to produce a new product or render a new service, it will form a subsidiary company as a vehicle for the new venture. Why is this, why not have the new venture conducted by the original company?

9.4 What is an associated company and what are the consequences for accounting of one company being the associated company of a group of companies?

Exercises

Exercises 9.1 to 9.4 are more advanced that 9.5 to 9.8. Those with a coloured number have answers at the back of the book, starting on p. 441.

9.1 Giant plc bought a majority shareholding in Jack Ltd, on the 31 March. On that date the balance sheet of the two companies were as follows:

Balance sheets as at 31 March

	Giant plc		Jack Ltd	
	£m	£m	£m	£m
Non-current assets				
Property, plant and equipment				
Land	27		12	
Plant	55		8	
Vehicles	18	100	7	27
Investment				
10 million shares of Jack Ltd		30		–
		130		27
Current assets				
Inventories	33		13	
Trade receivables	42		17	
Cash	22	97	5	35
Total assets		227		62
Equity				
Called-up share capital:				
ordinary shares of £1 each, fully paid	50		10	
Share premium account	40		5	
Revaluation reserve	–		8	
Retained earnings	46	136	7	30
Non-current liabilities				
Borrowings – Loan notes		50		13
Current liabilities				
Trade payables		41		19
Total equity and liabilities		227		62

Required:

Assume that the balance sheet values of Jack Ltd's assets represent 'fair' values. Prepare the group balance sheet immediately following the takeover.

9.2 The balance sheets of Jumbo plc and of Nipper plc, on the date that Jumbo plc bought the shares in Nipper plc, were as follows:

Balance sheets as at 31 March

	Jumbo plc £m	Jumbo plc £m	Nipper plc £m	Nipper plc £m
Non-current assets				
Property, plant and equipment				
Land	84		18	
Plant	34		33	
Vehicles	45	163	12	63
Investment				
12 million shares of Nipper plc		24		–
		187		63
Current assets				
Inventories	55		32	
Trade receivables	26		44	
Cash	14	95	10	86
Total assets		282		149
Equity				
Called-up share capital:				
ordinary shares of £1 each, fully paid	100		20	
Share premium account	–		12	
Retained earnings	41	141	8	40
Non-current assets				
Borrowings – Loan notes		100		70
Current liabilities				
Trade payables		41		39
Total equity and liabilities		282		149

Required:

Assume that the balance sheet values of Nipper plc's assets represent fair values. Prepare the group balance sheet immediately following the share acquisition.

9.3 An abridged set of consolidated financial statements for Toggles plc is given below.

Toggles plc
Consolidated income statement for the year ended 30 June

	£m
Revenue	172.0
Operating profit	21.2
Taxation	(6.4)
Profit after taxation	14.8
Minority interest	(2.4)
Profit for the year	12.4

Consolidated balance sheet as at 30 June

	£m	£m
Non-current assets		
Intangible asset		
Goodwill on consolidation		7.2
Property, plant and equipment		85.6
Current assets		92.8
Inventories	21.8	
Trade receivables	16.4	
Cash	1.7	39.9
Total assets		132.7
Equity		
Share capital	100.0	
Retained profit	16.1	116.1
Minority interest		1.3
		117.4
Current liabilities		
Trade payables		15.3
		132.7

Required:

(a) Answer, briefly, the following questions:

1 What is meant by 'minority interest' in both the income statement and the balance sheet?

2 What is meant by 'goodwill on consolidation'?

3 Why will the 'retained profit' figure on the consolidated balance sheet usually be different from the 'retained profit' as shown in the parent company's balance sheet?

(b) Explain the purposes and advantages in preparing consolidated financial statements for the parent company's shareholders.

9.4 Arnold plc owns 75 per cent of the ordinary shares of Baker plc. The outline income statements of the two companies for the year ended on 31 December are as follows:

Income statements for the year ended 31 December

	Arnold plc		Baker plc	
	£m	£m	£m	£m
Revenue		83		47
Cost of sales		(36)		(19)
Gross profit		47		28
Administration expenses	(14)		(7)	
Distribution expenses	(21)	(35)	(10)	(17)
Operating profit		12		11
Taxation		(4)		(3)
Profit for the year		8		8

Required:

Prepare the consolidated (group) income statement for Arnold plc and its subsidiary for the year ended 31 December.

9.5 The summary balance sheets for Apple Limited and Pear Limited are set out below.

Balance sheets as at 30 September

	Apple Limited		Pear Limited	
	£000	£000	£000	£000
Non-current assets				
Property, plant and equipment		950		320
Investment				
Shares in Pear Limited		240		–
		1,190		320
Current assets				
Inventories	320		160	
Trade receivables	180		95	
Cash at bank	41	541	15	270
Total assets		1,731		590
Equity				
£1 fully paid ordinary shares		700		200
Reserves		307		88
		1,007		288
Non-current liabilities				
Loan notes		500		160
Current liabilities				
Trade payables	170		87	
Taxation	54	224	55	142
Total equity and liabilities		1,731		590

Apple Ltd purchased 150,000 shares in Pear Ltd at a price of £1.60 per share on 30 September (the above balance sheet date). The balance sheet of Pear Ltd reflects all of the assets of the company, net of liabilities stated at their fair values.

Required:
Prepare a consolidated balance sheet for Apple Ltd as at 30 September.

9.6 Abridged financial statements for Harvest Limited and Wheat Limited as at 30 June this year are set out below. On 1 July last year Harvest Limited acquired 800,000 ordinary shares in Wheat Limited for a payment of £3,500,000. Wheat Ltd's share capital and share premium were each the same at both dates. At that date and at 30 June this year, the assets in the balance sheet of Wheat Limited were shown at fair market values.

Balance sheets as at 30 June this year

	Harvest Limited		Wheat Limited	
	£000	£000	£000	£000
Non-current assets				
Property, plant and equipment	10,850		4,375	
Investment				
Shares of Wheat Limited	3,500	14,350	–	4,375
Current assets		3,775		1,470
Total assets		18,125		5,845

Equity

Share capital (£1 shares)		2,000		1,000
Share premium account		3,000		500
Revenue reserves at				
1 July last year	2,800		375	
Profit for current year	399	3,199	75	450
		8,199		1,950
Non-current liabilities				
Bank loans		7,000		2,500
Current liabilities		2,926		1,395
Total equity and liabilities		18,125		5,845

Required:

Prepare the consolidated balance sheet for Harvest Ltd as at 30 June this year, using the data given above.

9.7 A year ago Pod Limited bought 225,000 £1 fully paid ordinary shares of Pea Limited for a consideration of £500,000. Pea Limited's share capital and share premium were each the same as at today's date. Simplified balance sheets for both companies as at today's date, after having traded as a group for a year, are set out below. The balance sheet of Pea Ltd reflects all of the assets of the company, net of liabilities stated at their fair values.

Balance sheets as at today

	Pod Limited		Pea Limited	
	£	£	£	£
Non-current assets				
Property, plant and equipment		1,104,570		982,769
Investments				
Shares in Pea Limited		500,000		–
		1,604,570		982,769
Current assets				
Inventories	672,471		294,713	
Trade receivables	216,811		164,517	
Amounts due from				
subsidiary company	76,000		–	
Cash	2,412	967,694	1,361	460,591
Total assets		2,572,264		1,443,360
Equity				
Share capital: £1 ordinary shares		750,000		300,000
Share premium		250,000		50,000
Reserves at 1.7.2004	449,612		86,220	
Profit for year	69,504		17,532	
Reserves at 30.6.2005		519,116		103,752
		1,519,116		453,752
Non-current liabilities				
Bank loan		800,000		750,000
Current liabilities				
Trade payables	184,719		137,927	
Amounts owing to holding company	–		76,000	
Borrowings – Overdraft	68,429	253,148	25,681	239,608
Total equity and liabilities		2,572,264		1,443,360

Required:

Prepare a consolidated balance sheet for Pod Ltd and its subsidiary company as at today's date.

9.8 The balance sheets for Maxi Limited and Mini Limited are set out below.

Balance sheets as at 31 March this year

	Maxi Limited		Mini Limited	
	£000	£000	£000	£000
Non-current assets				
Property, plant and equipment		23,000		17,800
Investment				
1,500,000 shares in Mini Limited		5,000		–
		28,000		17,800
Current assets				
Inventories	5,000		2,400	
Trade receivables	4,280		1,682	
Amounts owed by				
Maxi Limited	–		390	
Cash at bank	76	9,356	1,570	6,042
Total assets		37,356		23,842
Equity				
10,000,000 £1 ordinary shares fully paid	10,000			
2,000,000 50p ordinary shares fully paid			1,000	
Share premium account	3,000		2,000	
Retained earnings at beginning of year	3,100		2,080	
Profit for the year	713	16,813	400	5,480
Non-current liabilities				
Bank loans		13,000		14,000
Current liabilities				
Trade payables	3,656		2,400	
Other payables	1,047		1,962	
Amounts owed to Mini Limited	390		–	
Borrowings – Overdraft	2,450	7,543	–	4,362
		37,356		23,842

On 1 April last year, Maxi Limited bought 1,500,000 shares of Mini Limited for a total consideration of £5 m. At that date Mini Limited's share capital and share premium were each the same as shown above. The balance sheet of Mini Ltd reflects all of the assets of the company, net of liabilities stated at their fair values.

Required:

Prepare a consolidated balance sheet for Maxi Limited at 31 March this year.

10

Governing a company

Introduction

We saw in Chapter 4 that corporate governance, which concerns the way in which companies are directed and controlled, has become an important issue. Strenuous efforts have been made in recent years to improve standards of corporate governance, particularly for large listed companies. In this final chapter, we consider the framework of rules that has been created to try to protect the interests of shareholders. We also consider some of the key issues and problems associated with monitoring and controlling the behaviour of directors.

Learning outcomes

When you have completed this chapter, you should be able to:

- Discuss the need for corporate governance rules and the principles upon which such rules should be based.

- Explain the role and composition of the board of directors and discuss the issues and problems associated with the roles of chairman and non-executive director.

- Describe the audit process and the contribution of the key players to this process.

- Explain the main issues and problems associated with the remuneration of directors.

- Discuss the importance of shareholder involvement in the corporate governance process and outline the different forms of shareholder involvement that may be found.

Corporate governance

As we saw in Chapter 4, larger companies tend to have a separation of ownership from day-to-day control of the business. A potential conflict of interest can, therefore, arise between the directors and the shareholders. There is a risk that the directors will spend their time pursuing their own interests rather than those of shareholders. If this occurs, it is clearly a problem for the shareholders; however, it may also be a problem for society as a whole. Where members of the investing public feel that their funds are likely to be mismanaged, they will be reluctant to commit those funds. A shortage of funds will mean that companies can make fewer investments. Also, the costs of finance will increase as companies compete for what funds are available. Thus, a lack of concern for shareholders can have a profound effect on the performance of individual companies and, with this, the health of the economy. To avoid these problems, most competitive market economies have a framework of rules to help monitor and control the behaviour of directors.

These rules are usually based around three guiding principles:

- *Disclosure*. This lies at the heart of good corporate governance. An OECD report (see reference 1 at the end of chapter for details) summed up the benefits of disclosure as follows:

  > Adequate and timely information about corporate performance enables investors to make informed buy-and-sell decisions and thereby helps the market reflect the value of a corporation (company) under present management. If the market determines that present management is not performing, a decrease in stock [share] price will sanction management's failure and open the way to management change.

- *Accountability*. This involves defining the roles and duties of the directors and establishing an adequate monitoring process. In the UK, company law requires that the directors of a company act in the best interests of the shareholders. This means, among other things, that they must not try to use their position and knowledge to make gains at the expense of the shareholders. The law also requires larger companies to have their annual financial statements independently audited. The purpose of an independent audit is to lend credibility to the financial statements prepared by the directors. We shall consider this point in more detail later in the chapter.

- *Fairness*. Directors should not be able to benefit from access to 'inside' information that is not available to shareholders. As a result, both the law and the London Stock Exchange place restrictions on the ability of directors to buy and sell the shares of the company. One example of these restrictions is that the directors cannot buy or sell shares immediately before the announcement of the annual trading results of the company or before the announcement of a significant event such as a planned merger or the loss of the chief executive.

Strengthening the framework of rules

The number of rules designed to safeguard shareholders has increased considerably over the years. This has been in response to weaknesses in corporate governance procedures, which have been exposed through well-publicised business failures and frauds, excessive pay increases to directors and evidence that some financial reports were being 'massaged' so as to mislead shareholders. (This last point was discussed in some detail in Chapter 5.)

Many believe, however, that the shareholders must shoulder some of the blame for any weaknesses. Not all shareholders in large companies are private individuals owning just a few shares each. In fact, ownership, by market value, of the shares listed on the London Stock Exchange is dominated by investing institutions such as insurance businesses, banks, pension funds and so on (see Real World 10.6, p. 335–6). These are often massive operations, owning large quantities of the shares of the companies in which they invest. These institutional investors employ specialist staff to manage their portfolios of shares in various companies. It has been argued that the large institutional shareholders, despite their size and relative expertise, have not been very active in corporate governance matters. Thus, there has been little monitoring of directors. However, we shall see in a later section that things seem to be changing. There is increasing evidence that institutional investors are becoming more proactive in relation to the companies in which they hold shares.

The board of directors

→ Just before we come on to consider the **Combined Code** in more detail, it might be helpful to make clear the make up and role of the board of directors. The board governs the company on behalf of the shareholders and is responsible for promoting their interests. It is led by a chairman and, for a listed public company, will normally include both executive and non-executive directors.

The chairman

→ The **chairman** is the senior director, elected by the other directors, who chairs meetings of the board.

Executive directors

→ **Executive directors** are salaried employees. For example, the finance director of most large companies is a full-time employee. This person is a member of the board of directors and, as such, takes part in the key decision making at board level. At the same time, the finance director is also responsible for managing the departments of the company that act on those board decisions as far as finance is concerned.

Non-executive directors

→ **Non-executive directors** act purely as directors; they are not full-time employees of the company. They often have business experience gained from past or present activities concerned with businesses and/or administration, apart from the company concerned. Many non-executive directors are, at the same time directors of other companies. The role of non-executive directors has taken on increasing significance in recent years and reflects the increased importance given to corporate governance issues.

The Combined Code draws a distinction between non-executive directors and *independent* non-executive directors. The term 'independent' in this context implies freedom from other significant links to the company, its directors, and to major share-holders. For example, according to the Combined Code, a non-executive director could not be regarded as an independent non-executive director if that person had been a employee of the company concerned in the previous five years.

The distinction between non-executive directors and independent non-executive directors should not be taken to mean that non-executive directors of both types need not take an independent attitude towards their roles. Independence of mind should be vital for any non-executive director. They should be able to bring an objectivity of approach that can be difficult for executive directors whose working life is so bound up in the affairs of the company. Indeed, this is one of the main reasons for having non-executive directors.

To ensure an effective presence of independent non-executive directors, the Combined Code states that, for large listed companies, at least half the board, excluding the chairman, should consist of independent non-executive directors. The chairman should also be an independent non-executive director, at the time of being appointed. For smaller listed companies, at least two independent non-executive directors should be on the board.

Although executive directors are much more deeply involved in running a company than non-executive directors, both have the same legal obligations towards the share-holders of the company.

The role of the non-executive directors will be discussed in more detail later in the chapter.

The Combined Code

During the 1990s there was a real effort by the accountancy profession and the London Stock Exchange to address the problems mentioned above. A Code of Best Practice on Corporate Governance emerged in 1992. This was concerned with accountability and financial reporting. In 1995, a separate code of practice emerged which dealt with directors' pay and conditions. These two codes were revised, 'fine tuned' and amalgamated to produce the Combined Code, which was issued in 1998.

The Combined Code was revised in 2003, following the recommendations of the Higgs Report. These recommendations were mainly concerned with the roles of the company chairman (the senior director) and the other directors. It was particularly concerned with the role of non-executive directors. The Combined Code, which underwent some minor modifications in 2006, has the backing of the London Stock Exchange. This means that companies listed on the London Stock Exchange must 'comply or explain'. That is, they must comply with the requirements of the Code or must give their shareholders good reason why they do not. Failure to do one or other of these can lead to the company's shares being suspended from listing. This is an important sanction against non-compliant directors. This is because companies will find it hard and, therefore, expensive to raise funds from existing or potential share-holders where there is any doubt about those investors' ability to sell their shares as and when they choose.

The Combined Code sets out a number of principles relating to such matters as the role of the directors, their relations with shareholders, and their accountability. **Real World 10.1** outlines some of the more important of these.

Real World 10.1

The Combined Code

Some of the key elements of the Combined Code are as follows:

- Every listed company should have a board of directors to lead and control the company.
- There should be a clear division of responsibilities between the chairman and the chief executive officer of the company to ensure that a single person does not have unbridled power.
- There should be a balance between executive and non-executive (who are often part-time and independent) members of the board, to ensure that small groups of individuals cannot dominate proceedings.
- The board should receive timely information that is of sufficient quality to enable it to carry out its duties.
- Appointments to the board should be the subject of rigorous, formal and transparent procedures.
- All directors should submit themselves for re-election at regular intervals, subject to satisfactory performance.
- Remuneration levels should be sufficient to attract, retain and motivate directors of the quality required to run the company.
- There should be formal and transparent procedures for developing policy on directors' remuneration.
- The board should ensure that a satisfactory dialogue with shareholders occurs.
- Boards should use the annual general meeting to communicate with private investors and encourage their participation.
- Institutional shareholders should ensure that they use their votes and enter into a dialogue with the company based on a mutual understanding of objectives.
- The board should publish a balanced and understandable assessment of the company's position and future prospects.
- Internal controls should be in place to protect the shareholders' wealth.
- Formal and transparent arrangements for applying financial reporting and internal control principles and for maintaining an appropriate relationship with auditors should be in place.
- The board should undertake a formal and rigorous examination of its own performance each year.

Source: www.fsa.org.uk.

Strengthening the framework of rules in this way has been generally agreed to have improved the quality of information available to shareholders, resulted in better checks on the powers of directors, and provided greater transparency in corporate affairs. However, rules can only be a partial answer. A balance must be struck between the need to protect shareholders and the need to encourage the entrepreneurial spirit of directors – which could be stifled under a welter of rules. This implies that rules should not be too tight, and so unscrupulous directors may still find ways around them.

We shall see in a later section that the shareholders can also play an important role in preventing the directors from acting inappropriately.

Activity 10.1

Can you think of ways in which the shareholders may try to ensure that the directors act in the shareholders' best interests?

Two ways are commonly used in practice:

● Shareholders may insist on monitoring closely the actions of the directors and the way in which they use the resources of the company.
● They may impose incentive schemes on directors, which link their pay to changes in shareholder wealth. In this way, the interests of the directors and shareholders will become more closely aligned.

Real World 10.2 provides some idea of the make-up of the board of directors of a typical large listed company, Cadbury Schweppes plc, the well-known sweets and drinks business.

Real World 10.2

The Cadbury board at 28 March 2007

Chairman (non-executive director) Sir John Sunderland	Former chief executive officer of the company (1996 to 2003) Non-executive director of The Rank Group plc Non-executive director of Barclays plc
Deputy chairman and senior independent non-executive director Roger Carr	Non-executive chairman of Centrica plc Non-executive chairman of Mitchells and Butlers plc
Chief executive officer (executive director) Todd Stitzer	Non-executive director of Diageo plc
Chief financial officer (executive director) Ken Hanna	Non-executive director of Inchcape plc
Chief human resources officer (executive director) Bob Stack	Non-executive director of J. Sainsbury plc Visiting professor at Henley Management College
Independent non-executive director Wolfgang Berndt	Non-executive director of Lloyds TSB Group plc Non-executive director of Inchcape plc
Independent non-executive director Rick Braddock	Non-executive director of Eastman Kodak Company Non-executive director of Marriott International Inc.
Independent non-executive director Lord Patten	Former UK Conservative Party politician and government minister Former governor of Hong Kong Former European Commissioner Chancellor of Oxford University

Independent non-executive director David Thompson	Former finance director of The Boots Company plc Chairman of Nottingham Building Society
Independent non-executive director Rosemary Thorne	Finance director of Ladbrokes plc
Independent non-executive director Sanjiv Ahuja	Chief executive officer of Orange SA Non-executive director of Mobistar SA Non-executive director of Williams Sonoma Inc.
Independent non-executive director Raymond Viault	Former vice-chairman of General Mills Inc. Non-executive director of Safeway Inc. Non-executive director of Newell Rubbermaid Inc.
Group secretary (executive director) Hester Blanks	

Note that of the 13 directors, four are executives each with his or her own clear role in the management of the company. All of the other nine (including the chairman) are *independent* non-executive directors. Most of the directors also hold directorships of other major companies and/or have senior roles in non-business organisations. They also have experience of management/administration at a high level.

Source: Cadbury Schweppes plc website (www.cadburyschweppes.com).

The tasks of the board

To ensure that the company succeeds in its purpose, the board is charged with various tasks. The main tasks are to:

1 *Decide on the strategic direction of the company.* The degree of involvement in strategy setting tends to vary between boards. In some cases, the full board will establish the strategic aims but will delegate responsibility for developing a strategic plan to an **executive committee**. This is a committee made up of particular members of the board, which usually includes the **chief executive officer**, who leads the management team, and the other executive directors. Once the committee has developed a plan, it will be put before the full board for approval.

2 *Exercise control.* If things are to go according to plan and resources are only allocated to achieve the company's purpose, the board must exercise control. This is often done through particular board committees, each made up of board members who report to the full board on their progress and findings. Some of these committees are mentioned below. Different committees are made up of different board members.

Particular directors may be members of more than one committee.
The main areas over which the board must exercise control are:

● *Carrying out the strategic plan.* Having developed a strategic plan, the executive committee will usually be charged with its successful implementation.

● *The integrity of the financial statements.* The Combined Code states that a separate board committee, known as the **audit committee**, should be set up to promote the reliability of the financial reporting systems.

● *The evaluation and management of risk.* Although a separate **risk management committee** may be formed, the audit committee may take on this responsibility.

● *The ways in which directors are nominated and remunerated.* The Combined Code states that a **nomination committee** and a **remuneration committee** should each be established to help provide formal and transparent procedures in these areas.

- *The performance of the board of directors*. Appraisals based on contributions made, or outcomes achieved, should be carried out on individual directors and on the board as a whole.

The control function of the board will be discussed in more detail in later sections.

3 *Maintain external relations*. The board is responsible for promoting the interests of the company and establishing good relationships with shareholders. Relationships with major shareholders are often helped through informal meetings involving key board members. These meetings, which usually involve a free exchange of views between board members and shareholders, may encourage the shareholders to adopt a long-term perspective to company performance and may help in securing their support when the board has to make difficult decisions.

Chairing the board

We have seen that the role of chairman is to lead and manage the board of directors. The chairman should ensure that the board operates as an effective decision making body and that board meetings are conducted in a professional and business-like manner. Board members should be in a position to contribute fully to board discussions and to make timely decisions. Chairmen are frequently non-executive directors (for example the chairman of Cadbury Schweppes plc in **Real World 10.2**). To fulfil the role, the chairman will normally be expected to:

- hold board meetings at frequent intervals so that key issues and problems can be dealt with at the appropriate time;
- ensure that the board agenda properly reflects the key issues and problems confronting the company;
- provide board members with relevant, reliable and timely information to help in their deliberations;
- provide enough time at board meetings for key issues and problems to be discussed thoroughly;
- allow all directors the opportunity to voice their opinions at board meetings;
- guide discussions so that the focus does not deviate from key strategic issues and problems.

The chairman should try to foster a good working relationship between board members. The chairman can also help the work of the board by providing a supportive environment where directors are made to feel valued and where a climate of trust prevails.

Activity 10.2

In trying to establish good working relations, should the chairman seek to ensure that boardroom conflict is avoided?

No. There are occasions when conflict between board members is beneficial. It can help ensure that issues are thoroughly aired and that important proposals are given proper scrutiny.

The chairman will act as an important link between the board and the shareholders. When the board wishes to inform shareholders of its recent proposals and decisions, the chairman will normally take a lead role in presenting this information. Similarly, when shareholders wish to respond to board proposals and decisions, or to raise other concerns that they may have, they will often relay their views to the board through the chairman. Good communication skills are, therefore, a vital ingredient of a successful chairman.

Finally, the chairman must take responsibility for ensuring that the performance of the board is subject to proper scrutiny and that improvements are made where necessary. The performance of individual directors, as well as the board as a whole, should be evaluated on a regular basis, at least annually. The criteria for assessing board performance will be considered in a later section.

The relationship between the chairman and CEO

The role of the chairman is to lead the board of directors and the role of the chief executive officer (CEO) is to lead the management team. Given the power and authority vested in each role, the Combined Code states that both roles should not be occupied by the same individual. Nevertheless, this does occur in practice.

Activity 10.3

What risks are associated with a single individual occupying both roles?

The main risk is that the authority of the board will be undermined. A single individual may dominate key discussions and decisions and other directors may feel they have limited influence. Proposals may not be rigorously examined and, as a result, poorer decisions will be made.

There is also is a risk that the rewards provided to the individual occupying the two roles will not be subject to proper scrutiny. This may lead to excessive benefits being awarded in the form of large bonuses, luxury travel, lavish offices, expensive cars and so on. Good corporate governance requires appropriate checks and balances to be in place so that no single individual has unfettered power.

Some chairmen, who also act as CEO, can find it difficult to relinquish one of the roles. This was the case with Sir Ken Morrison, the former chairman and CEO of William Morrison Supermarkets plc. Sir Ken had built up the business over his lifetime, from very small beginnings to becoming a major UK supermarket business. Things came to a head in 2005 when the takeover by Morrisons of Safeway plc, which had taken place in 2004 appeared to be running into problems. Some of the Morrisons shareholders started to express their concerns about Sir Ken's role in the company. They were also concerned about the lack of non-executive directors. **Real World 10.3** is a *Financial Times* article that explains what happened in 2005. It must be added that the Morrisons/Safeway amalgamation problems seem now to have been solved.

Real World 10.3

Beyond our Ken

FT

Sir Ken Morrison, executive chairman of William Morrison, is today expected to take action on corporate governance issues at the UK's fourth largest supermarket group in response to shareholder dissatisfaction that was sparked by last week's surprise profits warning.

Unveiling the retailer's results, Sir Ken, who is 73, is expected to outline succession plans. It is thought he is thinking of appointing a chief executive to head the company, which has been struggling to integrate Safeway, the supermarket group it acquired for £3.35 bn last March.

Morrison is currently run on a day-to-day basis by Robert Stott and Marie Melnyk, both long-serving employees.

Sir Ken is also likely to tell the City he is committed to finding more non-executives to beef up corporate governance at the group. Morrison has just two non-executives on the nine-strong board, although it is thought Sir Ken is close to appointing a third. The executive chairman, who was locked in a board meeting late last night, will today brief analysts on the results.

They will seek more details on last week's profits warning, which Morrison blamed on accounting issues linked to the Safeway acquisition. Some have been calling for the head of Martin Ackroyd, finance director. It is thought his fate was hanging in the balance last night.

The profits warning was the second in eight months. Morrison said it would take a £40 m provision to cover lower than expected supplier income from Safeway, having warned in July that profits would be £130 m lower than expected because of the same issue.

The warning came after an audit committee meeting chaired by David Jones – chairman of Next and one of Sir Ken's two non-executive directors – which decided that Morrison should take a provision because it was unclear whether those funds were recoverable. The other non-executive is Duncan Davidson, chairman of Persimmon.

Sir Ken has been criticised in the past for not fronting Morrison results. On top of today's briefing to analysts, he will spend tomorrow visiting shareholders, who are eager to discuss Safeway's integration with him.

'He is the ultimate architect of this deal', said one. Another shareholder said they wanted to see progress on corporate governance and a better dialogue with the Bradford-based retailer.

'It is now time for Sir Ken to realise that he doesn't own the company. Eighty per cent is held by institutions and it is time he started listening to us.'

Source: Rigby, Elizabeth and Tucker, Sundeep 'Morrison Chairman Is Set to Beef Up Corporate Governance', *Financial Times*, 23 March 2005.

Separation of the two roles, however, brings with it potential problems. Unless a good working relationship can be established between the chairman and the chief executive, the effectiveness of the board will be undermined. To avoid unproductive conflict, the responsibilities associated with each role should be clearly set out and agreed. This, however, is easier said than done; some overlap of responsibilities can easily occur. Much will therefore depend on the willingness of the individuals occupying the roles to discuss possible areas of overlap and to resolve any problems that arise. Mutual respect for each other's abilities and for the authority and powers vested in each role is at the core of a good working relationship.

Real World 10.4 sets out the division of responsibilities between the chairman and the chief executive of J. D. Wetherspoon plc, the pub operator.

Real World 10.4

Divide and rule

The following table sets out the respective responsibilities of the company's two most senior officials.

Chairman's responsibility	Chief executive's responsibility
Delegated responsibility of authority to exchange contracts on behalf of the company	Develop and maintain effective management controls, planning and performance measurements
Provide advice, support and feedback to the chief executive	Develop and maintain an effective organisational structure
Support the company strategy and encourage the chief executive with development of strategy	External and internal communications, in conjunction with the chairman, on any issues facing the company
Maintain relations with investors	Implement and monitor compliance with board policy
Chair general meetings, board meetings operational meetings and agree board agendas	Timely and accurate reporting of the above to the board
Manage chief executive's contract, appraisal and remuneration by way of making recommendations to the remuneration committee	Recruit and manage senior managers within the company
Provide support to executive directors and senior managers of the company	Develop and maintain effective risk management and regulatory controls
Provide 'ethos' and 'vision' of the company	Maintain primary relationships with shareholders
Provide operational presence throughout the estate	Chair the management board responsible for implementing the company strategy

Source: J. D. Wetherspoon plc Annual Report and Accounts 2006, p. 18.

Occasionally, a chief executive will go on to become the chairman of the board of the same company, to be replaced by a new CEO (as with Sir John Sunderland and Cadbury Schweppes plc in **Real World 10.2**), despite the fact that this conflicts with the recommendations set out in the Combined Code. The result is often a difficult working relationship between the two most powerful individuals within the company.

Activity 10.4

Why might this situation result in a difficult working relationship?

The chairman may find it hard to relinquish the former role and may try to interfere in the decisions of the new chief executive. Such behaviour will almost inevitably lead to conflict and a climate of mistrust. The chairman may also seek to justify decisions made during his/her period as chief executive and may resist any attempts to overturn those decisions by the new chief executive. The new chief executive, on the other hand, may wish to begin a new chapter in the company's history and to justify a change of direction may be critical of earlier decisions.

To avoid such defensive behaviour, both parties must avoid raking over past decisions and should look to the future.

The role of non-executive directors

Not so long ago, the image of the non-executive director was that of an avuncular figure offering kindly guidance and advice to the board concerning the direction of the company. This was not seen as an unduly onerous role and any time spent on the company's affairs could be confined to board meetings and in perusing background documents for the various agenda items. Whatever truth such an image may have contained, it is certainly not a faithful portrayal of the current role of the non-executive director of a UK listed public company. An important consequence of strengthening corporate governance standards, which was referred to earlier, has been greatly to increase the demands placed on the non-executive directors.

Non-executive directors are expected to contribute towards each of the functions of the board mentioned above and the contribution that they make will largely depend on the background, experience and personal qualities that they possess. As we have seen, often non-executives of a listed public company are, or have been, executive directors of another listed public company and so will usually have considerable experience of the commercial world as well as expertise in a particular field, such as finance or marketing. As a result non-executive directors can often play a valuable role in discussions on strategy. They may contribute by making useful suggestions concerning the future direction to be taken and by challenging the assumptions and decisions of the executive directors.

The fact that non-executive directors do not engage in the day-to-day running of the company allows them to become more detached from company problems and issues which, in turn, allows them to provide objective and independent advice to the board of directors. This should be of particular value during periods of change or crisis, when a detached view can help the executive directors to maintain perspective.

Non-executive directors can also play an important role in monitoring and controlling the activities of the company. In working towards the strategic plan, control mechanisms involving, plans, budgets, quality indicators and benchmarking may be used. The experience and skills of non-executive directors may enable them to identify weaknesses in the current control systems and to suggest ways of improving them. They may also be able to highlight areas of poor performance.

Non-executives play an important role in the various board committees that are set up to control the activities of the company. It was mentioned earlier that, to promote the integrity of financial information, an audit committee is normally established. The Combined Code states that this committee should consist entirely of non-executive directors, the majority of whom should be independent non-executive directors. Members of the committee are expected to ask challenging questions of the executive directors and the auditors and must be strong enough to take a robust stand against any decisions of the executive directors that may undermine the integrity of the financial statements. The role of audit committee members is particularly onerous in today's highly regulated business environment. Any failure to show due care, skill and diligence in carrying out their duties is liable to expose them to the threat of legal action. It can also expose them to the loss of their good reputation. The audit committee will be considered in more detail later in the chapter.

A further aspect of control concerns the remuneration of the executive directors. As mentioned earlier, listed companies normally have a remuneration committee that is charged with recommending to the board the remuneration of the executive directors. The Combined Code states that this committee should consist of independent non-executive directors. This means that non-executives have enormous influence over the remuneration of executive directors, and where there are performance-related elements, will be involved in setting targets and in monitoring the performance of the executive directors.

A final aspect of control concerns the nomination of new directors. We saw earlier that listed companies normally have a nominations committee. Its role is to lead the nomination process by identifying the skills, knowledge and experience required for the board and by preparing appropriate job specifications. The Combined Code states that this committee should have a majority of independent non-executive directors as members.

The board and large shareholders often maintain a dialogue through informal meetings, which non-executives may attend. This can help them to appreciate the concerns of shareholders. At times, non-executives may become the shareholders' communications channel to the board of directors. Shareholders may be particularly reliant on this channel if they have already voiced concerns to the chairman, or to the executive directors, and have not received satisfactory replies.

Finally, non-executive directors may help to raise the profile of the company. They often enjoy a good reputation within their particular field and may have strong links with a wide range of bodies, including government agencies and foreign companies. These links may be extremely valuable in developing new contacts and in promoting the company's interests.

Role conflict

The different roles that non-executives are expected to play provide the potential for conflict. In developing strategy, cooperation between the executive and non-executive directors is required. All the directors are expected to work together as part of a team in pursuit of a common purpose. However, the monitoring role that non-executive directors must carry out requires that non-executives assess the performance of executive directors. Disputes between executive and non-executive directors can easily arise over the financial systems, control systems and remuneration systems that are in place. Given the potential conflict between the two roles, non-executive directors must tread carefully and may have to retain a certain distance from the executive directors to maintain a degree of independence.

Relations with the executive directors

There is a risk that the potential for disputes will make the non-executive and executive directors wary of each other. Executive directors may resent the presence of the non-executives on the board because they feel that:

● non-executive directors are monitoring their behaviour and, effectively, acting as 'corporate policemen';
● non-executive directors do not fully understand the nature of the company's business;

- non-executive directors do not devote enough time and effort in carrying out their duties.

Non-executives, on the other hand, may feel that executives are acting in an unhelpful or guarded manner towards them. They may feel that executive directors are seeking to undermine their position by:

- withholding key information or reports;
- failing to provide important information at the required time;
- holding informal meetings on important matters to which the non-executives are not invited.

The chairman of the board can play an important role in overcoming these problems. A lack of information is often at the root of many problems and the chairman must ensure that all directors receive timely and relevant information. **Real World 10.5** sets out the policies of J. D. Wetherspoon plc on this matter.

Real World 10.5

Time gentlemen please!

Information is normally furnished to all board members in the week before a board meeting, to enable the directors to consider the issues for discussion and to request clarification or additional information.

All directors are provided with, and have full access to, information which enables them to make informed decisions on corporate and business issues, including operational and financial performance. In particular, the board receives monthly information on the financial trading performance of the company and a comprehensive finance report which includes operational highlights. All directors receive sales and margin information for the company weekly by trading unit.

Source: J. D. Wetherspoon plc Annual report and accounts 2006, p. 19.

The chairman should also ensure that the board's procedures are transparent and that informal meetings of cliques are discouraged. Where doubts exist over the competence of particular directors, the chairman should see that appropriate training and development opportunities are made available. Finally, the chairman may arrange meetings between executive and non-executive directors to allow suspicions and problems to be aired.

Maintaining independence

There is a risk that non-executive directors will fail to provide an independent voice. They may come under the influence of the executive directors and fail to challenge decisions and promote proper accountability. It is worth remembering that non-executives are often executive directors of other companies and so may feel some empathy with executive director colleagues on the board.

Activity 10.5

How might this risk be avoided?

Shareholders could become involved in the appointment of the non-executive directors, perhaps by identifying and proposing suitable candidates. Once appointed, regular meetings with shareholders may help to strengthen their independence from the executive directors, as well as their commitment to the shareholders' interests.

The increasing burdens placed on non-executive directors means that a significant amount of time must be spent in dealing with company affairs. One survey of large listed companies revealed that non-executive directors spend an average of 18 days working on company business (see reference 2 at the end of the chapter). However, some individuals have been accused of accepting too many non-executive director appointments, which undermines their ability to devote time to increasingly complex board issues. Some restriction on the number of non-executive directorships held should help overcome this problem.

To encourage a diligent attitude, non-executives should be properly rewarded for the time spent on company business. Listed companies have recognised the growing burdens placed on non-executives and in recent years their pay has been rising. There is a potential problem, however, with paying non-executives too handsomely for their efforts.

Activity 10.6

What problem may arise from paying non-executives large salaries?

Where the salaries paid to non-executives are modest and form only a small proportion of their total income, they may retain a higher degree of independence when making decisions.

There is normally a considerable gulf between the total remuneration received by part-time, non-executive directors and that of full-time, executive directors. According to its annual report, Tesco plc paid its non-executive directors (excluding the chairman) between £17,000 and £100,000 each and its executive directors between £2.2 million and £4.0 million each for the year to February 2006.

Real World 10.6 is a *Financial Times* article that discusses a survey of fees paid to non-executive directors of UK listed companies.

Real World 10.6

Time to get on board   FT

Basic fees for non-executive directors and company chairmen are continuing to rocket, well ahead of the increase in average earnings, latest data from the pay and remuneration analyst Income Data Services show.

Average fees for non-executive directors in both FTSE 100 and FTSE 350 companies jumped by more than 13 per cent last year, on top of increases of about 21 per cent the year before.

→

Real World 10.6 continued

The rises of about a third over two years are roughly four times the increase in average earnings over the same period.

'In the past a non-executive directorship was seen as something of a reasonably well-paid sinecure for people with titles', said Steve Glenn, deputy director of IDS's executive compensation review.

'Now it is becoming a distinctly well-paid job, although one that carries a lot more responsibility and legal risk.'

Companies attributed the rise, IDS said, to increased workloads and tougher corporate governance duties in the wake of Enron and the Higgs report in 2003, which put non-executive directors in the line of fire for allowing governance lapses or obviously failed corporate strategies. The effect has been that the average basic fee for a non-executive director on a FTSE 100 company is now £48,826 for about 25 days' work a year. For those in the middle of the FTSE 250 it is now £35,000.

Average fees for chairmen of the top 100 companies are now above £300,000, at £311,276, and just over £140,000 for a mid-FTSE 250 company.

The averages hide a considerable range, with standard non-executive director fees running from £20,000 to £95,000. Additional fees for chairing audit committees appear to have risen by half, from £10,000 to £15,000 in FTSE 100 companies and from £5,000 to £7,500 in FTSE 250 companies.

'The days when a non-executive director turned up at board meetings simply to ratify the managing director's decisions seem to be long gone', IDS said. But even so the increases in fees in recent years had been 'pretty substantial by any standard'.

The extra pay may or may not match the additional responsibility. But IDS noted an Ernst and Young survey of 50 non-executive directors at the end of last year in which one in three said they would be less likely to accept a non-executive position than they would have been 12 months earlier. Almost half would be less likely to accept the chairmanship of an audit committee.

The findings are based on an analysis of actual fee rates in the annual accounts up to May 2006 of 332 FTSE 350 companies, including all the FTSE 100 companies.

They also show a marginal increase in the proportion of women on company boards, up from 12 to 13.4 per cent among the top 100 companies and from 6.3 to 8.3 per cent among the next 250.

Source: Timmins, Nicholas 'Fees for Non-execs and Chairmen Rocket', *Financial Times*, 16 October 2006.

The audit process

External audit

External audit forms an important element of corporate governance. To understand what it entails, we must first be clear about the roles and responsibilities of directors and auditors concerning the published financial statements.

As we saw in Chapter 5, company law requires that the directors prepare annual financial statements that provide a true and fair view of the state of affairs of the company. This will involve:

● selecting suitable accounting policies and applying them consistently;
● making estimates and judgements that are prudent and practical;
● stating whether appropriate accounting standards have been adopted;
● applying the going concern convention where it is appropriate to do so.

The annual financial statements that are prepared by the directors must be published and made available to shareholders, lenders and others. In addition to preparing the annual financial statements, the law also obliges the directors to keep proper accounting records and to safeguard the assets of the company.

External auditors are appointed by, and report to, the shareholders. They are normally an independent firm of accountants and their role is to examine the annual financial statements that have been prepared by the directors. They must assess the reliability of these statements by examining the underlying accounting records on which the statements are based and by reviewing the key assumptions and estimates used in their preparation. Following this, the auditors will provide shareholders with an independent opinion as to whether the financial statements provide a true and fair view of the state of affairs of the company and comply with legal and other regulatory requirements. This opinion is contained within an audit report, which becomes part of the published annual reports.

The external auditor must inform shareholders of any significant problems that have been unearthed during the audit process and so the audit report must include instances where:

● proper accounting records have not been kept;
● information and explanations required to undertake the audit have not been received;
● information specified by the law or by regulatory bodies, such as the UK listing authority, has not been disclosed;
● the directors report contains information that is inconsistent with the financial statements.

For companies listed on the London Stock Exchange, the auditors must also review the corporate governance statement, which is also prepared by the directors, to see whether it complies with the provisions of the Combined Code. Where the auditor has no concerns over the reliability and integrity of the financial statements, an 'unqualified' opinion is provided, which should lend credibility to the statements.

Although the scope of an external audit is wide, it does not cover all aspects of corporate governance. Thus, statements made by the board of directors concerning the company's corporate governance and internal control procedures, which are usually contained in the annual reports of listed companies, are not subject to scrutiny.

Internal audit

Many large companies have an **internal audit** function, although there is no legal requirement to have one. The main purpose of internal audit is to provide the directors with reassurance concerning the reliability of the company's control and financial reporting systems. Internal auditors are employees of the company and so do not have the same independence as external auditors. They will normally report to the directors, who will determine the nature and scope of the internal audit process. In other words, internal auditors are not independent of the directors.

Although some variation will be found in practice, internal audit will usually involve a review of:

● the internal control systems to see whether they are effective in safeguarding the company's assets and in preventing errors and fraud;
● the accounting systems to see whether they provide reliable information, which meets the needs of management and complies with relevant regulations;
● internal operations and processes to see whether they are efficient and provide value for money.

Real World 10.7 reveals how serious failures in the internal control systems of one major carmaker put its business plan at risk.

Real World 10.7

Losing control

Struggling carmaker General Motors has warned that ineffective internal controls over financial reporting might make it difficult for it to execute on its business plan.

GM said weaknesses include poor 'maintenance of records that, in reasonable detail, accurately and fairly reflect the transactions and dispositions of the assets of the corporation', as well as failing to ensure that 'receipts and expenditures of the corporation are being made only in accordance with authorisations of management and directors of the corporation'.

GM said that its management recognised the problems and is taking steps to correct them – but declined to comment further on the matter.

Source: 'Ineffective Internal Controls Hurting GM', AccountancyAge.com, 16 May 2007.

In recent years, the risk management processes of a company have been identified as a further element of good corporate governance. An important consequence of this has been to widen the remit of the internal audit function to include a review of these processes. Thus, internal auditors are now often expected to provide assurances to the directors concerning the adequacy and effectiveness of the company's risk management procedures. They may also be involved in promoting a risk management philosophy within the company through employee risk awareness and risk management programmes.

Real World 10.8 sets out the particular internal controls and risk management systems used to protect shareholder wealth at J. D. Weatherspoon plc, the pub operator, during the 2006 financial year.

Real World 10.8

Keeping control

During the year, the company and the board continued to support and invest in resources to provide an internal audit and risk-management function. The system of internal control and risk mitigation is deeply embedded in the operations and culture of the company. The board is responsible for maintaining a sound system of internal control and reviewing its effectiveness. The function can only manage, rather than eliminate entirely, and can only provide reasonable and not absolute assurance against material misstatement or loss. Ongoing reviews and assessments took place continually throughout the year.

The company has an internal audit function which is discharged as follows:

- adequate regular audits of the company stock (inventories);
- unannounced visits to the retail units;
- monitoring systems which control the company cash.

The company has key procedures in place as follows:

- clearly defined authority limits and controls over cash-handling, purchasing commitments and capital expenditure;
- comprehensive budgeting process, with a detailed operating plan for 12 months and a mid-term financial plan, both approved by the board;
- company results are reported weekly (for key times), with a monthly comprehensive report in full, and compared with budget;
- forecasts are prepared regularly throughout the year for review by the board;
- complex treasury instruments are not used; decisions on treasury matters are reserved by the board.

The directors confirm that they have reviewed the effectiveness of the system of internal control.

Source: J. D. Wetherspoon plc, Annual Report and Accounts 2006, p. 20.

The presence of internal auditors within a company can influence the external audit process. As internal auditors regularly review the reliability of the company's accounting and internal control systems, the external auditor is likely to take this into account when planning the scope and nature of the external audit work to be undertaken. Although the external auditor must retain full responsibility for the external audit, it may be possible to place confidence in certain work carried out by a well-resourced and competent internal audit team. This may allow the external auditor to focus on other areas.

Audit committees

The Combined Code places audit committees at the heart of the financial reporting process and they are regarded as vital to good corporate governance. The responsibilities placed on the audit committee have increased in recent years as a result of the introduction of international financial reporting standards and tougher overseas corporate governance rules, such as the Sarbanes-Oxley Act in the US. This act was introduced in the wake of accounting scandals and applies to a number of large UK listed companies that also list their shares in the US.

The role of the audit committee

There is always a risk that the role of the directors as preparers of the financial statements and the role of external auditor as 'watchdog' will not be carried out satisfactorily. We saw in Chapter 5 that there have been several accounting scandals involving directors preparing financial statements that portray the financial performance and position of a company in a way that bears little resemblance to economic reality. Unfortunately, to say the least, external auditors have sometimes failed to spot the irregular accounting practices used by directors to obscure the true financial health of the company. This has cast doubt over the quality of the audit process and, in some cases, over the independence of auditors. It has been argued that where the accountancy firm that carries out the audit also does a large amount of non-audit work for the company, its ability to audit the financial statements on behalf of the shareholders will be compromised. Examples of non-audit work include financial, and more general management, consultancy. This is because they may lack the independence from the directors that their audit role demands. The audit committee is designed to deal with these problems.

The Combined Code requires the setting up of an audit committee with delegated authority for ensuring that financial reporting and internal control principles are properly applied and for maintaining an appropriate relationship with the external auditors. The committee should consist of at least three, or in the case of smaller companies, two, independent, non-executive directors. The Combined Code sets out the main role and responsibilities of the audit committee as follows:

- to monitor the integrity of the financial statements;
- to review the company's internal controls;
- to make recommendations concerning the appointment and removal of the external auditor and to approve the terms of engagement;
- to review and monitor the independence, objectivity and effectiveness of the external auditor;
- to establish and implement policies concerning the supply of non-audit services by the external auditor.

In addition to these duties, the audit committee may also take responsibility for reviewing the risk management systems of the company where the board, or a separate risk committee, does not specifically address this issue.

Fulfilling the role

The audit committee will receive its terms of reference from the board of directors, which, in practice, are normally in line with the recommendations set out in the Combined Code. Although the terms of reference will define its role and responsibilities, the board of directors must also ensure that the committee has the authority and resources to carry out its responsibilities: without these, the committee will have no real 'teeth'.

It is vitally important to establish the right membership of the committee. It should consist of individuals with the integrity, judgement and strength of character to deal with the difficult issues that may have to be confronted. They must be prepared to pursue enquiries, even when faced with determined opposition from senior managers or executive directors. The Combined Code recommends that at least one member should have 'recent and relevant financial experience,' however, other members should also bring skills and experience that contribute to the work of the committee.

The audit committee should meet regularly and the time allocated to each meeting must be appropriate. Some of the meetings should be planned to coincide with important events such as the start of the annual audit, the publication of interim financial statements and the announcement of the preliminary results for the year. In practice, it seems that audit committees of most large UK listed companies meet at least four times a year. Those companies that are also registered with the US Securities and Exchange Commission (SEC) must comply with strict US requirements and are likely to meet more frequently. Figure 10.1 below shows the frequency of meetings of SEC registered and non-SEC registered companies that are in the FTSE 100.

If the audit committee is to be effective, clear lines of communication must be in place with key individuals such as the chief executive, the finance director and the heads of the internal and external audit teams. These individuals should provide the audit committee with timely and relevant information and, where appropriate, attend meetings of the audit committee.

When reviewing internal controls, the audit committee should receive details on the effectiveness of the processes in place by both the internal and external audit teams. The committee must be satisfied that the internal controls have operated satisfactorily during the year and that any recommendations for improvement were implemented. When reviewing the company's risk management systems, the committee will need to be satisfied that the key risk areas are being monitored and that any control failures or emerging risks are quickly identified and dealt with. The committee must also be satisfied that risk management is not seen as simply a 'box-ticking' exercise and that there is widespread recognition of its importance.

Internal auditors should provide assistance to the audit committee by reporting on the effectiveness of internal control and risk management procedures. They can become the 'eyes and ears' of the audit committee and may prove invaluable in providing necessary assurances. The internal auditors can benefit from a close relationship with the audit committee as it can strengthen their independence and status within the company. The audit committee can help foster greater independence through meetings with the internal auditors where management is excluded. The audit committee can also strengthen the authority of internal auditors by insisting that management cooperates with them. (See reference 3 at the end of the chapter.)

| Figure 10.1 | Frequency of audit committee meetings |

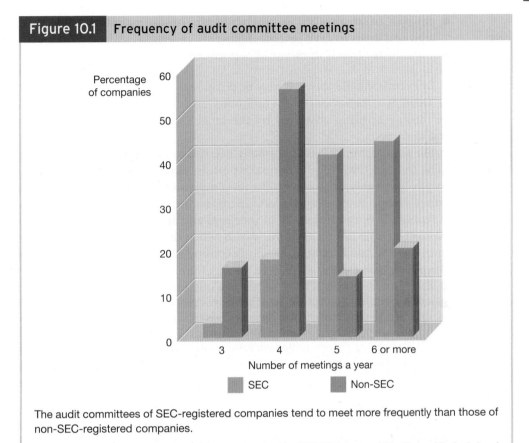

The audit committees of SEC-registered companies tend to meet more frequently than those of non-SEC-registered companies.

Source: based on a survey of annual reports of 84 companies from the FTSE 100 that were published between the beginning of November 2004 and the end of June 2005, Independent Audit Ltd, 'Audit Committee Reporting in 2005', www.boydeninterim.co.uk.

When reviewing the external audit process, the audit committee should consider the experience and expertise of the audit team. The committee should also review the audit plans and procedures that are being proposed and should check to see that there is an appropriate fit with the work carried out by the internal audit team. The committee will need to check that the time devoted to the audit process is sufficient and that the key issues and risks will be addressed. To help monitor progress, meetings with the external auditor should take place during which a review of the auditors' actual performance against earlier planned performance should be undertaken. The amount of non-audit services provided by the external auditors must also be reviewed on a regular basis to see whether their independence is being compromised. To help maintain a fresh perspective to the audit process, the audit committee may wish to ensure that the head of external audit and/or the audit firm is rotated on a regular basis.

When reviewing the financial statements, the audit committee should pay particular attention to the following:

● the accounting policies adopted and whether they conform to the industry norm;
● any changes to accounting policies;
● the estimates and judgements that have been made in key areas such as bad debts; provisions, depreciation and so on;

- any unusual items, such as large write offs, or unusual relationships, such as a very high bad debts to sales revenue figure;
- any unusual trends in financial performance or position.

By examining the above, it may be possible to identify irregular accounting practices or fraudulent behaviour. Any questions arising from such an examination should be capable of being answered by the chief executive, finance director and external auditors.

The audit committee will normally be expected to produce a report for shareholders to be contained within the annual report. In practice, the quality of these reports can vary considerably. In some cases they simply describe the main features of the committee such as its constitution and membership, its role, the names and qualifications of its members, the frequency of meetings and so on. This kind of information, however, offers little insight as to the way in which the committee has gone about its work. Independent Audit Limited, which is committed to improving corporate governance procedures, has argued:

> Good committees don't distinguish themselves by statements of compliance. They stand out by explaining to shareholders how they went about their duties, and by doing so in clear English which shows they are describing real activity rather than aspirations. They leave the reader with a sense that the committee understands its role and what being effective means, and that they care enough about what they have been doing to want the reader to understand it.
>
> (See reference 4 at the end of the chapter.)

The audit committee report will be presented to the annual general meeting, which the chairman of the audit committee should attend. This will provide shareholders with the opportunity to question the chairman on any matters for which the committee has responsibility.

The audit committee must also review its own effectiveness. This should be done on a regular basis and, ideally, should involve external parties in the assessment process. It should involve a review of the terms of reference and the way in which the committee has carried out its responsibilities. The contribution of individual members should be assessed, which should include some assessment as to whether they have kept up to date with financial reporting and corporate governance issues.

Are audit committees worthwhile?

Audit committees are a relatively new addition to the corporate governance framework and it is difficult to assess just how effective they are in dealing with the problems identified earlier. It seems, however, that at least many audit committee members *believe* that these committees are effective. A recent survey by the Audit Committee Institute asked audit committee members of leading UK and US companies whether they believed that losses incurred by the high profile financial reporting scandals of the last few years could have been avoided, or reduced, if the financial and auditing processes of the company had been overseen by an effective audit committee. The results are shown in Figure 10.2 below.

We can see that roughly two-thirds of audit committee members believe that effective audit committees would have been beneficial. There seems to be little difference between the responses of UK and US committee members. (See reference 5 at the end of the chapter.)

Figure 10.2	Would effective audit committees have avoided or reduced the losses caused by accounting scandals?

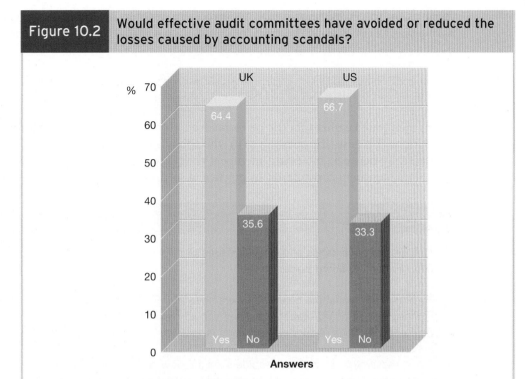

Although a clear majority believe that audit committees are effective in reducing accounting scandals, there is a significant minority of audit committee members in both the UK and US that do not believe that this is so.

Activity 10.7

Why might the above results give some cause for concern?

Sceptics might argue that the survey results shown above provide little more than self-justification. To vote against the proposition is really to cast doubt on the effectiveness of one of the key functions of the audit committee. Thus, the fact that roughly one third of committee members voted against the proposition may be interpreted as cause for concern.

Only the passage of time will reveal whether audit committees can really offer some protection from accounting scandals.

There are potential costs in placing heavy responsibilities on the audit committee and in scrutinising its activities and decisions. There is always a risk that such pressure will cultivate an increasingly cautious approach among committee members, which, in turn, may inhibit managers from taking risks. A 'compliance' mentality may develop which promotes conformity and caution at the expense of creativity and risk taking, which are essential to long-term prosperity. (See reference 6 at the end of the chapter.)

There is also a danger that the responsibilities placed on the audit committee, and the scrutiny to which its activities are subjected, may dissuade individuals from chairing, or even becoming a member of, the audit committee. A great deal of time and effort is normally required to carry out the committee's work and there is considerable risk to an individual's reputation if things go wrong. It is, perhaps, not surprising that a fairly recent survey has shown that non-executive directors are increasingly reluctant to take on the role of chairing the audit committee. (See reference 7 at the end of the chapter.)

Assessing board performance

It was mentioned earlier that the performance of the board should be subject to regular evaluation. This raises the question as to who should carry out the evaluation. The choice is effectively between the board members themselves or an external party, such as a firm of management consultants. In practice, it seems that boards prefer self-evaluation.

Activity 10.8

What are the advantages and disadvantages of board members, rather than an external party, evaluating board performance?

The advantage is that the board members have an intimate knowledge of the company's business and of board operations. They should therefore be in a position to ask more searching questions. A further advantage is that there is no risk that confidentiality will be breached.

A disadvantage is that shareholders might view this as being rather too cosy an arrangement. They may feel that an external party would provide a more objective and a more rigorous assessment of board performance. This may give more credibility to the process (although the cost is likely to be much higher).

A second question raised concerns the areas of performance that should be evaluated. As the evaluation of board performance is a fairly new process, there is still no consensus on this matter. However, some possible areas, based on the Combined Code and other sources of good practice are set out in Table 10.1.

Table 10.1 Evaluating board performance

Company objectives	• Are the objectives of the company clearly set out? • Is the board fully committed to these objectives? • Are the objectives used as a framework for board decisions? • Is there a regular board review of progress towards the achievement of the objectives?
Controlling the company	• Is the system of internal control and reporting regularly reviewed by the board? • Are the risk management and reporting systems regularly reviewed by the board?
Board structure and roles	• Are the roles and responsibilities of the board clearly defined? • Is the relationship between the board and key board committees appropriate and clear? • Are the roles of the chairman and non-executive directors appropriate and clear?
Board meetings	• Are board meetings called with sufficient frequency to permit timely decisions? • Is relevant material, including written agendas and minutes of previous meetings, sent to directors prior to a board meeting? • Are all directors required to attend board meetings and what is their attendance record?

Table 10.1 (*Continued*)

	• Do the discussions at board meetings focus on strategic rather than operational issues?
	• Are urgent problems arising between board meetings properly managed and reported?
Board composition	• Is there a separation of the roles of chairman and chief executive?
	• Does the board reflect an appropriate balance between executive and non-executive directors?
	• Does the board membership reflect an appropriate mix of age, skills and experience?
	• Is the membership of important board committees, such as remuneration and audit committees, appropriate?
	• Do the tenure agreements of board members provide the opportunity to refresh the board over time?
Board discussions and decisions	• Does the board work together in an effective manner?
	• Do board discussions result in appropriate decisions being made?
	• Are board decisions implemented and monitored?
	• Are board members given the time and opportunity to express their views on key issues?
	• Is the contribution of all directors at board meetings satisfactory?
	• Are board discussions and decisions dominated by key individuals?
Board relations with shareholders	• Are there appropriate policies in place for communicating with shareholders?
	• Are the communication channels established between the board and institutional and private shareholders appropriate?
	• Are shareholders satisfied that their views are heard and considered by the board?
Board appointments and development	• Are rigorous procedures in place for the appointment of new directors?
	• Are there clearly defined and appropriate procedures in place for appraising the performance of individual directors?
	• Are appropriate training and development programmes (including induction programmes) available to board members?
	• Has the board developed clear succession plans?

Self-assessement question 10.1

Required:

You have been asked to evaluate the performance of the board of directors of a large listed company and intend to use the checklist, set out in Table 10.1, as the basis for carrying out this task.

What sources of information would you use to help you undertake your evaluation?

The answer to this question can be found at the back of the book on p. 408.

Remunerating directors

Setting directors' remuneration at an appropriate level is not an easy task. Nevertheless, it is often vitally important to the success of the company. In the sections below we consider some of the key issues and problems that must be considered.

Remuneration policy

The Combined Code states that the level of directors' remuneration should be sufficient to attract, retain and motivate individuals of the right quality. The Code also states that remuneration should be linked to performance and that a significant proportion of the total remuneration awarded to executive directors should be based on company and individual performance.

The emphasis given to performance-related remuneration reflects a concern that executive directors have too often been rewarded for poor performance. By linking pay to performance, some of the risks and rewards of being a shareholder are passed to the directors. If a particular course of action yields good returns, the directors will benefit: if it fails to make a return the directors will not. This may encourage them to think more like shareholders and to take tough decisions where they are likely to benefit shareholders.

The remuneration package of an executive director of a large listed company will normally reflect the emphasis given to performance contained within the Combined Code. Although some variation will be found in practice, it is usually made up of two major elements:

● a fixed element, which is largely in the form of a base salary but will also include benefits, such as pension contributions, medical insurance and so on;
● a variable element, which rewards directors on the basis of both short-term and long-term performance.

The variable element is normally dependent on the executive directors achieving clearly defined targets, which reflect the goals of the company. The rewards for achieving these targets are usually taken in the form of cash and/or shares.

The main elements of the remuneration package for an executive director of a listed public company are shown in Figure 10.3.

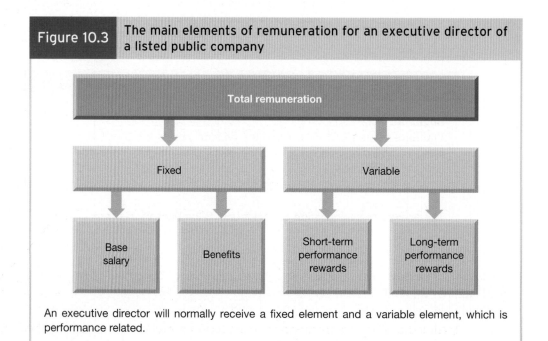

Figure 10.3 The main elements of remuneration for an executive director of a listed public company

An executive director will normally receive a fixed element and a variable element, which is performance related.

Activity 10.9

Should non-executive directors, as well as executive directors, have a performance-related element to their remuneration?

The view usually taken is that non-executive directors should be rewarded on the basis of the time spent and responsibilities undertaken on behalf of the company. By offering performance-related remuneration there is a risk that their independence will be compromised.

A recent survey of the largest 100 companies listed on the Stock Exchange revealed that around 55 per cent of the total remuneration paid to executive directors was performance related (see reference 8 at the end of the chapter). **Real World 10.9**, however, tells of one well-known US company that has decided to make directors' pay entirely performance related.

Real World 10.9

Going the whole hog
FT

Warren Buffett, the billionaire investor, on Thursday defended Coca-Cola's decision to make boardroom pay entirely dependent on company performance, arguing that the unprecedented move would align the interests of directors and shareholders.

Coke said on Wednesday that from this year its directors would be paid only if the beverage company met a target of 8 per cent compounded annual earnings growth over a three-year period.

Mr Buffett, a Coke director and the company's largest shareholder, said the scheme gave directors greater incentive to ensure the company met its full potential. 'We want a board that cares about whether management achieves its goals', he told the *Financial Times*.

The all-or-nothing compensation marks the most radical shift by any large US company to performance-related pay for directors. Some corporate governance experts expressed concern that the approach will make directors fixated on earnings and undermine their role as watchdogs.

Source: 'Buffett Backs Coke's Board Pay Scheme', FT.com site, 6 April 2006.

The targets and rewards that might be included in directors' incentive schemes will be discussed in more detail later in the chapter.

Tenure and service contracts

The emphasis on performance extends to the issue of tenure. The Combined Code states that all directors should be submitted for re-election, by shareholders, at regular intervals, subject to continued satisfactory performance. Executive directors are normally required to submit themselves for re-election at intervals of three years or fewer and non-executive directors, who are appointed for specific periods, are also subject to re-election. These provisions are designed help to keep directors on their toes and to allow the board to be refreshed over time.

Although directors are normally given service contracts, these do not provide immunity against poor performance. Where a director has underperformed the board should be prepared to consider dismissal. The Code states that any compensation for loss of office should be reasonable and should be spread over time. To prevent the risk of over compensation when contracts are terminated, they should not contain excessive notice periods. Normally the notice period should be one year at the longest.

Remuneration committee

The Combined Code states that no director should be allowed to determine his or her remuneration. We saw earlier that a remuneration committee is normally given the task of setting the pay and benefits for the executive directors and the chairman. Furthermore, members of the committee are all expected to be independent, non-executive directors.

Whilst this arrangement is designed to prevent executive directors being over rewarded for their efforts, some question its effectiveness. Critics point to the fact that, in recent years, directors' pay and benefits have increased considerably compared to that of other occupations.

Activity 10.10

Why might the setting up of a remuneration committee, made up of non-executive directors, not prevent executive directors from being over rewarded?

It can be argued that the arrangement is based on directors determining the rewards of other directors. As many non-executive directors are also executive directors of other companies, they may be sympathetic to a high-reward culture.

Setting up a remuneration committee, of course, does not deal with the problem of who determines the pay of the non-executive directors.

Activity 10.11

Who do you think should determine the remuneration of the non-executive directors?

The Combined Code states that the board of directors, or perhaps the shareholders, should take responsibility for doing this. Where the board sets their pay, the executive directors will have an influence over the pay of the non-executive directors (a point which may not be lost on those non-executive directors serving on the remuneration committee!).

Reporting directors' remuneration

The law requires that UK listed companies prepare a directors' remuneration report on an annual basis. This report must be submitted to shareholders for approval, which will normally take place at the annual general meeting of the company. The report should include details of the remuneration of each director and should set out details of salaries, fees, expense allowances, compensation for loss of office, share options and retirement benefits received. The chairman of the remuneration committee will normally attend the shareholders' meeting to deal with any issues relating to directors' remuneration that may arise.

Activity 10.12

How might shareholders benefit from these requirements?

The requirement to report directors' remuneration may have a moderating effect on the amounts paid to them, particularly as shareholders are required to give their approval.

Setting performance targets

We saw earlier that a significant proportion of the remuneration received by executive directors should be performance related. There are various performance targets that can be used as a basis for rewarding directors and below we consider some of the more popular of these. Before doing so, however, it is useful to reflect on what characteristics, or qualities, a good performance target should possess. Perhaps the key characteristics are that it should:

● be in line with the goals of the company;
● lead to a convergence of directors' and shareholders' interests;
● reflect the achievement of the directors;
● be robust and not easily distorted by particular policies, financing arrangements or manipulative practices.

No single performance target will perfectly encapsulate all of these qualities. Nevertheless, a number of potentially useful performance targets exist, as we shall now see.

Total shareholder return

A widely-used performance target is based on **total shareholder return (TSR)**. The total return from a share is made up of two elements: the increase (or decrease) in share value over a period plus any dividends paid during the period. To illustrate how total shareholder return is calculated, let us assume that a company commenced trading by issuing shares of £0.50 each at their nominal value (P_0) and by the end of the first year of trading the shares had increased in value to £0.55 (P_1). Furthermore, the company paid a dividend of £0.06 (D_1) per share during the period. We can calculate the total shareholder return as follows:

$$\text{Total shareholder return} = \frac{D_1 + (P_1 - P_0)}{P_0} \times 100\%$$

$$= \frac{0.06 + (0.55 - 0.50)}{0.50} \times 100\%$$

$$= \underline{22\%}$$

The figure calculated has little information value when taken alone. It can only really be used to assess performance when compared with some benchmark.

Activity 10.13

What benchmark would be most suitable?

Perhaps the best benchmark to use would be the returns from similar businesses operating in the same industry over the same period of time.

The reason that this benchmark is usually suitable is because it will compare the returns generated by the company with those generated from other investment opportunities that have the same level of risk. As a general rule, the level of return from an investment should be related to the level of risk that has to be taken.

Many large companies now publish total shareholder returns in their annual reports. **Real World 10.10** provides an example.

Real World 10.10

Tesco's TSR

Tesco plc, a major food retailer, publishes its total shareholder returns (TSR) for a five-year period, along with movements in the FTSE 100 index for the same period. The company uses this index as a benchmark as it reflects the performance of companies of similar size. However, when using TSR as a basis for rewarding directors, the company also uses other leading food retailers as a benchmark.

The TSR for the company, which is displayed graphically, is reproduced in Figure 10.4.

Figure 10.4	Tesco plc: total shareholder returns February 2001– February 2006

We can see from this graph that shareholder returns vary over time and so a measure of TSR is likely to be sensitive to the particular time period chosen.

Source: Annual Report and Financial Statements 2006.

British Sky Broadcasting Group (BSkyB) plc also uses TSR as a performance target for its executive directors. **Real World 10.11** explains how awards are made, or 'vested', using this target.

Real World 10.11

Sky high

BSkyB awards part of the performance-related element of executive directors' remuneration using a TSR target. TSR is measured over a three-year period and compared to the TSR of the FTSE100 companies. If the TSR is below the median of the FTSE100 companies, no awards are vested to the directors. If the TSR achieves the median, one third of awards available is vested and if the TSR is in the upper quartile, the whole of the awards available is vested. If the TSR lies somewhere between the median and upper quartile of the TSR of FTSE 100 companies, the awards available are vested on a straight-line basis. This is shown graphically in Figure 10.5.

Figure 10.5   TSR vesting schedule

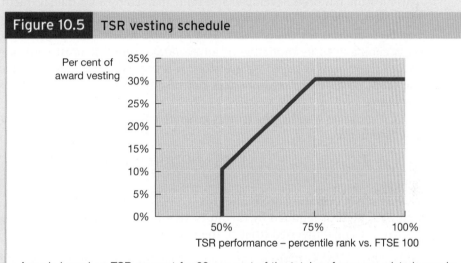

Per cent of award vesting / TSR performance – percentile rank vs. FTSE 100

Awards based on TSR account for 30 per cent of the total performance-related awards for executive directors. If TSR achieves the upper quartile range of FTSE 100 companies, all of the award (that is, 30 per cent of the total awards) is vested. If TSR achieves the median $1/3$ of the awards (that is, $1/3 \times 30\% = 10\%$ of the total awards) is vested. If the TSR lies somewhere between the median and the upper quartile, the awards are vested on a straight-line basis.

Note that BSkyB compares TSR performance against companies of a similar scale, presumably because it is impossible to find companies with similar operations.

Source: British Sky Broadcasting Group plc Annual Report 2006, p. 66.

Problems with TSR

TSR measures changes in shareholder wealth and, therefore, has obvious appeal as a basis for rewarding executive directors. It is also a fairly robust measure which can accommodate different operating and financing arrangements. Nevertheless, care must be taken when using it. In particular, the issue of risk must be given consideration. Higher returns may be achieved by simply taking on higher-risk projects and directors should not necessarily be remunerated for increasing returns in this way.

To provide a meaningful performance target, TSR must be compared to that of similar companies to assess relative performance. There may, however, be difficulties in finding similar companies as a suitable basis for comparison, as with BSkyB for example. (There is also a risk that unsuitable companies will be deliberately chosen in an attempt to make the company's performance seem better than is justified by the facts, leading to higher directors remuneration.) Other problems such as the inability to identify the contributions of individual directors to the overall performance of the company, the inability to identify changes in share price that are outside the control of the directors, and the fact that TSR can be manipulated over the short-term, all conspire to make this a less than perfect measure.

Economic value added (EVA®)

→ Performance targets based on **economic value added (EVA®)** offer another approach. This measure has been developed and trade marked by a US management consultancy firm, Stern Stewart. EVA®, however, is based on the idea of economic profit, which has been around for many years. The measure reflects the point made earlier that for a company to be profitable in an economic sense, it must generate returns that exceed the returns required by investors. It is not enough simply to make an accounting profit because this measure does not take full account of the returns required by investors.

EVA® indicates whether the returns generated exceed the returns required by investors. The formula is:

$$EVA® = NOPAT - (R \times C)$$

Where
NOPAT = Net operating profit after tax
R = Returns required by investors (that is, the weighted average cost of capital)
C = Capital invested (that is, the net assets of the company)

Only when EVA® is positive can we say that the company is increasing shareholder wealth. To maximise shareholder wealth, managers must increase EVA® by as much as possible.

Activity 10.14

What can managers do in order to increase EVA®? (*Hint*: use the formula shown above as your starting point.)

The formula suggests that in order to increase EVA®, managers may try to:

● Increase NOPAT. This may be done by either reducing expenses or by increasing sales revenue.
● Use capital invested more efficiently. This means selling off assets that are not generating returns that exceed their cost and investing in assets that do.
● Reduce the required rates of return for investors. This may be achieved by changing the capital structure in favour of loan capital (which is cheaper to service than share capital). This strategy, however, can create problems as discussed in Chapter 7.

EVA® relies on conventional financial statements to measure the wealth created for shareholders. However, the NOPAT and capital figures shown on these statements are used only as a starting point. They have to be adjusted because of the problems and limitations of conventional measures. According to Stern Stewart, the major problem is that profit and capital are understated because of the conservative bias in accounting measurement. Profit is understated as a result of arbitrary write-offs such as goodwill written off or research and development expenditure written off and as a result of excessive provisions being created (such as allowances for trade receivables (doubtful debts)). Capital is also understated because assets are reported at their original cost (less amounts written off), which can produce figures considerably below current market values. In addition, certain assets such as internally generated goodwill and brand names are omitted from the financial statements because no external transactions have occurred.

Stern Stewart has identified more than 100 adjustments that could be made to the conventional financial statements to eliminate the conservative bias. However, the firm believes that, in practice, only a handful of adjustments to the accounting figures of any particular business tend to be needed. Unless an adjustment is going to have a significant effect on the calculation of EVA® it is really not worth making. The adjustments made should reflect the nature of the particular business. Each business is unique and so must customise the calculation of EVA® to its particular circumstances. (This aspect of EVA® can be seen as either indicating flexibility or as being open to manipulation depending on whether you support this measure!)

The main advantage of EVA® is the discipline to which managers are subjected as a result of the charge for capital invested (the R × C term in the EVA® calculation). Before any increase in shareholder wealth can be recognised, an appropriate deduction is made for the use of business resources. Thus, EVA® encourages managers to use these resources efficiently. Where managers are focused simply on increasing profits, there is a danger that the resources used to achieve any increase in profits will not be taken into proper account. **Real World 10.12** provides an example of one business that is using EVA® to help managers refocus.

Real World 10.12

VW changes gear

FT

Volkswagen, Europe's biggest carmaker, is shaking up executive pay in an attempt to make managers more cautious about investment and increase loyalty to the group rather than the seven individual brands.

VW will base up to 40 per cent of this year's bonus on returns above the cost of capital, a big step in an industry renowned for destroying capital – and a move that is likely to lead to a lower payout.

The switch to economic value added measures to determine pay is part of an attempt by Bernd Pischetsrieder, chief executive, and Hans Dieter Pötsch, incoming finance director, to make managers think harder before making investments.

The company has abandoned return on sales targets in favour of measuring return on invested capital. It is also clamping down on investment and research spending, widely seen as out of control.

'People will understand that this is probably the main driver to end up with a higher bonus', Mr Pötsch told the *Financial Times*. 'We think it will be a good motivator.'

In addition to EVA, the bonus structure adds group performance measures to the individual and brand measures used in an attempt to make the brands work with each other, rather than competing.

Real World 10.12 continued

The system is being introduced this year, although the poor performance of the company – which saw operating profits fall severely in the first six months of this year – means the first bonus will be small.

All managers have been on a course on EVA, a measure created by Stern Stewart, the management consultants. The idea of EVA is to gauge return on investment above the cost of raising the capital to fund it – measured by the cost of paying dividends on shares and interest on bonds or loans.

VW made a return on invested capital of 7.4 per cent last year, below its 7.7 per cent cost of capital – equivalent to destroying €134 m ($147 m) of value.

Source: 'VW to Alter Management Focus', FT.com, 31 August 2003.

Under EVA®, managers can receive bonuses based on actual achievement during a particular period. If management rewards are linked to a single period, however, there is a danger that managers will place undue attention to increasing EVA® during this period rather than over the long term. This might be achieved in the short term, for example, by cutting back on necessary investment. The objective should be to maximise EVA® over the longer term. Where a business has a stable level of sales revenue, operating assets and borrowing, a current-period focus is likely to be less of a problem than where these elements are unstable over time. A stable pattern of operations minimises the risk that improvements in EVA® during the current period are achieved at the expense of future periods. Nevertheless, any reward system for managers must encourage a long-term perspective and so rewards should be based on the ability of managers to improve EVA® over a number of years rather than a single year.

Real World 10.13 describes the way in which one large listed company uses EVA® to reward its managers.

Real World 10.13

Banking on a bonus

Hanson plc, a major supplier of heavy building materials, adopts a bonus system for its directors based on EVA®. EVA® generated is accumulated in a 'bonus bank' and the directors are paid a portion of the EVA® bonus bank during a particular year; the remainder is carried forward for payment in future years. The following is an extract from the 2006 Annual Report of the business.

Annual bonus scheme

The annual bonus scheme for the Executive Directors and other senior executives is aligned with changes in shareholder value through the economic value added methodology. The main principle of economic value added is to recognise that over time a company should generate returns in excess of its cost of capital – the return that lenders and shareholders expect of the Company each year.

The annual bonus scheme is calibrated by reference to target levels of bonus and, for the Executive Directors and other senior executives, works on a bonus banking arrangement whereby each year the improvement in the group's overall economic value added for that year determines whether there is a bonus bank addition or deduction. Following the addition or deduction, the participant receives one-third of the accumulated bonus bank. There is neither a cap (maximum addition into the bonus bank each year) nor a floor (maximum deduction from the bonus bank each year).

The bonus bank has two main functions; firstly it encourages individuals not to make short-term decisions such as deferring essential expenditure from one year to the next and receive a bonus for doing so; and secondly, the bonus bank can act as a retention tool.

Source: Hanson plc 2006 Annual report www.hanson.com.

The amount of EVA® generated during a period is rarely reported to shareholders. This means that shareholders will be unable to check whether rewards given to directors are appropriate.

Earnings per share

Earnings per share (EPS) was considered in Chapter 8 and we may recall that it is calculated as follows:

$$\text{Earnings per share} = \frac{\text{Earnings available to ordinary shareholders}}{\text{Number of ordinary shares in issue}}$$

When used as a basis for directors' incentive plans, a particular level of growth in earnings per share is usually required in order to trigger rewards.

EPS can pose difficulties when used as a performance target for rewarding directors. A major problem is that an increase in EPS does not necessarily lead to an increase in shareholder wealth. EPS may be increased by embarking on risky ventures and an increased level of risk may be reflected in a decrease in share price. A further problem is that EPS is sensitive to manipulation by managers. It can, for example, be increased in the short term by restricting expenditure on discretionary items such as training, research and in nurturing brands. Accounting policy changes, such as changing the point at which revenue is recognised, can also increase it.

Where a company is suffering losses, caused perhaps by uncontrollable changes in economic conditions, it may take time to turn around the company's fortunes. The directors may be required to make tough decisions and to work hard over many years before there is any real prospect of generating profits. In such circumstances, an annual EPS target is unlikely to help in attracting, retaining or motivating directors.

Other accounting ratios

In practice, other ratios based on profits, such as return on capital employed and return on shareholders' funds, may be used to reward executive directors. They suffer, however, from the same sort of problems that afflict EPS.

Directors' share options

→ One way in which long-term performance can be rewarded is through the granting of **directors' share options**. This type of reward, however, has provoked considerable controversy. For years a debate has raged over whether granting share options to directors is consistent with good corporate governance. Peter Drucker, an eminent management thinker, has been a vociferous critic of this practice and has referred to it as 'an encouragement to loot the corporation'. We shall now consider the main features of directors' share options and then go on to explore the case for and against using options to reward directors. We shall see that a company implementing a directors' share option scheme must grapple with a variety of issues and problems.

What are directors' share options?

A directors' share option scheme gives directors the right, but not the obligation, to buy equity shares in their company at an agreed price. The conditions of the scheme will usually stipulate that the option to buy must be exercised either on, or after, a specified future date. A final date for exercising the option will also usually be specified.

Directors' share options will only be exercised if the market value of the shares exceeds the option price. Where the option is exercised, the company must issue the agreed number of shares to the director, who will make a profit from the transaction. Unlike most financial options, a director will not normally be required to pay for the option rights: they are granted at no cost to the directors concerned. Directors' share options, however, cannot be traded and will usually be forfeited if the director leaves the company before the option can be exercised.

In the UK, directors' share options are normally issued at the current market price of the underlying shares. In the past, share options were sometimes issued at a discount to the market price, however, the Combined Code has discouraged this practice. The terms of a share option scheme often allow the directors to exercise their option no earlier than three years, but no later than ten years, after the option has been granted. Inland Revenue rules and best practice guidelines from institutional investors limit the value of options to £100,000 or four times current salary (see reference 9 at the end of the chapter). The exercise of the option may be subject to certain performance targets, such as growth in earnings per share, being met (see reference 10 at the end of the chapter).

Share options are normally awarded only to executive directors. The Combined Code states that non-executive directors should not be rewarded in this way.

What are the benefits of granting options?

Directors' share option schemes have been a popular method of rewarding the directors of large listed companies and various arguments have been put forward to support their use. It is often suggested, for example, that a well-designed scheme will benefit shareholders as it will help to align the interests of directors with those of shareholders. The rationale provided is that share options give directors a financial incentive to increase the value of the company's shares, and thereby to increase the wealth of shareholders.

Some argue that share options may even help to strengthen the psychological bond that a director has with the company. Through exercising an option and acquiring shares, the directors may identify more closely with the company and feel a sense of shared purpose with other shareholders. This argument does depend, however, on the directors retaining, rather than selling, the shares acquired under the option agreement.

It has also been suggested that share options may help to retain board members. The fact that a director's share options are normally forfeited if a director leaves the company can provide a strong incentive to stay. Thus, options can provide a set of 'golden handcuffs' for talented directors who have other employment opportunities.

Unlike other forms of directors' remuneration, share options involve no financial outlay for the company at the time that they are granted. If the share price does not perform well over the option period, the option will be allowed to lapse and the company will incur no cost. If, on the other hand, the shares perform well and the options are exercised, they represent a form of deferred payment to the directors. This deferral of rewards may be particularly attractive to a growing company that is short of cash.

It should be emphasised that where directors exercise their options and the company, therefore, issues shares at below their current market value, there is a very real cost to the company. Were the company to issue those same shares to an ordinary investor, it would receive the current market price for them.

What are the problems of options?

Many believe that share options are a poor means of rewarding directors. Warren Buffett, one of the world's shrewdest and most successful investors, has made clear his opposition to the use of options. One problem that concerns him is that share option schemes cannot differentiate between the performances achieved by individual directors. He argues:

> Of course stock (share) options often go to talented, value-adding managers and sometimes deliver them rewards that are perfectly appropriate. (Indeed, managers who are really exceptional almost always get far less than they should.) But when the result is equitable, it is accidental. Once granted, the option is blind to individual performance. Because it is irrevocable and unconditional (so long as a manager stays in the company), the sluggard receives rewards from his options precisely as does the star. A managerial Rip Van Winkle, ready to doze for ten years, could not wish for a better 'incentive' system . . .
>
> (See reference 11 at the end of the chapter.)

A further problem concerning the incentive value of share options, to which Buffett refers, is that, where the share price falls significantly below the exercise price, the prospects of receiving benefits from the share options may become remote and any incentive value will be lost.

It is worth remembering that both rises and falls in share price may be beyond the control of the directors and may simply reflect changes in economy-wide or industry-wide factors. Any incentive scheme that is subject to the vagaries of the stock market is, therefore, likely to present problems. There is always a risk that directors will either be under-compensated or over-compensated for their achievements.

Buffett's criticism of share options is not confined to their dubious incentive value. He also challenges the view that share options place directors in the same position as that of shareholders. He argues:

> . . . the rhetoric about options frequently describes them as desirable because they put owners and managers in the same financial boat. In reality, the boats are far different. No owner has ever escaped the burden of capital costs, whereas a holder of a fixed-price option bears no capital costs at all. An owner must weigh upside potential against downside risk: an option holder has no downside. In fact, the business project in which you would wish to have an option frequently is a project in which you would reject ownership. (I'll be happy to accept a lottery ticket as a gift – but I'll never buy one.)   (See reference 11 at the end of the chapter.)

This latter point, concerning the lack of 'downside' risk associated with the acquisition of options, may have an impact on the directors' risk-taking behaviour.

Activity 10.15

How might this affect the risk-taking behaviour of directors?

As options are granted for free, the directors have an incentive to take risks when these options are 'underwater' (that is, when they cannot be exercised at a profit). By taking risks, there is a prospect of a rise in share prices and resulting benefits. If, on the other hand, by taking risks there is a fall in share prices, the directors will incur no financial loss.

Where share options are exercised, the directors may find themselves holding a large proportion of their total wealth in the form of company equity. The concentration of wealth in this form may have a number of unintended consequences. Firstly, it may lead to risk-averse behaviour as directors may be concerned with maintaining their wealth intact. This behaviour may not, however, find favour with the shareholders, who are likely to have a more diversified portfolio of investments and so may be more willing to take risks. Secondly, it may reduce the value of further share options in the eyes of the directors, who may feel that their wealth is insufficiently diversified. For this reason, the value of a share option to a director is likely to be lower than the value of the option to the company granting it, in terms of the opportunity cost of selling the option in the market. As a result, share options can be an expensive way of motivating directors from the company's perspective.

Share option schemes are based on the assumption that shareholders are concerned with share price increases and that directors' behaviour and incentives should reflect this concern. An excessive focus on share price, however, may not be in the best interests of shareholders. Share price represents only one part of the shareholders' total return from the company: the other part is dividend income.

Activity 10.16

How might directors behave as a result of this focus on share price increases rather than dividends?

There is a risk that this may lead the directors to restrict dividend payments so that profits are retained to fuel share price growth. Indeed, as directors are rewarded on the basis of share price growth rather than dividend growth, they have an incentive to act in this way. (This potential problem has led some companies to incorporate dividend protection conditions in the share option schemes offered to directors.)

Using similar reasoning, it can be argued that directors also have an incentive to have the company re-purchase its own shares as this too may lead to increases in share price.

Directors' share options have declined in popularity in recent years and various factors appear to have contributed towards this decline. One factor is likely to have been the changes in the corporate governance environment. In the UK, an influential report on directors' remuneration discouraged the use of share option schemes and a number of large institutional investors have voiced their concern over their cost and effectiveness. A further factor is likely to have been that international accounting standards now require the 'fair value' of share option schemes to be included in the financial statements. Shareholders can now see more clearly the cost incurred by granting share options as it is shown as a charge against profits. A final factor is likely to have been that share option schemes are open to abuse. The particular forms of abuse that have been identified usually relate to the conditions of the share option scheme and to the pricing of options.

For UK companies in particular, a share option scheme will often include a condition that certain performance targets, such as earnings per share, must be met before the directors can exercise their options. There have been allegations, however, that some companies have set performance targets too low for them to have any real incentive effect. **Real World 10.14** reveals how one major bank has recently toughened its performance targets in response to pressure from major shareholders.

Real World 10.14

Time to stretch

FT

RBS (Royal Bank of Scotland) has assured institutional investors it will set tougher pay targets for executive directors.

The world's fifth-biggest bank, led by Sir Fred Goodwin, has been cultivating relationships with shareholders since last year, following concerns it had been pursuing acquisitions at the expense of shareholder value.

RBS has assured Rrev, the powerful institutional investor group, that it will set tougher targets for board executives in its executive share option plan.

The scheme now pays out when the bank's earnings per share growth exceeds 3 per cent plus Retail Price Index growth.

But Rrev believes a 'tougher target could be applied during appropriate parts of the [banking] cycle', it said in a report ahead of the RBS annual meeting.

'All or nothing [option schemes] have not been in line with market practice for several years', it added.

In response, RBS has undertaken to Rrev – which is a joint venture between the National Association of Pension Funds and Institutional Shareholder Services – that there will be no further grants of options under the scheme to executive directors using the current performance target.

Instead, before future share grants, RBS told the shareholder group, the remuneration committee would consider the most appropriate measure in the light of market conditions and future performance conditions would 'be more stretching than the current one'. The scheme is due to be reviewed in 2007.

Source: 'RBS Will Set Tougher Targets for Executive Directors' Pay Packets', FT.com, 20 April 2006.

The pricing of options has often been a target for manipulation by unscrupulous individuals and, in the US, several scandals have been unearthed. Some high-profile US companies have been found to have reissued share options to directors at a lower price when the share price of the company fell below the option price. This practice effectively eliminates any risks for directors and may also eliminate any incentive effect that share options may have. (See reference 12 at the end of the chapter.)

Activity 10.17

Can you think of any circumstances under which reissuing share options at a lower price to directors might be justified?

It is sometimes argued that, by 're-pricing' options in this way, it may be possible to re-incentivise directors, particularly when stock market prices are falling.

More recently, there have been accusations that directors have benefited from the backdating of options. **Real World 10.15** describes one high-profile case concerning backdated options.

Real World 10.15

Sour Apple   **FT**

Try as it may, Apple seems unable to put its stock options backdating scandal to rest. While the company has already cleared all of its current executives of blame and Steve Jobs, the chief executive, has apologised for the lapses, the matter continues to shed an unflattering light on internal practices at one of the world's most successful technology and consumer electronics companies.

In the latest sign of Apple's continuing problems, Mr Jobs himself received at least one grant of options that was made without proper authorisation and was apparently backdated. The grant of 7.5 m options, made in late 2001, was never approved by Apple's full board of directors, as required by its internal rules, according to two people familiar with the matter; yet documents were falsified to show that this meeting had indeed taken place.

Since that supposed board approval was recorded some time after the date at which the exercise price on the options was set, it also indicates that the benefits were backdated.

Apple had already reported in October this year that Mr Jobs was 'aware' of backdating at the company in a small number of instances, though it also said he 'did not receive or otherwise benefit from these grants and was unaware of the accounting implications'. It also said an internal investigation had raised 'serious concerns' about the actions of two former officers, believed to be Fred Anderson, former chief financial officer, and Nancy Heinen, former general counsel, and had handed details to the Securities and Exchange Commission.

The latest revelation adds several new twists to this picture. One, not directly related to the backdating issue, suggests Apple's internal controls on compensation were surprisingly lax.

Source: 'Stock Options Backdating Haunts Apple', FT.com, 28 December 2006.

The above is far from an isolated case. One recent study found that 1,400 directors of 460 US companies benefited from the backdating of share options to the lowest price in a monthly period. (See reference 13 at the end of the chapter.)

Deciding on a target

Given the strengths and weaknesses of each of the performance targets and incentives described, companies rarely rely on a single target. Instead, they employ a range of targets in the hope of capturing various aspects of performance and of overcoming the weaknesses of a particular target. In addition to the quantitative targets described, a company may also use qualitative targets, which are again related to the objectives of the company.

To give some idea of the arrangements that a listed company might put in place, **Real World 10.16** sets out the basis for rewarding the executive directors of Tesco plc.

Real World 10.16

Tesco rewards

The executive directors of Tesco plc receive a fixed base salary (plus benefits) but are also eligible for performance-related cash bonuses and shares. Short-term performance is rewarded by an annual cash bonus and by deferred shares, while long-term performance is rewarded by shares issued under a share plan and by share options. The details of each element of remuneration and the performance targets used are as follows:

Part of remuneration	Performance measure	Purpose
Base salary	Individual contribution to business success	To attract and retain talented people
Annual cash bonus (up to 100% of salary)	Earnings per share and specified corporate objectives	Motivates year-on-year earnings growth and delivery of business priorities
Annual deferred share element of bonus (up to 100% of salary)	Total shareholder return, earnings per share and specified corporate objectives	Generates focus on medium-term targets and by incentivising share price and dividend growth ensures alignment with shareholder interest
Performance share plan (up to 150% of salary)	Return on capital employed over a three-year period	Assures a focus on long-term business success and shareholder returns
Share options	Earnings per share relative to retail price index	Incentivises earnings growth and executive director shareholding

The performance-related element represents a large proportion of total remuneration. For example, during the year ended 25 February 2006, the chief executive officer received total remuneration of nearly £4.0 million, of which almost £2.8 million was performance related.

Source: Tesco plc Annual Report and Accounts 2006, p. 28.

The rise of shareholder activism

Improving corporate governance has, in the UK, focused mainly on developing a framework of rules for the management of companies listed on the London Stock Exchange. Whilst such rules are important, there are many who take the view that it is also important for those who own the companies to play their part by actively monitoring and controlling the behaviour of directors. In this section, we identify the main shareholders of listed companies and discuss their role in establishing good corporate governance. We also consider why there has been greater shareholder activism in recent years.

Who are the main shareholders?

Real World 10.17 provides some impression of the ownership of London Stock Exchange listed shares.

Real World 10.17

Becoming institutionalised

At 31 December 2004, 33 per cent of the shares (by market value) of London Stock Exchange listed companies were owned by investors (individuals and institutions) that are based overseas. Of those owned by UK residents (individuals and institutions), the break-down of ownership is as shown in Figure 10.6.

| Figure 10.6 | Beneficial ownership of UK shares by UK investors, end 2004 |

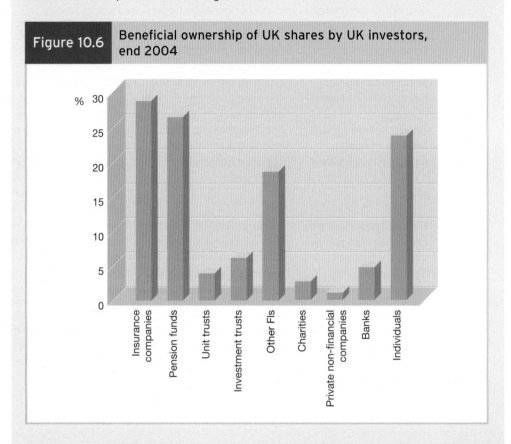

Large financial institutions such as insurance companies, banks, pension funds, unit trusts and investment trusts, are now the most important investors in shares listed on the London Stock Exchange. These institutions have increased their hold on the ownership of Stock Exchange listed shares over time, whilst, the proportion of listed shares held directly by individuals has decreased. The proportion of shares (by market value) owned by vari-ous financial institutions is now around 79 per cent of the total market value of those London Stock Exchange listed shares, with only 21 per cent held by individuals.

Looking at the changes in the ownership of listed shares over the past four decades shows two striking features:

1. The value of listed shares owned by overseas residents has gone up progressively from just 7 per cent in 1963 (to 33 per cent in 2004), and
2. of those held by UK residents, the value of listed shares held by individuals has fallen fairly steadily from 58 per cent in 1963 (to 21 per cent in 2004).

Source: Office for National Statistics.

The rise of the institutions should not be interpreted as meaning that individuals have less investment in listed shares. It simply means that individuals are now tending to invest through the institutions, for example by making pension contributions, rather than by buying shares directly. Ultimately, all of the investment finance must come from individuals.

This concentration of ownership of listed shares means that financial institutions have enormous voting power and, as a result, the potential to exercise significant influence over the way in which Stock Exchange companies are directed and controlled. In the past, however, they have been reluctant to exercise this power and have been criticised for being too passive and for allowing the directors of companies too much independence.

Most financial institutions have chosen to take a non-interventionist approach and have preferred to confine their investment activities to determining whether to buy, hold or sell shares in particular companies. They appear to have taken the view that the costs of actively monitoring directors and trying to influence their decisions are too high in relation to the likely benefits. It is also worth pointing out that these costs are borne by the particular financial institution undertaking the monitoring whereas the benefits are spread across all of the company's shareholders. (This phenomenon is often referred to as the 'free-rider' problem.)

Waking the sleeping giants

In recent years, however, financial institutions have begun to play a more active role in corporate governance. More time is being devoted to monitoring the actions of directors and in engaging with the directors over key decisions. This change of heart has occurred for a variety of reasons. One important reason is that the increasing concentration of share ownership has made it more difficult for financial institutions simply to walk away from an investment in a poorly performing company by selling its shares. A substantial number of shares is often held and so a decision to sell can have a significant impact on the market price, leading to heavy losses.

A further reason why it may be difficult to disinvest is that a company's shares may be included in a stock market index (such as the FTSE 100 or FTSE 250). Certain types of financial institutions, such as investment trusts or unit trusts, may offer investments that are designed to 'track' the particular index and so they become locked into a company's shares in order to reflect the index. In both situations outlined, therefore, a financial institution may have little choice but to stick with the shares held and try to improve performance by seeking to influence the actions and decisions of the directors.

It is also worth mentioning that financial institutions have experienced much greater competitive pressures in recent years. There have been increasing demands from clients for them to demonstrate their investment skills, and thereby justify their fees, by either outperforming benchmarks or beating the performance of similar financial institutions. These increased competitive pressures may be due, at least in part, to the fact that economic conditions have not favoured investors in the recent past; they have experienced a period of relatively low stock market returns. Whatever the reason, the increased pressure to enhance the wealth of their clients has led financial institutions, in turn, to become less tolerant towards underperforming boards of directors.

The regulatory environment has also favoured greater activism on the part of financial institutions. The Combined Code, for example, urges institutional shareholders to use their votes and to enter into a dialogue with companies.

Financial institutions are likely to take an interest in a wide range of issues affecting a company. Some of the more important issues that are likely to attract their attention include:

- objectives and strategies adopted;
- trading performance;
- internal controls;
- policies regarding mergers and acquisition;
- major investments and disinvestments;
- adherence to the recommendations of the Combined Code;
- corporate social responsibilities;
- directors' incentives schemes and remuneration.

This is not an exhaustive list. As owners of the company, anything that might have an impact on their wealth should be a matter of concern to the shareholders.

It is worth pointing out that listed companies have become more vulnerable to takeover, particularly by private equity funds. Takeovers very often lead to existing directors losing their positions. This makes the directors particularly sensitive to the views and aspirations of the large shareholders that have the power to resist a takeover by refusing to sell their shares.

Forms of activism

It is important to be clear as to what is meant by the term 'shareholder activism' as it can take various forms. In its simplest form it involves taking a more active role in voting for or against the resolutions put before the annual general meeting or any extraordinary general meeting of the company. This form of activism is seen by the government as being vital to good corporate governance. The government is keen to see much higher levels of participation than currently exists and expects institutional shareholders to exercise their right to vote. In the past, financial institutions have often indicated their dissent by abstaining from a vote rather than outright opposition to a resolution. There is some evidence, however, that they are now more prepared to use their vote to oppose resolutions of the board of directors.

Much of the evidence available remains anecdotal rather than based on systematic research. One such example concerns the recent merger of two large media companies – Carlton and Granada. The chairman of Carlton, Mr. Michael Green, was nominated as independent chairman of the combined company but some financial institutions felt he was unsuitable and succeeded in opposing his appointment by voting against the resolution. **Real World 10.18** provides a more recent example of where shareholders have acted to try to make changes to the board.

Real World 10.18

Revolting shareholders   **FT**

Dissident investors in SkyePharma have finally ran out of patience with the board of the drug delivery company and launched a coup attempt to oust Ian Gowrie-Smith, chairman, and replace him with industry heavyweight Bob Thian.

North Atlantic Value, the shareholder activist group, joined forces with Insight Investment and Morley Fund Management and other investors to call for an extraordinary meeting to vote on the proposed management change.

It is believed that the final trigger for the revolt was SkyePharma's plan to announce the appointment of two executives, including a chief executive, without consulting investors.

NAV said: 'We did not intend to do this but rushing out two executives is not negotiating in good faith.'

The dissident group, which has named itself the Requisitionists, said Skye-Pharma had repeatedly failed to listen to the concerns of large shareholders.

Investors have increasingly become frustrated with the lack of progress in finding a buyer for all or part of the business, following Skye-Pharma's announcement in November that it had appointed Lehman Brothers to conduct a strategic review.

The Requisitionists, who have a combined 13.15 per cent stake, firmly placed the blame for what they described as a corporate strategy of over-promising on performance but under-delivering on the shoulders of Mr Gowrie-Smith.

'Their entire strategy has been delay, delay, delay and time just ran out for them', said one large shareholder.

Other shareholders, including Legal and General and Fidelity, who between them have a 12 per cent holding in SkyePharma, are also believed to be prepared to support the move to change the management.

Source: 'Move to Oust SkyePharma Chairman', FT.com, 20 January 2006.

A particularly rich source of contention between shareholders and directors concerns directors' remuneration and there have been several shareholder revolts over this issue. Shareholders are often upset by what they regard as the setting of undemanding performance targets or unjustified, 'one-off' payments to directors. **Real World 10.19** provides an example of a fairly recent falling out.

Real World 10.19

Easy money

FT

Lord Hollick, outgoing chief executive of United Business Media, is facing an embarrassing shareholder revolt at the company's annual meeting next week over plans to award him a special £250,000 bonus.

The chance of UBM's remuneration report being voted down at the meeting increased on Wednesday when the Association of British Insurers, a powerful investor group, issued 'red-top' guidance to members, indicating its highest level of concern.

The National Association of Pension Funds is urging its members to rebel against the report. The Research, Recommendations and Electronic Voting advisory service, which is half-owned by the NAPF, says investors should also vote against the re-election of Chris Powell as a non-executive director because he chairs the committee that approved the bonus.

Investor anger was sparked last month when the company revealed in its annual report that Lord Hollick would receive the unusual bonus for helping to ensure a 'successful handover' to David Levin, the incoming chief executive.

Most of the company's largest institutional investors plan to register their fury by voting against the company's remuneration report. Few expect UBM to win the vote; a loss would force the company to back down or ignore its leading investors.

One shareholder said: 'I predict UBM will lose this vote. We simply cannot allow these types of payments. Why should Lord Hollick be paid extra simply to hand over to a successor?'

Peter Montagnon, ABI's head of investment affairs, said: 'We have reached our decision after careful discussion with members and their view is firm. These payments are not appropriate.'

Companies work hard to avoid losing the remuneration vote. The last high-profile casualty was GlaxoSmithKline in May 2003, when shareholders voted down the pay package of Jean-Pierre Garnier, chief executive.

UBM on Wednesday refused to say whether it would withdraw the bonus if it lost the vote. The company said: 'It is too early to pre-judge the outcome of the annual meeting but UBM takes all representations from shareholders seriously.'

Source: 'UBM Investors in Bonus Revolt', FT.com, 4 May 2005.

Although the examples mentioned above are widely reported and catch the newspaper headlines, they do not happen very often. Nevertheless, the benefits for shareholders of flexing their muscles and voting against resolutions put forward by the directors may go beyond their immediate, intended objective: other boards of directors may take note of shareholder dissatisfaction and adjust their behaviour in order to avoid a similar fate. The cost of voting need not be high as there are specialist agencies which offer research and advice to financial institutions on how their votes should be cast.

Another form of activism involves meetings and discussions between representatives of a particular financial institution and the board of directors of a company. This requires a fairly high degree of involvement with the company and some of the larger financial institutions have dedicated teams for this purpose. This can be, therefore, a costly exercise. **Real World 10.20** below is an extract from the website of one major financial institution that is committed to this form of activism and which gives an insight to the approach taken.

Real World 10.20

Getting active

Jupiter International Group plc, a major provider of unit trusts and investment trusts, believes that, when monitoring investments:

> An important part of the process is the dialogue (usually private) between institutional shareholders and the companies in which it invests. As such, its fund managers and analysts host and attend regular meetings with the management of the investee companies, with a high percentage of companies being seen twice a year where corporate strategy, performance and other management issues are discussed.

Source: www.jupiteronline.co.uk.

Such meetings can be a useful mechanism for exchanging views and for gaining a greater understanding of the needs and motivations of each party. This may help to pre-empt public spats between the board of directors and financial institutions, which is rarely the best way to resolve issues.

The final form of activism involves intervention in the affairs of the company. This, however, can be very costly, depending on the nature of the problem. Where strategic and operational issues raise concerns, intervention can be very costly indeed. Identifying the weaknesses and problems relating to these issues requires a detailed understanding of the nature of its business. This implies close monitoring by relevant experts who are able to analyse the issues and then propose feasible solutions. The costs associated with such an exercise would normally be prohibitive, although the costs may be mitigated through some kind of collective action by financial institutions. Not all forms of intervention in the affairs of a company, however, need be costly. Where, for example, there are corporate governance issues to be addressed, such as a failure to adhere to the recommendations of the Combined Code, a financial institution may nominate individuals for appointment as non-executive directors who can be relied upon to ensure that necessary changes are made. This should involve relatively little cost for the financial institution.

The future of shareholder activism

The rise of shareholder activism raises two important questions that have yet to be answered. Firstly, is it simply a passing phenomenon? It is no coincidence that shareholder activism took root during a period when stock market returns were fairly low. There is a risk that financial institutions will become less active and less vigilant in monitoring companies when stock market returns improve. Secondly, does shareholder activism really make a difference to corporate performance? The research on this topic so far has been fairly sparse but early research in the US is not encouraging for those who urge financial institutions to take a more active approach. We may have to wait some while, however, for clear answers to these questions.

Complying with the Combined Code

Despite the general agreement that the Combined Code provides a useful set of principles on which good corporate governance can be based, not all companies seem to follow it. **Real World 10.21** is an article that appeared in the *Financial Times* that discusses the results of a survey on compliance.

Real World 10.21

Code breaking

FT

Non-executive directors are failing to challenge their boards on departures from best practice corporate governance, says a leading accountancy firm.

Only a third of the largest companies claim full compliance with the UK's Combined Code, according to a report released today by Grant Thornton.

The code, which was introduced in 2003 after a series of corporate scandals, sets out standards of good practice on issues such as board composition, pay and relations with shareholders.

The remaining two-thirds of the FTSE 350 companies still do not claim to be in full compliance with the provisions and are obliged under the code to justify where and why they diverge from it. However, only 30 of the top 350 companies do so, says Grant Thornton.

Simon Lowe, head of Grant Thornton's risk management services practice, said: 'Non-executive directors in particular must now take a stand and challenge the [executive members of the] board to clarify why departure is better for the company and indeed their stakeholders, than full compliance.'

Of the 207 top companies that do not comply with the code, more than half have not changed their explanations for non-compliance since last year. Less than a third have made any substantial changes.

Meanwhile, a separate study of executives of top UK companies, also out today, says there is a strong demand for some provisions of the code to be overhauled.

Close to 40 per cent of those surveyed by search firm Hanson Green said the Higgs report on board governance – which led to the creation of the Combined Code – had not resulted in more effective board governance. More than 60 per cent thought the provision on complying or explaining was not working.

Source: Burgess, Kate 'Few Top Companies Follow Code on Corporate Governance', *Financial Times*, 28 December 2006.

Summary

The main points of this chapter may be summarised as follows:

Corporate governance

- Corporate governance issues arise because of the separation of ownership from control of the company.
- Corporate governance rules are based around the principles of disclosure, accountability and fairness.
- The Combined Code, which apples to UK Stock Exchange listed companies, adopts a 'comply-or-explain' approach to the rules that it sets out.

The board of directors

- The board governs the company on behalf of the shareholders.
- The board is responsible for setting the strategic direction of the company, controlling the company and nurturing relations with shareholders and other parties.
- The chairman must lead and manage the board of directors.
- The chairman's role involves ensuring that the board operates effectively, providing advice and support to directors, communicating with shareholders, and ensuring that the performance of the board and the directors is subject to regular scrutiny.
- The board is made up of executive and non-executive directors, all of which have the same legal obligation to the shareholders of the company.

Non-executive directors

- Are part-time and do not engage in the day-to-day running of the company.
- This more detached role allows them to take a more objective view of the issues confronting the company.
- Non-executive directors are meant to contribute to the main tasks of the board identified earlier and will play a key role in board committees concerned with the nomination of directors, the remuneration of executive directors and the integrity of financial statements.
- The role of non-executive directors contains the potential for conflict between the need to work with executive directors as part of a team and the need to monitor and assess the performance of executive directors on behalf of the shareholders.

The audit process

- An external audit is required by all but the smallest companies.
- External auditors are appointed by, and report to, the shareholders and their role is to examine the annual financial statements that have been prepared by the directors.
- Many large companies have an internal audit function, the main purpose of which is to provide the directors with reassurance concerning the reliability of the company's control and financial reporting systems.
- The presence of internal auditors can help the external auditors, who may be able to place reliance on some of the work undertaken by them.
- The Combined Code states that an audit committee should be created with delegated authority for ensuring that financial reporting and internal control principles are

properly applied and for maintaining an appropriate relationship with the external auditors.

- The terms of reference of the committee will be determined by the board of directors.
- An audit committee report will be prepared for shareholders and presented at the AGM.
- The value of audit committees in preventing audit scandals is, so far, unproven.

Assessing board performance

- The board should be subject to regular evaluation, which may be carried out by the board itself or by an external party, such as a firm of management consultants.
- Areas of performance to be evaluated may include achievement of company objectives, control exercised over the company's activities, board structure and roles, board meetings, board composition, board discussions and decisions, relations with shareholders and board appointments and development.

Remunerating directors

- The Combined Code states that directors' remuneration should be sufficient to recruit and retain directors of the right calibre and that a significant proportion of total remuneration should be linked to performance.
- The remuneration package of executive directors will usually have a fixed element and a variable element, which is linked to the achievement of clearly defined performance targets.
- Performance targets should be consistent with the overall aims of the company, align the interests of directors with those of shareholders, reflect the achievement of the directors and be robust.
- TSR (total shareholder return) is a popular performance target and measures changes in shareholder wealth. To assess relative performance, similar companies must be used as a benchmark.
- EVA® (economic value added) indicates whether the returns generated exceed the returns required by investors. It relies on conventional financial statements to measure the wealth created but adjusts these to reflect the conservative bias in accounting measurement.
- EPS (earnings per share) can be used as a performance target by setting a particular level of growth required.
- Share options may be used to reward directors. However, these have been criticised for their failing to align the interests of directors with those of shareholders.
- Most listed public companies use a variety of measures and incentives to reward executive directors rather than relying on a single measure.

The rise of shareholder activism

- Institutional shareholders, who dominate the London Stock Exchange, have taken a more active role in the affairs of listed companies in recent years.
- Activism takes the form of using their votes, meetings with directors and intervention in a company's affairs.
- It is not clear whether such activism will continue when share prices rise and returns from the stock market increase.

→ **Key terms**

Combined Code p. 323	**Nomination committee** p. 327
Chairman p. 323	**Remuneration committee** p. 327
Executive directors p. 323	**External audit** p. 336
Non-executive directors p. 323	**Internal audit** p. 337
Executive committee p. 323	**Total shareholder return (TSR)** p. 349
Chief executive officer p. 327	**Economic value added (EVA®)**
Audit committee p. 327	p. 352
Risk management committee p. 327	**Directors' share options** p. 355

References

1 OECD (1998) *Corporate Governance: Improving Competitiveness and Access to Capital in Global Markets*, report by Business Sector Advisory Group on Corporate Governance, Organisation for Economic Co-operation and Development (OECD), p. 14.

2 'Non-executive Directors' Pay Jumps 38%', FT.com, 6 December 2004.

3 Haigney, N., 'Relationship Between Audit Committee and Internal Audit', HM Treasury, www.nationalschools.gov.uk.

4 Independent Audit Ltd, *Audit Committee Reporting in 2005*, www.boydeninterim.co.uk.

5 'UK Audit Committees More Confident and Involved Than US Counterparts', *Audit Committee Quarterly*, Issue 11. Audit Committee Institute.

6 Sulkowicz, K. (2003) 'New Organisational and Psychological Challenges of the Audit Committee', *Audit Committee Quarterly*, Issue 8. Audit Committee Institute.

7 Reported in Tucker, S. (2005) 'UK Chiefs Reluctant to Take on Audit Role', FT.com, 30 January.

8 Richards, M. (2006) 'More Link Directors Pay to Performance', FT.com, 18 December.

9 Pope, P. and Young, S., 'Executive Share Options: An Investor's Guide', www.manifest.co.uk.

10 Bender, R. (2005) 'Just Rewards for a New Approach to Pay', *Financial Times*, 2 June.

11 Buffet, W. (1985) *Annual Report to Shareholders*, Berkshire Hathaway, Inc., p. 12.

12 Monks, R. and Minow, N. (2001) *Corporate Governance*, 2nd edn, Blackwell, p. 226.

13 Quoted in Guerrera, F. (2006) 'Study Links Directors to Options Scandal', *Financial Times*, 18 December.

Further reading

If you would like to explore the topics covered in this chapter in more depth, we recommend the following books:

Elliott, B. and Elliott, J. (2006) *Financial Accounting and Reporting*, 11th edn, Financial Times Prentice Hall, Chapter 30.

Stiles, P. and Taylor, B. (2001) *Boards at Work*, Oxford University Press, Chapters 4–6.

Monks, R. and Minow, N. (2001) *Corporate Governance*, 2nd edn, Blackwell Publishing, Chapters 2–4.

Kothari, J. and Barone, E. (2006) *Financial Accounting: An International Approach*, Financial Times Prentice Hall, Chapters 17 and 18.

Review questions

Answers to these questions can be found at the back of the book on p. 417.

10.1 Identify the main ways in which a large listed company may communicate with its shareholders.

10.2 Can you think of any arguments against a listed public company having an audit committee?

10.3 A large public company wishes to improve its payroll accounting systems and is seeking outside help to do this. The external auditors of the company are a large firm of accountants that has a consultancy arm. What are the advantages and disadvantages of allowing the external auditors to undertake this task?

10.4 Why have institutional shareholders become more active in corporate governance issues in recent years?

Exercises

Exercises 10.3 and 10.4 are more advanced than 10.1 to 10.2. Those with a coloured number have an answer at the back of the book, starting on p. 443.

If you wish to try more exercises, visit the students' side of the Companion Website.

10.1 Assume that the chairman of the board of directors of a large public, listed company has asked you to develop a set of criteria against which the performance of a non-executive director could be appraised. Try to identify at least six criteria, based on the discussion of the role found in the chapter, which you might select.

10.2 Reviewing the risk management systems within a company goes beyond the traditional role of internal audit. What changes may have to be made to the internal audit function to enable it to carry out this enhanced role?

10.3 The board of directors of a listed company is likely to place considerable emphasis on maintaining good communications and strong relationships with its institutional shareholders. What are the main benefits and problems of doing this?

10.4 The newly appointed chairman of Vorak plc has been told that considerable tension and suspicion exists between the executive and non-executive directors on the board. The executive directors question the competence of the non-executive directors and the non-executive directors believe that important information is being withheld from them. Assuming that the concerns of each group are well founded, what advice would you give to the chairman concerning how to ease the tension and promote a better working relationship between the two groups?

Appendix A
Recording financial transactions

Introduction

In Chapters 2 and 3, we saw how the financial transactions of a business may be recorded by making a series of entries on the balance sheet and/or the income statement. Each of these entries had its corresponding 'double', meaning that both sides of the transaction were recorded. However, adjusting the financial statements, by hand, for each transaction can be very messy and confusing. With a reasonably large number of transactions it is pretty certain to result in mistakes.

For businesses whose accounting systems are on a computer, this problem is overcome because suitable software can deal with a series of 'plus' and 'minus' entries very reliably. Where the accounting system is not computerised, however, it would be helpful to have some more practical way of keeping accounting records. Such a system not only exists but, before the advent of the computer, was the routine way of keeping accounts. It is this system that is explained in this appendix. We should be clear that the system we are going to consider follows exactly the same rules as those that we have already met. Its distinguishing feature is its ability to provide those keeping accounting records by hand with a methodical approach that allows each transaction to be clearly identified and errors to be minimised.

Learning outcomes

When you have completed this Appendix you should be able to:

- Explain the basic principles of double-entry bookkeeping.
- Write up a series of business transactions and balance the accounts.
- Extract a trial balance and explain its purpose.
- Prepare a set of financial statements from the underlying double-entry accounts.

The basics of double-entry bookkeeping

When we record accounting transactions by hand, we use a recording system known as **double-entry bookkeeping**. This system does not use plus and minus entries on the face of a balance sheet and income statement to record a particular transaction, in the way described in Chapters 2 and 3. Instead, these are recorded in accounts. An **account** is simply a record of one or more transactions relating to a particular item, such as cash, fixtures and fittings, borrowings, sales revenue, rent payable and capital. A business may keep few or many accounts, depending on the size and complexity of its operations. Broadly, businesses tend to keep a separate account for each item that appears in either the income statement or the balance sheet.

An example of an account, in this case the cash account, is as follows:

Cash

£		£

We can see that an account has three main features:

- a title indicating the item to which it relates;
- a left-hand side, known as the **debit** side;
- a right-hand side, known as the **credit** side.

One side of an account will record increases in the particular item and the other will record decreases. This, of course, is slightly different to the approach we used when adjusting the financial statements. When adjusting the balance sheet, for example, we put a reduction in an asset or claim in the same column as any increases, but with a minus sign against it. However, when accounts are used, a reduction is shown on the opposite side of the account.

The side on which an increase or decrease is shown will depend on the nature of the item to which the account relates. For example, an account for an asset, such as cash, will show increases on the left-hand (debit) side of the account and decreases on the right-hand (credit) side. However, for claims (that is, capital and liabilities) it is the other way around. An increase in the account for capital or for a liability will be shown on the right-hand (credit) side and a decrease will be shown on the left-hand (debit) side.

To understand why this difference exists, we should recall from Chapter 2 that the balance sheet equation is:

$$\text{Assets} = \text{Capital} + \text{Liabilities}$$

We can see that assets appear on one side of the equation and capital and liabilities appear on the other. Recording transactions in accounts simply expresses this difference in the recording process. Increases in assets are shown on the left-hand side of an account and increases in capital and liabilities are shown on the right-hand side of the account. We should recall the point made in Chapter 2 that each transaction has two aspects. Thus, when we record a particular transaction, two separate accounts will be affected. Recording transactions in this way is known as double-entry bookkeeping.

It is worth going through a simple example to see how transactions affecting balance sheet items would be recorded under the double-entry bookkeeping system. Suppose a new business started on 1 January with the owner putting £5,000 into a newly opened business bank account, as initial capital. This entry would appear in the cash account as follows:

The corresponding entry would be made in the capital account as follows:

It is usual to show, in each account by way of note, where the other side of the entry will be found. Thus, someone looking at the capital account will know that the £5,000 arose from a receipt of cash. This provides potentially useful information, partly because it establishes a 'trail' that can be followed when checking for errors. Including the date of the transaction provides additional information to the reader of the accounts.

Now suppose that, on 2 January, £600 of the cash is used to buy some inventories. This would affect the cash account as follows:

Cash

	£		£
1 January Capital	5,000	2 January Inventories	600

This cash account, in effect, shows 'positive' cash of £5,000 and 'negative' cash of £600, a net amount of £4,400.

Activity A.1

As you know, we must somehow record the other side of the transaction involving the acquisition of the inventories for £600. See if you can work out what to do in respect of the inventories.

We must open an account for inventories. Since inventories are assets, an increase in it will appear on the left-hand side of the account, as follows:

Inventories

	£		£
2 January Cash	600		

What we have seen so far highlights the key rule of double-entry bookkeeping: each left-hand entry must have a right-hand entry of equal size. Using the jargon, we can say that *every* **debit** *must have a* **credit**.

It might be helpful at this point to make clear that the words 'debit' and 'credit' are no more than accounting jargon for left and right, respectively. Generally, in English (that is when not referring to accounting), people tend to use credit to imply something good and debit something undesirable. Debit and credit have no such implication in accounting. Each transaction requires both a debit entry and a credit one. This is equally true whether the transaction is a 'good' one, like being paid by a credit customer, or a 'bad' one like having to treat a credit customer's balance as worthless because that customer has gone bankrupt.

Recording trading transactions

The rules of double entry also extend to 'trading' transactions – that is, making revenue (sales and so on) and incurring expenses. To understand how these transactions are recorded, we should recall that in Chapter 3 the extended balance sheet equation was set out as follows:

$$Assets = Capital + (Revenues - Expenses) + Liabilities$$

This equation can be re-arranged so that:

$$Assets + Expenses = Capital + Revenues + Liabilities$$

We can see that increases in expenses are shown on the same side as assets and this means that they will be dealt with in the same way for recording purposes. Thus, an increase in an expense, such as wages, will be shown on the left-hand (debit) side of the wages account and a decrease will be shown on the right-hand (credit) side. Increases in revenues are shown on the same side as capital and liabilities and so will be dealt with in the same way. Thus, an increase in revenue, such as sales, will be shown on the right-hand (credit) side and a decrease will be shown on the left hand (debit) side.

To summarise, therefore, we can say that:

- Debits (left-hand entries) represent increases in assets and expenses and decreases in claims and revenues.
- Credits (right-hand entries) represent increases in claims and revenues and decreases in assets and expenses.

Let us continue with our example by assuming that on 3 January, the business paid £900 to rent business premises for the three months to 31 March. To record this transaction, we should normally open a 'rent account' and make entries in this account and in the cash account as follows:

Rent

		£			£
3 January	Cash	900			

Cash

		£			£
1 January	Capital	5,000	2 January	Inventories	600
			3 January	Rent	900

The fact that assets and expenses are dealt with in the same way should not be altogether surprising since assets and expenses are closely linked. Assets actually transform into expenses as they are 'used up'. Rent, which, as here, is usually paid in advance, is an asset when it is first paid. It represents the value to the business of being entitled to occupy the premises for the forthcoming period (until 31 March in this case). As the three months progress, this asset becomes an expense; it is 'used up'. We need to remember that the debit entry in the rent account does not necessarily represent either an asset or an expense; it could be a mixture of the two. Strictly, by the end of the day on which it was paid (3 January), £30 would have represented an expense for the three days; the remaining £280 would have been an asset. As each day passes, an additional £10 (that is, £900/90 (there are 90 days in January, February and March altogether)) will transform from an asset into an expense. As we have already seen, it is not necessary for us to make any adjustment to the rent account as the days pass.

Assume, now, that on 5 January the business sold inventories costing £200 for £300 on credit. As usual, when we are able to identify the cost of the inventories sold at the time of sale, we need to deal with the sale and the cost of sales as two separate issues, each having its own set of debits and credits.

Firstly, let us deal with the sale. We now need to open accounts for both 'sales revenue' and 'trade receivables' – which do not, as yet, exist. The sale gives rise to an increase in revenue and so there is a credit entry in the sales revenue account. The sale also creates an asset of trade receivables and so there is debit entry in trade receivables:

Sales revenue

	£			£
		5 January	Trade receivables	300

Trade receivables

	£		£
5 January Sales revenue	300		

Let us now deal with the inventories sold. Since the inventories sold have become the expense 'cost of sales', we need to reduce the figure on the inventories account by making a credit entry and to make the corresponding debit in a 'cost of sales' account, opened for the purpose:

Inventories

	£			£
2 January Cash	600	5 January	Cost of sales	200

Cost of sales

	£		£
5 January Inventories	200		

We shall now look at the other transactions for our hypothetical business for the remainder of January. These can be taken to be as follows:

January 8   Bought some inventories on credit costing £800
January 11   Bought some office furniture for £600 cash
January 15   Sold inventories costing £600 for £900, on credit
January 18   Received £800 from trade receivables
January 21   Paid trade payables £500
January 24   Paid wages for the month £400
January 27   Bought inventories on credit for £800
January 31   Borrowed £2,000 from the Commercial Finance Company

Naturally, we shall have to open several additional accounts to enable us to record all of these transactions in any meaningful way. By the end of January, the set of accounts would appear as follows:

Cash

		£			£
1 January	Capital	5,000	2 January	Inventories	600
18 January	Trade receivables	800	3 January	Rent	900
31 January	Comm. Fin Co	2,000	11 January	Office furniture	600
			21 January	Trade payables	500
			24 January	Wages	400

Capital

		£			£
			1 January	Cash	5,000

Inventories

		£			£
2 January	Cash	600	5 January	Cost of sales	200
8 January	Trade payables	800	15 January	Cost of sales	600
27 January	Trade payables	800			

Rent

		£		£
3 January	Cash	900		

Sales revenue

	£			£
		5 January	Trade receivables	300
		15 January	Trade receivables	900

Trade receivables

		£			£
5 January	Sales revenue	300	18 January	Cash	800
15 January	Sales revenue	900			

Cost of sales

		£		£
5 January	Inventories	200		
15 January	Inventories	600		

Trade payables

		£			£
21 January	Cash	500	8 January	Inventories	800
			27 January	Inventories	800

Office furniture

	£		£
11 January Cash	600		

Wages

	£		£
24 January Cash	400		

Borrowings – Commercial Finance Company

	£		£
		31 January Cash	2,000

All of the transactions from 8 January onwards are quite similar in nature to those up to that date, which we discussed in detail, and so we should be able to follow them using the date references as a guide.

Balancing accounts and the trial balance

Businesses keeping their accounts in the way shown would find it helpful to summarise their individual accounts periodically – perhaps weekly or monthly – for two reasons:

● to be able to see at a glance how much is in each account (for example, to see how much cash the business has left);
● to help to check the accuracy of the bookkeeping so far.

Let us look at the cash account again.

Cash

		£			£
1 January	Capital	5,000	2 January	Inventories	600
18 January	Trade receivables	800	3 January	Rent	900
31 January	Comm. Fin. Co.	2,000	11 January	Office furniture	600
			21 January	Trade payables	500
			24 January	Wages	400

Does this account tell us how much cash the business has at 31 January? The answer is partly yes and partly no!

We do not have a single figure showing the cash **balance** but we can fairly easily deduce this by adding up the debit (receipts) column and deducting the sum of the credit (payments) column. However, it would be better if a cash balance were provided for us.

To summarise or balance this account, we add up the column with the largest amount (in this case, the debit side) and put this total on *both* sides of the account. We then put in, on the credit side, the figure that will make that side add up to the total that appears in the account. We cannot put in this balancing figure only once, as the double-entry rule would be broken. Thus, to preserve the double entry, we also put it in on the other side of the same account below the totals, as follows:

Cash

		£			£
1 January	Capital	5,000	2 January	Inventories	600
18 January	Trade receivables	800	3 January	Rent	900
31 January	Borrowings	2,000	11 January	Office furniture	600
			21 January	Trade payables	500
			24 January	Wages	400
			31 January		
				Balance carried down	4,800
		7,800			7,800
1 February					
	Balance brought down	4,800			

Note that the balance carried down (usually abbreviated to 'c/d') at the end of one period becomes the balance brought down ('b/d') at the beginning of the next. Now we can see at a glance what the present cash position is, without having to do any mental arithmetic.

Activity A.2

Try balancing the inventories account and then say what we know about the inventories position at the end of January.

The inventories account will be balanced as follows:

Inventories

		£			£
2 January	Cash	600	5 January	Cost of sales	200
8 January	Trade payables	800	15 January	Cost of sales	600
27 January	Trade payables	800	31 January	Balance c/d	1,400
		2,200			2,200
1 February	Balance b/d	1,400			

We can see at a glance that the business held inventories that had cost £1,400 at the end of January. We can also see quite easily how this situation arose.

We can balance all of the other accounts in a similar fashion. However, there is no point in formally balancing accounts that have only one entry at the moment (for example, the capital account) because we cannot summarise one figure; it is already in as summarised a form as it can be. After balancing, the remaining accounts will be as follows:

Capital

	£			£
		1 January	Cash	5,000

Rent

	£		£
3 January Cash	900		

Sales revenue

	£		£
31 January Balance c/d	1,200	5 January Trade receivables	300
		15 January Trade receivables	900
	1,200		1,200
		1 February Balance b/d	1,200

Trade receivables

	£		£
5 January Sales revenue	300	18 January Cash	800
15 January Sales revenue	900	31 January Balance c/d	400
	1,200		1,200
1 February Balance b/d	400		

Cost of sales

	£		£
5 January Inventories	200	31 January Balance c/d	800
15 January Inventories	600		
	800		800
1 February Balance b/d	800		

Trade payables

	£		£
21 January Cash	500	8 January Inventories	800
31 January Balance c/d	1,100	27 January Inventories	800
	1,600		1,600
		1 February Balance b/d	1,100

Office furniture

	£		£
11 January Cash	600		

Wages

	£		£
24 January Cash	400		

Borrowings – Commercial Finance Company

	£		£
		31 January Cash	2,000

Activity A.3

If we now separately total the debit balances and the credit balances, what should we expect to find?

We should expect to find that these two totals are equal. This must, in theory be true since every debit entry was matched by an equally sized credit entry.

Let us see if our expectation in Activity A.3 works in our example, by listing the debit and credit balances as follows:

	Debits £	Credits £
Cash	4,800	
Inventories	1,400	
Capital		5,000
Rent	900	
Sales revenue		1,200
Trade receivables	400	
Cost of sales	800	
Trade payables		1,100
Office furniture	600	
Wages	400	
Borrowings		2,000
	9,300	9,300

This statement is known as a **trial balance**. The fact that it agrees gives us *some* indication that we have not made bookkeeping errors.

This situation, does not, however, give us total confidence that no error could have occurred. Consider the transaction that took place on 3 January (paid rent for the month of £900). In each of the following cases, all of which would be wrong, the trial balance would still have agreed:

● The transaction was completely omitted from the accounts; that is, no entries were made at all.
● The amount was misread as £9,000 but then (correctly) debited to the rent account and credited to cash.
● The correct amount was (incorrectly) debited to cash and credited to rent.

Nevertheless, a trial balance that agrees does give some confidence that accounts have been correctly written up.

Activity A.4

Why do you think the words 'debtor' and 'creditor' are used to describe those who owe money or are owed money by a business?

The answer simply is that debtors have a debit balance (that is, a balance brought down on the debit side) in the books of the business, whereas creditors have a credit balance.

Preparing the financial statements (final accounts)

If the trial balance agrees and we are confident that there are no errors in recording, the next stage is to prepare the income statement and balance sheet. Preparing the income statement is simply a matter of going through the individual accounts, identifying those amounts that represent revenue and expenses of the period, and transferring them to the income statement, which is itself part of the double-entry system.

We shall now do this for the example we have been using. The situation is complicated slightly for three reasons:

1 As we know, the £900 rent paid during January relates to the three months January, February and March.
2 The business's owner estimates that the electricity used during January is about £110. There is no bill yet from the electricity supply business because they normally only bill customers at the end of each three-month period.
3 The business's owner believes that the office furniture should be depreciated by 20 per cent each year (straight line).

These three factors need to be taken into account. As we shall see, however, the end-of-period adjustments of these types are very easily handled in double-entry accounts. Let us deal with these three areas first.

The rent account will appear as follow, after we have completed the transfer to the income statement:

Rent

		£			£
3 January	Cash	900	31 January	Income statement	300
				Balance c/d	600
		900			900
1 February	Balance b/d	600			

At 31 January, because two months' rent is still an asset, this is carried down as a debit balance. The remainder (representing January's rent) is credited to the rent account and debited to a newly opened income statement. As we shall shortly see, the £600 debit balance remaining will appear in the 31 January balance sheet.

Now let us deal with the electricity. The electricity account will be as follows following the transfer to the income statement:

Electricity

	£			£
		31 January	Income statement	110

Because there has been no cash payment or other transaction recorded so far for electricity, we do not already have an account for it. It is necessary to open one. We need to debit the income statement with the £110 of electricity used during January and credit the electricity account with the same amount. At 31 January, this credit balance reflects the amount owed by this business to the electricity supplier. Once again, we shall shortly see that this balance will appear on the balance sheet.

Next we shall consider what is necessary regarding the office furniture. The depreciation for the month will be 20% × £600 × $^1/_{12}$, that is £10. Normal accounting practice is to charge (debit) this to the income statement, with the corresponding credit going to a 'provision for depreciation of office furniture' account. The latter entry will appear as follows:

Provision for depreciation of office furniture account

	£			£
		31 January	Income statement	10

This £10 balance will be reflected in the balance sheet at 31 January by being deducted from the office furniture itself, as we shall see.

The balances on the following accounts represent straightforward revenue and expenses for the month of January:

- sales revenue
- cost of sales
- wages.

The balances on these accounts will simply be transferred to the income statement.

To transfer balances to the income statement, we simply debit or credit the account concerned, such that any balance amount is eliminated, and make the corresponding credit or debit in the income statement. Take sales revenue, for example. This has a credit balance (because the balance represents a revenue). We must debit the sales revenue account with £1,200 and credit the income statement with the same amount. So a credit balance on the sales revenue account becomes a credit entry in the income statement. For the three accounts, then, we have the following:

Sales revenue

		£			£
31 January	Balance c/d	1,200	5 January	Trade receivables	300
			15 January	Trade receivables	900
		1,200			1,200
31 January	Income statement	1,200	1 February	Balance b/d	1,200

Cost of Sales

		£			£
5 January	Inventories	200	31 January	Balance c/d	800
15 January	Inventories	600			
		800			800
1 February	Balance b/d	800	31 January	Income statement	800

Wages

		£			£
24 January	Cash	400	31 January	Income statement	400

The income statement will now look as follows:

Income statement

		£			£
31 January	Cost of sales	800	31 January	Sales revenue	1,200
31 January	Rent	300			
31 January	Wages	400			
31 January	Electricity	110			
31 January	Depreciation	10			

We must now transfer the balance on the income statement (a debit balance of £420).

Activity A.5

What does the balance on the income statement represent, and to where should it be transferred?

The balance is either the profit or the loss for the period. In this case it is a loss as the total expenses exceed the total revenue. This loss must be borne by the owner, and it must therefore be transferred to the capital account.

The two accounts would now appear as follows:

Income statement

		£			£
31 January	Cost of sales	800	31 January	Sales revenue	1,200
31 January	Rent	300			
31 January	Wages	400			
31 January	Electricity	110			
31 January	Depreciation	10	31 January	Capital (loss)	420
		1,620			1,620

Capital

		£			£
31 January	Income statement (loss)	420	1 January	Cash	5,000
31 January	Balance c/d	4,580			
		5,000			5,000
			1 February	Balance b/d	4,580

The last thing done was to balance the capital account.

Now all of the balances remaining on accounts represent either assets or claims as at 31 January. These balances can now be used to produce a balance sheet, as follows:

Balance sheet as at 31 January

	£
Non-current assets	
Property, plant and equipment	
Office furniture: cost	600
depreciation	(10)
	590
Current assets	
Inventories	1,400
Prepaid expense	600
Trade receivables	400
Cash	4,800
	7,200
Total assets	7,790
Capital	4,580
Non-current liability	
Borrowings	2,000
Current liabilities	
Accrued expense	110
Trade payables	1,100
	1,210
Total equity and liabilities	7,790

The income statement could be written in a more stylish manner, for reporting to users, as follows:

Income statement for the month ended 31 January

	£
Sales revenue	1,200
Cost of sales	(800)
Gross profit	400
Rent	(300)
Wages	(400)
Electricity	(110)
Depreciation	(10)
Loss for the month	(420)

The ledger and its division

The book in which the accounts are traditionally kept is known as the **ledger** and 'accounts' are sometimes referred to as 'ledger accounts', even where they are computerised.

In a handwritten accounting system, the ledger is often divided into various sections. This tends to be for two main reasons:

1 Having all of the accounts in one book means that it is only possible for one person at a time to use the accounts, either to make entries or to extract useful information.
2 Dividing the ledger along logical grounds can allow specialisation, so that various individual members of the accounts staff can look after their own part of the system. This can lead to more efficient record keeping. It can also lead to greater security,

that is less risk of error and fraud by limiting an individual's access to only part of the entire set of accounts.

There are no clear, universal rules on the division of the ledger, but the following division is fairly common:

- *The cash book.* This tends to be all of the accounts relating to cash either loose or in the bank.
- *The sales (or trade receivables) ledger.* This contains the accounts of all of the business's individual trade receivables.
- *The purchases (or trade payables) ledger.* This consists of the accounts of all of the business's individual trade payables.
- *The nominal ledger.* These accounts tend to be those of expenses and revenue, for example, sales revenue, wages, rent, and so on.
- *The general ledger.* This contains the remainder of the business's accounts, mainly those to do with non-current assets and long-term finance.

Summary

The main points in this appendix may be summarised as follows:

Double-entry bookkeeping = a system for keeping accounting records by hand, such that a relatively large volume of transactions can be handled effectively and accurately.

- A separate account for each asset, claim, expense and liability that needs to be separately identified.
- Each account looks like a letter T.
- Left-hand (debit) side of the account records increases in assets and expenses and decreases in revenues and claims.
- Right-hand (credit) side records increases in revenues and claims and decreases in assets and expenses.
- There is an equal credit entry in one account for a debit entry in another.
- Double-entry bookkeeping can be used to record day-to-day transactions.
- Double entry can also be used to generate the income statement.
- Balance sheet is a list of the net figure (the 'balance') on each of the accounts after appropriate transfers have been made to the income statement.
- The accounts are traditionally kept in a 'ledger' a term that persists even with computerised accounting.
- The ledger is traditionally broken down into several sections, each containing particular types of account.

→ Key terms

Double-entry bookkeeping p. 373	**Balance** p. 378
Account p. 373	**Trial balance** p. 381
Debit p. 373	**Ledger** p. 385
Credit p. 373	

Further reading

If you would like to explore the topics covered in this appendix in more depth, we recommend the following books:

Dodge, R. (1997) *Foundations of Business Accounting*, 2nd edn, Thomson Business Press, Chapter 3.

Thomas, A. (2005) *An Introduction to Financial Accounting*, 5th edn, McGraw-Hill, Chapters 3 to 8.

Benedict, A. and Elliott, B. (2007) *Practical Accounting*, Financial Times Prentice Hall, Chapters 2 to 5.

Bebbington, J., Gray, R. and Laughlin, R. (2001) *Financial Accounting*, 3rd edn, Thomson Learning, Chapters 2 to 7.

Exercises

The answers to all three of these exercises are at the back of the book, starting on p. 444.

A.1   In respect of each of the following transactions, state in which two accounts must an entry be made and whether the entry is a debit or a credit. (For example, if the transaction were buying inventories for cash, the answer would be debit the inventories account and credit the cash account.)

(a)   Bought inventories on credit.
(b)   Owner made cash drawings.
(c)   Paid interest on business borrowings.
(d)   Bought inventories for cash.
(e)   Received cash from a credit customer.
(f)   Paid wages to employees.
(g)   The owner received some cash from a credit customer, which was taken as drawings rather than being paid into the business's bank account.
(h)   Paid a credit supplier.
(i)   Paid electricity bill.
(j)   Made cash sales.

A.2   (a)   Record the following transactions in a set of double-entry accounts:

1 February	Lee (the owner) put £6,000 into a newly opened business bank account to start a new business
3 February	Bought inventories for £2,600 for cash
5 February	Bought some equipment (non-current asset) for cash for £800
6 February	Bought inventories costing £3,000 on credit
9 February	Paid rent for the month of £250
10 February	Paid fuel and electricity for the month of £240
11 February	Paid general expenses of £200
15 February	Sold inventories for £4,000 in cash; the inventories had cost £2,400
19 February	Sold inventories for £3,800 on credit; the inventories had cost £2,300
21 February	Lee withdrew £1,000 in cash for personal use
25 February	Paid £2,000 to trade payables
28 February	Received £2,500 from trade receivables

(b)   Balance the relevant accounts and prepare a trial balance (making sure that it agrees).
(c)   Prepare an income statement for the month and a balance sheet at the month end. Assume that there are no prepaid or accrued expenses at the end of the month and ignore any possible depreciation.

A.3   The following is the balance sheet of David's business at 1 January of last year.

	£		£
Non-current assets		**Capital (owner's equity)**	25,050
Property, plant and equipment			
Buildings	25,000	**Non-current liability**	
Fittings: cost	10,000	Borrowings	12,000
dep'n	(2,000) 8,000		
Current assets		**Current liabilities**	
Inventories of stationery	140	Trade payables	1,690
Trading inventories	1,350	Accrued electricity	270
Prepaid rent	500		
Trade receivables	1,840		
Cash	2,180		
Total assets	39,010	**Total equity and liabilities**	39,010

The following is a summary of the transactions that took place during the year:

1 Inventories were bought on credit for £17,220.
2 Inventories were bought for £3,760 cash.
3 Credit sales revenue amounted to £33,100 (cost £15,220).
4 Cash sales revenue amounted to £10,360 (cost £4,900).
5 Wages of £3,770 were paid.
6 Rent of £3,000 was paid. The annual rental amounts to £3,000.
7 Electricity of £1,070 was paid.
8 General expenses of £580 were paid.
9 Additional fittings were purchased on 1 January for £2,000. The cash for this was raised from additional borrowings of this amount. The interest rate is 10 per cent a year, the same as for the existing borrowings.
10 £1,000 of the borrowing was repaid on 30 June.
11 Cash received from trade receivables amounted to £32,810.
12 Cash paid to trade payables amounted to £18,150.
13 The owner withdrew £10,400 cash and £560 inventories for private use.

At the end of the year it was found that:

(a) The electricity bill for the last quarter of the year for £290 had not been paid.
(b) Trade receivables amounting to £260 were unlikely to be received.
(c) The value of stationery remaining was estimated at £150. Stationery is included in general expenses.
(d) The borrowings carried interest of 10 per cent a year and was unpaid at the year end.
(e) Depreciation to be taken at 20 per cent on the cost of the fittings owned at the year end. Buildings are not depreciated.

***Required*:**
1 Open ledger accounts and bring down all of the balances in the opening balance sheet.
2 Make entries to record the transactions 1 to 13 (above), opening any additional accounts as necessary.
3 Open an income statement (part of the double entry, remember). Make the necessary entries for the items a to e (above) and the appropriate transfers to the income statement.
4 List the remaining balances in the same form as the opening balance sheet (above).

Appendix B
Glossary of key terms

Account A section of a double-entry bookkeeping system that deals with one particular asset, claim, expense or revenue. *p. 373*

Accounting The process of identifying, measuring and communicating information to permit informed judgements and decisions by users of the information. *p. 2*

Accounting conventions Accounting rules that have evolved over time in order to deal with practical problems rather than to reflect some theoretical ideal. *p. 48*

Accounting information system The system used within a business to identify, record, analyse and report accounting information. *p. 10*

Accounting (financial reporting) standards See financial reporting standards. *p. 148*

Accruals accounting The system of accounting that follows the accruals convention. This is the system followed in drawing up the balance sheet and income statement. *p. 80*

Accruals convention The convention of accounting that asserts that profit is the excess of revenue over expenses, not the excess of cash receipts over cash payments. *p. 80*

Accrued expense An expense that is outstanding at the end of an accounting period. *p. 76*

Acid test ratio A liquidity ratio that relates the current assets (less inventories) to the current liabilities. *p. 223*

Allotted share capital *See* Issued share capital. *p. 123*

Allowance for trade receivables An amount set aside out of profit to provide for anticipated losses arising from debts (trade receivables) that may prove irrecoverable. *p. 96*

Asset A resource held by a business, that has certain characteristics. *p. 34*

Associate company A company over which considerable influence, but not full control, may be exercised by another company. *p. 309*

Audit committee A committee of the board of directors, comprising of non-executive directors, that is charged with ensuring that financial reporting and internal control principles are properly applied and for maintaining an appropriate relationship with the external auditors. *p. 327*

Auditor A professional whose main duty is to make a report as to whether, in his or her opinion, the financial statements of a company do that which they are supposed to do, namely show a true and fair view and comply with statutory, and financial reporting standard, requirements. *p. 153*

Average settlement period for trade payables ratio   The average time taken for a business to pay its trade payables. *p. 217*

Average settlement period for trade receivables ratio   The average time taken for trade receivables to pay the amounts owing. *p. 216*

Average inventories turnover period   An efficiency ratio that measures the average period for which inventories are held by a business. *p. 215*

Bad debt   An amount owed to the business that is considered to be irrecoverable. *p. 95*

Balance   The net of the debit and credit totals in an account in a double-entry book-keeping system. *p. 378*

Balance sheet   A statement of financial position that shows the assets of a business and the claims on those assets. *p. 30*

Bonus issue   Reserves that are converted into shares and given 'free' to shareholders. *p. 122*

Bonus shares   *See* Bonus issue. *p. 122*

Business entity convention   The convention that holds that, for accounting purposes, the business and its owner(s) are treated as quite separate and distinct. *p. 48*

Called-up share capital   That part of a company's share capital for which the shareholders have been asked to pay the agreed amount. It is part of the claim of the owners against the business. *p. 124*

Capital   The owner's claim on the assets of the business. *p. 36*

Capital reserve   A reserve that arises from an unrealised 'capital' profits or gains rather than from normal realised trading activities. *p. 119*

Carrying amount   The difference between the cost (or fair value) of a non-current asset and the accumulated depreciation relating to the asset. The carrying amount is also referred to as the 'written down value' (WDV) and the 'net book value' (NBV). *p. 83*

Cash flow   The movement of cash in and out of the business. *p. 36*

Cash flow statement   A statement that shows the sources and uses of cash for a period. *p. 30*

Cash generated from operations per ordinary share ratio   An investment ratio that relates the cash generated from operations and available to ordinary shareholders to the number of ordinary shares. *p. 245*

Cash generated from operations to maturing obligations ratio   A liquidity ratio that compares the cash generated from operations to the current liabilities of the business. *p. 223*

Chairman   The director who is appointed to lead the board of directors. *p. 323*

Chief executive officer   The director who is appointed to lead the management team. *p. 327*

Claims   Obligations on the part of a business to provide cash or some other benefit to outside parties. *p. 34*

Combined Code   A code of practice for companies listed on the London Stock Exchange that deals with corporate governance matters. *p. 323*

Common-size financial statements   Normal financial statements (such as the income statement, balance sheet and cash flow statement) that are expressed in terms of some base figure. *p. 254*

Comparability   The requirement that items, which are basically the same, should be treated in the same manner for measurement and reporting purposes. Lack of comparability will limit the usefulness of accounting information. *p. 7*

Consistency convention   The accounting convention that holds that, when a particular method of accounting is selected to deal with a transaction, this method should be applied consistently over time. *p. 94*

Consolidated financial statements   *See* Group financial statements. *p. 133, 283*

Consolidating   Reducing the number of shares by increasing their nominal value. *p. 121*

Conventions of accounting   The generally accepted rules that accountants tend to follow when preparing financial statements. *p. 14*

Corporate governance   The process of directing and controlling a company. *p. 116*

Corporation tax   Taxation that a limited company is liable to pay on its profits. *p. 115*

Cost of sales   The cost of the goods sold during a period. Cost of sales can be derived by adding the opening inventories held to the inventories purchases for the period and then deducting the closing inventories held. *p. 68*

Creative accounting   Adopting accounting policies to achieve a particular view of performance and position that preparers would like users to see rather than what is a true and fair view. *p. 163*

Credit   An entry made in the right-hand side of an account in double-entry bookkeeping. *p. 373*

Current assets   Assets that are held for the short-term. They include cash itself and other assets that are held for sale or consumption in the normal course of a business's operating cycle. *p. 42*

Current liabilities   Claims against the business which are expect to be settled within the normal course of the business's operating cycle or within 12 months of the balance sheet date or they are held primarily for trading purposes; and the business does not have the right to defer settlement beyond 12 months after the balance sheet date. *p. 44*

Current ratio   A liquidity ratio that relates the current assets of the business to the current liabilities. *p. 222*

Debit   An entry made in the left-hand side of an account in double-entry bookkeeping. *p. 373*

Depreciation   A measure of that portion of the cost (or fair value) of a non-current asset that has been consumed during an accounting period. *p. 80*

Direct method   An approach to deducing the cash flows from operating activities, in a cash flow statement, by analysing the business's cash records. *p. 182*

Director   An individual who is appointed (normally by being elected) to act as the most senior level of management of a company. *p. 116*

Directors' report   A report containing information of a financial and non-financial nature that the directors must produce as part of the annual financial report to shareholders. *p. 154*

Directors' share options   The right given to directors to buy equity shares in their company at an agreed price. This right will only be exercised if the value of the shares exceeds the agreed price at the time that the right may be exercised. *p. 355*

Discriminate function   A boundary line, produced by multiple discriminate analysis, which can be used to identify those businesses that are likely to suffer financial distress and those that are not. *p. 261*

Dividend   The transfer of assets (usually cash) made by a company to its shareholders. *p. 117*

Dividend cover ratio   An investment ratio that relates the earnings available for dividends to the dividend announced, to indicate how many times the former covers the latter. *p. 244*

Dividend payout ratio   An investment ratio that relates the dividends announced for the period to the earnings available for dividends that were generated in that period. *p. 243*

Dividend per share   An investment ratio that relates the dividends announced for a period to the number of shares in issue. *p. 244*

Dividend yield ratio   An investment ratio that relates the cash return from a share to its current market value. *p. 244*

Double-entry bookkeeping   A system for recording financial transactions where each transaction is recorded twice, once as a debit and once as a credit. *p. 373*

Dual aspect convention   The accounting convention that holds that each transaction has two aspects and that each aspect must be recorded in the financial statements. *p. 50*

Earnings per share   An investment ratio that relates the earnings generated by the business during a period, and available to shareholders, to the number of shares in issue. *p. 245*

Economic value added (EVA®)   A measure of business performance that concentrates on wealth generation. It is based on economic profit rather than accounting profit and takes full account of the costs of financing. *p. 351*

Equity   Ordinary shares and reserves of a company. *p. 116*

Executive committee   A committee of the board of directors comprising the executive directors and normally chaired by the chief executive officer. The committee may be given the task of developing and implementing the strategic plan of the company. *p. 327*

Executive directors   Directors that normally work for the company on a full-time basis and have executive responsibilities for certain key business functions, such as finance, marketing and so on. *p. 323*

Expense   A measure of the outflow of assets (or increase in liabilities) incurred as a result of generating revenue. *p. 65*

External audit   An independent examination of the accounting records to see whether the financial statements provide a true and fair view of the state of affairs of the company and comply with legal and other regulatory requirements. The person conducting this examination will express an opinion, which is contained within an audit report and which becomes part of the published annual reports. *p. 336*

Fair values   The value ascribed to assets as an alternative to historic cost. They are usually the current market value (that is, the exchange values in arm's-length transactions). *p. 54, 301*

Final accounts   The income statement, cash flow statement and balance sheet taken together. *p. 33*

Financial accounting   The measuring and reporting of accounting information for external users (those users other than the managers of the business). *p. 12*

Financial gearing   The existence of fixed payment-bearing sources of finance (for example, borrowings) in the capital structure of a business. *p. 226*

First in, first out (FIFO)   A method of inventories costing, which assumes that the earliest acquired inventories are used (in production or sales) first. *p. 90*

Framework of principles   The main principles that underpin accounting, which can help in identifying best practice and in developing accounting rules. *p. 152*

Fully paid shares   Shares on which the shareholders have paid the full issue price. *p. 124*

Gearing ratio   A ratio that relates the contribution of finance that required a fixed return (such as borrowings) to the total long-term finance of the business. *p. 229*

Going concern convention   The accounting convention that holds that it is assumed that the business will continue operations for the foreseeable future, unless there is reason to believe otherwise. In other words, there is no intention, or need, to liquidate the business. *p. 50*

Goodwill arising on consolidation   Anything paid in excess of the underlying net asset value of the subsidiary's shares. *p. 290*

Gross profit   The amount remaining (if positive) after trading expenses (for example, cost of sales) have been deducted from trading revenue. *p. 68*

Gross profit margin ratio   A profitability ratio relating the gross profit to the sales revenue for a period. *p. 213*

Group balance sheet   A balance sheet for a group of companies, prepared from the perspective of the parent company's shareholders. *p. 283*

Group cash flow statement   A cash flow statement for a group of companies, prepared from the perspective of the parent company's shareholders. *p. 307*

Group financial statements   Sets of financial accounting statements that combine the performance and position of a group of companies under common control. *p. 133, 275*

Group income statement   An income statement for a group of companies, prepared from the perspective of the parent company's shareholders. *p. 305*

Group of companies   A situation that arises where one company is able to exercise control over another or others. *p. 275*

Historic cost   What was paid for an asset cost when it was originally acquired. *p. 48*

Historic cost convention   The accounting convention that holds that assets should be recorded at their historic (acquisition) cost. *p. 48*

Holding company   See Parent company. *p. 133, 275*

Horizontal analysis   An approach to common-size financial statements where all the figures in equivalent statements over time are expressed in relation to an equivalent figure for the base period (year, month and so on). So, for example, the sales revenue figure for each year will be expressed in terms of the sales revenue figure for the base year. *p. 257*

Income statement   A financial statement (also known as *profit and loss account*) that measures and reports the profit (or loss) the business has generated during a period. It is derived by deducting from total revenue for a period, the total expenses associated with that revenue. *p. 30, 65*

Indirect method   An approach to deducing the cash flows from operating activities, in a cash flow statement, by analysing the business's financial statements. *p. 182*

Intangible assets   Assets that do not have a physical substance (for example, patents, goodwill and trade receivables). *p. 36*

Interest cover ratio   A gearing ratio that divides the operating profit (that is, profit before interest and taxation) by the interest payable for a period. *p. 229*

Internal audit   Investigations carried out by employees of the company to provide the directors with reassurance concerning the reliability of the company's control and financial reporting systems. *p. 337*

International Financial Reporting Standards   Transnational accounting rules that have been adopted, or developed, by the International Accounting Standards Board and which should be followed in preparing the published financial statements of listed limited companies. *p. 144*

Issued share capital   That part of the share capital that has been issued to shareholders. Also known as allotted share capital. *p. 123*

Last in, first out (LIFO)   A method of inventories costing, which assumes the most recently acquired inventories are used (in production or sales) first. *p. 90*

Ledger   The book in which accounts are traditionally kept. *p. 385*

Liabilities   Claims of individuals and organisations, apart from the owner, that have arisen from past transactions or events such as supplying goods or lending money to the business. *p. 37*

Limited company   An artificial legal person that has an identity separate from that of those who own and manage it. *p. 18, 109*

Limited liability   The restriction of the legal obligation of shareholders to meet all of the company's debts. *p. 111*

Loan notes   Long-term borrowings usually made by limited companies. *p. 124*

Management accounting   The measuring and reporting of accounting information for the managers of a business. *p. 12*

Margin of safety   The extent to which the equity investment in a company provides security for creditors. *p. 128*

Matching convention The accounting convention that holds that, in measuring income, expenses should be matched to revenue, which they helped generate in the same accounting period as that revenue was realised. *p. 75*

Materiality The requirement that material information should be disclosed to users in financial statements. *p. 7*

Materiality convention The accounting convention that states that, where the amounts involved are immaterial, only what is expedient should be considered. *p. 79*

Minority interests That part of the net assets of a subsidiary company that is financed by shareholders other than the parent company. Also known as 'outsiders' interests'. *p. 288*

Mission statement A statement made by an organisation that expresses its ultimate purpose. *p. 21*

Multiple discriminate analysis A statistical technique that can be used to predict financial distress; it involves using an index based on a combination of financial ratios. *p. 261*

Negative goodwill arising on consolidation The amount by which the underlying net asset value of the subsidiary's shares exceeds the amount paid for the shares. *p. 290*

Net profit The amount remaining (if positive) after the total expenses have been deducted from total revenue. *p. 68*

Nominal value The face value of a share in a company. (Also called *par value*.) *p. 117*

Nomination committee A committee of the board of directors, comprising of a majority of independent, non-executive directors, that is charged with leading the process for nominating new directors. *p. 327*

Non-current assets Assets held that do not meet the criteria of current assets. They are held for the long-term operations of the business rather than continuously circulating within the business. Non-current assets can be seen as the tools of the business. (Also known as *fixed assets*.) *p. 43*

Non-current liabilities Those amounts due to other parties that are not current liabilities. *p. 44*

Non-executive directors Directors that normally work for the company on a part-time basis and who do not have executive responsibilities but nevertheless have the same legal obligations towards the shareholders as executive directors. *p. 323*

Operating and financial review A narrative report that helps users to understand the operating and financial results of a business for a period. *p. 158*

Operating cash cycle (OCC) The period between the outlay of cash to buy supplies and the ultimate receipt of cash from the sale of goods. *p. 224*

Operating profit The profit achieved during a period after all operating expenses have been deducted from revenues from operations. Financing expenses are deducted after the calculation of operating profit. *p. 68, 131*

Operating profit margin ratio A profitability ratio relating the operating profit to the sales revenue for the period. *p. 212*

Ordinary shares Shares of a company owned by those who are due the benefits of the company's activities after all other stakeholders have been satisfied. *p. 117*

Overtrading   The situation arising when a business is operating at a level of activity which cannot be supported by the amount of finance that has been committed. *p. 255*

Paid-up share capital   That part of the share capital of a company that has been called and paid. *p. 124*

Par value   *See* Nominal value. *p. 117*

Parent/holding company   A company that has a controlling interest in another company. *p. 133, 275*

Partnership   A form of business unit where there are at least two individuals, but usually no more than twenty, carrying on a business with the intention of making a profit. *p. 17*

Preference shares   Shares of a company owned by those who are entitled to the first part of any dividend that the company may pay. *p. 118*

Prepaid expenses   Expenses that have been paid in advance at the end of the accounting period. *p. 78*

Price/earnings ratio   An investment ratio that relates the market value of a share to the earnings per share. *p. 246*

Private company   A limited company that cannot offer its shares for sale to the general public. *p. 111*

Private placing   An issue of shares that involves a limited company arranging for the shares to be sold to the clients of particular issuing houses or stockbrokers, rather than to the general investing public. *p. 124*

Profit   The increase in wealth attributable to the owners of a business that arises through business operations. *p. 65*

Profit and loss account   See *income statement.*

Property, plant and equipment   Non-current assets that have a physical substance (for example, plant and machinery, motor vehicles). *p. 54*

Prudence convention   The accounting convention that holds that financial statements should err on the side of caution. *p. 49*

Public company   A limited company that can offer its shares for sale to the general public. *p. 111*

Reducing-balance method   A method of calculating depreciation that applies a fixed percentage rate of depreciation to the carrying amount of an asset in each period. *p. 83*

Relevance   The ability of accounting information to influence decisions; regarded as a key characteristic of useful accounting information. *p. 6*

Reliability   The requirement that accounting information should be free from significant errors or bias and should represent what it purports to represent. Reliability is regarded as a key characteristic of useful accounting information. *p. 6*

Remuneration committee   A committee of the board of directors, comprising of independent, non-executive directors, that is charged with the task of setting the pay and benefits for the executive directors and the chairman. *p. 327*

Reserves   Part of the owners' claim (equity) on a limited company that has arisen from profits and gains, to the extent that these have not been distributed to the shareholders or reduced by losses. *p. 116*

Residual value   The amount for which a non-current asset is sold when the business has no further use for it. *p. 82*

Return on capital employed (ROCE) ratio   A profitability ratio expressing the relationship between the operating profit (that is, profit before interest and taxation) and the long-term funds (equity and borrowings) invested in the business. *p. 211*

Return on ordinary shareholders' funds (ROSF) ratio   A profitability ratio that compares the amount of profit for the period available to the ordinary shareholders with their stake in the business. *p. 210*

Revenue   A measure of the inflow of assets (for example, cash or amounts owed to a business by credit customers), or a reduction in liabilities, arising as a result of trading operations. *p. 65*

Revenue reserve   Part of the owners' claim (equity) of a company that arises from realised profits and gains, including after-tax trading profits and gains from disposals of non-current assets. *p. 117*

Rights issue   An issue of shares for cash to existing shareholders on the basis of the number of shares already held. *p. 124*

Risk management committee   A committee of the board of directors that is charged with reviewing the adequacy and effectiveness of the company's risk management procedures. *p. 327*

Sales revenue per employee ratio   An efficiency ratio that relates the sales revenue generated during a period to the average number of employees of the business. *p. 219*

Sales revenue to capital employed ratio   An efficiency ratio that relates the sales revenue generated during a period to the capital employed. *p. 218*

Segmental financial reports   Reports that break down the operating results of a business according to its business or geographical segments. *p. 156*

Share   A portion of the ownership, or equity, of a company. *p. 5, 109*

Share premium account   A capital reserve reflecting any amount, above the nominal value of shares, which is paid for those shares when issued by a company. *p. 120*

Sole proprietorship   An individual in business on his or her own account. *p. 17*

Statement of changes to equity   A financial statement, required by IAS 1, which shows the effect of gains/losses and capital injections/withdrawals on the equity base of a company. *p. 149*

Stock Exchange   A market where 'second-hand' shares may be bought and sold and new capital raised. *p. 5*

Straight-line method   A method of accounting for depreciation that allocates the amount to be depreciated evenly over the useful life of the asset. *p. 82*

Subsidiary company   A company over which another (parent) company is able to exercise control, usually, but not necessarily, because a majority of its shares are owned by the parent company. *p. 275*

Summary financial statement   A summarised version of the complete annual financial statements, which shareholders may receive as an alternative to the complete statements. *p. 162*

Takeover   The acquisition of control of one company by another, usually as a result of acquiring a majority of the ordinary shares of the former. *p. 134, 275*

Tangible assets   Assets that have a physical substance (for example, plant and machinery, motor vehicles). *p. 36*

Target company   A company that has been identified by another company as a suitable target for a takeover. *p. 278*

Total shareholder return   A measure of the total return from a share, which is made up of two elements: the increase (or decrease) in share value over a period plus (minus) any dividends paid during the period. *p. 349*

Transfer price   The price at which goods or services are sold, or transferred, between divisions of the same business. *p. 157*

Trial balance   A totalled list of the balances on each of the accounts in a double-entry bookkeeping system. *p. 381*

Understandability   The requirement that accounting information should be understood by those for whom the information is primarily compiled. Lack of understandability will limit the usefulness of accounting information. *p. 7*

Univariate analysis   A method that can be used to help predict financial distress, which involves the use of a single ratio as a predictor. *p. 259*

Vertical analysis   An approach to common-size financial statements where all of the figures in the particular statement are expressed in relation to one of the figures in that same statement, for example, sales revenue or total long-term funds. *p. 257*

Weighted average cost (AVCO)   A method of inventories costing, which assumes that inventories entering the business lose their separate identity and any issues of inventories reflect the weighted average cost of the inventories held. *p. 90*

Written-down value (WDV)   See *Carrying amount*.

Appendix C

Solutions to self-assessment questions

Chapter 2

2.1 The balance sheet you prepare should be set out as follows:

Simonson Engineering
Balance sheet as at 30 September 2006

	£
Non-current assets	
Property, plant and equipment	
Property	72,000
Plant and machinery	25,000
Motor vehicles	15,000
Fixtures and fittings	9,000
	121,000
Current assets	
Inventories	45,000
Trade receivables	48,000
Cash in hand	1,500
	94,500
Total assets	215,500
Capital (owners' equity)	
Opening balance	117,500
Profit	18,000
	135,500
Drawings	(15,000)
	120,500
Non-current liabilities	
Long-term borrowings	51,000
Current liabilities	
Trade payables	18,000
Short-term borrowings	26,000
	44,000
Total equity and liabilities	215,500

Chapter 3

3.1 TT and Co

Balance sheet as at 31 December 2006

Assets	£	Claims	£
Delivery van (12,000 – 2,500)	9,500	Capital (50,000 + 26,900)	76,900
Inventories (143,000 + 12,000 – 74,000 – 16,000)	65,000	Trade payables (143,000 – 121,000)	22,000
Trade receivables (152,000 – 132,000 – 400)	19,600	Accrued expenses (630 + 620)	1,250
Cash at bank (50,000 – 25,000 – 500 – 1,200 – 12,000 – 33,500 – 1,650 – 12,000 + 35,000 + 132,000 – 121,000 – 9,400)	750		
Prepaid expenses (5,000 + 300)	5,300		
Total assets	100,150	Total equity and liabilities	100,150

Income statement for the year ended 31 December 2006

	£
Sales revenue (152,000 + 35,000)	187,000
Cost of goods sold (74,000 + 16,000)	(90,000)
Gross profit	97,000
Rent	(20,000)
Rates (500 + 900)	(1,400)
Wages (33,500 + 630)	(34,130)
Electricity (1,650 + 620)	(2,270)
Bad debts	(400)
Van depreciation [(12,000 – 2,000)/4]	(2,500)
Van expenses	(9,400)
Profit for the year	26,900

The balance sheet could now be rewritten in a more stylish form as follows:

Balance sheet as at 31 December 2006

	£
Non-current assets	
Property, plant and equipment	
Motor van at cost	12,000
Accumulated depreciation	(2,500)
	9,500
Current assets	
Inventories	65,000
Trade receivables	19,600
Prepaid expenses	5,300
Cash	750
	90,650
Total assets	100,150
Capital (owners' equity)	
Original	50,000
Retained profit	26,900
	76,900
Current liabilities	
Trade payables	22,000
Accrued expenses	1,250
	23,250
Total equity and liabilities	100,150

Chapter 4

4.1 Dev Ltd

(a) The summarised balance sheet of Dev Ltd, immediately following the rights and bonus issue, is as follows:

Balance sheet as at 31 December 2006

	£
Net assets [235 + 40 (cash from the rights issue)]	275,000
Equity	
Share capital: 180,000 shares @ £1 [(100 + 20) + 60]	180,000
Share premium account (30 + 20 − 50)	–
Revaluation reserve (37 − 10)	27,000
Retained earnings	68,000
Total equity	275,000

Note that the bonus issue of £60,000 is taken from capital reserves (reserves unavailable for dividends) as follows:

	£
Share premium account	50,000
Revaluation reserve	10,000
	60,000

More could have been taken from the revaluation reserve and less from the share premium account without making any difference to dividend payment possibilities.

(b) There may be pressure from a potential lender for the business to limit its ability to pay dividends. This would place lenders in a more secure position because the maximum buffer or safety margin between the value of the assets and the amount owed by the business is maintained. It is not unusual for potential lenders to insist on some measure to lock up shareholders' funds in this way as a condition of granting the loan.

(c) The summarised balance sheet of Dev Ltd, immediately following the rights and bonus issue, assuming a minimum dividend potential objective, is as follows:

Balance sheet as at 31 December 2006

	£
Net assets [235 + 40 (cash from the rights issue)]	275,000
Equity	
Share capital: 180,000 shares @ £1 ((100 + 20) + 60)	180,000
Share premium account (30 + 20)	50,000
Revaluation reserve	37,000
Retained earnings (68 − 60)	8,000
Total equity	275,000

(d) Before the bonus issue, the maximum dividend was £68,000. Now it is £8,000. Thus, the bonus issue has had the effect of locking up an additional £60,000 of the business's assets in terms of the business's ability to pay dividends.

(e) Before the issues, Lee had 100 shares worth £2.35 (£235,000/100,000) each or £235 in total. Lee would be offered 20 shares in the rights issue at £2 each or £40 in total. After the rights issue, Lee would have 120 shares worth £2.2917 (£275,000/120,000) each or £275 in total.

   The bonus issue would give Lee 60 additional shares. After the bonus issue, Lee would have 180 shares worth £1.5278 (£275,000/180,000) each or £275 in total.

None of this affects Lee's wealth. Before the issues, Lee had £235 worth of shares and £40 more in cash. After the issues, Lee has the same total wealth but all £275 is in the value of the shares.

(f) The things that we know about the company are as follows:

(i) It is a private (as opposed to a public) limited company, for it has 'Ltd' (limited) as part of its name, rather than plc (public limited company).

(ii) It has made an issue of shares at a premium, almost certainly after it had traded successfully for a period. (There is a share premium account. It would be very unlikely that the original shares, issued when the company was first formed, would have been issued at a premium.)

(iii) Certain of the assets in the balance sheet have been upwardly revalued by at least £37,000. (There is a revaluation reserve of £37,000. This may just be what is left after a previous bonus issue had taken part of the balance.)

(iv) The company has traded at an aggregate profit (though there could have been losses in some years), net of tax and any dividends paid. (There is a positive balance on retained earnings)

Chapter 5

5.1 J. Baxter plc

We can see from the table below that the Italian segment generates the highest revenue, but also generates the lowest profit. We shall be considering financial ratios in detail in Chapters 7 and 8, however, it is helpful to compare the profit generated with the sales revenue for each geographical segment. We can see from the table below that the French segment generates the most profit in relation to sales revenue. Fifteen per cent or £0.15 in every £1, of profit is derived from the sales revenue generated. However, for the Italian segment, only 2.1 per cent, or £0.02 in every £1, of profit is derived from the sales revenue generated.

We can also compare the profit generated with the net assets employed (that is, total assets – total liabilities) for each segment. We can see from the table below that the UK segment produces the best return on net assets employed: £0.36 for every £1 invested. Once again, the Italian segment produces the worst results.

The reasons for the relatively poor results from the Italian segment need further investigation. There may be valid reasons; for example, this segment may have deliberately engaged in low pricing during the period in an attempt to increase market share. However, it may suggest that the business needs to re-evaluate its presence in this geographical region.

It is interesting to note that the Italian segment benefited most from capital expenditure during the period. The reason for such a large investment in such a poorly-performing segment needs to be justified. It is possible that the business will reap rewards for the investment in the future; however, we do not have enough information to understand the reasons for the investment decision.

The reasons why the depreciation charges in the Italian segment are significantly lower than in the other geographical segments should also be investigated. The depreciation charge as a percentage of total assets is much lower. It is possible that the mix of assets is different in the Italian segment from that in the other two segments. If, however, this is not the case and a higher depreciation charge is really warranted, the profitability of this segment would be even worse.

Table of key results

	UK	France	Italy
Total revenue	270	200	390
Segment result	34	30	8
Net assets (assets – liabilities)	94	122	94
Segment result as a percentage of sales revenue	12.6%	15.0%	2.1%
Segment result as a percentage of net assets employed	36.2%	24.6%	8.5%
Capital expenditure	£20 m	£15 m	£35 m
Depreciation as a percentage of total assets	21.7%	23.3%	9.5%

Chapter 6

6.1   Touchstone plc

Touchstone plc
Cash flow statement for the year ended 31 December 2007

	£m	£m
Cash flows from operating activities		
Profit before taxation (after interest) (see Note 1 below)	60	
Adjustments for:		
Depreciation	16	
Interest expense (Note 2)	4	
	80	
Increase in trade receivables (26 – 16)	(10)	
Decrease in trade payables (38 – 37)	(1)	
Decrease in inventories (25 – 24)	1	
Cash generated from operations	70	
Interest paid	(4)	
Taxation paid (Note 3)	(12)	
Dividend paid	(18)	
Net cash from operating activities		36
Cash flows from investing activities		
Payments to acquire tangible non-current assets (Note 4)	(41)	
Net cash used in investing activities		(41)
Cash flows from financing activities		
Issue of Loan notes (40 – 20)	20	
Net cash used in financing activities		20
Net increase in cash and cash equivalents		15
Cash and cash equivalents at 1 January 2007 Cash		4
Cash and cash equivalents at 31 December 2007 Cash		4
Treasury bills		15
		19

To see how this relates to the cash of the business at the beginning and end of the year it can be useful to provide a reconciliation as follows:

Analysis of cash and cash equivalents during the year ended 31 December 2007

	£m
Cash and cash equivalents at 1 January 2007	4
Net cash inflow	15
Cash and cash equivalents at 31 December 2007	19

Notes

1 This is simply taken from the income statement for the year.
2 Interest payable expense must be taken out, by adding it back to the profit before taxation figure. We subsequently deduct the cash paid for interest payable during the year. In this case the two figures are identical.
3 Companies pay tax of 50 per cent during their accounting year and the other 50 per cent in the following year. Thus the 2007 payment would have been half the tax on the 2006 profit (that is, the figure that would have appeared in the current liabilities at the end of 2006), plus half of the 2007 tax charge (that is, $4 + (\frac{1}{2} \times 16) = 12$).
4 Since there were no disposals, the depreciation charges must be the difference between the start and end of the year's non-current asset values, adjusted by the cost of any additions.

	£m
Carrying amount, at 1 January 2007	147
Add Additions (balancing figure)	41
	188
Less Depreciation (6 + 10)	16
Carrying amount, at 31 December 2007	172

Chapter 7

7.1 Ali plc and Bhaskar plc

In order to answer this question you may have used the following ratios:

	Ali plc	Bhaskar plc
Return on ordinary shareholders' funds ratio	$99.9/687.6 \times 100 = 14.5\%$	$104.6/874.6 \times 100 = 12.0\%$
Operating profit margin ratio	$151.3/1{,}478.1 \times 100 = 10.2\%$	$166.9/1{,}790.4 \times 100 = 9.3\%$
Average inventories turnover period ratio	$592.0/1{,}018.3 \times 12 = 7.0$ months	$403.0/1{,}214.9 \times 12 = 4.0$ months
Average settlement period for trade receivables ratio	$176.4/1{,}478.1 \times 12 = 1.4$ months	$321.9/1{,}790.4 \times 12 = 2.2$ months
Current ratio	$\dfrac{853.0}{422.4} = 2.0$	$\dfrac{816.5}{293.1} = 2.8$
Acid test ratio	$\dfrac{(853.0 - 592.0)}{422.4} = 0.6$	$\dfrac{(816.5 - 403.0)}{293.1} = 1.4$
Gearing ratio	$\dfrac{190}{(687.6 + 190)} \times 100 = 21.6\%$	$\dfrac{250}{(874.6 + 250)} \times 100 = 22.2\%$
Interest cover ratio	$\dfrac{151.3}{19.4} = 7.8$ times	$\dfrac{166.9}{27.5} = 6.1$ times

Ali plc seems more effective than Bhaskar plc at generating returns for shareholders indicated by the higher ROSF ratio. This perhaps partly caused by Ali plc's higher operating profit margin.

Both businesses have a very high inventories turnover period; this probably needs to be investigated, particularly by Ali plc. Ali plc has a lower average settlement period for trade receivables than Bhaskar plc.

Ali plc has a much lower current ratio and acid test ratio than Bhaskar plc. The acid test ratio of Ali plc is substantially below 1.0: this may suggest a liquidity problem.

The gearing ratio of each business is quite similar. Neither business seems to have excessive borrowing. The interest cover ratio for each business is also similar. The ratios indicate that both businesses have good profit coverage for their interest charges.

To be able to draw really helpful comparisons between the two businesses, it would probably be necessary to calculate other ratios from the 2007 financial statements. It would also be helpful to have access to the ratios for both businesses over recent years and, possibly, the ratios of other businesses operating in the same industry.

Chapter 8

8.1   **Ali plc and Bhaskar plc**

	Ali plc	*Bhaskar plc*
Dividend payout ratio	$135/99.9 \times 100 = 135\%$	$95/104.6 \times 100 = 91\%$
Dividend yield ratio	$[(135/320)/(1 - 0.1)]/6.5 \times 100 = 7.2\%$	$[(95/250)/(1 - 0.1)]/8.20 \times 100 = 5.1\%$
Earnings per share	$99.9/320 = £0.31$	$104.6/250 = £0.42$
P/E ratio	$6.5/0.31 = 21.0$	$8.2/0.42 = 19.5$

Both of these businesses seem to have a rather imprudent dividend policy, Ali paying out more than its profit for the year and Bhaskar most of it. If the current year's level of profit is abnormally low and the businesses have the funds available this may not be quite as reckless as it seems, at first sight. The average payout ratio for all retailers listed on the London Stock Exchange is 59.5 per cent – much lower than either Ali or Bhaskar.

Given the high level of dividends paid by the two businesses, it is not surprising that the dividend yields are also high. The average dividend yield ratio for all retailers listed on the London Stock Exchange listed businesses is 2.44 per cent – again very much lower than either Ali or Bhaskar.

The EPS values are impossible to interpret without an historical series of past EPS values for each business. The EPS value is not directly comparable between businesses. This is partly because the par value of the shares (which varies from one business to another) and how each business is financed have profound effects on the EPS value.

The P/E ratios for both businesses are somewhat below the average for all retailers listed on the London Stock Exchange, which is 24.4. This ratio is seen as a measure of the level of confidence that investors have in the business's future. On the face of it, Ali is more highly regarded than Bhaskar, but both seem to be less well regarded than retailers generally.

Chapter 9

9.1 Great plc

Group balance sheet as at 31 December last year

	£m	£m
Non-current assets		
Property, plant and equipment (at cost less depreciation)		
Land (80 + 14 + 5)	99	
Plant	53	
Vehicles	31	183
Intangible asset		
Goodwill arising on consolidation (Note 1)		5
		188
Current assets		
Inventories	29	
Trade receivables	27	
Cash	22	78
Total assets		266
Equity		
Called-up share capital: ordinary shares of £1 each, fully paid	100	
Retained profit (Note 2)	81	181
Minority interests (Note 3)		13
		194
Non-current liabilities		
Loan notes		50
Current liabilities		
Trade payables		22
Total equity and liabilities		266

Note 1: Goodwill arising on consolidation: $53 - (80\% \times (20 + 35 + 5)) = 5$.

Note 2:

	£m
Great plc's retained profit balance	77
Great plc's share of Small plc's post-acquisition profits $(40 - 35) \times 80\%$	4
	81

Note 3: Minority interests: $(60 + 5) \times 20\% = 13$.

Group income statement for last year

	£m	£m
Revenue		118
Cost of sales		(59)
Gross profit		59
Administration expenses	(11)	
Distribution expenses	(8)	(19)
Operating profit		40
Interest payable		(3)
Profit before taxation		37
Taxation		(16)
Profit for the year		21
Attributable to minorities $(20\% \times 10)$		(1)
Profit for the year attributable to Great plc shareholders		20

Chapter 10

10.1   The sources of information that may be used could include the following:

- Documents setting out the:
  - strategic plan of the company;
  - board structure and roles;
  - board appointments procedures;
  - operations of the board;
  - minutes of board meetings;
  - meeting agendas and background information;
  - criteria for directors appraisal.
- Interviews with board members.
- Interviews with and/or questionnaires sent to senior management and shareholders.
- Attendance and observation at board meetings.
- Attendance and observation at meetings with shareholders, including the AGM.
- Company website and published material, including the annual reports.
- CVs of board members.
- Performance reports (such as monthly budget reports and sales reports) received by the board.
- Information relating to training and development programmes carried out.

This is not an exhaustive list. You may have thought of other sources of information.

Appendix D
Solutions to review questions

Chapter 1

1.1

Students	Whether to enrol on a course of study. This would probably involve an assessment of the university's ability to continue to operate and to fulfil students' needs.
Other universities and colleges	How best to compete against the university. This might involve using the university's performance in various aspects as a 'benchmark' when evaluating their own performance.
Employees	Whether to take up or to continue in employment with the university. Employees might assess this by considering the ability of the university to continue to provide employment and to reward employees adequately for their labour.
Government/ Funding authority	How efficient the university is in undertaking its various activities.
Local community representatives	Whether to allow/encourage the university to expand its premises. To assess this, the university's ability to continue to provide employment for the community, to use community resources and to help fund environmental improvements might be considered.
Suppliers	Whether to continue to supply the university at all; also whether to supply on credit. This would involve an assessment of the university's ability to pay for any goods and services supplied.
Lenders	Whether to lend money to the university and/or whether to require repayment of any existing loans. To assess this, the university's ability to meet its obligations to pay interest and to repay the principal would be considered.
Board of governors and other managers (faculty deans and so on)	Whether the performance of the university requires improvement. Here performance to date would be compared with earlier plans or some other 'benchmark' to decide whether action needs to be taken. Whether there should be a change in the university's future direction. In making such decisions management will need to look at the university's ability to perform and at the opportunities available to it.

1.2 In order to be justified in producing a particular piece of accounting information, strictly the person authorising its production should be satisfied that the economic cost of providing it is less than the economic benefit which will be derived from its production. This is to say that there should be a net economic benefit of producing it. Otherwise it should not be produced.

There are obvious problems in determining what is the value of the benefit. There are also likely to be difficulties in determining the amount of the cost. Thus, the judgement is not easy to make.

Economics is not the only issue, particularly in the context of financial accounting. Social and other factors may well be involved. It can be argued that society has a right to certain information about a large business, even though the information may not have an economic value to society.

1.3 Since we can never be sure what is going to happen in the future, the best that we can do is to make judgements on the basis of past experience. Thus, information concerning flows of cash and of wealth in the recent past is likely to be a useful source on which to base judgements about possible future outcomes.

1.4 The idea that we should provide simplified financial reports for less sophisticated users has gained increasing acceptance in recent years. Many large companies now offer simplified annual reports to private shareholders and to employees. However, there are dangers associated with this type of report. Companies are complex organisations and any attempt to simplify their activities or encapsulate their performance in a relatively few pages runs the risk that the message will be distorted. Perhaps we should not expect accountants to achieve what may be an impossible task. Instead, we should expect unsophisticated users to seek professional help or to study accounting!

Chapter 2

2.1 The confusion arises because the owner seems unaware of the business entity convention in accounting. This convention requires a separation of the business from the owner(s) of the business for accounting purposes. The business is regarded as a separate entity and the balance sheet is prepared from the perspective of the business rather than that of the owner. As a result, funds invested in the business by the owner will be regarded as a claim that the owner has on the business. In the balance sheet, this claim will be shown alongside other claims on the business from outsiders.

2.2 A balance sheet does not show what a business is worth for two major reasons:

- only those items which can be measured reliably in monetary terms are shown on the balance sheet. Thus, things of value such as the reputation for product quality, skills of employees and so on will not normally appear in the balance sheet; and
- the historic cost convention results in assets being recorded at their outlay cost rather than their current value. In the case of certain assets, the difference between historic cost and current value may be significant.

2.3 The balance sheet equation is simply the relationship between a business's assets, liabilities and capital. In the horizontal layout it is:

Assets (current and non-current) = Capital plus Liabilities (current and non-current)

In the vertical layout, the equation is the same but it is set out in columnar form. Assets are shown first and capital and liabilities are shown underneath.

2.4 Some object to the idea of humans being treated as assets for inclusion on the balance sheet. It can be seen as demeaning for humans to be listed alongside inventories, plant and machinery and other assets. However, others argue that humans are often the most valuable resource of a business and by placing a value on this resource will help bring to the attention of managers the importance of nurturing and developing this 'asset'. There is a saying in management that 'the things that count are the things that get counted'. As the value of the 'human assets' is not stated in the financial statements, there is a danger that managers will treat these 'assets' less favourably than other assets that are on the balance sheet.

Humans are likely to meet the first criterion of an asset listed in the chapter, that is, a probable future benefit exists. There would be little point in employing people if this were not the case. The second criterion concerning exclusive right of control is more problematic. Clearly a business cannot control humans in the same way as most other assets. However, a business can have the exclusive right to the employment services that a person provides. This distinction between control over the services provided, rather than control over the person, makes it possible to argue that the second criterion can be met.

Humans sign a contract of employment with the business normally and so the third criterion is normally met. The difficulty, however, is with the fourth criterion, that is, whether the value of humans (or their services) can be measured with any degree of reliability. To date, none of the measurement methods proposed enjoy widespread acceptance.

Chapter 3

3.1 At the time of preparing the income statement, it is not always possible to determine accurately the expenses that need to be matched to the sales revenue figure for the period. It will only be at some later point in time that the true position becomes clear. However, it is still necessary to try to include all relevant expenses in the income statement and so estimates of the future will have to be made. Examples of estimates that may have to be made include:

- expenses accrued at the end of the period such as the amount of telephone expenses incurred since the last quarter's bill;
- the amount of depreciation based on estimates of the life of the non-current asset and future residual value;
- the amount of bad and doubtful debts incurred.

3.2 Depreciation attempts to allocate the cost or fair value (less any residual value) of the asset over its useful life. Depreciation does not attempt to measure the fall in value of the asset during the period. Thus, the carrying amount of the asset appearing on the balance sheet normally represents the unexpired cost of the asset rather than its current market value.

3.3 The convention of consistency is designed to provide a degree of uniformity concerning the application of accounting policies. We have seen, that in certain areas, there may be more than one method of accounting for an item, for example inventories. The convention of consistency states that, having decided on a particular accounting policy, a business should continue to apply the policy in successive periods. Whilst this policy helps to ensure that users can make valid comparisons concerning business performance *over time* it does not ensure that valid comparisons can be made *between businesses*. This is because different businesses may consistently apply different accounting policies.

3.4 An expense is that element of the cost incurred that is used up during the accounting period. An asset is that element of cost which is carried forward on the balance sheet and which will normally be used up in future periods. Thus, both assets and expenses arise from costs being incurred. The major difference between the two is the period over which the benefits (resulting from the costs incurred) accrue.

APPENDIX D SOLUTIONS TO REVIEW QUESTIONS

Chapter 4

4.1 It does not differ. In both cases they are required to meet their debts to the full extent that there are assets available. To this extent they both have a liability that is limited to the extent of their assets. This is a particularly important fact for the shareholders of a limited company because they know that those owed money by the company cannot demand that the shareholders contribute additional funds to help meet debts. Thus, the liability of the shareholders is limited to the amount that they have paid for their shares, or have agreed to pay in the case of partially unpaid shares. This contrasts with the position of the owner or part owner of an unincorporated (non-company) business. Here all of the individual's assets could be required to meet the unsatisfied liabilities of the business.

4.2 A private limited company may place restrictions on the transfer of its shares; that is, the directors can veto an attempt by a shareholder to sell his or her shares to another person to whom the directors object. Thus, in effect, the majority can avoid having as a shareholder someone that they would prefer not to have. A public company cannot do this.

A public limited company must have authorised share capital of at least £50,000. There is no minimum for a private limited company.

The main advantage of being a public limited company is that they may offer their shares and debentures to the general public; private companies cannot make such an offer.

4.3 A reserve is that part of the equity (owners' claim) of a company that is not share capital. Reserves represent gains or surpluses that enhance the claim of the shareholders above the nominal value of their shares. For example, the share premium account is a reserve that represents the excess over the nominal value of shares that is paid for them on a share issue. The retained profit balance is a reserve that arises from ploughed-back profits earned by the company.

4.4 A preference share represents part of the ownership of a company. Preference shares entitle their owners to the first part of any dividend paid by the company, up to a maximum amount. The maximum is usually expressed as a percentage of the nominal or par value of the preference shares.

(a) They differ from ordinary shares to the extent that they only entitle their holders to dividends to a predetermined maximum value. Dividends to ordinary shareholders have no predetermined maximum. Usually preference shares attract a maximum payout equal to their nominal value on liquidation, the ordinary shareholders receive the residue after all other claimants, including the preference shareholders.

(b) They differ from loan notes in that these represent borrowings for the company, where normally holders have a contract with the company that specifies the rate of interest, interest payment dates and redemption date. They are often secured on the company's assets. Preference shareholders have no such contract.

Chapter 5

5.1 Accounting is still an evolving subject. It is not static and so the principles that are laid down at any particular point in time may become obsolete as a result of changes in our understanding of the nature of accounting information and its impact on users and changes in the economic environment within which accounting is employed. We must accept, therefore, that accounting principles will continue to evolve and that existing principles must be regularly reviewed.

5.2 Apart from increases in accounting regulation, financial reports have increased because of:

- increasing demands by influential user groups, such as shareholders and financial analysts, for financial information relating to the company;
- the increasing sophistication of influential user groups, such as financial analysts, to deal with financial information;
- the increasing complexity of business operations requiring greater explanation;
- increasing recognition of the need for greater accountability towards certain user groups (e.g. employees and community groups) requiring the need for additional reports, e.g. environmental reports and social reports.

5.3 There are various problems associated with the measurement of business segments. These include:

- the definition of a segment;
- the treatment of inter-segmental transactions, such as sales;
- the treatment of common costs.

There is no single correct method of dealing with these problems and variations will arise in practice. This, in turn, will hinder comparisons between businesses.

5.4 Preparing an OFR may present a problem for accountants. For information to be credible to all interested parties, accountants should be as neutral as possible in measuring and reporting the financial performance and position of the business. The OFR requires some interpretation of results and there is a danger that the directors will wish to portray the business activities in as favourable a light as possible. This will affect what items are reported and how they are reported. The OFR is not normally independently audited, so the risks of bias in reporting are increased. The board of directors, therefore, should accept full responsibility for preparing the OFR and this should be made clear to users.

Chapter 6

6.1 People and organisations will not normally accept other than cash in settlement of their claims against the business. If a business wants to employ people it must pay them in cash. If it wants to buy a new non-current asset to exploit a business opportunity, the supplier will normally insist on being paid in cash, normally after a short period of credit. When businesses fail, it is their inability to find the cash to pay claimants that actually drives them under. These factors lead to cash being the pre-eminent business asset and, therefore, the one that analysts and others watch carefully in trying to assess the ability of the business to survive and/or to take advantage of commercial opportunities as they arise.

6.2 With the 'direct method', the business's cash records are analysed for the period concerned. The analysis reveals the amounts of cash, in total, which have been paid and received in respect of each category of the cash flow statement. This is not difficult in principle, or in practice if it is done by computer as a matter of routine.

The 'indirect method' takes the approach that, while the profit (loss) for the year is not equal to the net inflow (outflow) of cash from operations, they are fairly closely linked to the extent that appropriate adjustment of the profit (loss) for the year figure will produce the correct cash flow one. The adjustment is concerned with depreciation charge for, and movements in relevant working capital items over, the period.

6.3 (a) *Cash flows from operating activities.* This would normally be positive, even for a business with small profits or even losses. The fact that depreciation is not a cash flow tends to lead to positive cash flows in this area in most cases.

(b) *Cash flows from investing activities.* Normally this would be negative in cash flow terms since assets become worn out and need to be replaced in the normal course of business. This means that, typically, old items of property, plant and equipment are generating less cash on their disposal than is having to be paid out to replace them.

(c) *Cash flows from financing activities.* There is a tendency for businesses either to expand or to fail. In either case, this is likely to mean that over the years more finance will be raised than will be redeemed or retired.

6.4 There are several reasons for this. These include the following:

- Changes in inventories, trade receivables and trade payables. For example, an increase in trade receivables during an accounting period would mean that the cash received from credit sales would be less than the credit sales revenue for the same period.
- Cash may have been spent on new non-current assets or received from disposals of old ones; these would not directly affect profit.
- Cash may have been spent to redeem or repay a financial claim or received as a result of the creation or the increase of a claim. These would not directly affect profit.

The taxation charged in the income statement would not be the same tax that is paid during the same accounting period.

Chapter 7

7.1 The fact that a business operates on a low operating profit margin indicates that only a small operating profit is being produced for each £1 of sales revenue generated. However, this does not mean necessarily that the return on capital employed will be low. If the business is able to generate a large amount of sales revenue during a period, the operating profit may be very high even though the operating profit per £1 of sales revenue is low. If the net generated is high, this can lead, in turn, to a high return on capital employed, since it is the total operating profit that is used as the numerator (top part of the fraction) in this ratio. Many businesses (including supermarkets) pursue a strategy of 'low margin, high turnover'.

7.2 Reducing the OCC requires one or more of the following:

- *Reducing the inventories turnover period.* This could lead to the business holding less inventories than is desirable, given its level of activity and the nature of the business. This could mean running out of inventories and not being able to offer customers the appropriate level of service. It might alternatively mean that the business might have to disrupt production due to a shortage of inventories.
- *Reducing the trade receivables collection period.* This might lead to a loss of customer goodwill and trade as a result of having to insist on a shorter period of credit. Offering discounts to encourage prompt payment could be effective, but costly.
- *Increasing the trade payables settlement period.* This could well cause a reduction in the level of goodwill among suppliers. This could lead to suppliers being reluctant to supply. A prolongation of the payment period could lead to the costly loss of prompt payment discounts.

7.3   Three possible reasons for a long inventories turnover period are:

- poor inventories controls, leading to excessive investment in inventories;
- inventories hoarding in anticipation of price rises or shortages;
- inventories building in anticipation of increased future sales.

A short inventories turnover period may be due to:

- tight inventories controls, thereby reducing excessive investment in inventories and/or the amount of obsolete and slow moving inventories;
- an inability to finance the required amount of inventories to meet sales demand;
- a difference in the mix of inventories carried by similar businesses (for example, greater investment in perishable goods which are held for a short period only).

7.4   Size may well be an important factor when comparing businesses:

- Larger businesses may be able to generate economies of scale in production and distribution to an extent not available to smaller businesses.
- Larger businesses may be able to raise finance more cheaply, partly through economies of scale (for example, borrowing larger amounts) and partly through being seen as less of a risk to the lender.
- Smaller businesses may be able to be more flexible and 'lighter on their feet' than can the typical larger business.

These and other possible factors may lead to differences in performance and position between larger and smaller businesses.

Chapter 8

8.1   The balance sheet is drawn up at a single point in time – the end of the financial period. As a result, the figures shown on the balance sheet represent the position at that single point in time and may not be representative of the position during the period. Wherever possible, average figures (perhaps based on monthly figures) should be used. However, an external user may only have access to the opening and closing balance sheets for the year and so a simple average based on these figures may be all that is possible to calculate. Where a business is seasonal in nature or is subject to cyclical changes, this simple averaging may not be sufficient.

8.2   Factors that could affect a company's decision on the level of dividend to pay include the following:

- *The level of profit for the period concerned.* Businesses tend to be reluctant to pay dividends at a higher level than that of after tax profits. They may be prepared to exceed this limit occasionally, when they have an abnormally poor year, but over a period of years, dividends typically fall well below profit levels.
- *The amount of cash available.* Businesses tend not to borrow to pay dividends though this would be perfectly legal. Only if they have sufficient liquidity will they normally pay dividends.
- *Other demands on funds.* Linked to the liquidity point, businesses may be constrained from paying dividends by the extent of other calls on their funds, particularly for investment. In theory, businesses will pay out any cash remaining only after all profitable investments have been undertaken.
- *Past practice.* Businesses tend to adopt a fairly consistent dividend policy, which they are often reluctant to vary. This is because it is believed that changes in dividend policy can send misleading 'signals' to inventors. For example, cutting the level of dividends might signal that the business is in difficulties.

8.3 The P/E ratio may vary between businesses within the same industry for the following reasons:

● *Accounting conventions*. Differences in the methods used to compute profit (for example inventories valuation and depreciation) can lead to different profit figures and, therefore, different P/E ratios.

● *Different prospects*. One business may be regarded as having a much brighter future due to factors, such as, the quality of management, the quality of products, location and so on. This will affect the market price investors are prepared to pay for the share and, hence, it will also affect the P/E ratio.

● *Different asset structure*. The business's underlying asset base may be much higher and this may affect the market price of the shares.

8.4 Three ratios that could be affected by overtrading are:

● *Acid-test ratio*. This is likely to fall if overtrading is occurring because the trade payables settlement period is likely to increase and overdraft finance is likely to exist. At the same time inventories and trade receivable levels could well fall.

● *Cash generated from operations to maturing obligations ratio*. This is likely to fall. Cash generated is likely to rise more slowly than maturing obligations if the business is overtrading.

● *Interest cover ratio*. This is likely to fall despite rising profits because interest, perhaps on short term borrowing (for instance, overdrafts), is likely to rise more steeply.

Chapter 9

9.1 A group is said to exist when one company is in a position to exercise control over another company. This almost always means that the parent owns a majority of the voting shares of the subsidiary. Where a group relationship exists, all companies in the group must prepare annual financial statements in the normal way, but, in addition, the parent company must prepare and publish a set of group financial statements.

9.2 The group balance sheet shows the assets and external claims of all members of the group (including the parent company) as if they were those of the parent company. Where there are minority shareholders in any of the subsidiary companies, the fact that the parent company shareholders do not supply all of the equity finance of the group is recognised. This recognition takes the form of an item 'minority interests' in the financing area of the group balance sheet.

9.3 There are probably two reasons for this:

● *Limited liability*. Each company has its own limited liability. Thus, one company's financial collapse will not affect the others directly. The group is a number of independent units as far as liability is concerned.

● *Individual identity*. Operating a large business as a group of separate semi-autonomous departments is generally seen as good management. One means of emphasising the autonomy is to establish each department or division as a separate company. This arrangement may also be seen as a good marketing ploy since customers may prefer to deal with, what they see as, a smaller unit.

9.4 One company will be treated as an associate of another where that other company or group has a long-term interest and can exercise significant influence over the operating and financial policies of that company. Usually ownership of 20 per cent or more of the voting shares will be seen as sufficient to make one company an associate of another. This is usually achieved through representation on the Board of Directors of the associated company and is supported by a substantial interest in the voting shares in that company.

The accounting consequences are that the group must include its share of the post-acquisition reserves of the associate in its own balance sheet. It must also show its share of the operating profit, interest charges and tax charges relating to the associate in its income statement.

Chapter 10

10.1 A large listed company may communicate with shareholders through:

- the published annual report;
- announcements made through the Stock Exchange concerning major events such as new contracts, new directors, proposed takeovers or mergers and so on;
- the annual general meeting (AGM);
- a dedicated company website;
- informal meetings with major shareholders;
- presentations to investment analysts.

10.2 There is a risk that the board of directors will feel that real responsibility for the integrity of the financial statements rests entirely with the audit committee and that they have no responsibility for this area. There is also a risk that the burdens placed on the committee have become so onerous that it will be difficult to appoint non-executive directors as they will be unwilling to serve on the committee.

10.3 The external auditors will have an intimate knowledge of the accounting and payroll systems that are currently in operation and should be well placed to suggest improvements that will suit the company's needs. There may therefore be a saving of time and cost if they are given the task. However, there is always a risk that the external auditors will receive too high a proportion of the total fees received from the company in the form of consultancy work. This runs of the risk of compromising the auditors' independence.

10.4 Institutional investors have become more active for the following reasons:

- *The difficulties of disinvesting in a large public company.* Institutional shareholders tend to have significant shareholdings in companies and attempting to sell a large quantity of shares may provoke a fall in price. Furthermore, an institutional shareholder may be locked into a company's shares if it offers funds to investors which attempt to track the market.
- *The pressure to perform.* Poor stock market returns in recent years have increased pressures on institutional shareholders to provide good returns. One way in which this may be done is through intervention in a company's affairs.
- *The changed regulatory environment.* There is pressure on large institutional shareholders through the Combined Code and government exhortations to engage with companies over corporate-governance issues.

Appendix E
Solutions to selected exercises

Chapter 2

2.1

Cash flow statement for Thursday

	£
Opening balance (from Wednesday)	59
Cash from sale of wrapping paper	47
	106
Cash paid to purchase wrapping paper	(53)
Closing balance	53

Income statement for Thursday

	£
Sales revenue	47
Cost of goods sold	(33)
Profit	14

Balance sheet as at Thursday evening

	£
Cash	53
Inventories of goods for resale (23 + 53 − 33)	43
Total business wealth	96

2.2

	£
Cash introduced by Paul on Monday	40
Profit for Monday	15
Profit for Tuesday	18
Profit for Wednesday	9
Profit for Thursday	14
	96

Thus, the wealth of the business, all of which belongs to Paul as sole owner, consists of the cash he put in to start the business plus the profit earned each day.

2.3

Income statement for day 1

	£
Sales revenue (70 × £0.80)	56
Cost of sales (70 × £0.50)	(35)
Profit	21

Cash flow statement for day 1

	£
Opening balance	40
Cash from sales	56
	96
Cash for purchases (80 × £0.50)	(40)
Closing balance	56

Balance sheet as at end of day 1

	£
Cash balance	56
Inventory of unsold goods (10 × £0.50)	5
Helen's business wealth	61

Income statement for day 2

	£
Sales revenue (65 × £0.80)	52.0
Cost of sales (65 × £0.50)	(32.5)
Profit	19.5

Cash flow statement for day 2

	£
Opening balance	56.0
Cash from sales	52.0
	108.0
Cash for purchases (60 × £0.50)	(30.0)
Closing balance	78.0

Balance sheet as at end of day 2

	£
Cash balance	78.0
Inventory of unsold goods (5 × £0.50)	2.5
Helen's business wealth	80.5

Income statement for day 3

	£
Sales revenue (20 × £0.80) + (45 × £0.40)	34.0
Cost of sales (65 × £0.50)	(32.5)
Profit	1.5

Cash flow statement for day 3

	£
Opening balance	78.0
Cash from sales	34.0
	112.0
Cash for purchases (60 × £0.50)	(30.0)
Closing balance	82.0

Balance sheet as at end of day 3

	£
Cash balance	82.0
Inventory of unsold goods	–
Helen's business wealth	82.0

2.5 (a)

Crafty Engineering Ltd
Balance sheet as at 30 June last year

	£000
Non-current assets	
Property, plant and equipment	
Property	320
Equipment and tools	207
Motor vehicles	38
	565
Current assets	
Inventories	153
Trade receivables	185
	338
Total assets	903
Capital (Owners' equity, which is the missing figure)	441
Non-current liabilities	
Long-term borrowings (Loan Industrial Finance Co)	260
Current liabilities	
Trade payables	86
Short-term borrowings	116
	202
Total equity and liabilities	903

(b) The balance sheet reveals a high level of investment in non-current assets. In percentage terms, we can say that more than 60 per cent of the total investment in assets (565/903) has been in non-current assets. The nature of the business may require a heavy investment in non-current assets. The investment in current assets exceeds the current liabilities by a large amount (approximately 1.7 times). As a result, there is no obvious sign of a liquidity problem. However, the balance sheet reveals that the business has no cash balance and is therefore dependent on the continuing support of short-term borrowing in order to meet obligations when they fall due. When considering the long-term financing of the business, we can see that about 37 per cent [260/(260 + 441)] of the total long-term finance for the business has been supplied by borrowings and about 63 per cent [441/(260 + 441)] by the owners. This level of long-term borrowing seems quite high but not excessive. However, we would need to know more about the ability of the business to service the borrowing (that is, make interest payments and repayments of the amount borrowed) before a full assessment could be made.

2.8 (a) The income statement shows the increase in wealth, as a result of trading, generated during the period (revenue), the decrease in wealth caused by the generation of that revenue (expenses) and the resulting net increase (profit) or decrease (loss) in wealth for the period. Though most businesses hold some of their wealth in cash, wealth is held in many other forms: non-current assets, receivables and so on.

(b) Assets, to be included in a balance sheet, must be judged as likely to produce future economic benefits. The economic benefit may come from selling the asset in the short term, in which case the statement is broadly true for those assets that it is the intention of the business to liquidate (turn into cash) in the short term. Many assets have an economic benefit that is not related to liquidation value but to use – for example, in production. For these types of asset, the statement is certainly not true.

There are other conditions that must be met in order for an item to be included in the balance sheet. These are:

- the business must have an exclusive right to control the asset
- the benefit must arise from some past transaction or event
- the asset must be measurable in monetary terms.

(c) The balance sheet equation is:

$$\text{Assets} = \text{Capital} + \text{Liabilities}$$

(d) Non-current assets are assets that do not meet the criteria for current assets. They are normally held for the long-term operations of the business. Some non-current assets may be immovable (for example, property) but others are not (for example, delivery vans).

(e) Goodwill may or may not have an infinite life – it will depend on the nature of the goodwill. There are no hard and fast rules that can be applied. Where this asset has a finite life, it should be amortised. Where it is considered to have an infinite life, it should not be amortised but should be tested annually for impairment.

Chapter 3

3.1 (a) Capital does increase as a result of the owners introducing more cash into the business, but it will also increase as a result of introducing other assets (for example, a motor car) and by the business generating revenue by trading. Similarly, capital decreases not only as a result of withdrawals of cash by owners but also by withdrawals of other assets (for example, inventory for the owners' personal use) and through trading expenses being incurred. For the typical business in a typical accounting period, capital will alter much more as a result of trading activities than for any other reason.

(b) An accrued expense is not one that relates to next year. It is one that needs to be matched with the revenue of the accounting period under review, but that has yet to be met in terms of cash payment. As such, it will appear on the balance sheet as a current liability.

(c) The purpose of depreciation is not to provide for asset replacement. Rather, it is an attempt to allocate the cost, or fair value, of the asset (less any residual value) over its useful life. Depreciation is an attempt to provide a measure of the amount of the non-current asset that has been consumed during the period. This amount will then be charged as an expense for the period in deriving the profit figure. Depreciation is a book entry (the outlay of cash occurs when the asset is purchased) and does not normally entail setting aside a separate amount of cash for asset replacement. Even if this were done, there would be no guarantee that sufficient funds would be available at the end of the asset's life for its replacement. Factors such as inflation and technological change may mean that the replacement cost is higher than the original cost of the asset.

(d) In the short term, it is possible for the current value of a non-current asset to exceed its original cost. However, nearly all non-current assets will wear out over time as a result of being used to generate wealth for the business. This will be the case for freehold buildings. As a result, some measure of depreciation should be calculated to take account of the fact that the asset is being consumed. Some businesses revalue their freehold buildings where the current value is significantly different from the original cost. Where this occurs, the depreciation charged should be based on the revalued amount. This will normally result in higher depreciation charges than if the asset remained at its historic cost.

3.3   The existence of profit and downward movement in cash may be for various reasons, which include the following:

- The purchase of assets for cash during the period (for example, motor cars and inventory), which were not all consumed during the period and are therefore not having as great an effect on expenses as they are on cash.
- The payment of an outstanding liability (for example, borrowings), which will have an effect on cash but not on expenses in the income statement.
- The withdrawal of cash by the owners from the capital invested, which will not have an effect on the expenses in the income statement.
- The generation of revenue on credit where the cash has yet to be received. This will increase the sales revenue for the period but will not have a beneficial effect on the cash balance until a later period.

3.5
(a)	Rent payable – expense for period	£9,000
(b)	Rates and insurance – expense for period	£6,000
(c)	General expenses – paid in period	£7,000
(d)	Interest (on borrowings) payable – prepaid	£500
(e)	Salaries – paid in period	£6,000
(f)	Rent receivable – received during period	£3,000

3.7

WW Associates
Balance sheet as at 31 December 2006

Assets	£	Claims	£
Machinery		Capital	
(+25,300 + 6,000 + 9,000		(+48,900 – 23,000 + 26,480)	52,380
– 13,000 + 3,900 – 9,360)	21,840*		
Inventory			
(+12,200 + 143,000 + 12,000			
– 127,000 – 25,000)	15,200		
		Trade payables	
		(+16,900 + 143,000 – 156,000)	3,900
Trade receivables		Accrued expenses	
(+21,300 + 211,000 – 198,000)	34,300	(+1,700 – 1,700 + 860)	860
Cash at bank (overdraft)			
(+8,300 – 23,000 – 25,000			
– 2,000 – 6,000 – 23,800			
– 2,700 – 12,000 + 42,000			
+ 198,000 – 156,000 – 17,500)	–19,700		
Prepaid expenses			
(+400 – 400 + 500 + 5,000)	5,500		
Total assets	57,140	**Total equity and liabilities**	57,140

	£
*	
Cost less accumulated depreciation at 31 December 2005	25,300
Less Carrying amount of machine disposed of (£13,000 – £3,900)	(9,100)
	16,200
Add Cost of new machine	15,000
	31,200
Depreciation for 2006 (£31,200 × 30%)	(9,360)
Carrying amount (written down value) of machine at 31 December 2006	21,840

Income statement for the year ended 31 December 2006

	£
Sales revenue (+211,000 + 42,000)	253,000
Cost of goods sold (+127,000 + 25,000)	(152,000)
Gross profit	101,000
Rent (+20,000)	(20,000)
Rates (+400 + 1,500)	(1,900)
Wages (−1,700 + 23,800 + 860)	(22,960)
Electricity (+2,700)	(2,700)
Machinery depreciation (+9,360)	(9,360)
Loss on disposal of the old machinery (+13,000 − 3,900 − 9,000)	(100)
Van expenses (+17,500)	(17,500)
Profit for the year	26,480

The loss on disposal of the old machinery is the carrying amount (cost less depreciation) less the disposal proceeds. Since the machinery had only been owned for one year, with a depreciation rate of 30 per cent, the depreciation on it so far is £3,900 (that is, £13,000 × 30%). The effective disposal proceeds were £9,000 because, as a result of trading it in, the business saved £9,000 on the new asset.

The depreciation expense for 2006 is based on the cost less accumulated depreciation of the assets owned at the end of 2006. Accumulated depreciation must be taken into account because the business uses the reducing-balance method.

The balance sheet could now be rewritten in a more stylish form as follows:

WW Associates
Balance sheet as at 31 December 2006

	£
Non-current assets	
Property, plant and equipment	
Machinery at cost less depreciation	21,840
Current assets	
Inventory	15,200
Trade receivables	34,300
Prepaid expenses	5,500
	55,000
Total assets	76,840
Capital (owners' equity)	
Original	48,900
Profit	26,480
	75,380
Drawings	(23,000)
	52,380
Current liabilities	
Trade payables	3,900
Accrued expenses	860
Borrowings – Bank overdraft	19,700
	24,460
Total equity and liabilities	76,840

3.8 An examination of the income statements for the two years reveals a number of interesting points, which include:

- An increase in sales value and gross profit of 9.9 per cent in 2006.
- The gross profit expressed as a percentage of sales revenue remaining at 70 per cent.

- An increase in salaries of 7.2 per cent.
- An increase in selling and distribution costs of 31.2 per cent.
- An increase in bad debts of 392.5 per cent.
- A decline in profit for the year of 39.3 per cent.
- A decline in the profit for the year as a percentage of sales revenue from 13.3 per cent to 7.4 per cent.

Thus, the business has enjoyed an increase in sales revenue and gross profits, but this has failed to translate to an increase in profit for the year because of the significant rise in overheads. The increase in selling costs during 2006 suggests that the increase in sales revenue was achieved by greater marketing effort, and the huge increase in bad debts suggests that the increase in sales revenue may be attributable to selling to less creditworthy customers or to a weak debt-collection policy. There appears to have been a change of policy in 2006 towards sales, and this has not been successful overall as the profit for the year has shown a dramatic decline.

Chapter 4

4.1 Limited companies can no more set a limit on the amount of debts they will meet than can human beings. They must meet their debts up to the limit of their assets, just as we as individuals must. In the context of owners' claim, 'reserves' mean part of the owners' claim against the assets of the company. These assets may or may not include cash. The legal ability of the company to pay dividends is not related to the amount of cash that it has.

Preference shares do not carry a guaranteed dividend. They simply guarantee that the preference shareholders have a right to the first slice of any dividend that is paid. Shares of many companies can, in effect, be bought by one investor from another through the Stock Exchange. Such a transaction has no direct effect on the company, however. These are not new shares being offered by the company, but existing shares that are being sold 'second-hand'.

4.2 (a) The first part of the quote is incorrect. Bonus shares should not, of themselves, increase the value of the shareholders' wealth. This is because reserves, belonging to the shareholders, are used to create bonus shares. Thus, each shareholder's stake in the company has not increased.

(b) This statement is incorrect. Shares can be issued at any price, provided that it is not below the nominal value of the shares. Once the company has been trading profitably for a period, the shares will not be worth the same as they were (the nominal value) when the company was first formed. In such circumstances, issuing shares at above their nominal value would not only be legal, but essential to preserve the wealth of the existing shareholders relative to any new ones.

(c) This statement is incorrect. From a legal perspective, the company is limited to a maximum dividend of the current extent of its revenue reserves. This amounts to any after-tax profits or gains realised that have not been eroded through, for example, payments of previous dividends. Legally, cash is not an issue; it would be perfectly legal for a company to borrow the funds to pay a dividend – although whether such an action would be commercially prudent is another question.

(d) This statement is partly incorrect. Companies do indeed have to pay tax on their profits. Depending on their circumstances, shareholders might also have to pay tax on their dividends.

4.4   Iqbal Ltd

Year	Maximum dividend £	
2002	0	No profit exists out of which to pay a dividend
2003	0	There remains a cumulative loss of £7,000. Since the revaluation represents a gain that has not been realised, it cannot be used to justify a dividend
2004	13,000	The cumulative net realised gains are derived as (–£15,000 + £8,000 + £15,000 + £5,000)
2005	14,000	The realised profits and gains for the year
2006	22,000	The realised profits and gains for the year

4.6   Pear Limited

Balance sheet as at 30 September 2006

	£000
Non-current assets	
Property, plant and equipment	
Cost (1,570 + 30)	1,600
Depreciation (690 + 12)	(702)
	898
Current assets	
Inventory	207
Receivables (182 + 18 – 4)	196
Cash at bank	21
	424
Total assets	1,322
Equity	
Shares capital	300
Share premium account	300
Retained earnings (104 + 41 – 25)	120
	720
Non-current liabilities	
Borrowings – 10% loan (repayable 2009)	300
Current liabilities	
Trade payables	88
Other payables (20 + 30 + 15 + 2)	67
Taxation	17
Dividend approved	25
Borrowings – Bank overdraft	105
	302
Total equity and liabilities	1,322

Income statement for the year ended 30 September 2006

	£000
Revenue (1,456 + 18)	1,474
Cost of sales	(768)
Gross profit	706
Salaries	(220)
Depreciation (249 + 12)	(261)
Other operating costs [131 + (2% × 200) + 2]	(137)
Operating profit	88
Interest payable (15 + 15)	(30)
Profit before taxation	58
Taxation (58 × 30%)	(17)
Profit for the year	41

4.7   **Chips Limited**

Balance sheet as at 30 June 2006

	Cost £000	Depreciation £000	£000
Non-current assets			
Property, plant and equipment			
Buildings	800	(112)	688
Plant and equipment	650	(367)	283
Motor vehicles (102 − 8); (53 − 5 + 19)	94	(67)	27
	1,544	(546)	998
Current assets			
Inventories			950
Trade receivables (420 − 16)			404
Cash at bank (16 + 2)			18
			1,372
Total assets			2,370
Equity			
Ordinary shares of £1, fully paid			800
Reserves at 1 July 2005			248
Retained profit for year			60
			1,108
Non-current liabilities			
Borrowings – Secured 10 per cent loan			700
Current liabilities			
Trade payables (361 + 23)			384
Other payables (117 + 35)			152
Taxation			26
			562
Total equity and liabilities			2,370

Income statement for the year ended 30 June 2006

	£000
Revenue (1,850 − 16)	1,834
Cost of sales (1,040 + 23)	(1,063)
Gross profit	771
Depreciation [220 − 2 − 5 + 8 + (94 × 20%)]	(240)
Other operating costs	(375)
Operating profit	156
Interest payable (35 + 35)	(70)
Profit before taxation	86
Taxation (86 × 30%)	(26)
Profit for the year	60

Chapter 5

5.1   Some believe that the annual reports of companies are becoming too long and contain too much information. A few examples of the length of the 2006 accounts of large companies are as follows:

Marks and Spencer plc	108 pages
Tesco plc	116 pages
BT Group plc	150 pages
3i Group plc	100 pages

There is a danger that users will suffer from 'information overload' if they are confronted with an excessive amount of information and that they will be unable to cope with it. This may, in turn, lead them to:

- fail to distinguish between important and less important information;
- fail to approach the analysis of information in a logical and systematic manner;
- feel a sense of confusion and avoid the task of analysing the information.

Lengthy annual reports are likely to be a problem for the less sophisticated user. This problem has been recognised and many companies publish summarised accounts for private investors, which include only the key points. However, for sophisticated users the problem may be that the annual reports are still not long enough. They often wish to glean as much information as possible from the company in order to make investment decisions.

5.3

I. Ching (Booksellers) plc
Income statement for the year ended 31 December 2006

	£000
Revenue	943
Cost of sales	(460)
Gross profit	483
Distribution costs	(110)
Administrative expenses	(212)
Other expenses	(25)
Operating profit	136
Finance costs	(40)
Profit before tax	96
Taxation	(24)
Profit for the period	72

5.4

Manet plc
Statement of changes in equity for the year ended 30 June 2007

	Share Capital £m	Share premium £m	Reval. reserve £m	Translat. reserve £m	Retained earnings £m	Total £m
Balance as at 30 June 2006	250	50	120	15	380	815
Changes in equity for the year ended 30 June 2007						
Gain on revaluation of properties			30			30
Exchange differences on translation of foreign operations	—	—	—	(5)	—	(5)
Net income recognised directly to equity			30	(5)		25
Profit for the period	—	—	—	—	160	160
Total recognised income and expense for the period			30	(5)	160	185
Dividends	—	—	—	—	(80)	(80)
Balance at 30 June 2007	250	50	150	10	460	920

5.5 Here are some points that might be made concerning accounting regulation and accounting measurement:

For

- It seems reasonable that companies, particularly given their limited liability, should be required to account to their members and to the general public and that rules should prescribe how this should be done – including how particular items should be measured. It also seems sensible that rules should try to establish some uniformity of practice. Investors could be misled if the same item appeared in the financial statements of two separate companies but had been measured in different ways.
- Companies would find it difficult to attract finance, credit and possibly employees without publishing credible information about themselves. An important measure of performance is profit, and investors often need to make judgements concerning relative performance within an industry sector. Without clear benchmarks by which to judge performance, investors may not invest in a company.

Against

- It could be argued that it is up to the companies to decide whether or not they can survive and prosper without publishing information about themselves. If they can, then so much the better for them as they will have saved large amounts of money by not doing so. If it is necessary for a company to provide financial information in order to be able to attract investment finance and other necessary factors, then the company can make the necessary judgement of how much information is necessary and what forms of measurement are required.
- Not all company managements view matters in the same way. Allowing companies to select their own approaches to financial reporting enables them to reflect their personalities. Thus, a conservative management will adopt conservative accounting policies such as writing off research and development expenditure quickly, whereas more adventurous management may adopt less conservative accounting policies such as writing off research and development expenditure over several years. The impact of these different views will have an effect on profit and will give the reader an insight to the approach adopted by the management team.

5.8 **Carpetright plc**

Table of key results

This table extracts some of the information from the segmental report and calculates a few ratios to help gain an insight to financial health. (Ratios will be explored in detail in Chapters 7 and 8.)

	2006		2005	
	UK and RoI £m	Rest of Europe £m	UK and RoI £m	Rest of Europe £m
Segment revenue	397.7	53.7	409.2	53.3
Gross profit	241.2	29.7	245.2	27.8
Operating profit	55.1	3.6	60.4	3.0
Total assets	162.7	74.8	147.9	64.2
Net assets (TA – TL)	52.7	60.2	47.0	52.4
Capital expenditure	30.8	4.3	23.6	9.5
Key ratios				
Gross profit as % revenue	60.6%	55.3%	59.9%	52.2%
Operating profit as % revenue	13.9%	6.7%	14.8%	5.6%
Operating profit as % of net assets	104.6%	6.0%	128.5%	5.7%
Capital expenditure as % of total assets	18.9%	5.7%	16.0%	14.8%

Comparing 2006 with the 2005 segment results

UK and RoI segment

- For the UK and RoI segment, revenue, gross profit and operating profit fell slightly in 2006 compared to the previous year.
- Operating profit as a percentage of revenue slipped slightly in 2006.
- Net assets increased during 2006.
- Given the decline in the operating profits and the increase in net assets, it was inevitable that the operating profits as a percentage of net assets would decline.
- Overall, some deterioration in financial results has occurred during 2006.

Rest of Europe segment

- Revenue increased slightly in 2006 compared to the previous year.
- Gross profit and operating profits increased by a greater amount than the increase in revenue compared to the previous year.
- Net assets increased by nearly 15 per cent in 2006 compared to the previous year.
- The increase in net assets was greater than the increase in operating profits.
- The operating profit as a percentage of net assets did not increase significantly.
- Overall, some improvement in financial results has occurred for the Rest of Europe during 2006.

Comparing the two segments

- There is a significant difference in the size of the two segments – the UK and RoI segment dwarfs the Rest of Europe segment.
- For 2006, sales revenue for the UK and RoI is more than seven times higher and operating profits are more than 15 times than for the rest of Europe.
- The UK and RoI segment is the more profitable segment in both years and across all measures.
- Capital expenditure, as a percentage of total assets, is much higher for the UK and RoI than for the Rest of Europe in both years.
- The Rest of Europe requires a much higher investment of assets to generate each £1 of sales revenue and each £1 of profit.

The reasons for the differences in profitability between the two segments are not clear from the information available. Possible reasons may include:

- a more difficult economic environment in the Rest of Europe segment;
- the Rest of Europe segment is not yet fully established in its markets;
- problems in applying, or adapting, the UK and RoI business model to the Rest of Europe.

Chapter 6

6.1 (a) An increase in the level of inventories would, ultimately, have an adverse effect on cash.

(b) A rights issue of ordinary shares will give rise to a positive cash flow, which will be included in the 'financing' section of the cash flow statement.

(c) A bonus issue of ordinary shares has no cash flow effect.

(d) Writing off some of the value of the inventories has no cash flow effect.

(e) A disposal for cash of a large number of shares by a major shareholder has no cash flow effect as far as the business is concerned.

(f) Depreciation does not involve cash at all. Using the indirect method of deducing cash flows from operating activities involves the depreciation expense in the calculation, but this is simply because we are trying to find out from the profit before taxation (after depreciation) figure what the profit before taxation and depreciation must have been.

6.3

Torrent plc
Cash flow statement for the year ended 31 December 2007

	£m	£m
Cash flows from operating activities		
Profit before taxation (after interest) (see Note 1 below)	170	
Adjustments for:		
Depreciation (Note 2)	78	
Interest expense (Note 3)	26	
	274	
Decrease in inventories (41 − 35)	6	
Increase in trade receivables (145 − 139)	(6)	
Decrease in trade payables (54 − 41)	(13)	
Cash generated from operations	261	
Interest paid	(26)	
Taxation paid (Note 4)	(41)	
Dividend paid	(60)	
Net cash from operating activities		134
Cash flows from investing activities		
Payments to acquire plant and machinery	(67)	
Net cash used in investing activities		(67)
Cash flows from financing activities		
Redemption of loan notes (250 − 150) (Note 5)	(100)	
Net cash used in financing activities		(100)
Net decrease in cash and cash equivalents		(33)
Cash and cash equivalents at 1 January 2007		
Bank overdraft		(56)
Cash and cash equivalents at 31 December 2007		
Bank overdraft		(89)

To see how this relates to the cash of the business at the beginning and end of the year it can be useful to provide a reconciliation as follows:

Analysis of cash and cash equivalents during the year ended 31 December 2007

	£m
Cash and cash equivalents at 1 January 2007	(56)
Net cash outflow	(33)
Cash and cash equivalents at 31 December 2007	(89)

Notes

1 This is simply taken from the income statement for the year.

2 Since there were no disposals, the depreciation charges must be the difference between the start and end of the year's plant and machinery values, adjusted by the cost of any additions.

	£m
Carrying amount, at 1 January 2007	325
Add Additions	67
	392
Less Depreciation (balancing figure)	78
Carrying amount, at 31 December 2007	314

3 Interest payable expense must be taken out, by adding it back to the profit before taxation figure. We subsequently deduct the cash paid for interest payable during the year. In this case the two figures are identical.

4 Companies pay 50 per cent of their tax during their accounting year and 50 per cent in the following year. Thus the 2007 payment would have been half the tax on the 2006 profit (that is, the figure that would have appeared in the current liabilities at the end of 2006), plus half of the 2007 tax charge (that is, $23 + (1/2 \times 36) = 41$).

5 It is assumed that the cash payment to redeem the debentures was simply the difference between the two balance sheet figures.

It seems that there was a bonus issue of ordinary shares during the year. These increased by £100 m. At the same time, the share premium account balance reduced by £40 m (to zero) and the revaluation reserve balance fell by £60 m.

6.6

Blackstone plc
Cash flow statement for the year ended 31 March 2007

	£m	£m
Cash flows from operating activities		
Profit before taxation (after interest) (see Note 1 below)	1,853	
Adjustments for:		
Depreciation (Note 2)	1,289	
Interest expense (Note 3)	456	
	3,598	
Increase in inventories (2,410 – 1,209)	(1,201)	
Increase in trade receivables (1,173 – 641)	(532)	
Increase in trade payables (1,507 – 931)	576	
Cash generated from operations	2,441	
Interest paid	(456)	
Taxation paid (Note 4)	(300)	
Dividend paid	(400)	
Net cash from operating activities		1,285
Cash flows from investing activities		
Proceeds of disposals	54	
Payment to acquire intangible non-current asset	(700)	
Payments to acquire property, plant and equipment	(4,578)	
Net cash used in investing activities		(5,224)
Cash flows from financing activities		
Bank borrowings	2,000	
Net cash from financing activities		2,000
Net decrease in cash and cash equivalents		(1,939)
Cash and cash equivalents at 1 April 2006		
Cash at bank		123
Cash and cash equivalents at 31 March 2007		
Bank overdraft		(1,816)

To see how this relates to the cash of the business at the beginning and end of the year it can be useful to provide a reconciliation as follows:

Analysis of cash and cash equivalents during the year ended 31 March 2007

	£m
Cash and cash equivalents at 1 April 2006	123
Net cash outflow	(1,939)
Cash and cash equivalents at 31 March 2007	1,816

Notes

1   This is simply taken from the income statement for the year.

2   The full depreciation charge was that stated in Note 3 to the question (£1,251 m), plus the deficit on disposal of the non-current assets. According to Note 3, these non-current assets had originally cost £581 m and had been depreciated by £489 m, that is a net carrying amount of £92 m. They were sold for £54 m, leading to a deficit on disposal of £38 m. Thus the full depreciation expense for the year was £1,289 m (that is, £1,251 m + £38 m).

3   Interest payable expense must be taken out, by adding it back to the profit before taxation figure. We subsequently deduct the cash paid for interest payable during the year. In this case the two figures are identical.

4   Companies pay tax at 50 per cent during their accounting year and the other 50 per cent in the following year. Thus, the 2007 payment would have been half the tax on the 2006 profit (that is, the figure that would have appeared in the current liabilities at 31 March 2006), plus half of the 2007 tax charge (that is, $105 + (^1/_2 \times 390) = 300$).

6.7

York plc
Cash flow statement for the year ended 30 September 2007

	£m	£m
Cash flows from operating activities		
Profit before taxation (after interest)		
(see Note 1 below)	10.0	
Adjustments for:		
Depreciation (Note 2)	9.8	
Interest expense (Note 3)	3.0	
	22.8	
Increase in inventories and trade receivables (122.1 – 119.8)	(2.3)	
Increase in trade payables (82.5 – 80.0)	2.5	
Cash generated from operations	23.0	
Interest paid	(3.0)	
Taxation paid (Note 4)	(2.3)	
Dividend paid	(3.5)	
Net cash from operating activities		14.2
Cash flows from investing activities		
Proceeds of disposals (Note 2)	5.2	
Payments to acquire non-current assets	(20.0)	
Net cash used in investing activities		(14.8)
Cash flows from financing activities		
Increase in long-term borrowings	3.0	
Share issue (Note 5)	5.0	
Net cash from financing activities		8.0
Net increase in cash and cash equivalents		7.4
Cash and cash equivalents at 1 October 2006		
Cash at bank		9.2
Cash and cash equivalents at 30 September 2007		
Cash at bank		16.6

To see how this relates to the cash of the business at the beginning and end of the year it can be useful to provide a reconciliation as follows:

Analysis of cash and cash equivalents during the year ended 30 September 2007

	£m
Cash and cash equivalents at 1 October 2006	9.2
Net cash inflow	7.4
Cash and cash equivalents at 30 September 2007	16.6

Notes

1 This is simply taken from the income statement for the year.

2 The full depreciation charge was the £13.0 m, less the surplus on disposal (£3.2 m), both stated in Note 1 to the question.

   According to the table in Note 4 to the question, the non-current assets disposed of had a net carrying value of £2.0 m. To produce a surplus of £3.2 m, they must have been sold for £5.2 m.

3 Interest payable expense must be taken out, by adding it back to the profit before taxation figure. We subsequently deduct the cash paid for interest payable during the year. In this case the two figures are identical.

4 Companies pay 50 per cent tax during their accounting year and the other 50 per cent in the following year. Thus the 2007 payment would have been half the tax on the 2006 profit (that is, the figure that would have appeared in the current liabilities at 30 September 2006), plus half of the 2007 tax charge (that is, $1.0 + (^1/_2 \times 2.6) = 2.3$).

5 This issue must have been for cash since it could not have been a bonus issue – the share premium is untouched and the 'Reserves' had only altered over the year by the amount of the 2007 retained profit (profit for the year, less the dividend). The shares seem to have been issued at par (that is, at their nominal value). This is a little surprising since the business has assets that seem to be above that value. On the other hand, were this a rights issue, the low issue price would not have disadvantaged the existing shareholders since they were also the beneficiaries of the advantage of the low issue price.

6.8

Axis plc
Cash flow statement for the year ended 31 December 2007

	£m	£m
Cash flows from operating activities		
Profit before taxation (after interest) (see Note 1 below)	34	
Adjustments for:		
Depreciation (Note 2)	19	
Interest expense (Note 3)	2	
	55	
Decrease in inventories (25 – 24)	1	
Increase in trade receivables (26 – 16)	(10)	
Increase in trade payables (36 – 31)	5	
Cash generated from operations	51	
Interest paid	(2)	
Taxation paid (Note 4)	(15)	
Dividend paid	(14)	
Net cash from operating activities		20
Cash flows from investing activities		
Proceeds of disposals (Note 2)	4	
Payments to acquire non-current assets	(25)	
Net cash used in investing activities		(21)
Cash flows from financing activities		
Issue of loan notes	20	
Net cash from financing activities		20
Net increase in cash and cash equivalents		19
Cash and cash equivalents at 1 January 2007		
Cash at bank		nil
Short-term investments		nil
		nil
Cash and cash equivalents at 31 December 2007		
Cash at bank		7
Short-term investments		12
		19

To see how this relates to the cash of the business at the beginning and end of the year it can be useful to provide a reconciliation as follows:

Analysis of cash and cash equivalents during the year ended 31 December 2007

	£m
Cash and cash equivalents at 1 January 2007	nil
Net cash inflow	19
Cash and cash equivalents at 31 December 2007	19

Notes

1 This is simply taken from the income statement for the year.
2 The full depreciation charge for the year is the sum of two figures labelled 'depreciation' and the deficit on disposal of non-current assets (that is, £2m + £16m + £1m = £19m). These were detailed in the income statement.

   According to the note in the question, the non-current assets disposed of had a net carrying amount of £5.0 m (that is, £15 m – £10 m). To produce a deficit of £1 m, they must have been sold for £4 m.
3 Interest payable expense must be taken out, by adding it back to the profit before taxation figure. We subsequently deduct the cash paid for interest payable during the year. In this case the two figures are identical.
4 Companies pay 50 per cent tax during their accounting year and the other 50 per cent in the following year. Thus, the 2007 payment would have been half the tax on the 2006 profit (that is, the figure that would have appeared in the current liabilities at 31 December 2006), plus half of the 2007 tax charge (that is, $7 + (^1/_2 \times 16) = 15$).

Chapter 7

7.1   I. Jiang (Western) Ltd

The effect of each of the changes on ROCE is not always easy to predict.

1 On the face of it, an increase in the gross profit margin would tend to lead to an increase in ROCE. An increase in the gross profit margin may, however, lead to a decrease in ROCE in particular circumstances. If the increase in the margin resulted from an increase in sales prices, which in turn led to a decrease in sales revenue, a fall in ROCE can occur. A fall in sales revenue can reduce the operating profit (the numerator (top part of the fraction) in ROCE) if the overheads of the business did not decrease correspondingly.
2 A reduction in sales revenue can reduce ROCE for the reasons mentioned above.
3 An increase in overhead expenses will reduce the operating profit and this in turn will result in a reduction in ROCE.
4 An increase in inventories held would increase the amount of capital employed by the business (the denominator (bottom part of the fraction) in ROCE) where long-term funds are employed to finance the inventories. This will, in turn, reduce ROCE.
5 Repayment of the borrowings at the year end will reduce the capital employed and this will increase the ROCE, assuming that the year-end capital employed figure has been used in the calculation. Since the operating profit was earned during a period in which the borrowings existed, there is a strong argument for basing the capital employed figure on what was the position during the year, rather than at the end of it.
6 An increase in the time taken for credit customers to pay will result in an increase in capital employed if long-term funds are employed to finance the trade receivables. This increase in long-term funds will, in turn, reduce ROCE.

7.2　Amsterdam Ltd and Berlin Ltd

The ratios for Amsterdam Ltd and Berlin Ltd reveal that the trade receivables turnover ratio for Amsterdam Ltd is three times that for Berlin Ltd. Berlin Ltd is, therefore, much quicker in collecting amounts outstanding from customers. On the other hand, there is not much difference between the two businesses in the time taken to pay trade payables.

It is interesting to compare the difference in the trade receivables and payables collection periods for each business. As Amsterdam Ltd allows an average of 63 days' credit to its customers, yet pays suppliers within 50 days, it will require greater investment in working capital than Berlin Ltd, which allows an average of only 21 days to its customers but takes 45 days to pay its suppliers.

Amsterdam Ltd has a much higher gross profit percentage than Berlin Ltd. However, the operating profit margin for the two businesses is identical. This suggests that Amsterdam Ltd has much higher overheads (as a percentage of sales revenue) than Berlin Ltd. The inventories turnover period for Amsterdam Ltd is more than twice that of Berlin Ltd. This may be due to the fact that Amsterdam Ltd maintains a wider range of inventories in an attempt to meet customer requirements. The evidence, therefore, suggests that Amsterdam Ltd is the one that prides itself on personal service. The higher average settlement period for trade receivables is consistent with a more relaxed attitude to credit collection (thereby maintaining customer goodwill) and the high overheads are consistent with incurring the additional costs of satisfying customers' requirements. Amsterdam Ltd's high inventories levels are consistent with maintaining a wide range of inventories, with the aim of satisfying a range of customer needs.

Berlin Ltd has the characteristics of a more price-competitive business. Its gross profit margin is much lower than that of Amsterdam Ltd, that is, a much lower gross profit for each £1 of sales revenue. However, overheads have been kept low, the effect being that the operating percentage is the same as Amsterdam Ltd's. The low inventories turnover period and average collection period for trade receivables are consistent with a business that wishes to minimise investment in current assets, thereby reducing costs.

7.6　Bradbury Ltd

(a)		2006	2007
(1)	*Operating profit margin ratio*		
	914/9,482 × 100%	9.6%	
	1,042/11,365 × 100%		9.2%
(2)	*ROCE ratio*		
	914/11,033 × 100%	8.3%	
	1,042/13,943 × 100%		7.5%
(3)	*Current ratio*		
	4,926/1,508	3.3:1	
	7,700/5,174		1.5:1
(4)	*Gearing ratio*		
	1,220/11,033 × 100%	11.1%	
	3,675/13,943 × 100%		26.4%
(5)	*Days trade receivables ratio*		
	(2,540/9,482) × 365	98 days	
	(4,280/11,365) × 365		137 days
(6)	*Sales revenue to capital employed ratio*		
	9,482/(9,813 + 1,220)	0.9 times	
	11,365/(10,268 + 3,675)		0.8 times

(b) The operating profit margin was slightly lower in 2007 than in 2006. Though there was an increase in sales revenue in 2007, this could not prevent a slight fall in ROCE in that year. The lower operating margin and increases in sales revenue may well be due to the new contract. The capital employed by the company increased in 2007 by a larger percentage than the increase in revenue. Hence, the sales revenue to capital employed ratio decreased over the period. The increase in capital during 2007 is largely due to an increase in borrowing. However, the gearing ratio is probably still low in comparison with other businesses. Comparison of the premises and borrowings figures indicates possible unused borrowing (debt) capacity. The major cause for concern has been the dramatic decline in liquidity during 2007. The current ratio has more than halved during the period. There has also been a similar decrease in the acid test ratio, from 1.7:1 in 2006 to 0.8:1 in 2007. The balance sheet shows that the business now has a large overdraft and the trade payables outstanding have nearly doubled in 2007.

The trade receivables outstanding and inventories have increased much more than appears to be warranted by the increase in sales revenue. This may be due to the terms of the contract that has been negotiated and may be difficult to influence. If this is the case, the business should consider whether it is overtrading. If the conclusion is that it is, increasing its long-term funding may be a sensible policy.

7.7 **Harridges Ltd**

(a)

Ratio	2006	2007
ROCE	$\dfrac{310}{1,600} = 19.4\%$	$\dfrac{350}{1,700} = 20.6\%$
ROSF	$\dfrac{155}{1,100} = 14.1\%$	$\dfrac{175}{1,200} = 14.6\%$
Gross profit margin	$\dfrac{1,040}{2,600} = 40\%$	$\dfrac{1,150}{3,500} = 32.9\%$
Operating profit margin	$\dfrac{310}{2,600} = 11.9\%$	$\dfrac{350}{3,500} = 10\%$
Current	$\dfrac{735}{400} = 1.8$	$\dfrac{660}{485} = 1.4$
Acid test	$\dfrac{485}{400} = 1.2$	$\dfrac{260}{485} = 0.5$
Days trade receivables	$\dfrac{105}{2,600} \times 365 = 15$ days	$\dfrac{145}{3,500} \times 365 = 15$ days
Days trade payables	$\dfrac{300}{1,560} \times 365 = 70$ days	$\dfrac{375}{2,350^*} \times 365 = 58$ days
Inventories turnover period	$\dfrac{250}{1,560} \times 365 = 58$ days	$\dfrac{400}{2,350} \times 365 = 62$ days
Gearing	$\dfrac{500}{1,600} = 31.3\%$	$\dfrac{500}{1,700} = 29.4\%$

* Used because the credit purchases figure is not available.

(b) There has been a considerable decline in the gross profit margin during 2007. This fact, combined with the increase in sales revenue by more than one-third, suggests that a price-cutting policy has been adopted in an attempt to stimulate sales. The resulting increase in sales revenue, however, has led to only a small improvement in ROCE and ROSF. Similarly, there has only been a small improvement in EPS.

Despite a large cut in the gross profit margin, the operating profit margin has fallen by less than 2 per cent. This suggests that overheads have been tightly controlled during 2007. Certainly, overheads have not risen in proportion to sales revenue.

The current ratio has fallen and the acid test ratio has fallen by more than half. Even though liquidity ratios are lower in retailing than in manufacturing, the liquidity of the business should now be a cause for concern. However, this may be a passing problem. The business is investing heavily in non-current assets and is relying on internal funds to finance this growth. When this investment ends, the liquidity position may improve quickly.

The trade receivables period has remained unchanged over the two years, and there has been no significant change in the inventories turnover period in 2007. The gearing ratio seems quite low and provides no cause for concern given the profitability of the business.

Overall, the business appears to be financially sound. Though there has been rapid growth during 2007, there is no real cause for alarm provided that the liquidity of the business can be improved in the near future. In the absence of information concerning share price, it is not possible to say whether or not an investment should be made.

7.8   Freezeqwik Ltd

The OCC may be calculated as follows:

	Number of days
Average inventories holding period:	
$\dfrac{\text{(Opening inventories + Closing inventories)}/2}{\text{Cost of sales}} \times 365 = \dfrac{(142 + 166)/2}{544} \times 365$	103
Average settlement period for trade receivables:	
$\dfrac{\text{Trade receivables}}{\text{Credit sales}} \times 365 = \dfrac{264}{820} \times 365$	118
	221
Less	
Average settlement period for trade payables:	
$\dfrac{\text{Trade payables}}{\text{Credit purchases}} \times 365 = \dfrac{159}{568} \times 365$	102
OCC	119

The business can reduce the length of the OCC in a number of ways. The average inventories holding period seems quite long. At present, average inventories held represent more than three months' sales requirements. Lowering the level of inventories held will reduce this. Similarly, the average settlement period for trade receivables seems long, at nearly four months' sales. Imposing tighter credit control, offering discounts, charging interest on overdue accounts and so on, may reduce this. However, any policy decisions concerning inventories and trade receivables must take account of current trading conditions.

Extending the period of credit taken to pay suppliers could also reduce the OCC. However, this option must be given careful consideration because it could lead to a loss of supplier goodwill that could be damaging to Freezeqwik Ltd.

Chapter 8

8.1   Next plc

The Next plc dividend yield is slightly below that for the retailers section average. This may mean that the business pays out relatively small proportion of its earnings as a dividend, which the dividend cover ratio reveals to be the case. Next only pays out less than one third of its earnings whereas the average for retailers listed on the London Stock Exchange is twice this. Compared to current (most recently reported) earnings, the current market price (P/E ratio) of Next is rather lower than the average for listed retailers. This possibly implies that the investing public has less confidence in the future prospects of Next than in listed retailers generally. However, P/E ratios can be difficult to interpret.

8.2   Telford Industrial Services plc

Common sized balance sheet at 31 December

	2004 £m	2005 £m	2006 £m	2007 £m
Non-current assets	100	83	106	102
Current assets				
Inventories	44	36	38	41
Trade receivables	71	69	56	46
Cash	–	5	–	–
	115	110	94	87
Total assets	215	193	200	189
Equity	100	100	100	100
Non-current liabilities	63	49	49	47
Current liabilities				
Trade payables	42	44	41	29
Short-term borrowings	10	–	10	13
	52	44	51	42
Total equity and liabilities	215	193	200	189

(The individual figures are calculated by dividing each of the original figures by the equity value for the year concerned and multiplying the result by 100. For example, the non-current liabilities figure for 2004 is $30/48 \times 100 = 63$. Since the revised values have been expressed in whole numbers (no decimal places), it was necessary to adjust to make the balance sheet agree, despite rounding errors.)

Summary of income statements for years ended 31 December

	2004 £m	2005 £m	2006 £m	2007 £m
Sales revenue	100	100	100	100
Operating profit	19	24	6	10
Interest payable	(3)	(2)	(4)	(3)
Profit before taxation	16	22	2	7
Taxation	(8)	(9)	–	(3)
Profit for the year	8	13	2	4

(The individual figures are calculated by dividing each of the original figures by the sales revenue value for the year concerned and multiplying the result by 100. For example, the profit for the year for 2004 is $12/152 \times 100 = 8$.)

8.3   Ali plc and Bhaskar plc

(a) The Altman model Z score model is as follows:

$$Z = 0.717a + 0.847b + 3.107c + 0.420d + 0.998e$$

Where a = Working capital/Total assets
b = Accumulated retained profits/Total assets
c = Operating profit/Total assets
d = Book (balance sheet) value of ordinary and preference shares/Total liabilities at book (balance sheet) value
e = Sales revenue/Total assets

For Ali plc, the Z score is:

$$0.717[(853.0 - 422.4)/1,300.0] + 0.847(367.6/1,300.0) + 3.107(151.3/1,300.0) \\ + 0.420[320.0/(190.0 + 422.4)] + 0.998(1,478.1/1,300.0) = \underline{2.193}$$

For Bhaskar plc, the Z score is:

$$0.717[(816.5 - 293.1)/1,417.7] + 0.847(624.6/1,417.7) + 3.107(166.9/1,417.7) \\ + 0.420[250.0/(250.0 + 293.1)] + 0.998(1,790.4/1,417.7) = \underline{2.192}$$

(b) The Z scores for these two businesses are virtually identical. This places them both in the category of businesses in the 'zone of ignorance' and, therefore, difficult to classify (a Z score between 1.23 and 4.14). This is quite unusual in that Altman model is able confidently to classify 91 per cent of businesses. Clearly, these two businesses fall into the remaining 9 per cent.

It is questionable whether the Altman model is strictly applicable to UK businesses, since it was derived from data relating to US businesses that had failed. On the other hand, it probably provides a useful insight.

8.5   Green Ltd

(a)

		2005		2006		2007	
(1)	Return on capital employed ratio	(0.2)/(8.4 + 6.5) × 100	(1.3)%	(2.0)/(4.0 + 8.2) × 100	(16.4)%	1.9/(4.4 + 7.4) × 100	16.1%
(2)	Acid test ratio*	2.8/4.1	0.68:1	2.6/5.8	0.45:1	4.1/6.1	0.67:1
(3)	Trade receivables settlement period ratio*	2.8/11.5 × 12	2.9 months	2.6/8.0 × 12	3.9 months	4.1/9.5 × 12	5.2 months
(4)	Interest cover ratio		No cover		No cover	1.9/1.5	1.3 times
(5)	Gearing ratio	6.5/(6.5 + 8.4) × 100	43.6%	8.2/(8.2 + 4.0) × 100	67.2%	7.4/(7.4 + 4.4) × 100	62.7%

* The year-end figures were used because it would not have been possible, with the information provided in the question, to use the average for all of the years.

In terms of profitability, Green Ltd seems to have improved in 2007, relative to the previous two years, particularly 2006. This has probably been the main reason for the improvement in liquidity since 2006. The increase in the time taken to collect the cash from credit customers is a concern. This has almost doubled since 2005. Over five months seems a very long time.

Gearing, which increased in 2006, has dropped a little in 2007. Given the level of profit, gearing still looks high, with the interest obligations not being very well covered by operating profit.

(b) Possibly the most useful help that your business could offer Green Ltd is some advice on reducing its level of working capital (current assets less current liabilities. As mentioned in (a), the trade receivable level in 2007 seems very high. This seems also to be true of inventories. At the same time, trade payables seem quite low (only 50 per cent of the level of inventories in 2007). It seems perfectly plausible that a combination of taking longer to pay suppliers, getting in cash from customers more quickly and reducing the level of inventories could generate sufficient funds to eliminate the bank overdraft.

Your business may be reluctant to involve itself in providing finance. It is not, presumably, in the business of doing so. It may prefer to suggest that Green Ltd looks for some bank or equity finance from a more traditional source. Given the already high level of gearing, even assuming that the overdraft can be eliminated, as suggested above, equity looks a better bet than loan financing. Given that it is your business's only source of certain of its needs, you may feel that supplying finance and gaining the influence that this may bring, is the best way to protect your business's interests.

If your business is able and willing to advance equity finance (buy new shares issued by Green Ltd), the following points need to be addressed:

- *Future profitability.* How profitable can Green Ltd be in the future, with the new machinery?
- *Influence.* If your business is to buy shares, it will need to be sure of some considerable influence over Green Ltd's management. A seat on Green Ltd's board of directors seems a minimum requirement.
- *Exit route.* How will your business be able to liquidate its investment, as and when it wishes to do so? Green Ltd is not a plc and cannot, therefore be Stock Exchange listed. This means that there is no ready and obvious market for the shares.

8.8   Genesis Ltd

(a) and (b)

These parts have been answered in the text of the chapter and you are referred to it for a discussion on overtrading and its consequences.

(c)

Current ratio = $\dfrac{232}{550}$ = 0.42:1

Acid test ratio = $\dfrac{104}{550}$ = 0.19:1

Inventories turnover period = $\dfrac{128}{1,248} \times 365$ = 37 days

Average settlement period for trade receivables = $\dfrac{104}{1,640} \times 365$ = 23 days

Average settlement period for trade payables = $\dfrac{184}{1,260} \times 365$ = 53 days

(d) Overtrading must be dealt with either by increasing the level of funding to match the level of activity, or by reducing the level of activity to match the funds available. The latter option may result in a reduction in operating profit in the short term but may be necessary to ensure long-term survival.

Chapter 9

9.1

Group balance sheet of Giant and its subsidiary as at 31 March

	£m	£m
Non-current assets (at cost less depreciation)		
Property, plant and equipment		
Land	39	
Plant	63	
Vehicles	25	127
Current assets		
Inventories	46	
Trade receivables	59	
Cash	27	132
Total assets		159
Equity		
Called-up share capital:		
ordinary shares of £1 each, fully paid	50	
Share premium account	40	
Retained profit	46	136
Non-current liabilities		
Loan notes		63
Current liabilities		
Trade payables		60
Total equity and liabilities		159

Note that the group balance sheet is prepared by adding all like items together. The investment in 10 million shares of Jack Ltd (£30 m), in the balance sheet of Giant plc, is then compared with the equity (in total) in Jack Ltd's balance sheet. Since Giant paid exactly the fair values of Jack's assets *and* bought all of Jack's shares, these two figures are equal and can be cancelled.

9.2 The balance sheet of Jumbo plc and its subsidiary will be as follows:

Balance sheet as at 31 March

	£m	£m
Non-current assets (at cost less depreciation)		
Property, plant and equipment		
Land	102	
Plant	67	
Vehicles	57	226
Current assets		
Inventories	87	
Trade receivables	70	
Cash	24	181
Total assets		407
Equity		
Called-up share capital:		
ordinary shares of £1 each, fully paid	100	
Retained profit	41	141
Minority interests		16
		157
Non-current liabilities		
Loan notes		170
Current liabilities		
Trade payables		80
Total equity and liabilities		407

Note that the normal approach is taken with various assets and external claims (that is, adding like items together). The 'minority interests' figure represents the minorities' share (8 million of 20 million ordinary shares) in the equity of Nipper plc.

9.3   Toggles plc

(a) (1) 'Minority interests' represents the portion, either of net assets (balance sheet) or profit for the year (income statement), which is attributable to minority shareholders. Minority shareholders exist where the parent company does not own all of the shares in its subsidiary. Since, by definition, the parent company is the major shareholder in each of its subsidiaries, any other shareholders in any other subsidiary must be a minority, in terms of number of shares owned.

(2) 'Goodwill on consolidation' is the difference, at the time that the parent acquires the subsidiary, between what is paid for the subsidiary company shares and what they are 'worth'. 'Worth' normally is based on the fair values of the underlying assets (net of liabilities) of the subsidiary.

These are not necessarily, nor usually, the balance sheet values. Goodwill, therefore, represents the excess of what was paid over the fair values of the (net) assets of the subsidiary.

As such goodwill on consolidation is an intangible asset that represents the amount that the parent was prepared to pay for the value of the fact that the subsidiary has a workforce in place and any possible synergies that will arise from the parent and the subsidiary having a close relationship.

(3) The retained profit of the parent company will be its own cumulative profits net of tax and dividends paid.

When the results of the subsidiaries are consolidated with those of the parent, the parent's share of the post-acquisition retained profits of its subsidiaries is added to its own retained profit figure. In this way the parent is, in effect, credited with its share of the subsidiaries' after tax profit, that has arisen since the takeover.

(b) The objective of preparing consolidated financial statements is to reflect the underlying economic reality that the assets of the subsidiary companies are as much under the control of the shareholders of the parent, acting through their board of directors, as are the assets owned directly by the parent. This will be true despite the fact that the subsidiary is strictly a separate company from the parent. It is also despite the fact that the parent may not own all of the shares of the subsidiaries.

Consolidated financial statements provide an example where accounting tends to put 'content' before 'form'. That is to say, that it tries to reflect economic reality rather than the strict legal position. This is to try to provide more useful information.

9.4   Arnold plc and Baker plc

Group income statement for the year ended 31 December

	£m	£m
Revenue (83 + 47)		130
Cost of sales (36 + 19)		(55)
Gross profit		75
Administration expenses (14 + 7)	(21)	
Distribution expenses (21 + 10)	(31)	(52)
Operating profit		23
Taxation (4 + 3)		(7)
Profit for the year		16
Attributable to minorities (25% × 8)		(2)
Profit for the year attributable to Arnold plc shareholders		14

9.5   The balance sheet of Apple Ltd and its subsidiary will be as follows:

Balance sheet as at 30 September

	£000	£000
Non-current assets (at cost less depreciation)		
Property, plant and equipment (950 + 320)		1,270
Goodwill arising on consolidation (see Note 2)		24
		1,294
Current assets		
Inventories (320 + 160)	480	
Trade receivables (180 + 95)	275	
Cash at bank (41 + 15)	56	811
Total assets		2,105
Equity		
£1 fully paid ordinary shares	700	
Reserves	307	1,007
Minority interests (see Note 3)		72
		1,079
Non-current liabilities		
Loan notes (500 + 160)		660
Current liabilities		
Trade payables (170 + 87)	257	
Taxation (54 + 55)	109	366
Total equity and liabilities		2,105

Notes
1 The normal approach is taken with various assets and external claims.
2 The goodwill arising on consolidation is the difference between what Apple Ltd paid for the shares in Pear Ltd (150,000 × £1.60 = £240,000), less the fair value of the net assets acquired (150,000/200,000 × £288,000 = £216,000). That is, £24,000.
3 The minority interest figure is simply the minority shareholders' stake in the net assets of Pear Ltd. This is 50,000/200,000 × £288,000 = £72,000.

Chapter 10

10.1   Non-executive directors

The following criteria may be used to evaluate the performance of a non-executive director:

- willingness to spend time in understanding the business and in acquiring additional skills to improve effectiveness;
- contribution made to board discussions on key issues such as strategy development;
- effectiveness in challenging proposals made by identifying key weaknesses and assumptions;
- independence of mind and ability to resist undue pressure from other directors;
- perseverance in following up unresolved issues and in defending positions taken;
- ability to work as part of a team, when required, and to establish effective relations with key individuals, including other board members.

This is not an exhaustive list, you may have thought of others.

10.3 **Institutional shareholders**

The benefits that may accrue from close ties with institutional shareholders are as follows:

- It provides the board of directors with the opportunity to explain the future direction of the company, which may lead to a better understanding of board proposals and decisions that have been made. This may, in turn, make institutional shareholders more willing to offer support during difficult times.
- It may encourage institutional shareholders to take a long-term view. If the board can provide a clear vision and strategy for the company, the shareholders may become less concerned with any short-term setbacks and become more concerned with achieving long-term goals.
- It can provide an external discipline on the board. The directors will be subjected to considerable scrutiny when meeting institutional shareholders. They will have to justify their decisions and be prepared to answer tough questions. This can, however, improve the quality of decisions made.
- It can provide valuable feedback on board proposals. Institutional investors may be sounded out on particular ideas that are under review. Their views can then be taken into account when making a final decision.
- It can help in future funding. Where institutional shareholders have good relations with the board and have confidence in the future direction of the company, they are more likely to be sympathetic to requests for additional funding.

There are various problems that can arise from close links with institutional shareholders. For example, there is a risk that certain commercially sensitive information provided to them will not be treated in confidence. There is also a risk in upsetting small shareholders, who may feel that large institutional shareholders are given undue influence over decisions. Finally, there is a problem in determining what are the acceptable limits to the discussions and information that is offered.

Appendix A

A.1

Account to be debited	Account to be credited
(a) Inventories	Trade payables
(b) Capital (or a separate drawings account)	Cash
(c) Interest on borrowings	Cash
(d) Inventories	Cash
(e) Cash	Trade receivables
(f) Wages	Cash
(g) Capital (or a separate drawings account)	Trade receivables
(h) Trade payables	Cash
(i) Electricity (or heat and light)	Cash
(j) Cash	Sales revenue

Note that the precise name given to an account is not crucial so long as those who are using the information are clear as to what each account deals with.

A.2 (a) and (b)

Cash

		£			£
1 Feb	Capital	6,000	3 Feb	Inventories	2,600
15 Feb	Sales revenue	4,000	5 Feb	Equipment	800
28 Feb	Trade receivables	2,500	9 Feb	Rent	250
			10 Feb	Fuel and electricity	240
			11 Feb	General expenses	200
			21 Feb	Capital	1,000
			25 Feb	Trade payables	2,000
			28 Feb	Balance c/d	5,410
		12,500			12,500
1 Mar	Balance b/d	5,410			

Capital

		£			£
21 Feb	Cash	1,000	1 Feb	Cash	6,000
28 Feb	Balance c/d	5,000			
		6,000			6,000
			28 Feb	Balance b/d	5,000
28 Feb	Balance c/d	7,410	28 Feb	Income statement	2,410
		7,410			7,410
			1 Mar	Balance b/d	7,410

Inventories

		£			£
3 Feb	Cash	2,600	15 Feb	Cost of sales	2,400
6 Feb	Trade payables	3,000	19 Feb	Cost of sales	2,300
			28 Feb	Balance c/d	900
		5,600			5,600
1 Mar	Balance b/d	900			

Equipment

		£		£
5 Feb	Cash	800		

Trade payables

		£			£
25 Feb	Cash	2,000	6 Feb	Inventories	3,000
28 Feb	Balance c/d	1,000			
		3,000			3,000
			1 Mar	Balance b/d	1,000

Rent

		£			£
9 Feb	Cash	250	28 Feb	Income statement	250

Fuel and electricity

		£			£
10 Feb	Cash	240	28 Feb	Income statement	240

General expenses

		£			£
11 Feb	Cash	200	28 Feb	Income statement	200

Sales revenue

		£			£
28 Feb	Balance c/d	7,800	15 Feb	Cash	4,000
			19 Feb	Trade receivables	3,800
		7,800			7,800
28 Feb	Income statement	7,800	28 Feb	Balance b/d	7,800

Cost of sales

		£			£
15 Feb	Inventories	2,400	28 Feb	Balance c/d	4,700
19 Feb	Inventories	2,300			
		4,700			4,700
28 Feb	Balance b/d	4,700	28 Feb	Income statement	4,700

Trade receivables

		£			£
19 Feb	Sales revenue	3,800	28 Feb	Cash	2,500
			28 Feb	Balance c/d	1,300
		3,800			3,800
1 Mar	Balance b/d	1,300			

Trial balance as at 28 February

	Debits	Credits
	£	£
Cash	5,410	
Capital		5,000
Inventories	900	
Equipment	800	
Trade payables		1,000
Rent	250	
Fuel and electricity	240	
General expenses	200	
Sales revenue		7,800
Cost of sales	4,700	
Trade receivables	1,300	
	13,800	13,800

(c)

Income statement

		£			£
28 Feb	Cost of sales	4,700	28 February	Sales revenue	7,800
28 Feb	Rent	250			
28 Feb	Fuel and electricity	240			
28 Feb	General expenses	200			
28 Feb	Capital (profit)	2,410			
		7,800			7,800

Balance sheet as at 28 February

	£
Non-current assets:	
Equipment	800
Current assets:	
Inventories	900
Trade receivables	1,300
Cash	5,410
	7,610
Total assets	8,410
Capital (owner's equity)	7,410
Current liabilities	
Trade payables	1,000
Total equity and liabilities	8,410

Income statement for the month ended 28 February

	£
Sales revenue	7,800
Cost of sales	(4,700)
Gross profit	3,100
Rent	(250)
Fuel and electricity	(240)
General expenses	(200)
Profit for the month	2,410

A.3

Buildings

		£		£
1 Jan	Balance brought down	25,000		

Fittings – cost

		£			£
1 Jan	Balance brought down	10,000	31 Dec	Balance carried down	12,000
	Cash	2,000			
		12,000			12,000
1 Jan	Balance brought down	12,000			

Fittings – depreciation

		£			£
31 Dec	Balance carried down	4,400	1 Jan	Balance brought down	2,000
			31 Dec	Income statement (£12,000 × 20%)	2,400
		4,400			4,400
			1 Jan	Balance brought down	4,400

General expenses

		£			£
1 Jan	Balance brought down	140	31 Dec	Income statement	570
	Cash	580		Balance carried down	150
		720			720
1 Jan	Balance brought down	150			

Inventories

		£			£
1 Jan	Balance brought down	1,350	31 Dec	Cost of sales	15,220
31 Dec	Trade payables	17,220		Cost of sales	4,900
	Cash	3,760		Capital	560
				Balance carried down	1,650
		22,330			22,330
1 Jan	Balance brought down	1,650			

Cost of sales

		£			£
31 Dec	Inventories	15,220	31 Dec	Income statement	20,120
	Inventories	4,900			
		20,120			20,120

Rent

		£			£
1 Jan	Balance brought down	500	31 Dec	Income statement	3,000
31 Dec	Cash	3,000		Balance carried down	500
		3,500			3,500
1 Jan	Balance brought down	500			

Trade receivables

		£			£
1 Jan	Balance brought down	1,840	31 Dec	Cash	32,810
31 Dec	Sales revenue	33,100		Income statement (bad debt)	260
				Balance carried down	1,870
		34,940			34,940
1 Jan	Balance brought down	1,870			

Cash

		£			£
1 Jan	Balance brought down	2,180	31 Dec	Inventories	3,760
31 Dec	Sales revenue	10,360		Wages	3,770
	Borrowings	2,000		Rent	3,000
	Trade receivables	32,810		Electricity	1,070
				General expenses	580
				Fittings	2,000
				Borrowings	1,000
				Trade payables	18,150
				Capital	10,400
				Balance carried down	3,620
		47,350			47,350
1 Jan	Balance brought down	3,620			

Capital

		£			£
31 Dec	Inventories	560	1 Jan	Balance brought down	25,050
	Cash	10,400		Income statement (profit)	10,900
	Balance carried down	24,990			
		35,950			35,950
			1 Jan	Balance brought down	24,990

Borrowings

		£			£
30 June	Cash	1,000	1 Jan	Balance brought down	12,000
31 Dec	Balance carried down	13,000		Cash	2,000
		14,000			14,000
			1 Jan	Balance brought down	13,000

Trade payables

		£			£
31 Dec	Cash	18,150	1 Jan	Balance brought down	1,690
31 Dec	Balance carried down	760	31 Dec	Inventories	17,220
		18,910			18,910
			1 Jan	Balance brought down	760

Electricity

		£			£
31 Dec	Cash	1,070	1 Jan	Balance brought down	270
31 Dec	Balance carried down	290	31 Dec	Income statement	1,090
		1,360			1,360
			1 Jan	Balance brought down	290

Sales revenue

		£			£
31 Dec	Income statement	43,460	31 Dec	Trade receivables	33,100
				Cash	10,360
		43,460			43,460

Wages

	£			£
31 Dec Cash	3,770	31 Dec	Income statement	3,770

Interest on borrowings

	£			£
		31 Dec	Income statement	1,350
			$[(6/12 \times 14,000) +$	
			$(6/12 \times 13,000)] \times 10\%$	

Income statement for the year to 31 December

	£			£
31 Dec Cost of sales	20,120	31 Dec	Sales revenue	43,460
Depreciation	2,400			
General expenses	570			
Rent	3,000			
Bad debts (Trade receivables)	260			
Electricity	1,090			
Wages	3,770			
Interest on borrowings	1,350			
Profit (Capital)	10,900			
	43,460			43,460

Balance sheet as at 31 December last year

		£		£
Non-current assets			Capital (owner's equity)	24,990
Property, plant and equipment				
Buildings		25,000		
Fittings: cost	12,000		**Non-current liabilities**	
depreciation	(4,400)	7,600	Borrowings	13,000
Current assets			Current liabilities	
Inventories of stationery		150	Trade payables	760
Inventories		1,650	Accrued electricity	290
Prepaid rent		500	Accrued interest on borrowings	1,350
Trade receivables		1,870		
Cash		3,620		
Total assets		40,390	Total equity and liabilities	40,390

Index